A
PARTNER
in
HOLINESS

VOLUME 1

A

PARTNER

in

HOLINESS

VOLUME 1

Genesis • Exodus

Deepening Mindfulness,

Practicing Compassion and

Enriching Our Lives through the Wisdom of

R. Levi Yitzhak of Berdichev's *Kedushat Levi*

RABBI JONATHAN P. SLATER, DMin

Foreword by **Arthur Green**
coauthor, *Speaking Torah: Spiritual Teachings
from around the Maggid's Table*

Preface by **Rabbi Nancy Flam**
codirector of programs, Institute for Jewish Spirituality

For People of All Faiths, All Backgrounds
JEWISH LIGHTS Publishing
Woodstock, Vermont

A Partner in Holiness:
Deepening Mindfulness, Practicing Compassion and Enriching Our Lives through
the Wisdom of R. Levi Yitzhak of Berdichev's Kedushat Levi—*Volume 1*

2014 Hardcover Edition, First Printing
© 2014 by Jonathan P. Slater
Foreword © 2014 by Arthur Green
Preface © 2014 by Nancy Flam

Library of Congress Cataloging-in-Publication Data
Slater, Jonathan P., 1952– author.
  A partner in holiness : deepening mindfulness, practicing compassion and enriching our lives through the wisdom of R. Levi Yitzhak of Berdichev's Kedushat Levi / Rabbi Jonathan P. Slater, DMin.
     volumes cm
  Includes bibliographical references.
    ISBN 978-1-58023-794-9 (hardcover) — ISBN 978-1-58023-809-0 (ebook)
  1. Spiritual life—Judaism. 2. Bible. Pentateuch—Commentaries. 3. Hasidism.
  4. Levi Isaac ben Meir, of Berdichev, 1740-1809—Teachings. I. Levi Isaac ben Meir, of Berdichev, 1740-1809. Kedushat Levi (Avot) II. Title.
  BM723.S6125 2014
  296.7—dc23
                                    2014019128
10 9 8 7 6 5 4 3 2 1

Manufactured in the United States of America
Jacket Design: Michael Myers
Interior Design: Michael Myers

For People of All Faiths, All Backgrounds
Published by Jewish Lights Publishing
A Division of LongHill Partners, Inc.
Sunset Farm Offices, Route 4, P.O. Box 237
Woodstock, VT 05091
Tel: (802) 457-4000 Fax: (802) 457-4004
www.jewishlights.com

To rabbis Nancy Flam, Sheila Peltz Weinberg, Rachel Cowan,
and Lisa Goldstein
With gratitude for faith, support, and love

To Arthur Green
Because you sent me out to find my path,
I have been able to trace it back to you

Contents: Volume 1

Here Is What You'll Find in Volume 2:

The Book of Leviticus

The Book of Numbers

The Book of Deuteronomy

Foreword

Arthur Green

Rabbi Levi Yitzhak of Berdichev is one of the most beloved folk heroes of Jewish tradition. He is best known for his love of ordinary people and his willingness to find holiness in all their deeds, even in their moral foibles. The tales about him repeatedly depict him arguing with God in defense of Jews, both individually and collectively. More than any other figure in the Jewish literary imagination, his life demonstrates the inseparable bond between love of God and love of humanity.

But Levi Yitzhak is also a real historical figure. He was among the leading disciples of Rabbi Dov Baer of Mezritch (1704–1772) and played a key role in the spread of the Hasidic movement. Persecuted and driven from several communal posts because of his then-controversial Hasidic faith, he finally became rabbi of Berdichev, one of the largest Jewish communities in the Ukraine, where he served from 1785 until his death in 1811. His book *Kedushat Levi*, published immediately after his death, is considered one of the great classics of Hasidic literature.

Like almost all of early Hasidic writings, *Kedushat Levi* is a collection of homilies following the weekly Torah portion and the holiday cycle. (One portion of it, that on Purim and Hanukkah, was published by Levi Yitzhak in 1798.) These homilies were first delivered orally in Yiddish, the only spoken language of Eastern European Jews. When prepared for publication, however, they were rendered into abbreviated Hebrew versions. Publication in the holy tongue, the literary language of the educated, was considered more respectable. Because of their summary nature, the texts are sometimes difficult to understand, the power of their original delivery lost in the course of abbreviation and rough translation. It is almost as if they reach us in dehydrated form and we have to add the liquid warmth of our own understanding to bring them back to full strength.

That is precisely what Jonathan Slater has sought to do in this collection. He has filtered a selected group of *Kedushat Levi* teachings through his own religious experience and inner life, making them accessible to a new generation of seekers. Each of the original oral teachings behind this volume was offered in a particular context, perhaps stimulated by the need or life situation of a specific disciple or member of Levi Yitzhak's community. All that has been lost to us in the course of transcription and the passage of generations. But Slater has not allowed that to make him give up. He addresses to the Hasidic sources precisely the question that these texts themselves constantly address to the Torah itself: How is this teaching relevant to us, living in our own time?

The teachings of Hasidism are extraordinarily rich and creative in exposition of prior Jewish texts, beginning with the Torah. They clearly attest to a deep faith and call constantly for personal spiritual openness and awareness of the divine presence throughout our lives. The cultivation of that awareness, *da'at*, and the attachment to God that results from it, *devekut*, constitute the heart of the Hasidic message. But the sources are not so strong in telling us precisely *how* to go about attaining these states. Surely both the life of the commandments and the study of Torah were seen as ways to enter God's service. Intense prayer, both liturgical and private, were also a part of the traditional spiritual "toolbox." But Slater correctly intuits that these are not enough, especially for the contemporary reader. Well known as a practitioner and teacher of meditation, he accompanies each text with questions for personal thought as well as devotional exercises, building bridges between texts that many today would find obscure and the widely popular practice of mindfulness meditation.

This book is made for contemplative practice, not for quick reading. You have before you the work of a contemporary mystical seeker reflecting on the teachings of a profound preacher of two hundred years ago. But that preacher himself was drawing on a rich array of prior sources. In entering the world of this book, you are invited to add another link to that great chain, allowing the wisdom of Jewish mystical teachings to enter your heart, leading you from the "sources to the great Source of all." That wisdom will be changed and renewed as it comes through you, just as it has been changed in coming through Jonathan Slater and in coming through Levi Yitzhak of Berdichev. But be prepared: as you make these teachings your own, they will seek to change and remake you as well. Only in allowing that to happen will you begin to understand the very important volume you have before you.

Preface

Rabbi Nancy Flam

When setting out to hike in unfamiliar terrain, I'm always pleased to find a display board posting a map in front of the trailhead. Of greatest value is the little red arrow with the essential words, "You are here."

So where are we as we set off on this path of *A Partner in Holiness* within the larger territory of Jewish learning? We are in the vast and ancient old-growth forest of Oral Torah known as *parshanut*, or explanations of the weekly Torah portion (*parashah*), within the broad field of homiletical *midrash*, or interpretive meaning-making based on the written words of Torah. We are on that part of the path forged relatively recently by the revolutionary insights of the Baal Shem Tov (1698–1760) and his students. The fruit of this revitalized Jewish mystical perspective was scattered on the footpath smoothed by post-Enlightenment, free-thinking Jews of the twentieth century (initially by such figures as Yosef Hayyim Brenner, Hillel Zeitlin, and Martin Buber) who rediscovered something of beauty, truth, and inspiration in these early Hasidic teachings. They cultivated the seeds hidden within this fruit in new social and historical environments to sprout what we call Neo-Hasidism. A related path of Hasidic teaching for non-Hasidic Jews was later pioneered in North America by Reb Zalman Schachter-Shalomi and Reb Shlomo Carlebach, and deeply enriched by Dr. Arthur Green, not only in the latter's translations of classic Hasidic homilies with modern-day commentary but also in his popular books rendering an accessible and compelling Neo-Hasidic theology for the contemporary Jewish seeker.

And then something new happened of which this book is an exquisite expression. American Neo-Hasidism met American Buddhist mindfulness through, in large part, the shared teaching of Arthur Green and renowned mindfulness teacher Sylvia Boorstein. Jonathan Slater became a keen student of them both through their collaborative teaching at the Institute for Jewish Spirituality. It is this synthesis of Neo-Hasidic worldview, language, and Torah interpretation with the worldview, language, and practice of American

Buddhist mindfulness meditation that marks the specific trail we will be walking together through the pages of this book, with Rabbi Slater as our guide.

The great gift of this fortuitous meeting stems from the way in which mindfulness meditation—and the understanding of mind that informs it—shines a penetrating light upon the words of Neo-Hasidic Torah that would otherwise remain opaque to us. The Hasidic masters' teachings were clearly rooted in personal experience, based on the truth of their own highly refined inner lives and reflection upon them. Additionally, the masters certainly engaged in their own practices to cultivate this inner territory of awareness and presence. But they did not generally share their precise methods of practice. Mindfulness meditation provides a systematic contemplative practice for training the mind and heart, cultivating the kind of consciousness that we believe the Hasidic teachers were advocating and encouraging. Mindfulness practice brings a depth and dimension to the masters' words that would otherwise elude us.

It is possible that mindfulness meditation practice and wisdom will provide a new hermeneutic to help Torah be relevant and compelling for our time and place, much as Maimonides applied the lens of Aristotle, or Bahya ibn Pakuda the lens of Sufism, to Torah in their times and places. If so, the small path we find ourselves on today may at some point become a much more widely trafficked route.

Introduction

In taking up this book, you have become my partner. Whenever one writes—except as a diary or journal—it is for an audience. And whenever one reads, it is through the heart and mind of the author. Writer and reader are partners, engaging together in the life of the book. This book has additional, more complex elements of partnership. I produced a set of translations and brief commentaries on *Kedushat Levi* as a study program for thirty-five other rabbis, participants with me in the first rabbinic cohort of the Institute for Jewish Spirituality. Having rededicated ourselves to Torah study as spiritual practice, for its own sake and for the sake of transforming the heart, we wanted to continue. Yet the program was over, and there were no texts or teachers to turn to. So as a colleague and fellow student, I undertook to provide something for us to work with. I was a novice student of Hasidic literature and Jewish mysticism. There was much I did not know, and I did not want to presume to "teach" others who might know more than I. So, I simply set out to share what I learned and experienced through my own studies.

That first year of translation and commentary—to my great surprise and delight—has now extended for twelve years. In the intervening years, I had the opportunity to return to study and teach *Kedushat Levi* to new colleagues and other students through the Institute. I had grown in the depth of my own knowledge and understanding of Hasidism and Jewish mysticism and felt prepared to offer more. In particular, I was interested in being more explicit about how these teachings resonate with mindfulness practice and how to take their lessons into our own daily experience, as spiritual practice. I do not believe that this impulse is new or innovative. R. Levi Yitzhak's students would have heard (or studied) these lessons and reflected themselves on their implications for their lives. They would have asked how the teachings were directed specifically to their own life situations, and they would have tried to live out the lessons they took.

So, these translations, commentaries, and practice suggestions came into being in partnership with my students. I was thinking of them, of their experience in the Institute, their work in the Jewish community, their personal struggles and hopes. And, I knew that many of them studied these teachings in partnership with a friend, in *chavruta*. Knowing that was a relief to me as a teacher: whatever I might advocate or teach would not be "definitive," rather considered, tested, and adapted to their lives, in their experience. Their engagement in study partnered with my study to make R. Levi Yitzhak's teachings meaningful.

Still, I studied on my own, wrote on my own, and sent out my teachings over the Internet, into the silent ether. I needed a partner. Over time I came to realize I had one, actually two: R. Levi Yitzhak and God. R. Levi Yitzhak led me through the Torah and through his heart and mind, opening up meanings I would never have seen, implications I never would have felt. It was a thrilling experience, challenging, poignant, inspiring. Yet I, too, had to bring these teachings into my own body, heart, mind, and soul. So I sat, holding my heart and mind open in meditation. I waited to sense how I was led, without any initiative or planning, to discern a practice for a given teaching. God was my partner in those moments, leading me, enlightening me, supporting me.

I invite you to make your study of *Kedushat Levi* a practice in partnership. Find a *chavruta*, share in a Torah study circle, blog about your experience, and invite responses. Ask your own questions—not only "What does this mean?" or "How does he get from here to there?"—but also "What does this mean in my life?" and "How can I apply this teaching in my relationships, in my devotional life, in the world?" Ask your rabbi, cantor, or educator for help and support. Seek out a teacher in your community who is willing to risk something new, to open heart and soul to study.

The words *Kedushat Levi* mean "the holiness of Levi." Surely R. Levi Yitzhak intended to play on his name. He sought to associate the holiness of the tribe of Levi with himself and his work. Perhaps he was thinking of the quality of the priest, in the mystical tradition associated with "love"; that of the Levites associated with "fear." Perhaps he had in mind *kedushah* as "dedication," an offering or a prayer. I've been thinking about this name for some time and suspect he may also have meant to pun on the word *levi*: as a verb (reflected in the role of the Levites as support and assistance to the priests), it suggests accompaniment, partnership.

In his teachings, R. Levi Yitzhak was offering his heart and mind, his body and soul to be our partner in seeking holiness. Our study together, our practice of mindful investigation, curiosity, openness, and compassion, can be our response as partners in holiness.

IF WE'RE TAKING THIS TRIP TOGETHER, LET ME INTRODUCE MYSELF

Among other things, I am a Conservative rabbi who served a congregation in Santa Rosa, California, for nineteen years. For many years I was the only full-time rabbi in Sonoma County, and my life was quite full. I was engaged in civic affairs and interfaith activities, in building a congregation and a religious school. Most important to me, though, was the time I spent in pastoral work, primarily visiting people in the hospital. I went to see everyone, whether they were congregants or not—sometimes even if they were not Jewish. Almost daily I was brought face to face with the varieties of human suffering, and searched in my heart for a way to hold it all. I found there snippets of prayers, lines from Psalms, teachings from rabbinic literature. As I wove them into my response to those I visited, and to my own pained heart, I learned an important lesson: the question "Why has this happened to me?" causes greater suffering, while the question "What are we to do now?" eases pain. Struggling with explanations often brought guilt or shame, or blame of others or the system, but never really relief. Accepting what is true right now, and investigating how to live the next moment, the next breath, did.

This was my introduction to mindfulness practice—although I had no idea that it had a name. It was simply how I made my way through each day with energy, hope, and a sense of joy in life. It kept me connected to my own experience and helped me stay open to whatever might come. I was pleased to find support and nurturance for my spiritual orientation in the short teachings from various Hasidic teachers that I found in the anthology *Iturei Torah*.[1] On my own I began to develop a sense of how Hasidic spirituality spoke my language, a language as yet not formally "mindfulness."

That changed in 1995 when Sylvia Boorstein came to my congregation. A founder of the Spirit Rock Meditation Center in Marin County and a well-known teacher of Buddhism, Sylvia was looking for a community in which she could ground her Jewish practice. We became friends, and slowly I found in her teachings a resonance with what I had learned on my own. In turn, we began to teach together in my synagogue, leading services that incorporated meditation and Jewish teachings that supported mindful awareness.

A few years later, Sylvia was invited to lead a series of silent meditation retreats for Jewish leaders and clergy. Soon those retreats became a full eighteen-month program of four retreats, with study and practice in between. With Sylvia's encouragement and support I applied to and participated in this program. In this manner I grounded my personal spirituality in the language and practice of mindfulness.

As that program was drawing to an end, another was about to begin: the first cohort of the Spirituality Institute at Metivta, which would later become the Institute for Jewish Spirituality. This, too, would be an eighteen-month program, based on four retreats and study in between, but this time only for rabbis. In this program, however, the mindfulness meditation would be joined to the study of classical Hasidic texts. The idea was that in weaving these two strands together, in the context of sustained practice and study, rabbis would be more able to bring this approach to spiritual life into the mainstream. Once again I would be practicing with Sylvia (and her student, Rabbi Sheila Peltz Weinberg). And I would also have the opportunity to study with Arthur Green and Rabbi Jonathan Omer-Man. While *Iturei Torah* introduced me to a Hasidic idiom of teaching, my studies with Art and Jonathan opened my heart, mind, and soul to the depths of these lessons. Over the course of those eighteen months, and along with a few other participants, I turned my hand to translating the texts that we were studying, in order to share them with the larger group. I delighted in the creativity, the liveliness, the power of these texts. And I benefited from studying with the leading teachers of this generation. Something clicked for me.

That laid the groundwork for the study we are about to undertake together. I moved back to New York and began working for the Institute for Jewish Spirituality. That work has afforded me the opportunity to continue studying and working with Art Green, and my appreciation for Hasidic thought and spirituality has deepened significantly. I have continued to engage in studying these texts and teaching them. I continue to hear in them the lessons of mindfulness, just as I did when I first encountered these texts. So let me invite you to take these steps with me, first through mindfulness, then Hasidism and Hasidic texts, and then how they work together.

WHAT DOES IT MEAN TO PRACTICE MINDFULNESS?

Have you ever had the experience of getting in the car or going for a walk and arriving at your destination without any clear recollection of how you got there? Or have you finished reading a page in a book and realized that you have no idea what you just read? Or finished a meal and realized that you cannot recall how it actually tasted, what it felt like to consume the food?

Perhaps you've found yourself standing in front of a full refrigerator or pantry thinking you were hungry but sensing that there is nothing there to eat. Or perhaps you've gone looking to take some aspirin for a headache only to find your back is in pain instead. Or possibly you found yourself stuck in a time of stress and all you could think was, "It's always this way" or "It will never get better."

Do you find that you argue with others and say things like, "You never X" or "You always Y"? Do you find yourself preoccupied with assessing who is to blame for your circumstances (for any circumstance) because, after all, *somebody* must be responsible? Do you worry about how things will turn out, hypervigilant to never make mistakes, crushed when things go wrong?

You are not alone. Most of us sleepwalk through much of our lives. Whatever we may be doing, our minds are on something else: memories, plans, fantasies, fears, bravado, distractions. Sometimes we are proud of our ability to multitask: to cook breakfast, read the paper, listen to the news, talk on the phone, and get ready for work at the same time. We may actually accomplish all of those things, but we have not actually been fully present in any one of them at all. We are also unaware of how we "work." When we meet difficult situations—conflicts with others, deadlines at work, stressful conditions in life—we may react with anger, resignation, fear, sleep. Rather than witnessing these reactions as phenomena, we take them to be natural, right, necessary. We so identify with our feelings and sensations that we function on automatic pilot, without recognizing how ineffective or unhelpful these behaviors are. We go through our lives engaged in what is going on without being fully attentive to or conscious of what is happening.

Mindfulness is paying attention to what is going on: direct, focused, unbiased, nonjudgmental attention. It is held lightly, with curiosity, compassion, and acceptance. This sort of attention immediately roots us in the moment: whatever is going on is happening right now, right here. When we bring mindfulness to our situation we realize that although it may be similar to previous events, the past is not repeating itself. This is different. Although we may fear potential outcomes, they are not happening yet. It is only this, right here, right now. When what is happening is pleasant, we are able to enjoy it fully, without worrying it might end or how to get more. When it is unpleasant, we need not get trapped in the distraction of assigning blame or caught in the fear it may never end. Even pain can be tolerated more easily when we do not project our fears into the future, when we notice we can bear it for this moment, and then the next. We can become sensitive to changes that take place moment to moment.

Paying attention from moment to moment reveals to us the fact that things are always changing. Nothing stays the same. We suffer when we try to keep things from changing, and we suffer when we fear they will never be different. There is release from suffering when we can acknowledge what is right now as it is. We can delight in it, acknowledge its pain, and prepare for whatever comes next.

Bringing our full attention to what is happening right now reveals that it is not happening only to us. Of course, there are times that conditions may prevent us from seeing beyond our own situation: deep pain, terrifying confusion, addled delusion. But when we stop to ask, "What is happening right now?" and we answer honestly, we realize that it is happening to everyone. Instead of thinking, "It is raining on me," we think, "It is raining." Even the thought "I am alone" brings us into relation with the people who are not there around us, or who are present but with whom we do not feel connected in the moment. Their absence from me is no less my absence from them. When we ask, "What is happening right now?" we are seeking concrete, factual, observable information. An honest answer will eschew attribution of motivation, inviting instead curiosity as to our own inner state, truthfulness about our assumptions, and what others are actually thinking and feeling. We discover that often what we assume about our situation is not actually what has happened. Others thought differently from us, intended good rather than ill, are as surprised as we at the circumstance. Mindfulness connects us to others; we realize that what is happening is happening to everyone, always.

In mindfulness practice, we come more directly into awareness of our own suffering in the face of loss and change because we experience directly the pain of our own confusion. If we are able to pause to simply feel the pain, to allow it to be present without rushing to change our circumstances or blame someone for them, then we might learn it is possible to be with our own suffering. And we may see it change before our eyes—simply because we are paying it attention. We realize how often our hearts are seized with pain, how much of our life is colored by our suffering. No longer confused by mindless flight from pain or rush to pleasure, we turn to ourselves, to our suffering, as we might to a friend: with compassion. Because we are responding to our direct experience of our own pain, we cannot hold ourselves at a distance. We cannot pity our situation and then walk away. We must attend instead with compassion: direct, felt concern to bring ease to suffering. This is not solipsistic, but natural. As I would comfort my child or best friend who is in pain, I comfort my own heart and soul. The consequence, though, is powerful. The compassion I offer myself releases me from self-concern. I know, deeply, internally, that I have been attended to, and so I can turn to attending to the needs of others.

MINDFULNESS AS PRACTICE, MEDITATION AS PRACTICE

Mindfulness is not a state that is attained once and for all. It is a practice, and it is supported by practice. Because what is happening now is only happening now, not five minutes from now when I choose to pay attention, I can only be mindful in this moment. That means that I have to work to bring my attention back to this moment, back to my experience, with as much clarity as possible all the time. To help me ground myself in this practice, I engage in mindfulness meditation. There are two aspects to this form of meditation: one is single-point focus or concentration practice; the other is open awareness. They are related and mutually supporting. And they help develop mindfulness.

Most people practice meditation seated (it is also possible to practice standing, walking, or lying down). First we notice that we are seated, feeling our connection to the floor, the seat bottom, and back. We bring our attention to the sensation of our skin, the temperature gradient across our bodies, the difference between what is clothed and what is exposed. We sense subtle sensations in the body: tingling, vibration, movement. Having brought awareness to the sensations of the body, we may notice the prominent experience of breathing. We notice our bellies rising and falling, breath entering the nose and filling the lungs. And we bring our attention to rest in one of these sensations, whichever is most prominent, whichever we feel most strongly.

We are not thinking about the breath, but sensing it, feeling it coming and going, arising and passing away. Yet perhaps precisely because we are focused on sensation and not thought, thoughts fill our minds. This is natural. The work of meditation is noticing when the thoughts are present and choosing, instead of thinking those thoughts, to witness that thought is happening and to return our attention to the breath. The goal is not to stop thoughts or to empty the mind. It is to find stillness in the midst of the turmoil, to become aware of the flow of thought without getting caught up in it. We train ourselves toward this by bringing the attention back to the breath over and over again. Each time we notice that our attention has wandered, in the noticing we have awakened to our experience in this moment (and not the reverie, flow of thoughts, planning, commenting that has occupied us up to now). We have connected intentionally, once again, to our attention. In that moment of awakening we are free to choose where to place our attention. There is nothing magical about returning to the breath. Rather, it is in the awakening, choosing, and returning that we build our capacity to pay attention in a focused manner to our lives, to come to know our experience more directly.

In the moment we realize that our attention has wandered we might notice a twinge of regret, anger, frustration, or loss. We are habituated to being "successful," and recognizing even such a small "failure" is painful. This momentary, passing seizure of pain is not insignificant, though. It is representative of all others, and it is important in our practice to turn toward that pain, to recognize it and, most critically, bring compassion to it. Treating ourselves with compassion in this moment liberates us to return to our intention, to remain connected to the breath. Were we not to fully connect to that momentary twinge, were we to deny ourselves that compassion, we would likely get caught in our habitual reactions to pain: denial, self-recrimination or chastisement, anger or shame. Instead, turning toward ourselves with compassion, we can let go of the commentary about "always" and "never" to connect instead with our intention: to remain connected with the breath in meditation. We train ourselves to return to our intention with compassion.

Deepening our concentration helps us remain connected to what is true in the moment. With a relatively concentrated mind, we will more likely recognize when we are distracted, or falling into habitual patterns of thought or reaction, and then return to clear attention. Yet it is possible to become too concentrated or perhaps too focused. With excessive concentration and will toward concentration, we may hold so tightly to our chosen focus that we miss the larger picture. So we balance concentration practice with open awareness. In this we begin sitting in the same manner, connecting with the sensations of the body, coming into relation with our current experience. Sensing our mind to be an expanse—like the sky—we can observe what arises in our consciousness. Thoughts, memories, stories, images, fantasies, plans, and ideas arise and pass through our minds. They are interesting, or painful, or unusual, or curious. We acknowledge their presence but allow them to pass away, like clouds in a breeze. We choose to let them go, intentionally, rather than allowing them to determine the content of our minds, the climate of our hearts. For this time, in meditation, our intention is to witness the fluid nature of experience, how things come and go. We discover that all that seems pressing, important, or necessary is not so. It arises and passes away, and if we choose, we can return to it later.

This practice helps us learn that we are not our thoughts. We do not have to think whatever arises in the moment. Thoughts and feelings are merely phenomena, like others, that arise and pass away. Because we are habituated to attach thoughts and feelings to narratives—"I feel this way because she did that to me," "This feels like the time X happened," "If I can just finish this thought, this plan, this idea, then I'll have it all solved and everyone will love me"—they feel solid. It seems as if they exist in the same way our bodies exist. Allowing them to pass away without reviving the narrative associated with them or creating a new story to go with them, we learn that they are not solid. They are ephemeral, transient.

Ultimately we may realize that the stories we tell attached to these thoughts and feelings are not really different from the stories we tell about our lives as a whole. They, too, are passing. The events that they recall happened and passed away. Our recollection brings them back as if they were happening once again, which is not true: we are thinking these thoughts, but they will pass away once again. All of the stories that we tell and retell, the history by which we know our selves to be solid, continuous, and separate are only stories, and like the thoughts and feelings, they are passing and ephemeral. We are not who we say we are.

This realization can be quite painful but also transformative. Knowing directly that our self-image is empty, that our story is a fiction, brings loss. All of the ways we build our selves up—or tear ourselves down—are false; our imagined future is just a projection; so many of our purported values are revealed as bias and preference. It is hard to give up this sense of self. To this pain, as well, we bring compassion. We are merely human, and like all people we have taken our thoughts to be real. For all of the ways that our thoughts have caused us pain, we offer compassion; for the ways that our feelings have brought us empty solace, we offer compassion; for the uncertainty of not knowing, the seeming emptiness of life without a story, we offer compassion. Resting in open awareness, however, we also discover that we are free. We are not bound by the past; we are not doomed to a fate. Each moment arises and passes away, and something new can come into being right now. We are liberated in each moment to do what is most wise, most compassionate, most skillful to ease the suffering of others.

Sitting in open awareness, however, we can also get lost. We can fall asleep—both literally and figuratively. Holding our awareness open can be relaxing, and we may simply fall into somnolence. Allowing thoughts and feelings to come and go without comment or attachment, we may lose touch with the world in which we live. We may then be asleep to the needs of others, who are not separate from us. Establishing some measure of concentration allows us to engage in open awareness without becoming overwhelmed or lost.

Mindfulness meditation trains us for mindfulness practice. We gain skills, develop habits, and nurture wholesome qualities in meditation that we can then bring to bear in the course of our lives. We practice these skills, habits, and qualities in our daily affairs as we pay attention from moment to moment. The quality of consciousness that we nurture in mindfulness practice is expansive, open, welcoming, curious, and connected. We become aware that what we experience in our lives is not different from what all people experience: we all grieve loss, we all fear death, we all wish to be recognized and known, loved and cared for, we all seek pleasure and run from pain. When we know how those feelings and desires drive our choices and shape our habits and witness how often our reactions only deepen our suffering, we respond to our selves—and then all others—with compassion. We learn, as well, that our happiness and well-being are interconnected with and interdependent on that of all others. We are always functioning in a web of relationships, dealing with conditions created by acts beyond our immediate, individual control. Not all that happens to us is our doing, yet we are implicated in all that takes place. We may fall victim to the deeds of others, yet our innocence does not free us from responsibility for what happens next. Compassion for our selves and for all others, the outcome and ground of mindfulness, provides a foundation for righteous, honest, and engaged living.

WHY ARE WE STUDYING A LATE-EIGHTEENTH-CENTURY HASIDIC BOOK?

The simplest answer is (to paraphrase the Talmud): "It is Torah and we need it!" While Hasidism became the predominant form of Jewish religious expression in Eastern Europe by the mid-nineteenth century, its impact on the West was negligible. Since the eighteenth century the mystical tradition had been ignored—or suppressed—in the West, its spiritual richness and inspiration thus unavailable. If for no other reason, it is important that we know what our ancestors thought, how they felt, and what they strove for in their religious and spiritual lives.

Yet, there is more. Hasidism in its heyday—which could be characterized as R. Levi Yitzhak's generation and those that followed—was immensely creative, inspirational, and transformative. There are many theories as to why Hasidic teaching became so popular and why Hasidic teachers were so influential. Still, whatever may have been true in the late eighteenth and early nineteenth centuries may not apply today. The teachings designed to address the concerns and everyday realities of our ancestors at that time may not be relevant to us. Therefore, we are studying Hasidic texts not to become Hasidim per se, but to glean from them their salient and lasting lessons for contemporary Jewish spiritual life. Of these there may be none more important than the core Hasidic teachings related to God.[2]

THE BAAL SHEM TOV'S TEACHINGS

The Baal Shem Tov, the founding figure in Hasidism, taught that God is present in the world, available to all to sense and perceive. Indeed, the whole aim of spiritual practice is to refine our capacity to connect with God in all things. He regularly quoted Isa. 6:3, as if to say, "'The whole of existence is filled with God's glory'—REALLY!" Before his time, to most people God seemed distant, too pure to be associated with this gross mundane plane and accessible only to those who were able to refine their minds and bodies through rigorous study and denial of the physical world. The Baal Shem Tov taught that everyone has the capacity and obligation to recognize divinity in all things, in every situation, everywhere. His instruction came with love and joy. Finding God in all things can transform each moment, offering a sense of blessing, intimacy, love, and joy in the encounter.

Just this sort of teaching can be meaningful today. There are many factors, of course, that work against it being received. In many ways we are too much the product of the Enlightenment, of capitalism and a post-industrial world to see beyond the material; to value experience over possession; to delight in being over doing, making, achieving. We are accustomed to asserting our power over nature, shaping it to our needs and desires, employing its resources wantonly for every whim and fancy. How can we then shift our perspective to see the world as alive with divine energy, filled with God's glory? But, it is precisely this shift that is so important today, when we are being forced to live with greater respect for the earth's limits, greater attentiveness to our interconnectedness with all other beings, greater awareness of how urgent it is for us to live in attunement with all of creation, and not as its masters.

This having been said, we might still balk at the idea that "God's glory" fills the earth. We are the children and grandchildren of the Shoah. We have inherited the world of atomic weapons and nuclear disaster; of genocides deaf to and unconcerned with "Never Again"; of images of unbearable human suffering offered incessantly, intrusively, 24/7 on every size screen and medium. Where is God in all of that?

Where God has been all along: *In* all of that. From the day Cain killed Abel, violence has plagued human society, yet love is present in greater supply. Since the crust hardened over the core of the earth, there have been "natural disasters" that destroy yet lay the ground for the evolution of new life. Altruism and self-interest, in constant dynamic, move us toward greater peace, greater justice, greater responsibility. While there may be no God external to creation who makes all this come to be, still none of this could get done (and would not exist) were it not for the divine force of love and curiosity, delight and challenge flowing through everything. Listening deeply to the Baal Shem Tov's insistent reminder—"There is no place, no moment, no interaction devoid of God"—may help us reconnect deeply to our own lives, to the lives of others, and to the life of our planet for the sake of more life.

THE MAGGID OF MEZRITCH'S TEACHINGS

The next great teacher in the Hasidic lineage, the man whose influence flows through *Kedushat Levi* and other books of his era, was R. Dov Baer, the Maggid of Mezritch. He surely inherited his teacher's passion to connect with God, to know God directly. Yet his approach was different, more internal, more a matter of contemplative consciousness. The Maggid emphasized *devekut*, cleaving to, even uniting, in God. This was attained through contemplative concentration practices—framed in kabbalistic terms—meant to diminish sensed awareness of the body and a separate "self." These practices were sometimes characterized as ascents of the soul, where the portion of divinity that is the soul reunites with its source, in God. The point of such practices was not for the sake of the experience or for personal gain. Rather, it was to transform consciousness and—through participating in God's inner life (as it were)—to bring blessing and well-being to others.

What is the point of transforming consciousness? In the Maggid's terms, it is to come to see the world from God's point of view, which is to say, to discover and fully know that there is nothing other than God. There is no separation between God and the world, between the spiritual and the material, between this and that, you and me. We are all part of divinity, as God's unity is absolute and infinite. Our experience of ourselves as a separate "self" is the necessary consequence of God constricting God's divine light, or divine Self, or power into coarser forms, into deeper dimensions of materiality so that there might emerge a "separate" consciousness to know, respond to, and love God. We are endowed with awareness—which includes our perception of distinctions, of the seemingly separate nature of things—for the sake of coming to know Unity, Oneness, God. Through contemplative practices, the Maggid and his students moved toward that unitive consciousness, seeing through separateness and knowing only God. In turn, they were more attuned to recognizing God's presence in every aspect of the manifest world. God, hidden in, constricted in, the physical world, was then revealed to be fully present there and no longer separate.

This spiritual orientation—that there is only God, nothing but God, and our perception of separateness is only for the sake of revealing God in all things—paradoxically heightens our awareness of self and other, as well as our appreciation for all things. Everything sparkles with the light of divinity. Yet, too often, we forget, or our vision is clouded, and things look like things, all seems separate, and nothing appears to be special. So the Hasidic tradition adopted the mystical conception of sparks of divine light, of holiness concealed and trapped in "shells" or "husks" in all things. The aim of spiritual practice was then to seek out awareness of these sparks in all moments of one's ordinary life: when using a tool, eating some food, meeting another person, transacting business. The quest to perceive these sparks is a practice that, similar to the Maggid's contemplations, reveals divinity in all things and that nothing is separate from God. All of spiritual practice, then, was toward the end of perceiving God in all things to then know, intimately, experientially, that there is nothing but God.

For some people, the assertion that there is nothing but God, that our self-perception as a separate being is "false" from God's point of view, may be dispiriting. We might wonder: what good is anything I do if there is no "me" who is doing it? And, what is the meaning of my suffering, my life's difficulties, if they are "only illusion"? Well, we are not separate from all the other aspects of creation in which we find divine light or in which God is garbed. We have equal significance as pointers toward God and God's oneness. Our particular experiences and our responses to them, our life choices, are real and matter. They are the way in which we demonstrate our awareness of God's presence in our lives, even in our suffering and difficulties. And, from the Maggid's perspective, our dedication to living our lives fully and deeply, dedicated to acknowledging God in the unfolding of our experience, brings delight to God. We fulfill God's intention in creating the context for our separate consciousness: to come to know, trust, love, and serve God. This brings God delight and is a life path in which we might find delight as well.

The Maggid's Views Have Practical Implications

Earlier I identified a second goal of the Maggid's mystical contemplative practice: to bring blessing and well-being to others. There are two ways to explain this. One has shamanic aspects, in which uniting with God, participating in God's inner life, affords the possibility of rearranging the order of Creation. Through contemplation one ascends through spiritual dimensions, drawing closer to the pure, undifferentiated, unified dimension of divinity. In these spheres, all is potential, as differentiation has not yet emerged. It is possible for the one who ascends to these heights to arrange for this potential to emerge into the concrete world as a different actuality. It is possible to annul the evil plans of oppressors, to provide sustenance to the hungry, to bring fertility to the barren. Within God all is possible, and the practitioner can help effectuate God's true desire, which is for all beings to be happy, satisfied in body and soul, and so freed to turn to God in love and devotion.[3]

The other way to understand how meditation might provide for the well-being of others has to do with the movement of the contemplative's awareness between mundane, separate consciousness and divine, unitive consciousness. In classical terms, this is the fluctuation between material, substantive existence (*yesh*) and divine, spiritual nothingness (*ayin*). When the practitioner turns attention toward God's oneness—letting go of connection with and perception of separation and difference—consciousness shifts from *yesh* toward *ayin*. Consciousness, unbounded by physical awareness or concerns, expands infinitely. The dimension of *ayin* is identified with the depths of God's own being, the core of all true existence. It is from there that the life force that permeates the material world emerges, giving our dimension of *yesh* vitality, allowing it to exist seemingly "separate" from God. In contemplation, then, one enters the core of creative power, and in returning to the dimension of *yesh*, one can bring new things into existence.

These processes were not just interesting consequences of the Maggid's theology and spiritual practice. They were central to the role that he and his students sought to play in their communities. Deputizing and deploying his students to bring the teachings of Hasidism out into the world, the Maggid both wished to transform the hearts and consciousness of the people and to bring them succor. These rabbis and teachers went out into their various communities to inspire spiritual passion, invigorate religious practice, and offer the possibility of personal redemption and freedom. But before the people they were to serve could hope to take on their practices or accept their teachings, these rabbis had to prove their worth. They did so by offering themselves—through their personal attention and in their spiritual practices—to make the lives of others better. Before the emergence of Hasidism, the figure of the spiritual "saint" was a recluse, dedicated to his own spiritual devotions and development. The new Hasidic rabbi, the tzaddik (the righteous one; the one who connected heaven and earth), went out to the people to attend to their needs: for food, work, family, and health. His spiritual devotions were dedicated to the good and well-being of his followers. Whether the wonder-working tzaddik actually changed the course of people's lives we cannot know. But, surely many experienced such changes for the better or trusted that the tzaddik had the power to bring such changes about.

That trust formed the foundation of the relationship of the tzaddik with his followers. While the Hasidim may have received material blessing through the tzaddik, more important was the spiritual inspiration they received. Although they might not be able to achieve *devekut* and so participate in cosmic transformations, the Hasidim were to do their best to follow the tzaddik's model. Thus, daily life—both ritual observance and making a living, holy time and mundane time—grew in significance. Everything mattered now, not out of fear of failure or punishment for sin, but because consciousness mattered to God. It brought God delight; it fulfilled the divine intention for Creation. The Hasidim, through their personal observance and their connection to the tzaddik, played a role in a cosmic process. In turn, the Hasidim experienced God's love through the tzaddik. Their self-worth was honored, buttressed, and vitalized through the tzaddik's attention. The Hasidim learned that God loved them, cared about their life, and honored their endeavors to live up to God's expectations.

THE EXPRESSION OF THESE VIEWS IN *KEDUSHAT LEVI*

These spiritual perspectives (and assumptions) fill the pages of *Kedushat Levi*.

- God is most often referred to as the "blessed Creator." The Creator's intention in bringing the world into being was for our good. The Creator's goodness and love fill this mundane world and so are accessible to us. We can respond to that love with love.

- God brought the world into being through divine speech. When we connect consciousness to speech and deed, we can inspire and direct the flow of divine blessing in this world. Through our intentional speech—in Torah study, in prayer, in holy conversation—we can return that divine energy, completing the cycle from *ayin* to *yesh* and *yesh* to *ayin*.

- The blessed Creator is still actively involved in creation. Each moment is a coming-into-being of existence once again, a new creation. Nothing is to be taken for granted, not even the laws of "nature." Even what is most natural—where the garment obscuring God's presence is most opaque—still testifies to God's infinite freedom to do whatever is needed for justice, love, and wholeness.

- Serving God without expectation of reward brings God delight. Our sole attention is on God, not on our selves. God delights in our efforts, which is then reflected in our experience: we feel more full, more blessed, more free.

That is because we have "nullified" our selfhood, our ego, for the sake of another, of the Other. In getting our selves "out of the way" we diminish our quantum of *yesh* to then testify to the greater truth of God's *ayin*.

- The blessed Creator is bound up in all creation, waiting to be discovered and met. Expanding and deepening our consciousness of God's presence in every thing, in each moment, brings us delight in meeting God over and over, and makes God more present in the world. We both testify to and make real God's oneness, the interconnectedness of all existence.

- The process of bringing our awareness back over and over to the truth of God's presence in all existence, of the renewal of creation by the blessed Creator, is the highest form of *teshuvah*, return (or repentance). Failure to observe the commandments or trespassing them is essentially a rejection of God, a denial of the fundamental structure of creation. Rectifying these mistakes requires not only a change in behavior (itself a powerful practice to bring God more fully into the world) but also a change in consciousness. Returning to God—in practice and in awareness—nullifies our *yesh* before God's *ayin*, fulfilling our role in the world.

BUT WE'RE NOT HASIDIM!

If we have doubts about shamanism and the capacity of Hasidic tzaddikim to actually change the order of nature for the sake of their Hasidim, then why should we be interested in all of this? Couldn't these teachings just be a charlatan's spiritualized sop to seduce new followers? There were, in fact, many contemporaries who felt just this way and who fought the new Hasidic teachers—including in particular R. Levi Yitzhak—with just these charges. Yet, whether the tzaddik actually provided sustenance or fertility to his people, something of his teachings rang true to his followers; some deeper message made sense beyond the claims of intervention in the divine realms to affect material reality. People were inspired by his teachings, and in response their lives were transformed. Their sense of themselves in the world, of their relationship to others, of their purpose in life was renewed.

This is why we may be interested in studying these teachings as well; we wonder if perhaps these teachings might inspire and transform our lives, too. We approach these teachings with these questions in mind: Can these teachings change how I understand myself in the world? Can I find instruction for living that will help me be happier, more compassionate, more righteous, more attuned to my responsibilities to all beings, to the life of this planet? I believe they can—and do. Some "translation" is necessary—not only of the Hebrew original in which they were published but also of the frame of reference of the time. The late eighteenth century is too far away from our time to take its "scientific," anthropological, historical, or sociological assumptions as true.[4] We have to listen deeply to these teachings to identify what their "meta-message" may be for us, and then bring the teaching and its meaning back into our lives in language we can understand and as practice.

In the end, these teachings present ideas that are meant to affect how we live. They are instructions for practice. For R. Levi Yitzhak and his followers, this meant both traditional Jewish observance and additional spiritual undertakings. It can mean the same for us, in our own terms. We may find a way into deeper Jewish observance through these teachings. And, we may discover that they suggest other practices to help us wake up to our lives, to the wonder of existence, to our interconnection with, dependence on, and responsibility to all others, our true calling as human beings.

My understanding of Hasidic teachings has been influenced by my practice of mindfulness, supported by mindfulness meditation. I did not take up meditation in place of traditional Jewish practice, but as a supplement. I have not taken on mindfulness as a substitute for Jewish spirituality, but as a method of deepening it. It is through my experience in meditation that I have gained access to the spiritual consciousness taught by R. Levi Yitzhak. I have found mindfulness to resonate with his teachings.

MINDFULNESS AND JEWISH LIFE

Jewish religious practice, in all of its forms and features, is meant to help us develop mindfulness. On its simplest level, this appears in those rituals and practices that force us to pay attention to some specific act, to some particular time, to some experience. Pausing to recite a blessing before eating can help me become aware of and connect directly to the experience of what I am about to eat. It reminds me to return to this moment, this act. The whole of the system of the dietary rules can do the same. The statutory prayers three times a day connect me to the passage of time and to the unique qualities of each part of the day, making it less likely that I will treat today as if it were no different from yesterday, as if it will be indistinguishable from tomorrow. This is true, as well, with Shabbat and the festivals. The study of Torah invites me to step out of my self-centered perspective to consider an alternative way of viewing myself, my neighbor, the world. The rules regulating the relationship between charity donor and recipient and the regulations of labor and capital force me to step out of my self-concern to place myself within the web of community and interdependence.

The mindfulness aspect of Jewish life extends beyond the practical aspects of religious observance. King David is reported to have said to Solomon, his son, "Know the God of your father, and serve Him" (1 Chron. 28:9). This suggests that Jewish religious life is fulfilled not only by performing prescribed acts, but also by doing so with consciousness. The purpose of practice—keeping the commandments, performing religious acts—is so that we might "know" God. Connection, intimacy with experience, is the goal of practice. Practice without consciousness may fulfill the mundane aspect of the commandments, but it fails the spiritual. Knowledge of God, intimacy, consciousness, and mindfulness are necessary components of Jewish spiritual life.

Hasidism has been described as a "revival" movement, rather than a revolution or reformation. The distinction is that the former sees the value in the tradition as received and wishes to inspire others to find that value. Often that comes with some new explanation for or interpretive relation to the tradition. This was true in Hasidism. The Jewish mystical tradition as expressed through Kabbalah was now adapted to make it accessible to the broad populace. Even the uneducated were (at least initially) empowered through their intentional acts to participate in cosmic transformation: redeeming sparks, bringing delight to the blessed Creator, attesting to God's infinite, undifferentiated oneness. All religious activity—and in the end, all human activity—was given cosmic significance when engaged with consciousness. Jewish religious life, now a practice of consciousness, was for the sake of deepening what I understand as mindfulness.

R. Levi Yitzhak, inspired by and engaged in promulgating this view of Jewish spiritual practice, expressed his experience of mindfulness through classical Jewish language. He spoke of God as the blessed Creator and the blessed Holy One, as if God were a being other than and outside of the material world. This God has a will and desire and is master of all existence. All that occurs comes about through the divine will, and all that happens to us is an expression of God's loving concern. We can call this way of speaking about God "dualistic," as it places us and God, the world and God, in a two-way relationship. Yet R. Levi Yitzhak also spoke of God in nondualistic ways. He employed a form of the four-lettered name of God commonly used by Hasidic teachers, *HVYH*. This name takes the untranslatable *YHVH*—the verb of being past-present-future—and renders it "Being." God, then, is the source from which all existence emerges, is the vital force that sustains all in existence, and is not separate from it. Even when speaking of *HVYH* as if in the third person, the implication is that it is actually all-inclusive, and all is embraced within the totality of Being. There is nothing other than God, as all is God, all is in God, all is enlivened by God's vitality.

These two experiences of God—as Other and as the All—point us back to the discussion of *yesh* and *ayin*. We meet God as Other, in the second person, when we meet the world in its expression as *yesh*. Every thing, each distinct aspect of creation, testifies to God's presence in the world. Each is an avenue to find God, to meet God, to enter into relation with God. Each demands full respect and attention, as God is present in it. At the same time, however, God's infinite, undifferentiated, all-encompassing Being negates any separateness to what we perceive as *yesh*. This leads us to sense its emptiness, its insubstantiality and insignificance as an "independent" thing. All dissolves into the One from the perspective of *ayin*.

R. Levi Yitzhak's close attention to the myriad manifest ways in which God can be known in the world directs our attention there as well. We are instructed not to take anything for granted, not to receive anything as "natural." His instructions can be understood as concentration practice. Pay attention. See beyond the surface flow of thoughts and experience. Connect to the truth in this moment:

what is true right now? While R. Levi Yitzhak might answer that last question by saying, "God is present in this moment, in this thing before you, in your immediate experience," he could just as easily say, in the way of plain mindfulness wisdom, "This is happening, just like this, in this moment, in the only way it can right here, right now." The God who is revealed to R. Levi Yitzhak we can know as the truth of our experience through mindful attention.

And while each instance of particular, embodied experience may reveal God's presence through concentrated attention, when R. Levi Yitzhak speaks of self-nullification, or serving without expectation of reward, or to bring delight to the blessed Creator, he is pointing toward open awareness. In open awareness we let go of our particular perspective, our personal concerns. We notice all unfolding in its own way, without our control and in spite of our preferences. We rest in the truth of this moment as it is, letting go of our attachment to our expectations and allowing things to be as they are. R. Levi Yitzhak would suggest that this is an experience of *ayin*. There is nothing but God, and we are nothing before God.

It may not have been fair to say, "R. Levi Yitzhak teaches mindfulness"; he would not have known the word (even though his use of *da'at*—knowledge, awareness—comes close) and worked from within his own integrated, holistic system. Yet, I read R. Levi Yitzhak as a mindfulness teacher. I do so for two reasons: I hope that in this way I can help make the rich spiritual teachings in *Kedushat Levi* accessible and meaningful to seekers who might otherwise not find themselves in a Jewish spiritual book. In addition, I find that reading R. Levi Yitzhak as a mindfulness teacher makes it possible for me, as a spiritual seeker and religious person, to employ the classical language of God-and-the-world and still know that I am talking about awareness and not about God as a separate "being," about consciousness of the totality of all existence and not a dualistic God.

These two are interconnected. The success of the Jewish community in America has been great—institutionally, economically, socially. Yet, there are signs that we have not found a spiritual language or religious approach that speaks to our experience and inspires dedication, commitment, or practice. The God of the intellect, the God of ethics, the God of peoplehood, and the God in heaven no longer sufficiently inspire. Yet, Jews have not given up altogether. They and others are still seeking spiritual inspiration, a grounding in the world that motivates concern for the other, mutual responsibility, and compassion, that nurtures interconnectedness and honors the truth of one's experience. They are looking for a way to be happy—to embrace life fully with joy and love—while facing the truth of human suffering and earthly peril without flinching. I believe that R. Levi Yitzhak speaks to these needs and concerns. And because he speaks from within the tradition in a nontraditional voice, I believe that he offers a way into Jewish religious and spiritual life for contemporary seekers.

THE KEY IS PRACTICE

Mindfulness is not a state of mind or a feeling. It is a practice. Each moment is new and presents new challenges, new experiences, new possibilities. The practice of mindfulness helps us connect to each moment so that we can become new as well. R. Levi Yitzhak knows that practice is the path to awareness: "Know the God of your father, and serve Him." Service (*avodah*) is how he would speak about spiritual practice. In every circumstance, whether under the purview of religious proscriptions or prescriptions or not, is an opportunity for *avodah*, a chance to awaken to God's presence in the world, to delight in being one form in which God expresses God's self in the world. Practices are forms by which we remind ourselves to remember what we know to be true. Through practice we deepen, sustain, and extend our mindfulness, our awareness, our connection to God.

R. Levi Yitzhak spoke to a community in which traditional Jewish religious practice was more or less a given. He could assume that his students were participating in those rituals. His goal was to help them engage those practices as a means to wake up, to become aware. It is therefore sometimes difficult to recognize that his teachings point to an injunction to practice. Yet, that is our goal as well. While his teachings may be emotionally, intellectually, and even spiritually inspiring, ultimately their importance lies in how they change us, prodding and leading us to become aware, so that we might live with greater integrity, for the sake of all beings.

A FEW WORDS ABOUT R. LEVI YITZHAK

R. Levi Yitzhak was born in 1740 to a distinguished rabbinic family in Hoshakov in Galicia. He distinguished himself in his studies in the nearby town of Yaroslav. A well-known merchant family in Libertov sought him out to marry the daughter of Israel Peretz, one of the four brothers. There he continued his studies in the company of other excellent students.

In 1754, R. Shmuel Shmelke Horowitz took up the post of rabbi of the town Ryczwol, where he drew young followers to his early Hasidic teachings. Levi Yitzhak was attracted as well and soon persuaded his father-in-law to permit him to travel there. R. Shmuel Shmelke saw Levi Yitzhak's promise and brought him to meet his teacher, the Maggid of Mezritch, and there R. Levi Yitzhak joined the circle of distinguished students who would ultimately spread Hasidism throughout Poland and Ukraine.

After 1761, R. Shmuel Shmelke was called to the rabbinate in Shinova. R. Levi Yitzhak's patron had since fallen on hard times, and so he acceded to the call to serve the community in Ryczwol. Although his predecessor was among the first Hasidic rabbis to serve in local communities and was known for his expressive prayer style, apparently R. Levi Yitzhak's manners were even more extreme. This drew the attention of the nascent "opposition" (*misnagdim*), who reacted negatively to his leadership and teaching, resisting his authority. Thinking that he might escape this difficult post, he accepted the invitation to serve as rabbi in Zelechow in 1765. He was the first Hasidic rabbi to serve in the area, and once again he encountered strenuous resistance to his teaching and authority.

Looking to find some stability and peace, R. Levi Yitzhak left Zelechow for Pinsk, to serve as community rabbi (around 1775). By this time, the forces of the *misnagdim* were stronger and more organized. In 1781, R. Levi Yitzhak engaged in a public debate with one of the chief opponents, R. Avraham Katzenellenbogen, rabbi of Brisk, yet failed to overcome the resistance of his community. While in Pinsk R. Levi Yitzhak found many supporters, the opposition of the Gaon of Vilna tipped the community against him. Soon after they expelled him from the town, throwing his belongings into the street after him.

In 1785, R. Levi Yitzhak was appointed rabbi of Berdichev, where he found peace and served to the end of his life.

While *Kedushat Levi* is known as R. Levi Yitzhak's primary work, he actually published a small section of the teachings—related to the nature of the miracles-in-nature of Hanukkah and Purim—in 1798. The larger and more significant portion of the book on the weekly Torah readings, which he authored but was finally organized for publication by his son (one had predeceased him) and his disciples, appeared posthumously in 1811 (R. Levi Yitzhak had died in 1809).

As we have noted, R. Levi Yitzhak teaches about the role of the tzaddik in providing for his followers. This was not merely a theoretical matter. Rather, it characterized his role as community leader and promoter of Hasidic values and practices. He devoted himself to the good of the people, engaging with them in their lives. There are many tales about R. Levi Yitzhak attesting to his love of the Jewish people, his understanding of their difficulties and the reasons for their failures in religious life, and his desire to find the good in them. This is possibly how R. Levi Yitzhak is known best, rather than through the teachings we'll share in this book. So here are a few examples of the way in which R. Levi Yitzhak held the Jewish people dearly, and stood for them before God. The first illustrates how he sought to raise up even the lowliest Jew, finding even in their flawed practice devotion to God:

> Once the rabbi of Berdichev saw a drayman arrayed for the Morning Service in prayer shawl and phylacteries. He was greasing the wheels of his wagon. "Lord of the world!" he exclaimed delightedly. "Behold this man! Behold the devoutness of your people. Even when they grease the wheels of a wagon, they still are mindful of your name!"[5]

In the following story, R. Levi holds up a mirror to the Jewish people, to chide them gently, while still arguing in their favor before God:

> The rabbi of Berdichev said: "What I see before me is a topsy-turvy world. Once the whole truth was in the alleys and marketplaces of Israel; there everyone told the truth. But when they came to the House of Prayer, they managed to tell lies. Now it is just the other way round. In the streets and in the squares they utter falsehoods, but when they enter the House of Prayer, they confess the truth. For once it was thus in Israel: Truth and faithfulness were the lamps lighting their steps, and when they went to the marketplace and into the world of trade, with their souls they proved the words: Your 'yes' be truth and your 'no' be true, and all their trading was done in good faith. But when they came to the House

of Prayer they beat their breasts and said: 'We have trespassed! We have dealt treacherously! We have robbed!' And all this was a lie because they had kept faith before God and Man. Today the reverse takes place: in trading they lie and cheat; in their prayer they profess the truth."[6]

For all that he might chastise his people for their failings in business, R. Levi Yitzhak still never despaired of them, or gave up praying for them.

> In the middle of a prayer Rabbi Levi Yitzhak said: "Lord of all the world! A time there was when you went around with that Torah of yours and were willing to sell it at a bargain, like apples that have gone bad, yet no one would buy it from you. No one would even look at you! And then we took it! Because of this I want to propose a deal. We have many sins and misdeeds, and you an abundance of forgiveness and atonement. Let us exchange! But perhaps you will say: 'Like for like!' My answer is: Had we no sins, what would you do with all your forgiveness? So you must balance the deal by giving us life, and children, and food besides!"[7]

In a similar vein we have this story:

> In the middle of a prayer, the rabbi of Berdichev once said to God: "Lord of the world, you must forgive Israel their sins. If you do this—good. But if you do not do this, I shall have to tell all the world that the phylacteries you wear are invalid. For what is the verse enclosed in your phylacteries? It is a verse of David's, of your anointed: 'Who is like thy people Israel, a unique nation on earth!' But if you do not forgive Israel their sins, then they are no longer a 'unique nation on earth,' the verse contained in your phylacteries is untrue, and they become invalid."
>
> Another time he said: "Lord of the world, Israel are your head-phylacteries. When the phylacteries of a simple Jew fall to the ground, he picks them up carefully, cleans them, and kisses them. Lord, your phylacteries have fallen to the ground."[8]

In the folk imagination, as reflected in these tales, R. Levi Yitzhak intervened on behalf of Israel through his prayer, and stood up for them. Yet, of course, as a Hasidic master, his true intent was to transform the hearts of Israel, to make them fully worthy before God. This we will learn as we study together the lessons in this book.

HOW TO USE THIS BOOK

It is surely possible to use this book simply to come to know a selection of teachings from a virtuoso Hasidic master of the late eighteenth century, and I am pleased to be able to open up even such a small portion of the lessons of *Kedushat Levi* to an English-reading audience. Yet, inasmuch as R. Levi Yitzhak intended his teachings as inspiration and support for personal transformation and spiritual awareness, there is surely more that we can take from this book.

I encourage you to approach this book as a guide for practice. Each week I have selected from one to four lessons from *Kedushat Levi* based on the weekly synagogue reading from Scripture, and offer an English translation (the Hebrew texts for each lesson can be found at www.jewishlights.com). These translations follow the original Hebrew fairly closely, sometimes leading to redundancies, lacunae, and long or convoluted sentences and sometimes pointing to references outside of the text itself. I have chosen not to interpolate too much into the translation or to overwrite R. Levi Yitzhak, for a number of reasons. One is personal: as I noted above, when I first began translating selections, it was for colleagues as a shared endeavor. I did not see myself as a "teacher" and so saw the translation only as a "prop," a tool to support other clergy engaged in studying the original Hebrew. And I believe (and hope) that this may still be true—that you (or others) will read the English alongside the Hebrew, looking for the English translation to open up the Hebrew text for you. Yet for many the Hebrew text is inaccessible. For them I wished to communicate a bit of R. Levi Yitzhak's writing style, bringing them into its internal logic and mode of expression. Finally, I chose to keep the translation close to the original because I also provided other resources to help unpack and interpret the lessons.[9]

Thus, following each lesson is a commentary meant to open up difficult, obscure, or unfamiliar aspects of the teaching. Sometimes I bring the full text of a citation referred to in the lesson; other times I reformulate the argument in a clearer, more linear, or less complex manner. In my commentary, I hope to clarify why I think this lesson is meaningful, how it relates to mindfulness practice, how it reveals something new about the scriptural passage it refers to, and how it reveals something interesting and powerful about human spirituality. With this in mind, I then pose three questions for reflection. Each refers to some specific aspect of the lesson: a phrase, an idea, a prop-osition, or an argument. I pose the questions without expectation of a particular "right" answer. Rather, I ask because they are questions I ask myself, and I think that in pursuing them we can learn more about ourselves, about Judaism, and about our own spiritual lives.

Finally, I propose a practice that I believe grows out of R. Levi Yitzhak's teaching. Again, the lessons in *Kedushat Levi* were not orig-inally intended as intellectual curiosities or as demonstrations of R. Levi Yitzhak's brilliance. They were meant to inspire religious pas-sion and deeper spiritual practice. I believe that these teachings will come to life in us when we bring them into our lives in practice. So when I say "as you make your way through your day" or "this week try this," I mean it literally. Try it. Practice. Notice what you notice; feel what you feel; learn from your experience.

I do mean for *Kedushat Levi* to become a partner for you in deep-ening your spiritual life. It may be sufficient. But, in my experi-ence—and as we have found at the Institute for Jewish Spirituality and as has been the central mode of Jewish education for millen-nia—you will learn more and take in the lessons more deeply if you study with an actual partner. Find someone in your community—in your synagogue or *chavurah*, at your gym or child care, a best friend across the country or someone new who is also on a spiritual path—and set aside an hour a week for study. Take your time. Sit for a minute before beginning so that you can both arrive and set an intention to meet the text with a full heart, with curiosity and an openness to change and grow. You might want to recite the tra-ditional blessing for Torah study before diving into the text. Offer yourself and your efforts for the sake of your partner, that your partner might find in the study and practice to follow what he or she needs in his or her life. Rest assured: you will be blessed as well. Turn your attention to one teaching (don't try to do all of them in one week—it is really too much and may be confusing). Read it out loud, taking turns. Go back over it and ask questions: What don't you understand? What seems unusual to you? What is surprising? What is new? In sharing your questions you invite each other into a new dominion: the realm of discovery. You are not seeking "the" answer (although to be sure it is important to know what the text is actually saying), but a response that touches you, that inspires you, that challenges you. As you work through your questions, seeking to understand not only what the text says but also how it says it, why, and to what end, remember to pause periodically to ask: Is this true in my experience? What is happening in me right now, as we are talking? How is this affecting me in this moment?

At the end of your time together, consider the practice suggestion. Discuss how—or if—you will take it on. In making a commitment to your partner, you should feel both strengthened in your commitment to engage the practice and a curiosity about what your partner will experience. We practice for ourselves and for our partners. And, of course, have compassion for yourself and your partner. Taking on new practices is difficult. Every change of habit meets resistance. Do your best, and support each other along the way. You may decide to stay with a practice for weeks on end, ignoring whatever suggestions may appear in subsequent weeks. That is fine. You may drop a practice after one week to move on to another. That is fine, too. But, if there is a practice—or a teaching that inspires a practice—that moves you in particular, stay with it. Sustaining a practice over time (several weeks or months) often reveals new and unexpected results and insights.

This form of study is also appropriate to Torah study groups, meditation groups, *chavurot*, and adult education programs. Remember: keep the focus of your study and practice on spiritual growth and transformation. The ideas are nice, but if they do not make their way inside, if they do not touch the heart or soul, then they have not hit their target. May your study with a partner help you sense yourself accompanied on your way by R. Levi Yitzhak and the blessed Holy One. May deepened mindfulness help release you from the "terminal uniqueness" of the separate self, to sense yourself in the presence of Presence, consciousness, and awareness in each moment. And, may you become a partner in holiness.

The Book of
Genesis

Bereishit

We can say more about: "In the beginning [God created the heaven and earth]" (Gen. 1:1).

"In the beginning" (*Bereishit*): we can read this as "two beginnings" (*b'reishit*): the blessed One pours out abundant, flowing blessing (*shefa*), and we, in our prayers, limit and shape this *shefa*, each of us, according to our needs. One person may constrict the flow with the letters of "life" for Life; another one with the letters of "wisdom" for Wisdom; and yet another one with the letters of "wealth" for Wealth. And, so it is for all good things, each of us according to our needs.

Now, just as this is so in the spiritual realm, it is also true in the physical. Thus, in the physical realm there are the qualities of sound (voice) and speech. "Sound" ("voice"; *kol*) is all-inclusive, while "speech" (*dibbur*) is the constriction or shaping of the sound through the letters of speech. Similarly, on Rosh Hashanah, the sound (*kol*) of the shofar is the outpouring of blessing (*shefa*) from the blessed Creator, and it is all-inclusive. But, our prayers of *Malkhuyot*, *Zikhronot*, and *Shofarot* are the constriction of this flow that we bring about through the letters (of speech), each of us shaping and constricting the flow from the blessed Creator according to our needs.

The all-inclusive *shefa* that comes forth from the blessed Creator is the Written Torah. And, the manner by which we constrict and shape the *shefa* is the Oral Torah. We create the Oral Torah according to our will, according to our interpretation of the Written Torah. This is the meaning of *Bereishit*—*b'reishit*, "two beginnings": Written Torah and Oral Torah.

FOR FURTHER THOUGHT

One might ask the question, How is it that God created a world in one moment, at one time, but that this same world continues to function beyond God's original Creation, as it were, on its own? One of the answers to that question is that we are mistaken to think that the original Creation was static, a onetime event. Rather, God "in goodness renews Creation every day." Still, having said that, we are left with the question, What is the significance of the story of Creation as it appears in the Torah? This is what Levi Yitzhak comes to tell us.

God's blessed, dynamic force pours forth in every instant, creating and sustaining all existence. This is called *shefa*. At its source, this force is pure, undifferentiated, containing all things. For the multiple, variegated, and diverse aspects of Creation to come into being, this flow has to be "stepped down" in power, constricted and contracted into gross forms. This is *tzimtzum*. The mystical tradition has imagined the process of *tzimtzum* taking the form of letters, chaining down in form and substance, their interconnections, combinations, and recombinations producing all of existence, both physical and spiritual. The pure outflow of blessing—all-inclusive, undifferentiated—is like the voice, like the sound of the shofar, like the original Written Torah. Speech, the cutting up of sound into letters, phonemes, syllables, words, and sentences, is the way that this pure flow becomes manifest creation. Our participation in creation is through our intentional application of our speech—in prayer and in Torah study, directing the flow to the betterment of all people; interpreting Torah, the blueprint of all Creation, so that its enlivening power might truly be a blessing.

We, speaking beings, have the capacity to join with God in the process of Creation. This power carries responsibility, and so on Rosh Hashanah we are reminded that we write the script of our own lives. We will most likely succeed in our role when we remember that we are indeed partners with God, bringing prayerful awareness to our every act and interaction, so that the Torah we write and the creation we manifest in this moment is worthy of its origins in the Torah of the first moment of Creation.

 ## Questions for Reflection

1. What is your experience of hearing the shofar on Rosh Hashanah? How does it make you feel? How is the sound of the shofar different for you from the sound of the prayer leader or the congregation in prayer?

2. How does seeing the Written Torah as the source of undifferentiated expression, rather than a book of detailed stories and laws, affect your relation to the text and to the significance of interpreting the text? Have

you ever experienced your interpretation of Torah as a process of creation? As *the* process of Creation? When, how?

3. When you are in conversation with someone, how much of your attention is in the specific words that are spoken by the other person, and how much in the larger, perhaps nonverbal communication? Have you been frustrated by your inability to communicate everything in your heart in words? How do these experiences affect your understanding of the nature of prayer or Torah study in light of this lesson?

 ## Taking It into Your Life

Sit quietly, allowing your body to relax, bringing your attention to the flow of your breath. Allow thoughts that arise to slip away, and when you find that your mind has wandered, bring it back to the awareness of your breath. When you find that you are settled, bring to mind the intention to produce the word "you." Hold that intention, notice how the thought arises, what it means to have an intention in potential, not yet expressed. When you are ready, move from the intention to producing the sound "ooo" on an out-breath. Notice the movement from potential to actual. Notice also the quality of a voiced, but unarticulated sound. When ready, add the consonant "y" to the beginning of the sound "ooo" on a slow out-breath. Notice the sensation of producing a recognizable word (world). Notice the thoughts, inner feelings, sensations, and associations that come from this experience. Then, return to simply attending to your breath. Come back to active awareness of the room. Journal about your experience, and relate it to our text.

The midrash (Gen. R. 8:5) teaches that when God was creating the world, Truth complained, saying, "Let it not be created," and the blessed Holy One cast Truth to the earth … as Scripture says, "Truth springs up from the earth" (Ps. 85:12).

In general, a person who lies cannot engage in the even mundane activities of this world, in making a living. No one wants to do business with someone who lies or to speak to him. Nevertheless, even if a person doesn't do any of the other mitzvot (heaven forbid!), he or she still can engage in business and mundane activities. Yet, how is it that without truth one cannot do anything in the world, even the most mundane activities, while this is not the case with all of the rest of the mitzvot?

In fact, Truth stands in a very high position, and it is not easy to attain it. If it were possible for the world to exist without the Truth, no one would move himself or herself to get it; they would not do anything to attain the level of Truth. It is for this reason that the Holy One made it such that without the Truth we are not able to do even the most mundane things, so that we will be aroused to seek out Truth through service of the blessed Creator. That is the meaning of the midrash "**the blessed Holy One cast Truth to the earth**": even when we are most base, in our lowest estate, or engaged in the world of this world we cannot survive without Truth.

FOR FURTHER THOUGHT

This passage starts out on the level of the mundane—that is, truth is necessary between people for even the most basic of interactions: commerce, communication, community. But, it does not stay there. The need for truth in mundane interactions leads us to "seek out Truth through service of the blessed Creator." This helps us locate ourselves in the world, to know what the purpose of Creation was and how we fit in it. This lesson helps us reflect on our lives, from moment to moment, from year to year.

In the original midrash, it is not clear why God casts Truth to the earth. Perhaps it is to get Truth out of the way, so that God could create human beings; perhaps so that Truth could emerge from the hard work of human beings. Levi Yitzhak suggests that Truth, despite its elevated status, had to be found in even the lowliest places for true life to go on. More than that, any mention of "earth" (*eretz*) suggests to a Hasidic teacher our "earthiness," our materiality and corporeality. So, at the end of the lesson Levi Yitzhak draws the connection to earthiness (*artzi'ut*), our "base, lowest estate." Even when we are disconnected from any spiritual concerns, we cannot survive without paying attention to the truth.

 Questions for Reflection

1. In your experience, is there a connection between being truthful with others—embodying the truth—and seeking out Truth in serving God? When, how? Can we do one without the other?

2. "Truth springs up from the earth." Is Truth on the earth or in "a very high position"? When does Truth spring up? How? Who makes this happen? When?

3. What are the barriers or obstacles to seeing clearly or knowing the truth? Why is it so difficult to attain this clarity, to know oneself, another person, or the nature of existence on this level of truth?

Taking It into Your Life

What is the Truth that we are seeking when we approach the Holy One? Fundamentally we seek to become transparent, where we hide nothing from God. Of course, we can try to hide, but God will know, and we will not be truthful. And sometimes we can be obtuse, ignorant of what we think or feel, or what we have done—and God will know that, too, even when we don't. So embodying the Truth requires that we pay close attention to all aspects of our lives, to see clearly who we are at all times.

Sylvia Boorstein has called mindfulness practice a discipline of "radical truth-telling." That means that we strive to see clearly precisely what we are feeling, precisely what we are doing each moment, without telling a story. So often we add details that protect our ego, to gain an edge, deflect fears, or fill our needs. In this sense we are not talking about some objective truth, or some philosophical Truth. Nor is it some relativistic subjective truth that we can use to cudgel others into submission or to protect our egos. Rather, we seek to meet each moment just as it is, learning to recognize that "it is just this."

As you make your way through the day, notice what you notice, what attracts your attention, what arises in your thoughts. Is your eye drawn to your reflection in the mirror? Notice your reaction—your rush to judgment, your wishes, desires, fears—and respond, "It is just this." Are you caught in traffic, jostled on the train? "It is just this." Interrupted at work, overloaded with work, frustrated at work? "It is just this." Over and over we tell the truth: we are not in control, we are not to blame, we only wish to be happy, everyone else is in the same boat. This truth, as mundane and earthy as it may be, can connect us directly to our lives, and to God.

An alternative explanation of the verse "A
river flows forth from Eden to water the

> garden [and it then divides and becomes
> four branches]" (Gen. 2:10).

What it means to be Jewish is to strive to cleave to good and upright qualities (*middot*) and in this manner to bring ease and pleasure to the blessed Creator. This sort of devotion is so that God might glorify, that is, take pride in our actions as reflected in this teaching in Pirke Avot (2:1): "Rabbi (Yehudah the Patriarch) used to say: What is the upright path that one should choose? That which brings glory to its doers, and which brings glory from people (i.e., brings attestation of glory from others)."

Now, this teaching is phrased with sweet precision. First, it says, "that which brings glory to its doers" (*osehah*): that is, God takes pride in human actions, yet in the end it is God who does everything (*oseh hakol*), so our actions bring glory to God. We might find this odd. After all, why would God be concerned at all about human deeds? Does God not have enough heavenly angels who constantly praise the Creator of all?

But this is precisely why God chose the people of Israel. Even when people exist on the lowest level of all creation, they may constantly devote themselves to God's service. And this is then the beauty of the second half of our lesson: "which brings glory from people" (*min ha'adam*). Even when our consciousness is limited yet we still serve God, surely the blessed Creator takes pride in us—this is what "brings glory from people." God gets delight from people and so glorifies in us. When we think of ourselves in this light, the Creator derives great delight, which in turn generates flow of goodness to all worlds. This is reflected in our opening verse. The image of a "river" suggests this flow of goodness. Thus, **"A river flows forth from Eden to water"**—that is, from the pleasantness (*eiden*) and delight that God receives from our devotions, a river of blessing and goodness flows forth. This flow is to **"water the garden,"** that is, all of existence; all the worlds of existence are known as a "garden."

FOR FURTHER THOUGHT

In this lesson we are introduced to one of the central themes of Hasidic spirituality and of Levi Yitzhak in particular: the ultimate purpose of our devoted service of God is to bring God delight. The joy that God derives from our actions—the product of the pride that

God takes in us and the glory that comes to God from our devotion—generates a response in God. That response is to direct blessing and goodness to all creation.

We should not minimize this point. Our actions in this world, in the limited realm of our personal existence, have cosmic consequences! When we act with awareness, seeking not our own satisfaction but the good and well-being of others, we attain the highest qualities of human existence. Our service—to others, to God—is of greater value even than that of the heavenly angels. God's response to our deeds is delight, joy, pleasure, ease (as we say in Yiddish: *naches*), which prompts God to pour out blessings and goodness on all creation.

This translation retains an ambiguity in the original. Levi Yitzhak begins speaking about the obligations incumbent on Jews. But influenced by the more generic language of the teaching in Pirke Avot, he shifts to speak about human beings in general. He alternates back to speak of the election of Israel but concludes generically (reflected in the terms "people" and "we" above). Levi Yitzhak in general sees the role of the Jewish people as unique and superior to that of others. But he is not consistent, and when he leaves the door open, we do well to adopt his teachings as a reflection of spiritual truths, applicable to all of God's devotees. We Jews serve God in our particular ways, but all who serve God and wish only God's glory bring delight as well.

Levi Yitzhak also performs a classical Hasidic shift. The teaching from Pirke Avot seems to be concerned with the perceptions of the actor and of those who see him or her; that is, the best way for us to act is such that we can take pride in our actions ourselves and that other people will attribute glory to us for our actions. It is a humanistic teaching, grounded in interpersonal relationships. Levi Yitzhak shifts the referent from humans to God. The best path we can follow is one in which God can take pride and through which we bring glory to God. He rereads that teaching, bringing in the divine concern, and thereby adds the cosmic/spiritual dimension to the ethical concern of Pirke Avot. Not only should we be concerned with our relations to others, but we must also give attention to, devote ourselves to, our relation to the Other.

How shall we read this passage as a lesson in mindfulness practice? Surely, Levi Yitzhak attributes feelings such as delight, pride, and glory to God, and he suggests that God cares that we bring glory to God. This may be off-putting or distracting to some people. But, it need not necessarily be so. If we consider that the first phrase—"that which brings glory to its doers"—is meant to shift our concern from self to God, it suggests that in all of our affairs we might seek to lift ourselves up out of our "story," out of our self-referential orientation, to one that seeks to see what is true in this moment. Acting only for God's glory is a way of saying, "I wish to act with wisdom, for the sake of easing the suffering of all beings, for the good of all creation." Further, when we act in this manner with awareness, as our truest intention, it generates even greater power. It expands the effect of our actions. In this sense, our attention to the "Other" (God, or the sense of "what is" as opposed to "what I wish were true") leads us to act for the benefit of the other.

 ## Questions for Reflection

1. Does it surprise you to read a sentence like "What it means to be Jewish is to strive to cleave to good and upright qualities (*middot*) and in this manner to bring ease and pleasure to the blessed Creator"? Is this what you think it means to be Jewish? How might this formulation of what it means to live a Jewish life affect your sense of yourself, of your spiritual life, of your expectations of the Jewish community?

2. God takes pride in the fact that we do things in which God's glory is made manifest. Why, then, does it appear that God glorifies even more when "we act in this manner out of awareness"? What is it about our awareness that makes our deeds more powerful?

3. That which brings God "ease and pleasure" is that we cleave to good and upright qualities. What is the relation between these qualities (*middot*) and God being made manifest, glorified, in the world? How does the fact that we connect to these qualities (which are also divine qualities), that we enact them in the world, bring God ease? What is the relationship between these qualities and divine service, devotion to God?

 ## Taking It into Your Life

Sit quietly, allowing your body to relax, bringing your attention to the flow of your breath. Allow thoughts that arise to slip away, and when you find that your mind has wandered, bring it back to the awareness of your breath.

Allow your breath to come and go in its own, natural rhythm. When you find that you are settled, give a bit more attention to the thoughts that arise from moment to moment. Notice their content, when they are about you—your feelings, your plans, your reflections—and when they are about other people—how you feel about them, plans you have with them, memories of them, and so on. As this awareness deepens, notice your attachment to these thoughts or your dissatisfaction with them. Notice how you engage with them, positively or negatively. Then, investigate: are these thoughts me, or are they thoughts? Can I allow these thoughts to pass away without comment, without regret, without relief? What does it feel like—in the moment and after you conclude this meditation—to be free of attachment to your thoughts, to this aspect of your "self"? How might this practice be a way of orienting ourselves to doing things for God's glory?

Noach

"[This is the line of Noah. —] Noah was a
righteous man; [he was blameless in his age;
Noah walked with God]" (Gen. 6:9).

Consider Rashi's comment on Gen. 7:7: "Even Noah's faith was
limited (lit., Noah was among those of limited faith)." How could
this be, since Scripture itself testifies that Noah was "**a righteous man;
he was blameless in his age**"? Further, it is troubling that Noah did
not pray that the decree be annulled (to stop the Flood).

We can explain it this way: there are two types of tzaddikim who
serve the Creator. There is the tzaddik who serves the Creator and
has no desire other than to be the servant of the Creator, and in that
he also believes that he has the power in the upper realms to direct
creation according to his will. This is the tzaddik who is reflected in
the passage in Mo'ed Katan (16b): "'The righteous rules the fear of
God' (2 Sam. 23:3): [God asks,] 'Who rules over me? The tzaddik.'
The blessed Holy One decrees, and the tzaddik annuls the decree in
favor of the good."

Yet, there is another sort of tzaddik, one who serves the blessed
Creator and who is very lowly in his own eyes. He thinks to himself,
"Who am I that I should pray to annul the decree?" and he therefore
does not pray to do so....

Even though Noah was a great and blameless tzaddik, he was very
small in his own eyes, and he did not have faith in himself that he was
a tzaddik with the capacity to annul decrees. Rather, he thought of
himself as only equal to the rest of his generation. He thought, "If I
am to be saved in this ark, and I am no more righteous than the rest
of this generation, they too will be saved." Therefore, he did not pray
to save that generation. This is what Rashi meant in his comment
that Noah's faith was limited. That is, Noah was small in his own
eyes, limited in faith in himself as a blameless tzaddik who is able to
annul decrees, since he did not consider himself much at all. That is

the intent of the verse "I am about to destroy them with the earth" (Gen. 6:13). That is, (God said,) "I will do according to My will. Since there is no tzaddik who will pray to annul this decree, therefore I will destroy them with the earth." Then, later God said, "I now establish My covenant with you" (9:9), even though there is no tzaddik who will pray to annul the decree, nevertheless I will keep My covenant with you."

FOR FURTHER THOUGHT

In the Talmud, the Rabbis debate Noah's standing as a tzaddik: was he truly righteous, or was he righteous only relative to his generation? In our lesson we assume that Noah is truly a tzaddik, yet his righteousness is limited by his lack of faith in himself, held passive by his fear of heaven and his humility. He saw himself only "in his generation," that is, as no better than the rest of his fellows. He did not recognize that as a pure and upright person, as a true tzaddik, he had the power to overturn God's decree, to save his generation.

One factor that contributed to the success of the Hasidic movement was the innovative relationship of its leaders to the people. Up to their day, the spiritual leaders, the tzaddikim, held themselves aloof from the populace, secluding themselves to deepen their personal piety. In contrast, the Hasidic leaders placed themselves among the people, demonstrating their concern for their well-being. They adopted a mystical view of the role of the tzaddik, understanding him to be a mediator between heaven and earth. The tzaddik was able, through contemplative practices, to ascend to the heavens and participate in the divine economy, rearranging the letters of Creation to bring blessing to his people. They believed that they could live out the Rabbinic assertion that God may decree (negative consequences for Israel), but the tzaddik can annul the decree.

This is how Levi Yitzhak solves the problem he set out at the start: how can Noah be called a tzaddik, yet not stand in the breach, serving as the prophetic "loyal opposition" to save his people? Well, he may be a tzaddik, but not of the higher (Hasidic) sort. In this manner, Levi Yitzhak uses Noah as a foil against which he can set up the Hasidic tzaddik, the wonder-worker, the protecting shepherd of Israel as the true leader for his time.

Questions for Reflection

1. We are very aware of the dangers of hubris, of ego, and of the excesses of power. What are the dangers of excess humility? On the other hand, can you be humble and still be powerful?

2. The Hasidic tradition relies on the verse "God fulfills the desires of those who revere Him" (Ps. 145:19), meaning that the devotion of the tzaddik is such that God will fulfill his desire, his will. Is this a phenomenon to which you can relate? How do you understand this verse? Is there any way in which you can perceive a human capacity to change God's will?

3. What kind of tzaddik would you prefer to be? Which God do you feel you serve—and when: the God of "what is" or the God of "what is supposed to be"? What are the benefits and dangers in each case? What might be the consequences of our choosing the wrong approach? Can we manage to do both?

Taking It into Your Life

We are constantly confronted with moments of decision: to act or not to act. Pay attention over the next week to those moments when you are called upon to act to protect another person (in your family, in your congregation or community, on the street) from another's anger or impatience, from injustice or wrongdoing, from violence or hostility. Notice when you are able to respond and when you hesitate. Pay attention to the inner voices that urge you on or hold you back. How do you feel when you are able to act, and how do you feel when you are held back? What is the source of your energy in acting, and what is the nature of the resistance to acting? Sit with your awareness and consider yourself in light of our lesson. When are you Noah (and when might that be appropriate), and when are you the tzaddik who can work for the benefit of others (and when might that lead you to overreaching)?

> Another interpretation of "[This is the line of Noah.—Noah was a righteous man; he was blameless in his age;] Noah walked with God" (Gen. 6:9).

This verse comes to teach us that Noah caused the blessed Creator to be garbed in the letters (of speech, of Creation). We learn this from the direct object, *et* (which here signifies "with")—its two letters, *aleph* and *tav*, representing all of the twenty-two letters of the Hebrew alphabet. With these letters Noah caused God to walk; he caused God to be present in the letters.

"[Make yourself an ark of gopher wood;] make it an ark with compartments, [and cover it inside and out with pitch]" (Gen. 6:14).

The word "**compartments**" (*kinim*) refers us to "a bird's nest" (*kan*) (cf. Deut. 22:6), that is, a dwelling place. This means that we are to be attached and connected to the word (*teivah*), that which we say when we speak in devotion, in Torah study or prayer.

Another interpretation of "[Make yourself an ark of gopher wood;] make it an ark with compartments, [and cover it inside and out with pitch]" (Gen. 6:14).

By means of your speech you are to cause the blessed Creator to dwell in this world. This is how we should read the verse: you should make "**compartments**" (*kinim*) (as above) "with the word" (*teivah*), that is, with your speech.

FOR FURTHER THOUGHT

These lessons build from a classical teaching of the Baal Shem Tov, focusing on the homonyms *teivah* = ark / *teivah* = word. Part of the revolution brought about by the Baal Shem Tov was a renewal and revitalization of the prayer experience. Under the influence of the Kabbalah of R. Isaac Luria, what was perceived to be "true" prayer, or effective prayer, had become recondite, inscrutable except to the most learned. Each word—indeed, even syllables and letters—had unique intentions connected to them, each meant to bring about some cosmic transformation. The Baal Shem Tov offered simple people the possibility that their prayer, with their simple but concentrated intention, would be acceptable, even a delight to God. What he asked, though, was focused concentration on each letter in prayer, such that through this the very essence of God's power and being hidden in that letter might be revealed.

We hear this in the following passage from *Tzava'at haRiVa"Sh*, a collection of teachings attributed to the Baal Shem Tov:

> "Make a light for the *teivah* (ark) [and finish it to (the width of) an *amah* (cubit) on high ...]" (Gen. 6:16). This means that the *teivah* (word) should shine.
>
> Every letter contains "worlds, souls, and divinity." These ascend and become bound up and united with one another, with divinity. The letters then unite and become bound together to form a word (*teivah*), becoming truly unified in divinity. We, therefore, must include our very soul in each of these aspects. All worlds will then be unified as one and ascend, and this effects immeasurably great joy and delight. (*Tzava'at haRiVa"Sh*, 75)

In this light, we can see a progression in Levi Yitzhak's thought from one teaching to the next. In the first, he presents Noah as a model for our study and prayer: we are to do as he did, causing God to "walk," to be present in the letters of the words we read, the words we speak. Such a practice will result in our being fully invested in our speech—both secular and religious. And, when we are fully present in our speech, then God can be present as well. When we dwell in our words, when we rest our consciousness in each letter and syllable we speak, we invest our words with divinity and reveal God's immanent presence in the world.

 ## Questions for Reflection

1. Levi Yitzhak leads us through three realms of awareness: the letters, the words, and the world, no one of them more truly God's realm than the other. When you look for God's presence, do you tend to look for something grand (the ocean, the heroic service of others, the mystery of space) or something small (the smile of a sleeping baby, the beauty of a snowflake or flower, small kindnesses between strangers)? If you only look in one place, might you be missing God in the other? How might you remember to find God in all moments, in every word and instance?

2. How do you imagine that your awareness of the words that you speak—in prayer, in study, even in conversation—might make God more present in the world? Which do you sense is more important to making God

more present in the world: the nature of speech ("religious" or comforting or comforting or business or rowdy) or the intention of speech? Are these qualities equally important? Why or why not? What might you bring from your "religious" speech into your "secular" speech to make it more a dwelling place for the Holy One or vice versa?

3. How might you make the words you speak a dwelling place for the Holy One? How would you "invite" God into your words? What kind of space does God need to dwell in? How might this effort connect to making a dwelling place for the Holy One in the world?

Taking It into Your Life

The letters of Creation are its building blocks. They make up the words by which everything came into being, and they are the constituent elements of the names by which we identify things. When we speak, we do not actually articulate letters, but the sounds we make are represented by them. When we say, "*Lechayyim*" ("To life") we energize the forces for life. There is power in speech. Reflect on your sense of connection to and responsibility for the words that you speak. When are you aware of the power that they carry? What reminds you to be concerned about how your words will be taken? Make an intention to pay attention to one aspect of speech— telling the truth, saying what is helpful, expressing gratitude in words, and so forth. When starting in this practice, focus it on a specific time of day or in certain limited situations: at a store, at meals, when dealing with co-workers. Observe when and how you fulfill your intention, and when you do not. What do you feel in those moments? How can this awareness help you sustain your effort, support you in your intention?

Another interpretation of "For your part, take of everything that is eaten [and store it away, to serve as food for you and for them]" (Gen. 6:21).

The word "**that is eaten**" (*ma'akhal*) grammatically suggests that which is provided as food for others (*ma'akhil et acherim*).

We have this principle: when we eat, we repair the defect caused by the first human, the blemish he brought into the world through eating. That is, the mitzvot we perform when eating—the blessings we recite when we eat, and all other mitzvot that we perform even before preparing a meal, since every food has mitzvot attached to its preparation (e.g., with meat: proper slaughter, proper preparation in salting and soaking)—repair Adam's mistake.

With this in mind we can interpret the following midrash (Gen. R. 19:12):

> "The man (Adam) said, 'The woman You put at my side—she gave me of the tree, and I ate'" (Gen. 3:12). R. Abba said: Scripture does not report that Adam said, "and I did eat [ve'akhalti]." Rather, he said, "va'okhel: I ate [akhalti], and I will eat [ve'okhal]."

The midrash has Adam say: "I did eat, and I will yet eat again." This is how we should understand the latter phrase: inasmuch as I will eat again, through the mitzvot that will accompany my eating I will repair my mistake. So, since Adam tarnished the world through eating, we have to eat in such a manner as to repair his mistake. In this way, Adam's original eating actually functions to provide food for others (ma'akhil le'acherim): because of his eating, we now have to eat (with intention).

This is hinted at in the words "take of everything that is eaten" (kach lekha mikol ma'akhal): since Noah brought all of the animals into the ark, and also provided them with food, he was later permitted to eat of them (Levi Yitzhak interprets the word "take," kach, to mean "acquire authority over"; having provided for the animals, he acquired the right to then later eat of them).

This interpretation is supported by the phrase "you shall eat eating" (va'akhaltem akhol) (Joel 2:26). "You shall eat": that which you are eating now comes to you by virtue of the original "eating" (reflected in the word akhol). You eat now to repair the mistake the first human made through eating, by means of the mitzvot related to eating.

FOR FURTHER THOUGHT

The Torah at first permits Adam and Eve (and their descendants) only grains, fruits, and vegetables as food. Only after the Flood are Noah and his descendants given permission to eat animal flesh. What is the significance of this shift? What brings it about? What was true in the Garden and in the world before the Flood (or, what did God think about human existence and its relation to the world), and what is true afterward (or, what does God think now)? There are those who connect the violence that filled the earth before the Flood to the "inclination" (yetzer) of the human heart and suggest that eating meat is meant as a means to redirect human violent energy. Humans could "shed blood" through slaughtering animals and perhaps dissipate some of their tendency toward bloodshed altogether.

Levi Yitzhak takes a different tack. Through an act of kindness, through taking responsibility for the lives of all animal-kind, Noah and his descendants acquire certain new rights relative to animal life. Before the Flood, humans had no rights over animal life (at least for personal benefit; apparently, sacrifice of animals to God was permitted). Now, having acted to save and sustain them, Noah has "taken" them to be his, for use as food (but not for destruction).

Levi Yitzhak further complicates this relationship by refracting it through the story of Adam's sin. Adam's mistake—eating the forbidden fruit—demanded repair. This comes about through how we eat now. When we eat properly—observing the mitzvot attendant on food preparation and consumption, eating with intention—we repair his sin. Sin generates a dynamic of obligation and responsibility; we eat in order to repair his mistake. When Noah acts with kindness and responsibility, he generates a dynamic through which his descendants are permitted to eat meat. We eat in gratitude for his generosity. Yet, it is also by acting with responsibility that we are able to rectify Adam's sin and create blessing.

Questions for Reflection

1. What characterized Adam's first mistaken bite? How aware was he of his relationship in the moment to Eve, to God, and to his own inner desires, fears, hungers, doubts, jealousies, and passions? If our manner of eating is to redeem his mistake, what do we need to be aware of?

2. If we are permitted to eat meat as a benefit derived from Noah's responsibility, do we have any obligations to follow suit? What might it mean to bring "Noah awareness" into your eating? How might we acquire permission to eat our food? What sort of responsibility for the production of our food might we need to take for our consumption to be fully permitted? What do we have to do, what do we have to give (give up?) to truly be in relationship with the food we eat?

3. How do you view the world: are animals independent beings with their own sets of rights, or are they dependent entities, subject to our needs and desires? What can we do to animals (those under our control), and what are the limits? What obligations might we have toward animals

that are not under our control (those that live in our neighborhoods, in our regions, in other parts of the world)? How are we to balance the permission to eat meat with the consequences of our actions on animals that we do not eat (e.g., pollution of environment, depletion of sources of food, spread of disease)?

Taking It into Your Life

When you say a blessing before eating, share food with the needy, intentionally choose to avoid food that is not traditionally considered kosher, or really pay attention when you are eating, do you have any sense that this is a way of repairing the world? What would it mean to you to bring this awareness to the foods you select to eat and to your eating habits?

Before eating each meal for one day, pause to consider the origins of the food you are eating. How did it reach your table? How did it come into your home? How did it get to the place where you purchased it? Who produced it, manufactured it, prepared it? What was it before it was prepared for market? If it is of animal origin, how did the animal live? How was this food prepared?

How might this reflection contribute to developing "Noah awareness" in your eating?

> Regarding the verse: "[YHVH smelled the
> pleasing odor, and YHVH said to Himself:
> 'Never again will I doom the earth because of
> man, since the devisings of man's mind are
> evil from his youth;] nor will I ever again smite
> every living being, as I have done" (Gen. 8:21).

What is the significance of that last phrase, "**as I have done**" (ka'asher asiti)? We should read it literally (suggesting that God had done something already that is now being referenced).

At the time of Creation, the aspect of judgment (middat hadin) said: "Ruler of the Universe, this human being is destined to sin and to provoke You." ... To which the blessed Holy One replied: "... Is it for nothing I am called 'compassionate and gracious'?" (Zohar III 35b). From this we learn that the essential intent of Creation was for it to function through the quality of compassion (middat harachamim). This is echoed in the midrash (Gen. R. 12:15) where God engaged the quality of compassion (*middat harachamim*) in the process of Creation so that the world might endure.

This is the sense of the phrase **"as I have done."** That is, God is saying, "As I acted at the time of Creation so that the world might function through the quality of compassion (*middat harachamim*), so shall it be now; and, that being so, '**Nor will I ever again smite every living being.**' Even if they sin and provoke Me, I will behave according to the quality of compassion and grace. That was the condition on which I created the world, and so it shall be."

FOR FURTHER THOUGHT

We might have thought that the phrase in question refers back to the destruction of the Flood. There are two problems with this, however: (1) not everything was destroyed, as Noah and his family, all the animals in the ark, and all the flora now blooming again testify and as manifest in Noah's sacrifice; (2) the verb used here—"to smite" (*lehakot*)—does not appear elsewhere in the Flood story, so there is no sense in which we might understand that God had already once destroyed all living things in this manner. These problems may seem minor, but they raise questions that demand explanation.

Further: God commits twice "never again" to doom or destroy the earth. The second time this is voiced, it begins with the word "and." This suggests that the first time may have reflected God's immediate awareness of need for or commitment to humankind and the desire to preserve them. What would the second time signify? And what can we learn to answer this question from the concluding phrase "as I have done"? Levi Yitzhak senses these textual anomalies are an invitation to investigate more deeply into the Flood story and to find a more powerful message of consolation: God is committed, from the start and forever, never to destroy all creation, to allow compassion to be the goal of existence.

Levi Yitzhak cites a passage in the Zohar, actually misrepresenting it. Here it is in full:

By the Torah, too, was humankind created, as it is written, "And God said, 'Let *us* make man'" (Gen. 1:26). The blessed Holy One said to the Torah, "I desire to create humans." She replied, "This human being is destined to sin and to provoke You. If you are not patient with him, how will he endure in the world?" God replied, "I and you shall maintain them; it is not for nothing that I am called 'slow to anger' (Exod. 34:6)." (An alternative version adds this conclusion: "For so long as they are engaged in studying Torah, the world will be preserved.")

This alternative ending is a wonderful and powerful teaching. The world is preserved through the study of Torah. But, this is not what interested Levi Yitzhak. Rather, he wanted to recall God's commitment to the Torah to be "slow to anger," a promise made long before human beings were created. God establishes, even before the first sin, long before violence and corruption, to be merciful and compassionate, full of grace. That is the foundation of the world, and it is to that commitment that God returns after the Flood.

This is a consoling message, one that even we might need to hear. Levi Yitzhak's world was one in which war and violence were well known (he lived from 1740 to 1809, and so knew of the wars of that century, the revolution in France and Napoleon's rise to power and the wars that followed). And certainly, violence against the Jews was never just a memory or a distant report. That his world, like ours, might have seemed as corrupt as that of the Flood does not seem a stretch to imagine. But, no matter how corrupted the world may become, no matter how much violence there is, Levi Yitzhak offers us a consolation: God's compassion for creation implies God's constant concern and involvement in the world; so long as we also study Torah, we will contribute to the survival of the world. For the author of the Zohar, for Levi Yitzhak, and for us, this latter message is not simply magical. It is not simply the study of Torah that offers protection: it is the constant attention to God that emerges from it, the transformation of the heart that follows, and the subsequent impetus to act for the benefit of others, to embody and express compassion that will bring relief and redemption.

 ## Questions for Reflection

1. Levi Yitzhak ignores the issue of the "devisings" of human hearts, the *yetzer* that pushes and pulls us, confusing us and leading to unwise action. Instead, he focuses on God's commitment to compassion. How does this affect your personal image of God? Does it add anything to God's character? Does it tell you something new about how God per-

ceives you, as well as the world? What are the implications of a God who is all compassion, rather than a God who is all judgment?

2. The "story" that Levi Yitzhak tells occurs after the destruction of the world in the Flood. It is (only) now that God recalls the commitment to conduct the world on the basis of compassion. Is it consoling to you that so much destruction can take place and yet the world survives? Is it infuriating that God might let such destruction occur (or even bring it about) and still claim to be a God of mercy, grace, and compassion? What would a world founded on compassion look like to you?

3. We noted above that Levi Yitzhak misquotes the passage from the Zohar. Another way in which he rewrote the passage was to substitute the pairing of "compassionate and gracious" (*rachum vechanun*) for God's self-description as "long-suffering" (*erekh apayim*). Why do you think he did so? What are the implications of emphasizing God's graciousness and compassion over God's forbearance? How do you sense the difference between being forbearing or long-suffering and being compassionate and gracious? How would you like God to relate to you—which qualities would you like to flow your way?

 ## Taking It into Your Life

As you make your way through your daily affairs, notice when you confront adversity or opposition (a difficult task, a recalcitrant person, other people's mistakes—or your own). In the moment, note how you respond. Is it with anger, frustration, fear, anxiety, silence, resentment, acceptance, interest, concern, forbearance, compassion, grace? In the moment, consider what might happen if you were to respond to the mistakes of others (or yourself) with forbearance? Feel that moment, that response in your body, your heart, your mind, your soul. Do the same with compassion and graciousness. What do you learn about your heart, your soul? What might it take for you to establish that you, too, function on the basis of the quality of compassion?

Lekh Lekha

"*YHVH* said to Abram, 'Go forth [from your
native land and from your father's house to
the land that I will show you']" (Gen. 12:1).

When reading through the narrative of Abraham's journey, many commentators find fault with him for endangering Sarah's life by taking her down to Egypt, particularly when God did not directly tell him to do so.

We have a response. God spoke to Abraham and told him to go "**to the land that I will show you.**" God meant: go to whichever land it appears conditions direct you. When Abraham arrived in the Land of Israel and then confronted a famine, he saw that these circumstances were from God, indicating that he was not to remain there. So, when the Torah says, "There was a famine in the land, and Abram went down to Egypt to sojourn there, for the famine was severe in the land" (Gen. 12:10), it means that he saw that this famine was a reason not to remain in this land, but to travel somewhere else. The impetus to go to another land where God's favor is present actually arises from God.

Or, to explain the verse: "[*YHVH* said to
Abram, 'Go forth from your native land and
from your father's house] to the land that I
will show you'" (Gen. 12:1).

Here is the rule: When you are uncertain if you should do something or not, pay attention: if you sense clarity in your thinking, in your inner awareness, then you should do this thing. This is the meaning of God's promise "**I will show you**" (*areka*): this word implies clarity of awareness.

An additional explanation: "*YHVH* said
to Abram, 'Go forth [from your native
land and from your father's house to
the land that I will show you']"
(Gen. 12:1).

This is a fundamental lesson: Wherever you might go, you are going
to your root-source. Wherever you go, you must raise up the sparks
in that place connected to your root-soul. That is what God meant in
saying, "**Go forth**" (*lekh lekha*): go to yourself, on your own, to your
source, and raise up those sparks.

This is in contrast to Moses, Aaron, and Samuel. They embodied
the whole of the people of Israel. That is why it says of Samuel, "There
was his home" (1 Sam. 7:17): wherever he went he was connected to
the source of his vital force, which is to say, in that place was his source,
inasmuch as he embodied the whole of Israel.

FOR FURTHER THOUGHT

These three texts each lead us to awareness of where we are—in
space, in time, in our lives—in each moment. The first two represent the experience of discernment as it emerges through spiritual
practice. That is, as we develop an awareness of God in our lives, we
may become more sensitive to the ways in which God moves in us,
through us, with us—in time frames both large and small. Similarly,
we may become sensitive to the push or pull of God on our hearts,
leading us toward or holding us away from particular acts, directing us toward more wholesome decision making. Through careful
personal attention, sometimes attended, witnessed, and encouraged
by a companion, we might come to more clearly discern what God
wants of us in the moment. That was God's direction to Abraham:
go "to the place I will show you"—watch out for the signs that indicate when and where it is appropriate to stay. I will show you where
to stop and when to go. But, how was Abraham to know this? He
could pay attention to external signs: "There was a famine in the
land." Alternatively, he might pay attention to the clarity of his
awareness in the moment—how uncluttered his heart, how clear
his ability to see, sense, respond—and employ that as a means of
discernment.

The third text offers a different model for understanding this dynamic. In general we act on the basis of our own impulses and needs to determine where to go and when. We plan for and then take a vacation. Factors combine and we take a trip for business. We check the fridge or pantry and determine to go to the market. But God says, *"Lekh lekha"*: wherever you go, go to yourself, go to your source, the root of your soul. When you set out on your journey in this manner—no matter what it may be that *you* plan to do—you will be better able to discern where God is present, where the holy sparks are hidden that you, and perhaps only you, are able to lift up. It may be possible, through regular practice and constant attention, to make this our sole mode of connection to the world. Like Moses, Aaron, and Samuel, we may find that we are at home, connected to God and to all others, wherever we are.

 ## Questions for Reflection

1. What is your sense of how to interpret "signs"? Would you have understood the famine in Abraham's time as a sign from God to leave for greener pastures or a test of faith in God's providence? Wasn't Elimelekh in the book of Ruth punished for just such an act, leaving his people during a famine? Didn't Jacob require a direct word from God to leave the land and go down to Egypt in time of famine? How can we tell when what is happening is a sign and then how to interpret it?

2. In the second text, is it self-evident to you what the experience of "clear awareness" is? Have you had experience of times of uncertainty suddenly becoming clear as to what to do? Of uncertainty continuing, holding you back from acting? What were the outcomes in each case? Have you found that one or the other is more likely to lead to positive outcomes? When, how, why? What might be the pitfalls of looking for signs of God's direction?

3. Here is Levi Yitzhak the Zen master: "Wherever you go, you are going to your root-source." What is the ultimate purpose of our existence from this teaching? What do you sense it might mean to return to your "root-source"? Would paying attention in this manner deepen your awareness of the uniqueness of each individual place you visit or smooth everything out into one ongoing search for holy sparks? What might it feel like to be "at home" wherever you are? How might you develop that sensibility? Would you want to?

Taking It into Your Life

Bring to mind a decision that you are facing or that you faced. Reflect on the options before you. Feel your body—the rhythm of your breath, your pulse, the tightness or ease of your belly or shoulders—as you consider each option. Observe the chatter in your mind—the voices that argue for each side, the names you call yourself for leaning one way or the other—as you consider each option. What is the difference between the inner responses to each option? Without judging yourself for having one or the other, can you sense where one path seems more likely the correct one? Notice when your thinking is clearer, when your awareness is brighter. How would it feel to allow these sensations to guide you in making a decision—beyond the "rational" process of evaluation, assessment, balancing factors, and so on? Might this be a way to sense God's will working through you? Reflect.

> "[I will make of you a great nation, and I will bless you; I will make your name great,] and you shall be a blessing" (Gen. 12:2).

The rule is that the letters of the divine name *Y"H* point to the Holy One, and *V"H* point to Israel. Until Abraham, there had been no one to arouse the outpouring of blessing (*shefa*) from above, so that flow derived from God alone. In that sense, *Y"H* (God's impulse to bless) preceded *V"H* (arousal of that impulse from below). But, from the time that Abraham arrived on the scene, there was arousal of the *shefa* from below, and *V"H* now preceded *Y"H*. That is the meaning of "*VeHeYeH berakhah*" ("**and you shall be a blessing**") (where *V"H* now precedes *Y"H*). That is what the midrash tells us: "The appearance of the word *VeHaYaH* [and it shall be] suggests joy [*simcha*]" (Gen. R. 42:3), which is to say, *V"H* preceding *Y"H* points us to the awareness of arousal from below.

FOR FURTHER THOUGHT

God's name, expressing God's love, is reflected in the name *YHVH*. That name suggests a flow of love and blessing emanating from God, instigated by God's spontaneous and self-generated love. But, there is another, more powerful and intentional expression of God's love: that which is stimulated from "below," when we serve God to bring God delight. For Levi Yitzhak, that our actions can bring joy (*ta'anug*) to the Holy One is a great blessing and vests in us great power, since the response to our action, God's joy, is the gushing forth of divine blessing (*shefa*). The world improved and the relationship between God and the world deepened when Abraham initiated this flow from below. He was the first person (so the Rabbis would have us believe) who was able to initiate the flow from below, reflected in the word *VeHeYeH*, to stimulate divine blessings. *VHYH* is the inverse of *YHVH*, reflecting this reversal. When *veheyeh* came into the world with Abraham, blessing truly began to flow.

The midrash cited in our lesson reflects the Sages' attempt to distinguish between two idiomatic forms by which a narrative is introduced in Scripture. Sometimes we read "*vayehi* / and it was / it came to pass," sometimes "*vehayah* / and it shall be / it shall come to pass." Although there are many inconsistencies, the Sages seem to arrive at a consensus that the former most often introduces a moment or narrative of sadness, in which the negative prevails; the latter, passages of joy, where the positive unfolds.

Levi Yitzhak employs this reading to support his creative interpretation of a confusing phrase: *veheyeh berakhah*, "and you shall be a blessing." What does that mean? How shall Abraham "be" a blessing? His answer is that Abraham was the first to instigate the flow of blessing from below and so brought (or became the source of) blessing. He reinforces this by noting that the consonants of the word *VeHeYeH* are the same as *VeHaYaH*. The latter, according to the midrash, signifies a moment of joy. In this case, it is the joy that God derived from Abraham's arousal from below.

 ## Questions for Reflection

1. The flow of blessing from God to the world comes at God's initiative. That is the divine intention. Abraham begins a new process, arousing the flow from below. Why do we have to evoke it? How is the flow different if it comes as God's joyful response to our actions (rather than God's natural inclination)?

2. We might think that by serving God to bring God joy we are not serving "in order to receive a reward" (Avot 1:3). But, if we also know that the blessing will flow more directly and more fully if we do so, is our service completely selfless? How can we avoid being self-serving? Is there any

way out of this? What do you sense are the characteristics of altruistic action?

3. We might think that if we are to serve God to bring joy, our actions also will have to be in joy. Is it possible to serve God always in joy? Can we perceive God in all things, at all times, in all places, such that we can find joy in God's presence and serve God with joy even in moments of pain?

Taking It into Your Life

Set a timer to go off every hour. In response, stop what you are doing and turn your mind and heart in prayer, thanking God for this breath, this piece of work or recreation you are engaged in, this life in this moment, and then simply hold yourself open and aware. Notice what arises. Notice impatience, anxiety, anticipation, fear, joy, peace, love, resistance, and so on. Whatever arises, whatever comes to your heart, do not judge it, but notice its presence, and turn again to God in prayer, with gratitude. Pay attention. After some time with this practice, notice if there is any change in your ongoing awareness of God's presence in your daily life, in your ongoing consciousness.

An alternative interpretation of "After these events, the word of *YHVH* came to Abram in a vision, saying, ['Fear not, Abram, I am a shield to you; your reward shall be very great']" (Gen. 15:1).

There are two sorts of devotees of the blessed Creator. One serves God with her intellect, able to perceive through experience and thought that there is a Creator deserving of devotion. The other serves only with God's help: he does the mitzvot, and God helps him to fulfill them. Now, the one who serves God with her intellect sees the Creator (as if it were possible), while the one who serves with God's help does not see the Creator. Further, the one who serves God with her intellect is able to bring blessing and awareness to others, and her actions produce effects. But the one who serves with God's help is not able to influence anyone else.

With this in mind, let us turn to our verse: "**After these events, the word of YHVH came to Abram in a vision, saying.**" This means that Abraham actually saw the Creator (as if it were possible) with his intellect. That is the implication of the word "**in a vision**" (*bamachazeh*). He was able to do so since he had only now attained the spiritual capacity to serve the Creator on his own, with his intellect. This attainment also explains what follows in verse 4: "The word of *YHVH* came to him, saying, 'This one will not inherit from you.'" It is here that Abraham receives the announcement that he will produce offspring. It is because he had developed his intellect that he will be able to produce effects that last after him.

FOR FURTHER THOUGHT

This lesson presents a number of paired concepts: serving with intellect / serving with God's help; seeing God directly / not seeing God; capacity to influence others and produce effects (*holadah*) / incapacity to influence and produce effects. We are invited to tease out of the nexus of these pairings what Levi Yitzhak wishes us to understand for our own spiritual work.

First, we should not get trapped in the term "intellect" (*sekhel*). This is not an invitation to philosophize or to engage in rational investigation of the material realm to determine if God exists. Rather, Levi Yitzhak uses this term to mean the application of our inner being to come to an awareness of God in the world. Opposed, as it is, to the one who serves "with God's help" (*besayyata deshemaya*), we might see this as another form of arousal from below versus heavenly initiative. That is, the one who serves with intellect makes an effort and stretches to come to perceive God, while the other relies on God to sustain his devotions. The energy of the former is what generates the awareness that is experienced in the intellect—an awareness that sustains grounded, tested faith rather than conventional, received faith.

How does Abraham come to intellectual awareness of God? This is not explicitly stated in our lesson. Rather, Levi Yitzhak relies on an earlier teaching: Until Abraham extended himself beyond his natural quality of love (*chesed*) to embrace also the divine quality of force and limitation (*gevurah*) by going to battle to save his nephew, his spiritual capacity was incomplete. Having done so, however, he was more balanced; he more truly embodied God's qualities. He therefore was able to truly perceive God, as well as have an impact in the world, to bear fruit through his deeds and through his body (*holadah*). By incorporat-

ing his native *chesed* with *gevurah*—the quality associated with Isaac—
and so implicitly also bringing about their resolution and balance in
tiferet—the quality associated with Jacob—Abraham embodied and so
became able to father the generations to succeed him. (This change is
reflected, perhaps, as well in the last word Levi Yitzhak quotes in citing our verse: "saying," *leimor.* The literal meaning of this word is "to
say." Not only is Abraham now able to "see" God, but he is also able
to extend his new awareness to others through speech, *leimor.*)

Seeing God and developing the capacity to bear fruit (bringing
forth children, having an effect on others) emerge from our
application of energy and intention to serve God with our
"intellect," or full awareness. This apparently has to do with risking
moving beyond our natural, familiar, preferred, or comfortable
mode to develop and expand our full capacities. We may have to
balance other qualities in our lives. Whatever we have to do, this
effort is what opens the way to deeper, fuller, and more enlivened
relationship with God.

Questions for Reflection

1. With what aspect of your being do you serve God? Heart? Body? What
   aspect of your awareness would you identify as your "intellect" (*sekhel*)?
   Is it your experience that when you serve God, you are thinking about
   serving God? Or do you strive to move beyond self-awareness/thinking
   in your devotions? How does your experience square with Levi Yitzhak's
   model?

2. Levi Yitzhak clearly presents the one who serves God with God's help
   as less spiritually developed. Does that make sense to you? Wouldn't
   it be a high rung to leave oneself fully open to being moved by the
   divine will, to act only through the instance of God's help? What do
   you think Levi Yitzhak is telling us here about the nature of religious
   practice and its relationship to spiritual work? Could he be prodding
   us to move beyond "just doing it" as a mode of religious and spiritual
   practice?

3. Abraham's nature and quality was *chesed.* What do you feel is your
   nature, the quality of your inner life that is most familiar, that presents
   itself most regularly in your inner-personal, interpersonal, and spiritual
   life? What quality do you feel you most need to develop to be balanced
   and whole in your life? How would attaining that balance help you be

generative in your life, to produce effects that would flower forth in positive ways?

Taking It into Your Life

Mindfulness meditation may be a model of how to serve God with our intellect. This may seem paradoxical, as meditation is not about "thinking." Yet, the practice of concentration, holding the mind steady so that it might become more balanced, supports the application of effort in a thoughtful, intentional manner. So, we might understand the one who "serves God with God's help" as someone who is confused and distracted by the comings and goings of thoughts, feelings, and reactions; the one who "serves God through the intellect" is clear-sighted, aware of the push and pull of the experience of "pleasant/unpleasant/neutral," nonjudging and free to be present to what is, and so open to experiencing, "seeing" God in all moments.

Further, mindfulness meditation may make more possible the process of identifying imbalance in one's approach to the world. That is, holding a nonjudging attitude toward our behavior, our thoughts, our reluctances and resistances, we are afforded more energy to discover what might be better ways to respond to the exigencies of our lives. We are freer to apply that energy—incrementally, perhaps; dramatically, possibly—to acting "against type" in a manner that brings more balance, more freedom, and more joy to our lives. In this, we will not be "thinking ourselves out" of our problems, but applying our awareness to the nature of our minds and hearts, and discovering new visions of how we might live, how to live with God.

Sit to practice mindfulness meditation. Allow the breath to rise and fall, maintaining your attention on the sensations of the breath. Thoughts may come, but allow them to pass without comment, without judgment. Allow an inner balance to appear behind the rush and tumble of thoughts and sensations. Connect with that dimension of awareness, returning over and over without grasping, without regret. What arises from that dimension of awareness? What do you learn about your prejudices, your preferences, your fears or desires? Let what you "see" offer you greater freedom of choice in your life.

Vayeira

"[He took curds and milk and the calf that had been prepared and set these before them;] he stood over them under the tree while they ate" (Gen. 18:8).

This is the principle: the householder should not behave before guests in a manner that appears superior to the guest, so that the guest will not become jealous of the householder.

A tzaddik is "one who walks"—since he walks, moving upward at all times from one spiritual level to another. An angel is "one who stands" (cf. Zech. 3:7). Here, Abraham did not want the angels to become jealous of him, so he garbed himself in the attribute of an angel, as one who stands. This is the significance of "**he stood over them.**"

FOR FURTHER THOUGHT

The verse from the book of Zechariah (3:7) reads, "Thus said *YHVH* of Hosts: If you walk in My paths and keep My charge, you in turn will rule My House and guard My courts, and I will permit you to move about [*mahelkhim*] among these attendants [*ha'omdim*]." Joshua, the high priest in Zechariah's time who was to restore the Temple ritual after the Babylonian exile, is promised that he will be given free access to the Temple. It is not clear who the "attendants" are, but since it is an angel of God who is speaking, it may be that he is talking about other angelic beings.

In any case, this image provides the terms to describe the spiritual life: one of constant motion. In spiritual work, either we are growing in awareness or diminishing, rising or falling, expanding or contracting. To stand still is to risk atrophy; stasis hardens into sclerosis. Thus, we "walk." In this humans are distinguished from angels. The spiritual nature of the angels is set; they "stand." They are assigned a task, which they fulfill with whole hearts, but from which they also are not free to desist. The human quality of will makes our endeavors meaningful, while also at risk for failure. Our efforts bring us merit.

In this brief lesson, Levi Yitzhak models the power of Hasidic teaching to communicate both spiritual lessons and moral instruction. Abraham, the paradigm of spiritual devotion, does indeed move around throughout his life. His spiritual quest, to find God, to live with God, to inherit the land and bequeath the covenant to his descendants, took him from one end of the Middle East to the other. We are invited to model ourselves after him, to remain attentive at every moment to what God desires of us so that we might move to respond.

At the same time, we are warned not to let our spiritual preoccupation blind us to our responsibilities to others. How we behave has an impact. We must pay attention to how our actions might affect the sensibilities of others, so as not to make them jealous (or, perhaps, even angry, depressed, revolted, confused, and so on). We may be superior to angels, and the tzaddik may be superior to us, but in no case are we to act in such a manner that we cause another pain.

 ## Questions for Reflection

1. Is it true, in your experience, that you are always moving in your spiritual life? Were there ever times in which you simply felt at ease, aware, balanced? Or possibly numb, dumb, and immobile? Is there never a time in which we can just rest in our lives; do we always have to keep moving? How do you respond to the movement and stillness of your spiritual life? Of your life in general?

2. Have you ever felt belittled by another person's spiritual demeanor? What was that like? How has that affected your own interest in or pursuit of spiritual growth? How has that affected your behavior toward others?

3. How might this lesson affect your own behavior toward your guests? Have you ever felt that your role as host made you "superior" to your guests? Should you have to change your behavior to please them? What do you and they gain from your attention in this regard?

 ## Taking It into Your Life

Pay attention to the movement of energy in your body. In meditation, when you sit, notice the rise and fall of your breath. How does your body respond to the in-breath, the out-breath? Is it the same? If not, how is it different? Is it possible to sit perfectly still, without moving at all, even the slightest bit?

You may wish to shift this experience from sitting to standing. While standing in one place, notice the shifting movement of energy in your body, tiny adjustments that help you to remain erect. Place your attention in the soles of your feet, and slowly move it up through your body to the crown of your head, truly seeking to experience the sensation of each part of the body. Having done this a few times, see if you are able to sense the energy in your feet and, if so, to raise it through your body to your head.

Pay attention to the sensations in your body as you move about during the day. When do you feel energetic, when do you feel sluggish? What can you learn about the movement of energy in your body and its effect on your awareness?

> "Now *YHVH* said, 'Shall I hide from Abraham
> [what I am about to do, since Abraham is
> to become a great and populous nation
> and all the nations of the earth are to bless
> themselves by him]? For I have singled him
> out, that [*lema'an*] he may instruct his children
> and his posterity to keep the way of *YHVH* by
> doing what is just and right, in order [*lema'an*]
> that *YHVH* may bring about for Abraham
> what He has promised him'" (Gen. 18:17–19).

What is the significance of the fact that the word **lema'an** appears twice in these verses? Moreover, there are many other problematic issues in these verses—but we will not address them.

This is what this passage is about: it tells of the righteousness of Abraham. All of his service of God, acting to serve God with love and an expansive consciousness, were like nothing to him compared to all of the goodness and miracles that were done for him. Therefore, that which he did was insufficient in his eyes. He said to himself, "Even if I were to perfect myself through all sorts of practices and devotions, still what would I be?" Therefore, he settled himself, and thought, "It is hardly enough that I keep the commandments with an expanded consciousness, so let me bring an additional intention—that whatever mitzvah I perform let me do so in the name of all Israel."

Indeed, all Jews were present in his thought and brain, since progeny derive from the father's potential. The root and collectivity of the whole of the congregation of Israel were in Abraham's mind, the seed of Abraham throughout all generations to the time of the Messiah. When, then, Abraham performed any mitzvah, he did so with all of his power, including in his thought all of the descendants who will in the future branch out from him. From this, two great benefits accrued to his descendants: (1) because he performed all of the mitzvot in the name of all Israel, including the mitzvot of the Rabbis (*derabanan*) down to the most minute detail, even including festival preparation (*eruv tavshilin*) (Yoma 28b), his service became that of the collective (*avodah derabim*)—and thereby, it is as if every Jew virtually performed the 613 commandments; (2) through his devotions he paved a way for his descendants after him, that they might discern the full inner meaning of the mitzvot and then do them, since they had already virtually done them once before in partnership with Abraham our father. Therefore, it is much easier for every Jew to bring these matters from the potential into the actual, doing the mitzvah in full, given that the gate has been open since the time of Abraham.

Understanding this helps us to explain the meaning of the teaching of the Sages, "A person should say, 'When will my deeds reach those of Abraham, Isaac, and Jacob?'" (*Tanna deBei Eliyahu Rabbah* 25:2). Really, how could anyone reach the spiritual level and degree of awareness of Abraham, the chariot supporting God's right hand of love? But, in truth, the Sages did not mean that we will attain the deeds of Abraham himself, but only that we should get to the point that we once attained when we were at our root-source in Abraham. Since each of us has already performed all of the commandments through Abraham's agency, therefore we only need return to our root-source, to Abraham's power, to thereby be able to bring deeds from potential to actual. In this manner, we will be able to attain the level performance that we had through Abraham's agency. That is why the teaching mentions Abraham's *deeds*, that is, when the deed was expressed through Abraham's agency.

So, back to our opening verses. When it says, "**Shall I hide [anything] from Abraham? For I have singled him out**" (*yedativ*), it means "I (God) love him (Abraham)." From this, God goes on to praise him and to tell of the high level at which he performs the mitzvot. When the text continues with the first instance of **lema'an,**

36

it means "in order that" he then would "charge (*asher yitzaveh*)," that is, "connect with" (*tzavvta*); his intention is to connect any mitzvah he performs—not only for himself alone—but with "**his children and his posterity.**" He performs all mitzvot with his progeny and his seed after him. When the verse continues "**to keep (*veshamru*) the way of YHVH**" it seems to be in the past tense—which suggests that they have already kept God's way, since they have already performed the mitzvot with Abraham. He has also paved the way for his descendants, making it easier for them afterward to do righteousness and justice. More, "**in order that YHVH may bring about for Abraham**"—his intention was to lead the blessed Creator to pour out blessing from the quality of Abraham on all root aspects of *HVYH*, that is, that God will act with *chesed* just as Abraham had, he will pour out blessings of compassion and love forever.

FOR FURTHER THOUGHT

We often speak of Abraham as "the first Jew." Levi Yitzhak apparently thought about this and found in these verses a way to make that particular status lively and relevant to us today. As the first Jew, Abraham is the progenitor of all Jews (including those who convert, of course). It is from him that we all descend. But, Levi Yitzhak is not so interested here in the physical elements of lineage as much as in the spiritual aspects of descent. In the classical tradition, the source of the male genetic component was in the brain/mind. That Abraham "thought" about Israel while he lived his life and acted out the commandments brought his deeds into the makeup of future generations. So, Abraham embodied not only the "genetic code" of all future Jews, but through his intention to act on their behalf he also embodied their "spiritual code." His actions in life had an impact on the future: he accomplished all of the spiritual tasks that his descendants would face; he made it easier for Jews in the future to do what comes to them because he had already done it.

To make this claim, Levi Yitzhak relies on the classical pun on the words *mitzvah* and *tzavvta* (connection). God loves that Abraham connects himself in his mind to all future Jews, acting on their behalf, making it possible for them to fulfill their mission to do "what is just and right." By doing mitzvot in the past, he made possible our good actions today. And through his loving deeds he influenced God to then shower his descendants with Abraham's quality of love.

Questions for Reflection

1. Abraham here is depicted as having performed the mitzvot "for the sake of all Israel" (*beshem kol yisrael*). In the mystical tradition, we are to perform all mitzvot with this intention as well. How have you understood the meaning of doing mitzvot for the sake of all Israel? How does this connect you to other Jews? How do your acts affect them? How are you affected by their acts?

2. You may be familiar with the experience of déjà vu. What Levi Yitzhak may be describing here is just that experience, the sense of doing something that you have already done. Have you ever had such an experience? When was it? How did you explain it to yourself? How did this experience affect your energy in carrying the action forward?

3. How do you feel knowing that you have already fulfilled all the mitzvot through Abraham? Do you feel empowered to engage in your spiritual life, or does this diminish your sense of agency? Does this help you feel that even difficult things may be possible for you to do? Do you feel accompanied on your way?

Taking It into Your Life

Levi Yitzhak speaks of fulfilling the mitzvot but may intend all of spiritual life. Sit in a comfortable position, and allow yourself to come to rest physically and internally—allowing thoughts to drift in and out without paying them heed, allowing emotions to arise and pass away. When you feel balanced, bring to mind an action, an activity, a conversation, or a practice that you are preparing to undertake (it need not be onerous or scary, but it may be something about which you feel some anxiety or anticipatory concern). Feel into your anticipation. Acknowledge the feeling without judging. See clearly what you are planning to do. Now imagine Abraham facing the same matter. See him experience his own anxiety, his own uncertainty, his own preparation. Allow Abraham in your mind's eye to actually enter into the activity you are anticipating and successfully navigate his way through. When you have finished this, come back to rest. Repeat, but this time imagine that Abraham has taken you by the hand as he made his way through the experience, holding you steady, lovingly keeping you connected to him, even in the midst of anxiety and concern. When you together have come through, rest with Abraham in that moment. See how you feel about Abraham's presence in this experience, how you feel about your presence in it. Later, reflect on how this might affect your own future experience of the actual matter before you.

> "*YHVH* took note of Sarah as He had spoken,
> and *YHVH* did for Sarah as He had said"
> (Gen. 21:1).

Consider the midrash (Gen. R. 53:4):

> "*YHVH*, Your word [*devarkha*] stands firm in heaven forever" (Ps. 119:89)—but not on earth? What it means is: That which you said to Abraham in heaven (cf. Gen. 15:5) [stands firm forever. Now, do what you said regarding: "I will return to you next year, and your wife Sarah will have a son" (Gen. 18:10). Hence, "**YHVH took note of Sarah as He had spoken** [*amar*], **and YHVH did for Sarah as He had said** [*dibbeir*]"].

What is Scripture's point in telling us that God took note of Sarah as He had spoken? Of course the blessed Holy One fulfills His word! "Would God speak and not act, promise and not fulfill?" (Num. 23:19). Didn't the Sages teach: "No word that God speaks for the good, even if conditional, goes unfulfilled" (Berakhot 7a).

The root of the matter is that there is a difference between "take note" (*pakad*) and "remember" (*zakhar*). The Zohar distinguishes between them, saying that *pakad* has a feminine quality and *zakhar* has a masculine quality. *Pakad* refers to that which is received from a previously existing source.

The root of the matter is this: regarding all of the promises that the blessed Holy One made to Israel, we trust that God certainly will fulfill them for us, to provide us with all goodness and blessing. Still, when the blessed Holy One promises to do some or another good it is still tied up in God, latent in God's power, and there is no distinction between past, present, and future. But for the recipients, when they need to experience it, they must bring it from potential to actual, to reveal it (may it be soon). For when it is still in God's mind, it is hidden (in concealment), waiting in the world that is yet to come, in the future; it will be revealed, yet it is still hidden. The means to bring this matter from the future into the present is faith. When a tzaddik has faith that God will certainly fulfill His promise, looking forward in every moment, burning with anticipation at its realization—this very yearning and enthusiasm and anticipation that comes from his faith connects with the supernal thought of the intended promise and helps to draw it—through that faith—into the world.

In this manner we can understand the connection made in the midrash to the verse "YHVH, Your word stands firm in heaven forever" (Ps. 119:89). God's promissory word to do good when it is still incorporeal is hidden, set in heaven. But, the sequel teaches, "Your faith is from generation to generation": that is, by means of faith, "You have established the earth" (119:90), You have established and prepared a vessel to reveal that word.

Now, Abraham [and Sarah] experienced both God's speech and word. Speech (amirah) is covert—so long as it is incorporeal and is hidden. But the word (dibbur) is revealed. Thus, Rashi was precise when he interpreted that "**as He had spoken**" (amar) relates to Sarah's conception. Sarah experienced two things. One was conception—that is to say, so long as God's word remained hidden in God's thought, she only experienced conception, which is also hidden. This is speech (amirah). But, "**YHVH did for Sarah**"—that is, established and prepared her as a vessel to receive the word, to come into revelation. This is speech, which is "**as He had said**" (dibbeir). From this speech did she give birth.

FOR FURTHER THOUGHT

So much of the mystical tradition is experienced through the tension of hidden and revealed. Through our senses we embrace all that is revealed: the concrete, physical world. But through our souls we sense that there is more, something hidden to the senses but accessible through spiritual work. Whatever we see and sense is real, but it is not the whole, and our role as spiritual seekers is to learn to perceive what is behind, beyond, hidden in the revealed.

God's intention, before it is drawn out into action, remains hidden. This echoes the process of emanation reflected in the theory of the sephirot. God's initial intention to create was hidden, obscured, in the highest reaches of existence. Its first manifestation was a movement in Chokhmah, which then generated a more manifest process in Binah leading to the emanation of the lower seven *sephirot*, and ultimately to the creation of the physical world. Even in *Binah*, no distinctions existed, not even in time: no past, present, or future. Only in the unfolding of the lower *sephirot* did these distinctions come into being. The spiritual quest is to retrace the unfolding of events back to their source in *Binah*, where all action is still potential and so, also, all good. In that manner will we (or, perhaps, the tzaddik) be able to effect outcomes, to shift God's intention from potential to actual.

That-which-is-to-be is concealed in God's thought, unbounded by time. The process of moving from potential to actual is the coming-into-being of God's intention, placing events in time in our world. The "world-to-come" is what will come into being as the hidden is revealed, as the potential is actualized in each moment. This comes about through the power of the tzaddik's faith, and the language of this text suggests that this is not an easy task. Yet, that is the work of the tzaddik and the power of the Hasidic movement and its teachings. We have the capacity to effect what is hidden; we can help God make actual what is yet only potential: the coming of the Messiah (may it be soon).

So, then, are God's as yet unfulfilled promises empty promises? Are we supposed to understand that they are nice ideas, but they are not really going to come about in our lives or in all of the existence of the people of Israel and the world? Or does the fact that they have not yet come about simply mean that there is work to do to help bring them from the potential to the actual? Or are they already present, pregnant, hidden, only waiting to become known, birthed into full existence? In the context of our parashah, God not only takes note of Sarah, but God also acts to accomplish what He had promised, to bring it from potential to actual. That result, apparently, comes about from Abraham's deep faith.

In this selection, we do not hear the rest of our teacher's explanation regarding the feminine and masculine aspects of "noting" and "remembering." It is easy to see the connection between "remembering" (*zekhirah*) and "maleness" (*zakhar*). Yet, even if we do not accept the essentialist identification of gendered terms from the past, we still need to understand the mind-set of our teacher, to recognize our own biases and prejudices, and to look beyond the gendered stereotypes to hear the deep teaching about relationship, faith, and action.

Questions for Reflection

1. For God, future, present, and past are all one. That is not so for us. What does it take to bring to God's attention that what is hidden in God's mind (and in a sense already fulfilled) has yet to be accomplished? Do we have a role in bringing about the fulfillment of God's intention or only in leading God to do so?

2. If God's promises actually exist, fulfilled, in God's mind, can we experience them as fulfilled in our lives, too? How? What does it mean to know that God intends for something to come about—for there to be a final reconciliation among all peoples and for peace to reign on earth—even when it has not yet happened? If you will not see their actual fulfillment, can you yet rejoice in knowing they are still "real"?

3. What about our promises and commitments? Is our intention enough? Have we accomplished what we mean by speaking our intention? Why do we have to do what we say to have it make a difference in the world, and why is that different for God?

 ## Taking It into Your Life

During this week pay attention to your own intentions. What do you commit to do—for yourself, for others, for God? Where does this commitment, this intention, emerge from in you: your heart, your mind, your soul, your conscience, your moral core? What is your sensation of the energy that is required to fulfill each sort of commitment? Which are harder and which easier? What commitments did you make that could not be fulfilled at this time, that require the participation of others, or that can only emerge from conditions outside of your control? How does it feel to make such commitments? Are you more or less energized to fulfill these? Why?

Hayyey Sarah

A further explanation of "[Abraham was now old, advanced in years, and] *YHVH* blessed Abraham in all things" (Gen. 24:1).

There is a tzaddik whose complete intention and desire is for the sake of the community (collective, totality), and there is a tzaddik whose intention is for his own sake. Abraham was the sort of tzaddik whose desire was for the sake of all.

This is how we should understand our verse. The conventional reading is: "**YHVH blessed Abraham in all things**" (*vaYHVH beirakh et avraham bakol*). But, the direct object *et* can also have the meaning of "with." So, read the verse instead: "*YHVH* blessed Abraham with all (the community)," according to his intention and desire.

This then helps us to understand the teaching "Abraham had a daughter [*bat*], and *bakol* was her name" (Baba Batra 16b). The word *bat* suggests measurement (*middah*; cf. 1 Kings 7:26, "its capacity was two thousand *bat*"). So Abraham's measure, his particular quality (*middah*), was "named *bakol*"—he influenced the flow of blessing to all.

FOR FURTHER THOUGHT

Once again Levi Yitzhak employs the trope of "two types of tzaddikim." This time the more desirable figure is the tzaddik whose concern is for all beings: that no one be excluded, that everyone benefit from God's blessings. This tzaddik, of course, is Abraham. We might also assume that Levi Yitzhak intends us to understand that this tzaddik is the Hasidic leader, the tzaddikim emerging in the nascent Hasidic communities as well. So in this lesson Levi Yitzhak both presents a new model of leadership and offers himself and his associates as those leaders, tzaddikim who care for all.

What is delightful here, though, is that he manages to make this political statement in the context of a very beautiful and powerful teaching. In classical Hasidic hyper-literal manner, he rereads our verse, emphasizing an acceptable but not self-evident meaning of the direct object *et*. His reading—"*YHVH* blessed Abraham with *bakol* (*all* that he desired: that *all* be blessed with him)"—shifts the focus of God's blessing from Abraham to the community of all beings. No blessing could be complete for Abraham unless everyone shared in it.

The conclusion may be confusing. Levi Yitzhak picks up the Rabbinic midrash that introduces the word "daughter" (*bat*) in relation to the term "all" (*bakol*). It may also be that Levi Yitzhak hears in this midrash (or in the word *bakol*) the term *bat kol*, signifying a heavenly voice, an echo of divine speech. The Zohar hears in this term a reference both to the *Shekhinah* (*bat*) and *Tiferet* (*kol*), speech and sound, articulation and undifferentiated voice. In addition, he associates the word *bat* with some sort of measure. Speech delimits and cuts sound into meaningful articulation, and in this manner the word *bat* suggests the way in which Abraham constricts, delineates, and directs the undifferentiated flow of God's outpouring of blessing (*shefa*). In what way does he do so? Where does he direct it? He does so for the sake of the blessing being experienced *bakol*, in all—places, beings, moments. And employing another double meaning, Levi Yitzhak tells us that Abraham's "measure" (*middah*) is just that: his personal quality is that he measures out God's blessing for all beings.

 ## Questions for Reflection

1. When do you sense yourself to be most generous? When do you sense yourself less generous? What affects your capacity to be giving?

2. What do you believe contributes to the quality of selfless joy, the capacity to truly rejoice in someone else's blessing and well-being, without even the passing sense of "why him?" or "why not me?" How might we develop this quality? Would you want to?

3. Levi Yitzhak clearly seems to disparage the tzaddik who is concerned only for himself. Under what circumstances do you believe that it is truly a righteous path to be more concerned for one's own sake than for that of others? What might be the work of the tzaddik whose intention is for his own sake? Where do you feel you fall on this spectrum?

Taking It into Your Life

A professor of psychology has suggested a procedure to eliminate child abuse and improve parenting universally: let every mother who gives birth go home with someone else's baby. Every parent then would know that the well-being of their biological child is dependent on the goodwill and love of some other person. In turn, they will care for their "child" with the love and concern they hope the "parent" of their child expresses.

Play with this mind experiment. If you have children of your own, imagine them to be someone else's biological child. If you do not have children, consider this to be the case with regard to your siblings or even your own parents. Do you love them less now? Would you have loved them less had you known before that they were not "yours"? Look around at the people nearby. Could one of the children, one of the teens, one of the adults be your child? Can you love them without knowing for sure? Feel through this experiment to observe how your heart opens; notice how you might become like Abraham, desiring only the good of all.

"The servant ran toward her [and said,
'Please, let me sip a little water from your
jar']" (Gen. 24:17).

Rashi says that he (the servant, Eliezer) knew she was the right woman for Isaac when he saw that the water in the well rose up toward her. Ramban clarified this comment: Just afterward it says, "and she drew for all of the camels" (Gen. 24:20), where previously there had been no mention of her drawing water. Apparently earlier she had had no need to draw, since the water had arisen in and of itself. Still there seems to be a contradiction here. That is, why, when she watered the camels did the water not rise of its own accord, as it had before?

This (with God's help) is my understanding: The Sages taught that mitzvot demand intention (Pesachim 114b), and the essence of a mitzvah is the thought that in doing this, one is complying with the divine will. In this light, we can understand that in the first instance, Rebecca's intention was to draw water for her personal needs, and for this reason the water rose on its own so that she would not have to work so hard (since her intention was to draw for her own needs and not to perform a mitzvah). This was hardly the case the second time, when her intention was to do an act of loving-kindness (*chesed*), drawing water for the camels of Eliezer, Abraham's servant. For this reason the water did not rise of its own accord: when one does a mitzvah, it is more meritorious to do something active to fulfill it, for in actively doing it for the sake of the mitzvah it is considered even more of a mitzvah.

FOR FURTHER THOUGHT

This text comes to teach us a number of lessons. We start with this: we need to bring our intention (*kavvanah*) fully to our actions. Mitzvot demand *kavvanah*. Further, when we bring our full intention to our deeds, we align ourselves with the divine intention. In turn, when our actions are in line with the divine intention, all of creation participates in accomplishing that deed in the most meritorious manner.

How is this expressed in our text? When Rebecca set out to the well, she was connected to her intention, but it was not turned to devotion. She was simply intent on serving her own needs. In that sense, she was not acting on the highest level, and her deeds did not reach the level of a mitzvah. Still, nature did respond to her, and the waters of the well rose to meet her. In this sense, she enjoyed the blessing of a righteous, conscious life. But when she turned to serving Eliezer, when she undertook the mitzvah of caring for a stranger and (perhaps especially) for his animals, her devotion to loving-kindness, *chesed*, brought her into line with the divine intention. Rebecca now attained the spiritual level of a *tzadeket*, a fully righteous woman. In turn, nature lined up to advance her merit, to make her service to Eliezer devotion to God as well. So, the water did not rise to meet her, to make her labors less onerous. Rather, she gained merit from her fully engaged, personal attention and devotions.

Mitzvot demand intention. We cannot really fulfill our obligations without thinking about what we are doing, and the fullest expression of serving God is to act beyond one's personal needs or desires, going beyond what "feels right." In this passage, we see the lessons connected with this principle play out in a beautiful way: her righteousness drawing response from nature, her righteousness demanding that she exercise her intention to serve God for the sake of others.

Questions for Reflection

1. In drawing water for Eliezer's camels, the text says that Rebecca's intention was to do loving-kindness (*chesed*). The implication is that this *chesed* was really "for the sake of heaven" (*leshem shamayim*), not for her sake at all. Is this always true of your actions for the sake of other people? Are you always clear about your personal motives when you do *chesed*—ego needs, role fulfillment, or otherwise? When, how, why?

2. Do you believe that sometimes there is a benefit when the fulfillment of a mitzvah is difficult or demanding? Is it your experience that difficult or onerous mitzvot are uplifting? When, why? Might Levi Yitzhak be trying to encourage his followers to engage more deeply in their spiritual practice? Does this inspire you?

3. What does Levi Yitzhak mean at the end of the lesson when he teaches that actively doing something for the sake of the mitzvah is considered even more of a mitzvah? How many mitzvot do we fulfill in our hearts, in intention, and how many must we act out? Is there some way that what we do in our hearts is also actually "doing"? When do you feel as if you have really "done" a mitzvah? In what way is the work that you do to remain connected to and committed to your intention experienced by others in the world?

 ## Taking It into Your Life

Pay attention to the sensations of your body as you move through your day. Make the experience of every action one of sensation, of rootedness in the bodily feeling of that action: "When we sit, we just sit; when we walk, we just walk." Notice when your mind is doing something other than what your body is doing. When you are engaged in nonphysical activity—writing, reading, even teaching, praying, meditating—stay in touch with your physical experience. Where are you hands? What is the sensation in your shoulders? How tight or loose is your throat as you speak? How deep or shallow is your breath? Reflect on ways that this practice changes (or does not change) your sense of connectedness to your surroundings, to the flow of your action, to the ease of your being in the world.

"And Isaac went out to meditate in the field
[before evening and, looking up, he saw
camels approaching]" (Gen. 24:63).

In general, subjugation to another leads us to feel dejection and sadness, since we no longer have the freedom to do as we desire. We cannot do what we want because we have submitted ourselves to another. But, when we serve the blessed Creator and subjugate ourselves before the blessed Creator, we thereby connect ourselves to the source of joy. Quite naturally, then, joy and rejoicing dwell in us.

This is the meaning of our verse "**Isaac went out to meditate in the field.**" "**Isaac**" (*yitzhak/tzhok*) signifies joy; "**meditate**" (*su'ach*) signifies self-subjugation; "**in the field**" (*basadeh*) signifies the realm of holiness (Zohar I 151b). So when is it that joy comes out? When self-subjugation is before, present to holiness (the divine, God), joy and rejoicing result.

Another interpretation of "And Isaac
went out to meditate in the field before
evening [and, looking up, he saw camels
approaching]" (Gen. 24:63).

Read this in light of the Sages' teaching (Pesachim 119a): "See how the way of the blessed Holy One is not like that of mortals. The way of mortals is that when they are defeated, they are dejected and saddened. But the way of the blessed Holy One is that when He is defeated, He rejoices!" This dynamic lies behind the teaching: the blessed Holy One may issue decrees, but tzaddikim can annul them (Mo'ed Katan 16b).

From this we can understand that when the blessed Holy One (as it were) directs the world according to His will, it is as if He were alone. But, when the blessed Holy One directs the world according to the dictates of the tzaddikim, it is as if God bends to the will of the tzaddikim. This is how we can understand the saying, "The *Shekhinah* is in the lower realms" (Gen. R. 19:13). And this is how we can understand the verse "*YHVH* descended on Mount Sinai" (Exod. 19:20): God came down to do the will of the tzaddikim. This is God's delight: when defeated by them.

We can find this in our verse: "**Isaac went out to meditate in the field.**" "**Isaac**" signifies joy—this is God's joy; "**meditate**" (*su'ach*) signifies descent; "**in the field**" (*basadeh*) signifies the will of the tzaddikim, who are known as "the workers in the field of the holy apples" (Zohar I 151b); **"before evening"** (*liphnot erev*) signifies the nullification of negative forces (negative forces are called "evening"; Zohar II 21a). Joy comes to God when the tzaddikim overturn the divine decree, nullifying negative forces.

FOR FURTHER THOUGHT

What a lovely dance these two texts describe. In the first, we are invited to experience the joy that comes from placing our will before God's will, subjugating ourselves before the Divine. In the second, we are invited to witness the joy that God experiences when the will of the tzaddikim overcomes (defeats) God's will. Our joy arises when we can truly, with a whole heart, say, "Not my will, God, but Yours." God's joy arises when God can experience, "Not My will, but yours."

While Levi Yitzhak does offer the verbal associations by which he builds these lessons, we should not get too hung up on how he makes each word mean what he wants. This is not to say that Levi Yitzhak is not precise in his interpretation or a consummate teacher. Rather, it is to acknowledge that for our purposes it is the larger message we are interested in, and not the quality or weight of the "proof-texts." Thus, we can understand the first reading of our verse to mean that joy arises when we are able to set aside our personal desires for what *should* be happening in the face of what is *actually* happening. When we allow ourselves to be fully present to what is, we are able to feel joy. Not that what may be happening in the moment is necessarily sweet, pain-free, or desirable. Rather, it simply is "what is" in this moment. When we accept this wholeheartedly, we connect with the "source of joy"—the totality of all being, the truth of all existence in this moment, in this configuration, in this unfolding of God's being.

In an amazing manner, Levi Yitzhak applies this truth to God as well. That is, God understands that true relationship can be built only from relinquishing the ego, from care for the other, from self-subjugation. Even God wants to "get out of the way," to experience the joy of being present fully to what is. God looks to us (to the tzaddikim) to help make this happen. So the capacity of acceptance, of loving self-subjugation to God's will on our part, generates the power to nullify or transform the unfolding of the divine will. Our capacity to receive what is true as "what is true" clears our vision, opens our heart, and energizes us to act in such a way that we can change the ultimate outcome of events. When we are not reactive but attentive, open, willing, and free, our actions are likely to be more felicitous and to bring greater blessing and less constriction. In short, changing ourselves we are able to nullify the divine decree. Our presence to the truth of the moment invites God's self-subjugation, God's willing "defeat" before our effort and activity.

 ## Questions for Reflection

1. What do you understand to be the "source of joy"? When, if ever, have you touched it? How did this come about? How would you try to connect with it again (or at all)?

2. Have you ever felt that your efforts to change the world, to undo injustice, to comfort those who hurt and ameliorate their condition, was like overcoming and defeating God and God's intention? How did you feel toward God at that moment? Alternatively, could you feel your efforts to be in partnership with God even when what was unfolding seemed unfair or unjust yet also "part of God's plan"?

3. These two texts might serve as the foundation for mindful engagement in social justice work. Is it possible to both accept what is true in the moment without contention and at the same time exert effort to change the situation? What would that feel like? Can we exert effort toward change without attachment to outcomes?

 ## Taking It into Your Life

Pay attention to the moments when you experience frustration, when what is happening is not to your liking. This need not be—and most frequently is not—of great consequence. Rather, notice when you register, "This is not what I want; I don't like this." Notice the quality of your response: How do you feel the sensation of "unpleasantness"? How do you feel in your heart? How do you feel in your body? What are the words that arise in response? Whose voice or what tone of voice speaks these words in your heart or mind?

After having noticed your response, examine what might happen if you were to respond, "This is not what I want, but I accept it." What do you notice about your sensation in body, heart, mind? Are you able to see in the situation anything new: a different feeling toward the other people involved, toward yourself; greater freedom of movement or thought; different energy? How is the quality of the effort that emerges from "I accept it" different from that which arises from "NO, NO, NO"?

Toledot

"[But the children struggled in her womb,
and] she said, 'If so, why do I exist?' [She
went to inquire of *YHVH*, and *YHVH*
answered her: 'Two nations are in your
womb, two separate peoples shall issue
from your body; one people shall be
mightier than the other, and the older shall
serve the younger']" (Gen. 25:22–23).

We can interpret this verse in the following manner. First, read it in light of the teaching of the AR"I *z"l*: righteous women do not suffer the pain of pregnancy or labor. Seeing that she was indeed suffering, Rebecca reasoned that she was not considered a righteous woman. If she were, she would not be suffering so through pregnancy.

Second: surely, someone who is not good cannot be a dwelling place for holiness (didn't the Sages teach this in their interpretation of "each raven with its own kind," Lev. 11:15; cf. Gen. R. 65:3, impure ones associate with their like?). Yet, the Sages taught that whenever she would pass by study-halls, Jacob would struggle to get out (Gen. R. 63:6). In this way, Rebecca saw that she had in her womb at least one child rooted in holiness, who when she passed a place of holiness wanted to get out.

And last: the source of holiness is called "I" (*anokhi*): "I [*anokhi*] am *YHVH* your God" (Exod. 20:2).

So, this is how we can understand this verse: "**the children struggled in her womb**" means that she suffered the pangs of pregnancy. Rebecca thereby reasoned that she was not good. She therefore said, "**If so, why do I exist**" (*im kein lamah zeh anokhi*), that is, (how can it also be that I bear) one child who yearns for holiness? This proves that his root is in goodness! Yet, how could something derived from good dwell in me if I am not good, which I understand to be the case since I am suffering so in pregnancy? God then responded to her saying, "**Two nations are**

> **in your womb, etc., and one people shall be mightier than the other."**
> That is, it is not as you reason, thinking that you are not good. Indeed,
> you are good, and your suffering is only because **"two nations are in**
> **your womb,"** one opposed to the other. Understand.

FOR FURTHER THOUGHT

Rebecca, as our Sages and teachers hold, is a *tzadkanit*, a fully righteous woman. It would be unbecoming for her to complain about her lot, to exhibit any sort of doubt of God's righteous judgment and perfect providence. Her outburst of pain and exasperation does not befit her character. Therefore, Levi Yitzhak seeks to hear through her words to some deeper message.

He finds a hint in her self-reference, in the pronoun "I," *anokhi*. Any reader of Torah will recognize that as the personal pronoun used by God as the first word of the Decalogue. And so, Levi Yitzhak reasons that her use of this pronoun was intentional, meant to refer to God, to the source of holiness. Further, since Rebecca was a *tzadkanit*, she would have been in touch with all of Torah, all that had been and would yet be revealed, including the teachings of the AR"I *z"l* (Rabbi Isaac Luria, the great kabbalist of Safed, late sixteenth century). These are the building blocks of Levi Yitzhak's lesson.

The point of the lesson, however, goes beyond the witty and creative reworking of the biblical text. Levi Yitzhak brings forward this matriarch to accomplish two ends: to make a place for women in the emerging Hasidic community, and thus include them in the realm of spiritual seekers, and to give voice to a common spiritual confusion. With regard to the former, Glenn Dynner in *Men of Silk: The Hasidic Conquest of Polish Jewish Society* (New York: Oxford University Press, 2006) argues that one factor that contributed to the successful expansion of Hasidism in Poland was the willingness, even the intention, of the early Hasidic masters to address women, to meet with them privately, and to express concern for their issues.

With regard to the latter, we can understand it in this way: All people experience suffering, and perhaps women—through childbearing—even more so. That distress generates the fundamental human inquiry: why do I suffer? We probe and inquire, we analyze and assess, all in the effort of coming to an answer. We try to plumb the nature of suffering and to know its source and meaning. Rebecca did just that and found herself boxed in a corner. She had two theories to explain her suffering, but they turned out to be contradictory. Moreover, she made the additional mistake of blaming herself, that she was the cause of her suffering. She was stymied, almost to the point of despair, of giving up on life. Levi Yitzhak, through this lesson, offers a response: Suffering arises from misunderstanding the nature of existence. It comes from seeing a world divided between holiness and impurity, between good and evil, between nation and nation. Suffering arises from participating in generating further conflict and opposition, in setting what is in contention with what we want, expect, or fear. The way out of suffering is not through reasoning, through dissecting, through analysis; it is not through seeking explanations. Rather, it is indeed through turning to God, where oppositions do not exist, where only good prevails.

Questions for Reflection

1. When have you found yourself wondering why you suffer in a particular manner? How did you work through your pain? What answers did you find? How did you arrive at them?

2. When have you felt yourself most at ease, balanced, and composed? What contributed to that experience? What might support you in developing such balance in the future?

3. How do you understand the presence of impulses toward good and bad in you? Where do you sense their source (in different aspects of your personality, your heart, your mind)? What have you found that helps you deal with that inner opposition? What brings you ease, and what creates tension, inner turmoil, contention, and stress?

Taking It into Your Life

One source of suffering is our attachment to our ego, to the story we tell ourselves about who we are, who we are supposed to be, how we are supposed to be happy, blessed, fortunate. We suffer because we present ourselves as "Anokhi"—as if we were God. In a way, we thereby reinforce a divided self, as if there were two opposed beings in us: the one who experiences life as it is, and the one who is always looking for it to be different. We struggle and therefore suffer.

Pay attention to the forms of sentences in which you refer to yourself: "I wish," "I hate," "I would never," "I did *X*," "I blew it," and so on. Observe when you make such statements how you are feeling: excited, engaged, distanced, angry, jealous? Allow the feelings to be present without the story. Don't justify your feelings, and do not criticize them; simply allow them to be as they are. Observe what impact that may have on your sense of the "I" in the feelings. If you sense any sort of ease, a resting in this moment, consider how you told the story that explained why you were feeling as you did. Examine how much of the story had to do with your sense of a separate self, a solo actor unaffected by others, separate from other people, other events, other factors, other conditions. Reflect on who the "I" is in that story and how it is relative to all of the other factors in the story. Who is the "*Anokhi*" in your story?

> "Dwell in this land, [and I will be with you
> and bless you; I will assign all these lands]
> to you and to your heirs, [fulfilling the oath
> that I swore to your father Abraham. I will
> make your heirs as numerous as the stars
> of heaven, and assign to your heirs all these
> lands, so that all the nations of the earth
> shall bless themselves by your heirs—]
> inasmuch as Abraham obeyed Me [and kept
> My charge: My commandments, My laws,
> and My teachings]" (Gen. 26:3–5).

On first inspection, this is startling, since it would seem that Isaac did not merit all of this blessing on his own!

Rather, consider it in this light: We know that all of Abraham's service was in raising up sparks, to bring them before the Holy One. Therefore, he had to travel about in foreign lands in order to gather up the sparks that had fallen there. Once Abraham had gathered all of these sparks under his wings, Isaac, too, was able to raise them up. But, he did not have to travel about to find them, since Abraham had extended this power to him: Isaac would be able to raise up any and all sparks that came under his sway.

Therefore, God said to him, "**Dwell in this land**, etc.," that is, you will not need to travel to other lands, "**inasmuch as Abraham has already obeyed Me.**" You, Isaac, have acquired "the merit of the ancestors" (*zekhut avot*): Abraham has already transferred this power to you, having gathered all the sparks under his influence. But this was not the case with Abraham, who had no inherited merit and therefore had to travel about in foreign lands.

FOR FURTHER THOUGHT

We are familiar with the concept of "merit of the ancestors" (*zekhut avot*). We invoke it in the opening paragraph of the *Amidah*; we rely on it in our prayers on the High Holy Days. But when and how was this merit developed? What is its nature, and how does it work in us? In this lesson, we see its beginnings, starting with Abraham and immediately enacted on behalf of Isaac. Abraham generated merit in having gathered the sparks to be found outside the Land of Israel. That is, he devoted his attention to finding God's presence everywhere, revealing the divine sparks even in places that—at least on the surface—are distant from holiness. This merit, in turn, allowed Isaac to concentrate on elevating those sparks that Abraham had gathered even further. Moreover, Abraham endowed him with the capacity to raise up other sparks without having to leave the Land. Isaac was able to concentrate his devotional efforts, freed of the distractions of travel, uncertainty, and exile.

We, then, stand at the end of the chain of merit, reaching back to Abraham and Isaac, and we are invited to engage in their work here and everywhere. Levi Yitzhak introduces into the biblical verses the mystical element of raising sparks, without connecting it to any specific words or phrases. Abraham raised up sparks by keeping God's "charge: commandments, laws, teachings." Perhaps spiritual devotion for Abraham's descendants is to be accomplished in the same manner. Further, being "in the land" may mean wherever we may live—there are sparks to be redeemed everywhere.

 Questions for Reflection

1. How shall we understand "outside the Land / in the Land" (*chutz la'aretz / ba'aretz*) in our time? Does it mean the same for us as it did for Levi Yitzhak's students? We are grateful that today we can live in the Land of Israel, and there are millions of Jews who do. Still, can the idea of "outside of the Land" also carry a spiritual valence, a meaning that is not

tied to the actual Land of Israel? Does this lesson ratify the possibility of full spiritual work taking place outside of the Land of Israel? How do you experience this?

2. Where do you have your greatest impact? At work or at home? In public forums or organizational work? In personal interactions? Do you have to go out to find sparks to then raise them, or can you raise sparks just from where you are? What is this experience for you?

3. America is the land of the "self-made man," of pulling oneself up by the bootstraps. Is there room in that schema for *zekhut*, for benefiting from the work of others? If we gain from the work of others, is the value of our own work lessened or the benefit we derive from it less rightfully ours? Do you have any reservations about the idea of "merit of the ancestors" (*zekhut avot*)? What *zekhut* do you rely on? Where or from whom does it derive? Over how many generations does it reach? What *zekhut* are you generating, and how far into the future will it stretch?

 ## Taking It into Your Life

The two modalities of spiritual work described in this selection seem to suggest action and rest, effort and relaxation, expansion and contraction. They are the qualities of Abraham and Isaac: expansive, loving extension and purposeful limitation and holding back. As you engage in your own spiritual practices, as you make your way through your day, pay attention to what endeavors require action and which require repose. After expending effort to bring about some purpose, do you remember to rest, to reflect on what has been accomplished, how it feels to have engaged in purposeful activity? When in repose, do you notice how previous effort has affected you, changed you, prepared you for what may come next? Does effort arise from effort, or does it arise from quiet? And is rest true or complete if it is not the product of effort or if it is not the ground out of which action arises?

We are generally more attuned to the sensation of effort in the body, so start there. Where in your body does effort arise? Is that dependent on the nature of the action? What might it feel like for action to arise always from the core, connected to the quiet of intention? If effort is tied to intention, might it be possible to notice effort in the mind, the heart, the spirit?

When you come to the end of action, where do you sense rest? Only in the limbs that were involved, or elsewhere? How does physical rest influence your sense of mental, emotional, or spiritual rest? How does your awareness of mental, emotional, or spiritual effort affect your sense of physical repose?

Bring this practice through your week and into Shabbat. Reflect.

> "May God give you of the dew of heaven
> [and the fat of the earth], abundance of new
> grain [and wine]" (Gen. 27:28).

That God desires (and delights in/approves/loves) Israel's devotions and derives delight from this is called *dalet*, as in poor (*dalah*) and impoverished. The blessed Creator ceaselessly yearns to delight in Israel's devotions. This is hinted at in the word *DaGa"N* (**new grain**): *dalet Ga"N*. A *gan* is a garden, a place of delight. From God's neediness (*dalet*), God derives constant delight from Israel's abundant devotions. Understand.

FOR FURTHER THOUGHT

It is quite common for Levi Yitzhak to emphasize the importance of God's delight in the devotions of Israel as the goal of spiritual practice. When we serve God without expecting a reward, when we direct our devotions solely to serving God and bringing God joy, we bring delight to the Holy One. In turn, God responds with blessing and care. Apparently, however, maintaining the inner awareness—the mental, emotional, and spiritual orientation—to sustain this relationship is difficult. God yearns for it, and we strive for it, but more often it seems either that we are simply serving God, devoted surely, but rooted in our own needs and concerns, or that God sends us blessings that we sense we do not deserve.

Levi Yitzhak recognizes this problem. He skillfully selected this verse, in which Isaac blesses Jacob (and so Israel after him), invoking God's blessings on him. When reading these verses in the Torah, we might fall into our conventional position: we need things—food, sustenance, protection—and rely on God to bless us with them. Levi Yitzhak explodes that model, turning it around to say, "God needs us." In fact, relative to us God might be considered "poor," "impoverished." It is we who sustain, who *feed* God, by bringing God the delight of our selfless service. That is the true source of our blessing. In the end, Levi Yitzhak reads the second phrase as that which brings about the first: "May God give you of the dew of heaven ..." surely, but let it come about through "abundance of *dalet gan*, our providing delight through sustaining God." Arousal from above follows arousal from below.

It is worth considering, as well, that this verse (and others like it) was selected to conclude the evening service at the end of Shabbat. It is, perhaps, on Shabbat that we are most likely to find ourselves without worries, cares, or needs. We are able to sense the turning in our hearts and souls toward God, with gratitude and love, with joy and delight. Our devotions on Shabbat come closest to that to which Levi Yitzhak points. It may be that his lesson here is intended to encourage us to hold on to the experience of Shabbat and its delight so that we might continue to feed God and bring delight through our devotions in the week to come.

 ## Questions for Reflection

1. How do you respond to the image of God as needy, poor, *dal*? What might it mean to you in your spiritual life that God can be needy? What might it mean to make your life one that creates a "Garden/*Ga"N*" in which God might dwell and be sustained?

2. What is your relationship to eating? Do you eat quickly, rushing through meals to get to something else? Are you a gourmand? Which foods do you look to for comfort? Which do you savor, hoping to make the experience last a long time? How might your experience with food help you understand the image of "feeding God"?

3. What is your experience of feeding others? What is your experience of being fed by others? What does it mean to nurture or sustain in this manner? How might your experience in this regard help you understand the image of "feeding God"?

 ## Taking It into Your Life

Consider this teaching of Mahatma Gandhi relating to working with the poor:

> I dare not take before them the message of God. I may as well place before the dog over there the message of God as before those hungry millions, who have no luster in their eyes

and whose only God is their bread. I can take before them a message of God only by taking the message of sacred work before them.

It is good enough to talk of God whilst we are sitting here after a nice breakfast and looking forward to a nicer luncheon. But how am I to talk of God to the millions who have to go without two meals a day? To them God can only appear as bread and butter.

How would you tie this teaching to that of Levi Yitzhak? How is feeding the poor, empowering the poor so that they can feed themselves, a form of devotion? How might this devotion be a means of feeding God? How might our capacity for selfless service of God help us become free enough to serve those in need?

As you make your way through the day, pay attention to when you "talk of God." Does it distance you from God or bring you closer? Does it distance you from the hungry or bring you closer? Does it bring the hungry and needy closer to God? Does it bring God closer to the hungry and needy? When is your "talk of God" verbal, and when is it action (like Heschel: "I felt my legs were praying")?

Vayeitzei

"He had a dream: there was a ladder [set on the ground and its head reached to the sky, and angels of God were going up and down on it]" (Gen. 28:12).

At first when we set out to serve God, our hearts fire up in us when we realize that we can direct the upper worlds. From our devotions all of the upper realms are raised up. This inspires us, and we become stronger in our divine service.

But later, when we have attained a degree of firmness in our practice, grounded in our intention, then our thoughts are directed solely toward God. And, God delights in us, as we then serve as a chariot for the *Shekhinah*.

This is the meaning of our verse. The word **"He had a dream"** (*vayachalom*) signifies strength, as in "You have restored me to health [*vetachalimeini*] and revived me" (Isa. 38:16; cf. Job 39:4). Thus, this signifies how we strengthen our heart in devotion to God; when we start out in our service, we need to strengthen ourselves. This encouragement comes about in this manner: **"There was a ladder set on the ground"**—we are set on the ground, human beings in this world; yet, **"its head reached to the sky"**—our service reaches and affects the heavens. **"Angels of God were going up and down on it"**— the exalted angels are raised up by our service (that is the significance of the word "on it," *bo*, that is, "by him," as a consequence of human action). (And, heaven forbid, it is also possible that humans can cause descent and decline, as the Sages taught, "Since the destruction of the Temple, the heavenly retinue has been diminished"; *Pesikta Rabbati, Bo*, 21:8.) But later, when we become more established in our service, we become aware that "*YHVH* is standing over him" (*nitzav alav*) (Gen. 28:13): because of our devotions, we have become a chariot for the *Shekhinah*.

FOR FURTHER THOUGHT

Levi Yitzhak uses this powerful scene to teach us about developing our spiritual practice. He recognizes the dynamic of many beginners: enthusiasm, commitment, determination, passion to succeed. He understands that these emotions are helpful, perhaps even necessary, to undertake spiritual practice and service of God. They make it possible to overcome self-doubt, fatigue, fear, and distraction. Employing them to encourage our spiritual devotion, strengthen our resolve, and build a strong practice is right and important. But, it is only when they truly help build a firm, steady, dependable practice will we be able to relinquish them, to realize that we have the capacity to shift our awareness from our own experience, from our self-awareness of being a servant of God to actually, deeply serving God. That is, when we in our practice are steady, and God (as it were) is made steady through our devotions, we become a "chariot for the *Shekhinah*."

From a literary point of view this is also an interesting passage. Levi Yitzhak begins with a general description of the process of development in spiritual practice. As is characteristic of Hasidic literature, he speaks of the devotee in the third person (masculine). When he shifts to interpreting the verse in question, which has Jacob as its subject, we might have expected Levi Yitzhak to make him, specifically, a model for our practice, by referring to Jacob's experience directly, by name. Instead, he continues his teaching in the generic form, carrying the third-person form forward. He thus invites us more directly to feel that he is speaking right to us, that this process is one in which we can engage, that he is offering us the possibility of becoming that chariot, like Jacob.

 Questions for Reflection

1. How do you experience beginnings? What does it take for you to undertake something new, something unfamiliar? What tools do you have to encourage yourself in your undertaking, to strengthen your resolve to carry on? Think of concrete examples (e.g., beginning to work out at the gym or exercising; committing to yoga/meditation/prayer on a regular basis; fulfilling your personal commitment to read all of Jane Austin).

2. How can you tell when your practice is established? How do you know when you are strong in your practice? Do you find that it is accompanied

by a shift in awareness of self? What is your sense of the interplay of self-awareness and non-awareness as your practice develops?

3. What is your sense of what it means to say that our actions affect the heavenly realms? Levi Yitzhak notes that we are rooted on the ground, in earthliness, and then that our heads reach the heavens. How do you sense he reads the connective *vav* (of the word *verosho*, "its head")? Is it disjunctive/contrasting ("*but* its head reached to the sky"), or is it truly connective ("*and* its head reached to the sky")? How do you sense this? Are we able to affect the heavenly realms despite our humanness, or is it because we are humans?

Taking It into Your Life

The image of becoming a chariot (*merkavah*) for the *Shekhinah* is inviting. You may wish to take this as the focus of a visualization. Sit comfortably, and allow your breath to come to a restful, easy rhythm. Closing your eyes, notice the flow of thought and ideas, and slowly allow them to drift away, bringing your awareness back to the breath.

Now, bring to mind your image of a chariot. What is its shape, its color, its size? Who might be riding in it? What do you sense as negative associations, and what aspects of this chariot are attractive? Begin to build up a positive image of a chariot and positive associations with who might be riding in it. As that person/being becomes clearer, allow yourself to identify with the chariot. Take pleasure in being the one to bear the rider of the chariot.

If it is not a distraction, morph your chariot rider into the *Shekhinah*. Be the one who bears the *Shekhinah*, bringing God's presence into the world. Perhaps expand your inner vision to include those who witness the *Shekhinah* riding on the chariot, which is you. Imagine the joy, the celebration, the sounds and actions of the crowds around you, the songs they sing, the words they use to celebrate you. Take pleasure in this scene, in your experience as the one who carries the *Shekhinah* in the world.

How do you sense the presence of the *Shekhinah*? Where in your body do you sense that you carry the *Shekhinah*? How might you continue to strengthen yourself in this area? How might you expand your capacity to bear the *Shekhinah* in the rest of your body, beyond that one physical experience? Having become aware of the physical presence of the *Shekhinah* in this meditation, how might you bring that into your moment-to-moment awareness during the rest of your day?

> "[Jacob then made a vow, saying, "If God remains with me, if He protects me on this journey that I am making, and gives me bread to eat and clothing to wear, and if I return safe to my father's house—] *YHVH* shall be my God" (Gen. 28:20–21).

The commentators have all struggled with how Jacob could make this request: **"Jacob then made a vow … 'If God remains with me'"**? Had not the blessed Holy One promised him everything already? Why would Jacob need to make a request after this promise?

Let us look at it this way (with God's help). Jacob actually requested a different detail that God had not promised him, and this was the true content of his petition. We know that when we set out to serve God, we need assistance from God, to help us to serve God in truth. But once we are whole in our devotions, we are naturally strengthened and encouraged and no longer need help to support us.

So God had promised Jacob, "I will be with you" now, when you need help. Further, God promised, "I will bring you back to this land," but did not promise to be with him after he returned to his father's house, to support him (Gen. 28:15). At that point, Jacob would no longer need help or support, since he would be able to strengthen himself.

So, Jacob's request was that *even after* his return to his father's house that God would be his help. Jacob did not want to rely on himself, that he would generate his own steadiness and strength in his devotions. Jacob's request truly emerged from his great humility. This detail was Jacob's actual request: **"and if I return safe to my father's house** (I want that) *YHVH* **shall** (still) **be my God."** Even when I return to my father, "Let *YHVH* be for me" (*li*), my help and support. This was a new detail that God had not previously promised him. God's promise of help and support had extended only until he returned to the Land, and not beyond. Understand.

FOR FURTHER THOUGHT

Once again, Levi Yitzhak turns his interpretation of the Torah to describing the process of growth in spiritual practice. When we set out in our devotions, we need God's help to support us. Only after much practice, after we have built a certain degree of stability and trust in our grounded devotion, can God "step back" (as it were) as we set out more fully on our own. This is an important lesson, a reminder that we do not have to do it all on our own. Indeed, it may be that we need to be reminded that we are not doing this spiritual work on our own at all. That is, when we turn our hearts toward God in devotion, we invite God to enter our lives, to move through us, to move us. Were we to think that we were in charge, that it is due to our efforts that we serve God, our self-consciousness might verge on egotism. Our initial turning toward God should be a response, one that is supported by God's initiative.

Moreover, when we set out in our devotions, we are in need of God's help. It is so hard to establish a practice, to overcome inertia, to believe in ourselves. Through God's assistance we learn that we have the capacity to turn from self-centered concerns, to open our hearts fully to God and the world. In both cases, we build our strength and ability to the point where God is able to step back and allow us full merit for our devotions, now turned wholly to God without self-concern.

In our passage, Jacob rejects this process. He turns to God to ask that God always be his help, that he not have to rely on himself, on his own merit or initiative. Our understanding of Jacob's resistance can be deepened in light of the passage that precedes this one in *Kedushat Levi*. There, Levi Yitzhak argues that for those who do not know how to pray effectively, God steps in and takes care of them. But for those who truly do know how to pray, God expects them to do so, so that God can then provide for them in response to their prayers (since God delights in the prayers of the righteous).

That former lesson continues: As Jacob set out on his journey, leaving the Land of Israel, moving into a time and place of diminished spiritual focus and power, he delighted in his full dependence on God's beneficence. He would not be able to depend on his own devotions, to pray effectively, to serve God fully. He realized that he would therefore enjoy God's blessing as a gift of grace, and not in response to any act on his part. He would then be able to serve God without any expectation of reward. But he feared that once he returned to the Land of Israel, and particularly to his father's house—the place of grounded, balanced, fully focused devotion—

he would be expected to pray, to make spiritual effort on his own. The blessings he would then receive might in some manner be a reward for his service. He did not want to rely on himself, on the merit of his devotions; he wanted still to depend on God's gifts of grace. He wanted to continue to be able to serve God without any expectation of reward. In that manner, as in our lesson, Jacob asks that God continue to be with him—to support him, to provide for him with grace—even after he returns to his father's house.

 ## Questions for Reflection

1. Our culture emphasizes autonomy, agency, independence. We feel ourselves to be most fully our "selves" when we control our lives and our destiny. Apparently, that was not true for Jacob (and possibly Levi Yitzhak). How do you feel about Jacob's rejection of God's expectation that he become responsible for sustaining his own spiritual life? Are you striving to build your spiritual practice to a point of self-sufficiency? What might it mean to turn your success back to God, to rely on God for your power, effort, and attainment?

2. The biblical text seems to suggest that God's presence (being "with" Jacob) is felt through the material blessings enumerated in God's promise to him. Levi Yitzhak senses that it is in the support for spiritual devotion and service. How do you experience God being "with" you?

3. When you set out in a new project, or when you seek to undertake a new spiritual practice, do feel that you need support, encouragement? Do you feel sufficient enthusiasm to sustain you in the early stages of your work/practice? Do you need more support later, to sustain your practice? How do you read Levi Yitzhak's teaching in light of your own experience?

 ## Taking It into Your Life

A church billboard read, "If your only prayer is always saying 'thank you' it will suffice." Serving God without expectation of reward is to relinquish any sense of connection between our acts and the unfolding of our lives—a very difficult challenge. We plan, we consider, we think things through to accomplish ends, to attain goals, to do the right thing. We are often disappointed when things do not turn out as we wished. What might be the spiritual and emotional outcome of saying "thank you" even in those moments of disappointment? What might be the spiritual and emotional outcome of saying "thank you" even in those moments when our hopes are fulfilled, suggesting that it was not our acts but God's grace that brought about the desired end?

As you move through your day, make a point of saying "thank you" at every instance, in every instant: When you wake up. When you fold back the covers. When you step out of bed. When you go to the toilet. When you brush your teeth. When you shower. When you dry off. When you open the door, when you smell the air, when you step outside. When you meet your co-workers, when you sit in your chair, when you pick up the phone. When you receive bad news, when you give bad news, when you are frustrated by incompetence, when you are pained by insensitivity. When your stomach growls for lunch, when you are out of breath from running late, when your back aches from sitting too long in a meeting / picking up the groceries the wrong way / stepping off the curb inattentively. When you shut off the car in the garage, when you hear the silence, when you enter your home again, when you realize there is work to do now at home.

What happens to your sense of what you deserve and what you don't deserve? How does this practice help you understand—and experience—God's gifts of grace?

> "And when Jacob saw Rachel, [the daughter
> of Laban, his mother's brother, and the flock
> of Laban, his mother's brother, Jacob went
> up and rolled the stone off the mouth of
> the well, and watered the flock of Laban, his
> mother's brother]" (Gen. 29:10).

This scene is suggestive of the joy of the bride and groom, which is like the joy of the pilgrimage festivals. We read, "[I will give them one heart and put a new spirit in them;] I will remove the heart of stone [from their bodies and give them a heart of flesh]" (Ezek. 11:19)—that (stone) is the "force for ill" (*sitra achra*) that rests on our hearts, preventing prophecy from our hearts. Scripture says, "A prophet (is one with) a heart of wisdom" (*venavi levav chokhmah*) (Ps. 90:11)—the heart is the font of prophetic wisdom. This is what the Torah means when it says, "**and rolled the stone**"—that is, the stumbling block (the *sitra achra*)—"**off the mouth of the well**"—and the well signifies the heart that gushes forth prophetic wisdom.

FOR FURTHER THOUGHT

In his customary manner, Levi Yitzhak removes the concrete actions of the narrative to place them in the realm of cosmic spiritual practices. The rock on the well that Jacob moves is the rock that sits on our hearts, closing us off from God, from clear awareness of how God might speak through us, directing us in our lives. The association of the *sitra achra* with a rock is found in the Talmud (Kiddushin 30b):

> The School of R. Yishmael taught: My child, if this repulsive one (the *yetzer hara* / *sitra achra*) assails you, lead it to the schoolhouse (*bet midrash*): if the *yetzer hara* is made of stone, it will dissolve; if iron, it will shatter, as Scripture says, "Behold, is not My word like fire—declares *YHVH*—and like a hammer that shatters rock!" (Jer. 23:29). If it is of stone, it will dissolve, as Scripture says, "Ho, all who are thirsty, come for water" (Isa. 55:1), and it also says, "Water wears away stone" (Job 14:19).

That rock seems to be present on our hearts as a matter of course, perhaps in the way that the *yetzer hara* seems to be part of our nature. But, its presence does not prescribe its power or persistence. We have the capacity to remove it, by force or by practice or by patience or through study.

Levi Yitzhak finds in our verse another practice, another process by which we might remove the stone that sits on our heart: joy. The "joy of the bride and groom," the union of two people in love, finding peace in each other, resolving loneliness and exile, is joyful for us as witnesses and participants. It is a metaphor, as well, for our relationship with God. The meeting of Israel with God at Sinai was conceived by the Rabbis as marriage (Exod. R. 33:7). This union was rehearsed and recalled on the festivals, when Israel came up to see God and to be seen by God. We would delight in God, and God would take joy in us at those moments. The joy of the festivals was like the joy of the bride and groom. When we recall this joy—when we develop joy in our own hearts—we have the power to break through and wear away the rock on our hearts. Developing the quality of joy in our lives may help us overcome or wear our way through and past the *yetzer hara*.

Questions for Reflection

1. How much have you learned to be aware of the intuitive, to rely on it for "inspiration," to answer difficult problems, to point you in the right direction? Is it helpful or confusing to consider that "prophetic wisdom"?

2. Hillel relied on the capacity of the Jewish people to know what to do, arguing, "If they are not prophets, they are yet the descendants of prophets" (Pesachim 66a). Do you have any sense that the Jews of today are in any manner "descendants of prophets"? Have you had any experience in which you sensed that the ideas or concerns of your study fellows or other Jews in your community flowed from prophetic wisdom?

3. How do you understand the role of joy in opening the heart to prophetic wisdom? Can the heart in its fullness know what the mind cannot in terms of truth? Is there an alternative mode of prophetic intuition, one that derives from joyous knowing, ecstasy, rather than quiet contemplation? What is the role of emotion in our spiritual life?

Taking It into Your Life

You might want to give some thought to the opening line of the lesson—having to do with the joy of the bride and groom and the joy of the festivals—and its connection to opening the heart. What techniques do you have to open your heart? Can you imagine mindfulness practice serving us in this way?

Consider setting your intention as "I wish to experience joy in my life." What might you have to do for that to happen? First, certainly, you would have to find a way to deal with the suffering in your life, in all life. Is it possible to experience joy when there is suffering? What is the source of that suffering, and what might create an opening, a relief, a release? If it is possible to accept that there is suffering but that one might still experience joy, then consider these other orientations, attitudes, and experiences to develop: Can you still experience gratitude or express appreciation for aspects of your life? Can you accept your role—and rolelessness—in the suffering in your life, as well as in your growing in happiness? Can you let go of the story that ties you—that holds you down like a rock—to your suffering or tell it in a manner that opens you to the possibility of joy?

Surely there are other aspects of this practice, but even carrying these questions in your heart as you move through your life may make the possibility of joy more likely, more apparent to you.

"I am the God [*el*] Beth-el, [where you
anointed a pillar and where you made a vow
to Me. Now, arise and leave this land and
return to your native land]" (Gen. 31:13).

Rashi comments, "This is like saying, 'The God of Beth-el.'" Here
is an analogy to help us understand: A house is a place where one
can live. But the people who live in it wear clothes. In a sense, then,
the house is the preparation, the context for human dwelling. This is
similar to the holiness that fills the fulfilled mitzvah. First, there has
to be a "house" in which that holiness can find a resting place. The
"house" is how we prepare ourselves: when we intend to do some
mitzvah, we direct our hearts to the blessed Creator even before we
actually perform it. This preparation is the house in which the holiness
of the mitzvah might dwell. And according to the expansiveness or
limits of our awareness in preparation will be its capacity to receive
that holiness.

This is what King David meant when he said, "I long, I yearn for
the courts of *YHVH*; my heart and my body shout for joy to the living
God" (Ps. 84:3). What he meant was, "The longing, the yearning of
my soul for You have become courts and a house for You, God." He
continued, noticing "'my heart and my body [shout for joy to the living
God]'—I realize that God has come to dwell there, because I built
courts for God with my yearning."

Now, this yearning has an additional quality. An act is not simply
the act itself. For example: when we put on tefillin, we have only the act
of putting on tefillin. But, the yearning and enthusiasm that we have
for that mitzvah—that it might bring ease and joy to the Creator—
ultimately extend to and include all other mitzvot. In doing this one
mitzvah in this manner, it is as if we had performed them all (as the
Sages suggested: "If one thinks of doing a mitzvah but is prevented
from performing it, it is considered as if one had indeed fulfilled it";
Kiddushin 40a).

This, then, helps us to understand this verse: "All the
commandment [*kol hamitzvah*] that I enjoin upon you today you
shall faithfully observe [*tishmerun la'asot*], [that you may thrive and
increase and be able to possess the land that *YHVH* promised on
oath to your fathers]" (Deut. 8:1). This means that you will be able to

fulfill even those mitzvot that are not observed at this time. You are to "keep" (*tishmerun*) them, in the sense of "his father took note [*shamar*] of the matter" (Gen. 37:11). That is, you should wait, anticipate, and yearn for the mitzvah thinking, "When will it be possible for me to observe it?" (cf. Berakhot 61b).

This is what King David meant as well when he said, "But I, in my poverty, set aside for the House of *YHVH* a hundred thousand talents of gold" (1 Chron. 22:14). It is as if he said: "Is it possible to fulfill the mitzvah of *tzedakah* only by giving to the poor? But even in my poverty, I was so excited that I urgently said, 'May it only be that I have the capacity to build a house for God,' and in this manner did I set aside the 'thousands' of talents of gold. Just my intention was considered as if I had actually done it." This, as well, is reflected in the verse "I have sworn to keep Your just rules, and I have kept my word" (*nishbati va'akayeima lishmor mishpetei tzidkekha*) (Ps. 119:106). I swore to do it, and immediately it was as if I had fulfilled my word, watching out (*lishmor*) to keep Your just rules.

So through longing, enthusiasm, and mental preparation, we can build a house in which the holiness of a mitzvah might dwell. This was implicit in Jacob's vow at the start of this parashah: "If God remains with me ... this stone, which I have set up as a pillar, shall be God's house" (Gen. 28:20–22). When he made this vow, he had nothing, only his intention and preparation for this mitzvah. In response to that intention, God now responds, "**I am the God of Beth-el**": as a consequence of your preparation for the mitzvah you built me a house. Therefore, "**return to your native land ... and I will be with you**" (Gen. 31:3). That is, I will even cause My *Shekhinah* Herself to dwell in you, since at first there was nothing but what you had vowed to me, which was only a house [prepared to receive your eventual devotions]. Understand.

FOR FURTHER THOUGHT

We can sense a few layers of meaning and interpretation in this text. We start with an etiological story. At the start of this parashah, Jacob anoints a pillar/stone and names it *bet-el*, "house of God." This is in reference to his revelation of the night before, where he came to understand that the place where he had slept was the "house of God" (*bet elohim*). Naming the stone would identify the place in which he received this revelation and serve as a concrete reminder of the event. Moreover, as the Torah reports, this event and the erection of this monument bring about a change in the name of the locality. In this way we learn how the town Luz came to be known as Beth-el.

Further, it is quite likely that this story reflects ancient religious belief, one that allowed for multiple gods, tied to specific events and/ or localities. Thus, the god whom Jacob met in his dream may have been identified as the god of that specific event and place. It would make sense, then, for this god to appear to Jacob in a dream at some later point and self-identify as "the god: Beth-el." What Rashi comes to tell us is that this narrative actually reflects an advance in ancient religion, rejecting that view, and presenting a new one: There is only one God, who is universal in time and space. The God whom Jacob met in his dream is the God of his ancestors, *and* is also the same God who will appear to him later in Haran, *and* is the same God who will be with him in Egypt. No longer is this a local deity, but one who is everywhere. Thus, Rashi tells us to read the opening phrase as "The God *of* Beth-el"—the one who appeared to you there, but who is with you everywhere.

Levi Yitzhak accepts Rashi's interpretation, of course, but still seems troubled by it. It cannot be enough for Rashi simply to teach us proper grammar or to rectify ancient religious beliefs (beliefs that had already been rejected by the time the Torah was written). Instead, Levi Yitzhak argues that these narratives come to tell us how to bring God's presence into our lives. Jacob awoke enlivened and enthused. He put his passion into erecting a monument and in that manner prepared for God to enter his life. His devotion to God, even when he was not able to do anything for God (when he was poor and had nothing yet to tithe in gratitude, for instance), was sufficient to create the relationship. In looking forward to serving God, he created the conditions by which he met God, implicitly fulfilling his wish already. His profound intention created the context, the house, in which God might dwell.

We can do the same. Our enthusiasm, our devotion to serving God, even when there is no concrete means to express that sentiment, creates a connection nonetheless. Our anticipation of performing mitzvot, even those we might never be able to do, is accounted as if we had actually fulfilled them. Our impassioned devotion to

God in our intention creates a house in which God might dwell, builds a temple in our hearts in which God can reside.

Questions for Reflection

1. Levi Yitzhak promotes intention as the key element of spiritual practice. What do you understand to be the relationship between intention (*hakhanah*—in the sense of preparation, anticipation) and *kavvanah* (intention in the sense of concentration, focused awareness in the moment)? How are they mutually reinforcing? How are they different, entailing different qualities of awareness? How have you experienced them in your practice?

2. Levi Yitzhak employs a common interpretation of the verb *lishmor*: often translated as "to guard" or "to keep"—and so "to maintain"—he suggests it also means "to take note" and so "to watch out for, to look forward to." Which mitzvot do you look forward to fulfilling? Which mitzvot are you on the lookout to do but that are not under your control to bring about? How does your frame of mind affect the possibility, or even the likelihood, that you will fulfill these mitzvot?

3. Do not pass by Levi Yitzhak's interpretation of Ps. 84:3 too quickly. He reveals the Hasidic attentiveness to bodily experience as a proper realm for spiritual awareness. David's preparation for serving God—expressed in longing and yearning—generates a bodily response: "My heart and my body shout for joy to the living God." What is your experience of sensation in the body as a response to spiritual experience? What does it feel like in the body to feel excited? To yearn? To long? To become enthused, aflame with passion? How might paying attention to your bodily sensations help you know different aspects of God's presence in your life?

Taking It into Your Life

It is out of intention that we enact the truth of our hearts. We cannot do what we wish in our lives until we clarify what we truly want to do. And having done so, it is the clarity of that intention that ultimately determines the "success" of our lives. That is, we may not actually be able to attain our intention because of external or internal/personal conditions, but when we can return over and over to that intention, we can create the conditions in which we recognize what is important to us and can remain dedicated to enacting and embodying that value, that goal. In this way, there is a deep connection between knowing and setting an intention and the capacity to truly do *teshuvah*.

Sit quietly, and allow your body to become still. Notice the rising and falling of your breath. Allow what thoughts arise to pass away without engaging in them. When you sense a degree of balance in your body and mind, pose this question: "What is my intention?" Simply ask the question, and allow it to be present. Alternatively, you may wish to ask it repeatedly, but slowly, allowing a time of quiet in between for the question to penetrate, to enter your being. Sit in its presence. Even if you do not attain a clear awareness of an inner response while you are sitting, do not despair. Return to this practice over the course of a few days, and pay attention throughout the day, and after. Some awareness likely will arise.

When an intention becomes clear, use it as a focus of meditation. Feel into your desire to do or be or enact this intention. Notice where it sits in your body. Notice what emotions may arise around the prospect of attaining your intention (and of not doing so). Notice how you think about yourself and how you imagine people will respond to your "success" or "failure." None of these are real, but they reveal some of what may stand in the way of enacting your intention or what may help you attain it. Noticing them may help you in those moments when you seem far from your intention. You will be able to remember, "Oh yes, I had that thought/feeling/ sensation—it was passing, so I can return now to my intention." Returning to the intention can energize you to remain faithful, devoted in your life. Knowing what you truly wish to do or be can help you return to a path that may more likely help you attain your intention. Watch this unfold over time.

Vayishlach

"[He instructed the one in front as follows,] 'When my brother Esau meets you and asks you, 'To whom are you connected? [Where are you going? And whose (animals) are these ahead of you?]" (Gen. 32:18).

In general, when we set out to draw nearer to God, the evil inclination (*yetzer hara*) rises up and overwhelms us. We should respond to it, thinking that from our service of God we will receive the rewards of this world, thereby convincing the *yetzer hara* not to oppose us for trying to cleave to God. That will allow us, later, when we succeed in more fully attaching ourselves to God, to make our devotions only for the sake of bringing ease and pleasure to our Creator, and not for the sake of the blessings of this world.

So, consider our verse: "**When my brother Esau meets you and asks you, 'To whom?'**" The *yetzer hara* is also called "Esau," and he will meet Jacob's messengers, that is, Jacob's holy thoughts from which angels are created. Esau will then challenge these thoughts, asking, "**Where are you going?**" "You shall respond, 'We belong to your servant Jacob'" (Gen. 32:19)—we are Jacob's angels, created by his good deeds. But do not challenge Jacob for his good deeds: "They are a gift sent to my lord Esau" (ibid.). The good that results from Jacob's good deeds affect you as well. By means of Jacob's good deeds Esau receives the blessings of this world, as this world is a gift to the *yetzer hara*.

FOR FURTHER THOUGHT

Underlying this teaching is the assumption that Jacob's true inheritance is the world-to-come (*olam haba*) and that of Esau is this world (*olam hazeh*). There is a problem with this, however. In order to live at all, one must make use of the goods of this world, so Jacob and his descendants wind up benefiting from some of Esau's portion.

R. Menahem Nahum of Chernobyl (R. Levi Yitzhak's contemporary and fellow Hasidic master) in his book *Me'or Einayim* (*Vayeitzei*, end) addresses this problem:

> For the descendants of Jacob, the blessings of this world are not considered blessings, but simply what is required for life. The goods of this world are a vessel for the blessings of the world-to-come. The world-to-come is garbed in the necessities of this world, for without this world it would be impossible to merit the world-to-come. The excesses of this world belong to the descendants of Esau, and not Jacob's seed, for they know that these things distance them from the Creator.

We can read our passage in this light: use the goods of this world as if you were seduced by the *yetzer hara* so that they can become "vessels" for your true spiritual development. Simply put, Levi Yitzhak deepens our understanding of the interchange between Jacob and Esau. Not only does Jacob send flocks and herds and servants to Esau as supplication and compensation for his earlier actions, but he also sends these goods to Esau as his due. The goods of this world belong to Esau, they are a gift to him in this world, as the world-to-come is a gift for the Jewish people. Moreover, sending a gift to Esau distracts Esau from his intention to oppose Jacob, so that Jacob can proceed in his spiritual development.

Yet, there is a deeper level to this teaching. Levi Yitzhak, following the Baal Shem Tov, is finely sensitive to the inner dynamics of the psyche. He recognizes that it is difficult to escape the self-centered (though necessary) needs, concerns, and focus of the ego. When we set out truly to serve God, should we experience difficulty in our devotions and contemplate giving up, that would be the work of the *yetzer hara*. And when we find some facility, some ease, some fluidity in our devotions, we might very well get caught in thinking, "How well I am doing." That, too, would be the voice of the *yetzer hara*. Further, if our only motivation to serve God is so that God will provide for us, protect us and our families, sustain us in life, then that again would be the work of the *yetzer hara*.

How can we free ourselves of this force in our hearts and minds? Levi Yitzhak invites us to engage in a little "Hasidic tae kwon do." That is, overcoming the ego and the *yetzer hara* directly is too hard. Should we seek to engage in battle with these feelings, we are likely to fail or to cause ourselves great grief (another impediment to truly serving God). Instead, Levi Yitzhak suggests that we harness the energy of the *yetzer hara* to help us in our early stages of devotion. We can acknowledge, without shame or reservation, that our initial desire is that God reward us for our service, all the while holding in our hearts and minds the possibility, the desirability, of attaining a higher level: to serve God for its own sake. Only by paying the *yetzer hara* its due, as it were, can we remove it from its place of opposition and use its energy to sustain us as we devote ourselves to truly serving God. Our devotions do produce good—good thoughts, good deeds—and these are not to be denied. They have an impact on the world. But the good that we do, and the good that we derive, is that they point us to God, to serving God out of love and fear, out of selfless devotion. When we sense that truth, we are able to let go of the physical, material goods of this world and offer them as a gift to the *yetzer hara*, freeing us to serve God in truth.

 ## Questions for Reflection

1. One might see in Levi Yitzhak's teaching a version of "that which is not for its own sake will ultimately be done for its own sake" (Pesachim 50b). Is it your sense that practice transforms experience? If you do not have a goal in mind, do you find that you change? If you do have a goal in mind, how do you deal with adversity, obstacles, and "failure"?

2. Do you trust yourself to undertake spiritual practice for personal, selfish, ulterior motives while holding in mind an ultimately selfless, impersonal goal? What do you do—or might you do—to guarantee that you do finally shift your orientation to that ultimate goal?

3. How do you feel about Levi Yitzhak's suggestion? Are you willing to pay off Esau, to dupe the *yetzer hara* to get past your own inner weakness? Is this a matter of spiritual martial arts, or is this another example of Jacob's trickery? When do the ends justify the means?

 ## Taking It into Your Life

Levi Yitzhak is quite sensitive to the qualities of heart and mind that hinder us from truly devoting ourselves to serving God. In Buddhist theory, there are five hindrances to steady, meaningful practice: distracting desire, anger or negative feelings, sloth or lack of energy, restlessness or worry, and doubt. We might say that in this instance Levi Yitzhak is pointing to the first of these hindrances. Yet, what distinguishes our Jewish practice from the Buddhist (and other) contemplative practice is that Levi Yitzhak recognizes the legitimate claim that physical needs (and their expression as desires) have on our lives and on God. So he suggests that we de-link the legitimate need from any sense of deservedness, of reward. Accept and fully experience the need simply as need, as what arises in a body, without making it more (or less) than what it is. The first effect is to lessen some of the pull of that need—to diminish the fear that the need will not be filled. The second effect is to free the energy that could have been turned to quelling that fear and filling that need so that it can be used in truly serving God—to balanced, pure, awareness of God's goodness in all moments.

When you engage in your primary spiritual practice (e.g., prayer, medi-tation, yoga, study) or when you are engaged in a key activity of your life (e.g., conversation with loved ones, interaction with others at work, exercise, eating), pay attention to when your attention wanders. That is a sign of some aspect of resistance. Pay attention to body sensations, ideas, or feelings associated with that moment of distraction. See if you can discern what is preventing you from devoting your full attention to this moment. Note what you discover, and at another time, return to con-sidering what it feels like. Sense it in your body. Notice again the associa-tions that arise in conjunction with it. See what sort of "hindrance" this might be. When you can sense its character, see if you can anticipate it the next time you are engaged in this key activity. Start with awareness of the hindrance or distraction. Allow the feeling to fill your body. Acknowl-edge the fear, anger, desire, fatigue, doubt, or confusion (or whatever else you might discover). Allow that to be the start of your practice, the background to your activity. Note that it need not take over, that you can persist despite its presence. Use the energy of that awareness to liberate you to fuller participation in the moment. Do this over time, and trace what happens in your practice.

"Said he, 'Your name shall no longer be
Jacob, but Israel, for you have striven with
God and man and have prevailed'"
(Gen. 32:29).

There are people who are always connected to the blessed Creator, even when they are talking with other people. And there are people who connect with the blessed Creator when they are immersed in devotions, in Torah study, and in doing mitzvot, but when they talk to other people, they are not able to attach their minds to the blessed Creator. The first sort of person is called "Israel" (*YiSRaEL*): this name is made up of the letters *YaShaR EL* ("straight with God"); and also *LY RoSh* ("the *yod* is at the start"). The second sort of person is called "Jacob" (*Ya'AKoV*): *Yod AKeV* ("the *yod* comes at the end").

This is how we should read our verse "**Your name shall no longer be Jacob, but Israel, for you have striven with God**"—you are connected to God even when you talk with other people. This is the sense of "**with God and man and have prevailed** [lit., you are able]"—you are able to attach your thoughts to the blessed Creator always.

FOR FURTHER THOUGHT

Once again Levi Yitzhak employs a two-sided typology, although it is interesting that he refers only to people (*adam*) and does not identify these two types as tzaddikim. In this manner he sets up the preferred mode of spiritual consciousness (connecting to God at all times) and offers it as an aspiration for all people. He does not denigrate the second class altogether—after all, they are still part of the "House of Jacob." Still, he makes clear that the higher level of spiritual practitioner, the true adept, is the one who deserves the name "Israel."

He achieves this through the classical game of mystical anagrams. *YiSRaeL* becomes *YaShaR EL*. Not only does this suggest "straight to God" but also seeing God directly (the verb *sh-u-r* = "behold, regard"). It also becomes *LY RoSh*: "the *yod* is at the start." This signifies connecting with the first letter of the divine name *YHVH*, cleaving directly to the root of God. These surely are apt for the person who is able to maintain unbroken attention to the Divine, mental attachment to God. Thus, the title given to those spiritual "knights" who never flag in their devotion to God is Yisrael. Their more lowly brothers are called Jacob/*Ya'AKoV*: *Yod AKeV*. The word *EKeV* means "heel"; the *yod* signifies the final letter of the divine name *Adonai*, signifying that they are mired in the lowest dimension of divinity, in this world. These people, then, are at the bottom, on the lowest spiritual rung.

They are, quite simply, the Jews. Although this term has its roots in earlier mystical texts, it is quite likely that Levi Yitzhak and his contemporaries heard in the word *yod* the familiar Yiddish word for Jew: *yud/yid*. These Jews on the bottom, then, may have been the majority, but they were not to be disparaged. They still strove to connect with God and deserved fully the name "House of Jacob."

 Questions for Reflection

1. When do you feel that you are most directly connected with God? Would you describe your experience as *devekut* (attachment to the Divine)? What do you think is similar to or distinguishes your experience from what Levi Yitzhak describes/assumes?

2. Levi Yitzhak lists three activities: *ba'avodato uvetorato uvemitzvotav.* In the translation above we present this as "immersed in devotions, in Torah study, and in doing mitzvot." How do you read this phrase? Are they three different activities? What distinguish one from the other, if anything? What do you consider to be your primary form of *avodah* (devotion, service to God)? When do you sense your Torah study to be devotional? When do you sense your engagement in doing mitzvot to be devotional? What other activities do you engage in that you consider to be *avodah*?

3. There is a story about the Alter Rebbe (R. Shneur Zalman of Lyadi, the founder of Chabad Hasidism) and his adult son, who lived in the same house. Once the son was immersed in studying when the crib of his son turned over. The child spilled out, and he started crying. His father did not hear him, did not pay attention. The Alter Rebbe heard the child, came and picked him up, and comforted him. He chastised his son, the father, telling him that studying that prevents one from hearing his own child crying in need is not proper studying. In your opinion, should there be anything that takes precedence over paying attention to other people? Can you imagine a way that one might pay attention to the needs and concerns of other people—even passing, casual, unimportant concerns— while still remaining connected to God?

 Taking It into Your Life

There is a traditional meditation practice that might be useful in developing the capacity to remain attached to God even when engaged in mundane activities. It does require some time in personal devotion, in meditation, before taking it out into the world, however. This means that we have to accept that initially we regard ourselves as "Jacob" even as we undertake to truly merit being "Israel."

Sit in a comfortable, yet attentive position: feet flat on the floor, knees bent, hips tilted slightly forward, spine erect, shoulders at ease, neck extended, and head floating on the top of the neck. Allow your breath to come to a regular, easy rhythm and your eyes to close. Rest in this position, sensing your body at ease, your breath flowing without being forced or restricted. Allow thoughts to come and go, without getting involved in them. When you feel at ease and attentive, bring to your mind's eye the four letters of God's name: *Yod, Hei, Vav, Hei.* Hold the four letters about a foot or so before your mind's eye and about six inches above your line of sight. Trace the letters with your inner eye. Allow them to become solid, fixed, before you. Endeavor to hold the letters steady before you for a period of time.

As you deepen this practice, you may find or you may wish to imagine that the letters take on the appearance of flames. When you find that you are able to hold this vision steady in your mind's eye for a period of time, move to the next step of this practice. Sitting in the same position, bring the letters to your mind's eye even as your physical eyes are open. Hold God's name before you with your eyes open. When this becomes steady, take the next step: rise from your seat and move around the room, even as you hold God's name before you with your eyes open. When this is steady, take the next step: leave your room/home and move on to the street, even as you hold God's name before you with your eyes open. Experiment. See what it is like to hold God's name constantly before you even as you engage in your daily routine.

"So Jacob named the place [Peniel, meaning,]
'I have seen God face-to-face, and my life
has been preserved [*vatinatzeil naphshi*]'"
(Gen. 32:31).

There are people who serve the blessed Creator in order that God shower them with good things when they serve God. But, there is a superior form of divine service, when people serve the blessed Creator "because He is Sovereign and Ruler" (Zohar I 11a). These people do not at all intend receiving God's goodness. This type of service is called "face-to-face" (*panim bephanim*): they serve God only because He is Sovereign and Ruler, and the blessed Creator, as it were, turns to them face-to-face. But, the first form is called "face-to-back" (*panim be'achor*): the blessed Creator turns to them face-to-face, but they turn their service into a means to receive good things from God.

This is the import of the phrase "**I have seen God face-to-face,**" like the second form of devotion. This is also hinted at in the phrase "**and my life has been preserved**" (*vatinatzeil naphshi*), meaning "separated out and lifted up." [Rashi, on Gen. 31:16, says that "every instance of *hatzalah* in the Torah means 'separating out and lifting up.'"] This suggests that it had never crossed Jacob's mind to serve God for any personal benefit, that is, in order to receive good things from the Holy One. When he says, "**My life has been preserved,**" he means that he has separated off from anything that has to do with his own life.

This form of service is truly "for its own sake" (*lishmah*), while the former is "not for its own sake" (*shelo lishmah*).

FOR FURTHER THOUGHT

Levi Yitzhak once again uses the form of "two types of people." This time he emphasizes the distinction between the one who serves God so that God will provide blessings (even if only sustenance, health, family) and the one who serves God out of awe and reverence for God. Recognizing that there is a God in the world who chose to create the universe and to allow humans to know of God's existence inspires passionate love, awesome fear, and true devotion. Those who serve God out of this awareness have no self-interest. They recognize that it is enough simply to live in God's presence, to bask in God's light, to know God and be known by God. They are fully present to God, without any inner reservations, without any ulterior concerns. These people truly relate to God face-to-face; they serve God in purity, for its own sake.

And again, Levi Yitzhak deeply understands the biblical situation and the meaning of the verse and interprets it in such a manner that it speaks directly to his listeners. We might be tempted to think that his interest is limited to promoting the fundamental Rabbinic value of serving God without ulterior motives (*lishmah*), without expectation of reward or response. But there is also more. He suggests that when we can attain that level of divine service, acting only for

God's sake, without concern for or awareness of our "selves," we can experience being saved, lifted up out of our mundane existence to another plane. The degree of transparency we attain, the lack of self-serving intention, allows us to stand face-to-face with God, where that divine image in us truly and fully mirrors its origin.

An additional note on reading a Hasidic text: a cue to the true interest of the teacher is the word (or words) he actually leaves out of the verse cited. In our case, Levi Yitzhak quotes virtually the whole verse, including the term "face-to-face," leaving out *only* the name of the place: Peniel, meaning "the face of God." What this suggests is that Levi Yitzhak meant to teach us not only what it takes to turn face-to-face toward God through our devotions, but also that in doing so we might, like Jacob, actually, truly, come to see God's face through selfless Torah study, performance of the mitzvot, and connection to other people.

 ## Questions for Reflection

1. How do you understand the difference between relating to God "face-to-back" and "face-to-face"? Why do you think that Levi Yitzhak employs these terms in this manner? After all, in both instances God turns to us directly. Why is it that when we serve God for our own sakes, we are portrayed as having turned our backs?

2. God speaks to Moses face-to-face, and Moses says that at Sinai God spoke to Israel in the same manner. Does Levi Yitzhak mean to suggest that in moments of divine service we might experience what they experienced? Does he mean a different experience? How would you recognize that you were face-to-face with God?

3. We tend to use the terms *lishmah* and *shelo lishmah* with regard to studying Torah and performing mitzvot. What would it mean to think that every mitzvah offers the opportunity to come face-to-face with God? What if we really like doing some mitzvot, if we love Shabbat and the holidays, feel better when we've done *tzedakah*—does this mean that we have not acted *lishmah*? Do we turn our backs on God when we want to have a good experience in doing a mitzvah?

 ## Taking It into Your Life

We can learn about relating to God face-to-face from examining our human relations. Indeed, classical sources (e.g., Gen. R. 8:1; p Zohar I 35a) depict

Adam and Eve as first being attached back-to-back and unable to help one another, unable to develop fully as human beings. Only once God severed one from the other so that they could turn face-to-face could they fulfill themselves and each other fully.

We turn away from others in many different ways. As you make your way through the day, pay attention to where you put your eyes. That is, observe when you look directly at what is before you, particularly the person you are engaged with, and when you look away. What runs through your mind that causes you to look away? What arises in your heart that you wish to ignore? What thought distracts you so that you disengage slightly? What question are you asked that you would rather not answer directly and so hide slightly?

Pay attention to where your eyes roam as you move about in the world. What do you look at? What attracts your attention? What do you look away from? What do you avoid?

Observe the moments in which you sense that you are fully engaged in what is before you, without distracting thoughts, reservations, projections into the future, fear, desire, or apathy.

Becoming sensitive to the ways in which we turn away from the world, the ways in which we hold ourselves back or allow self-concern to limit our engagement, may help us more fully present ourselves face-to-face to our loved ones, to our own lives, to God.

Vayeishev

"Now Jacob dwelt in the land of his father's sojourn, the land of Canaan" (Gen. 37:1).

Ramban writes in *Sefer Ha'emunah Vehabitachon* (ch. 15): Even though the blessed Holy One made a promise to our father Jacob [to be with him, and to protect him], Jacob still feared that perhaps some sin would impede its fulfillment, that perhaps he had not served the Creator appropriately—you can check it out there.

We are obligated to serve God in each and every moment and to be joyful always when we see that Israel is blessed with goodness in this world. And (heaven forbid) if we see that the opposite is the case, we must join them in their suffering, investigating with care whether perhaps some sin of ours [caused this] and we did not serve the Creator [properly]. Jacob was always at this spiritual level. He feared always that perhaps he had sinned and had not fulfilled his obligation to serve the Creator.

This is the meaning of our verse "**Jacob dwelt in the land of his father's sojourn**" (*megurei*). He always sensed fear (*megurei* is a synonym for "fear," *pachad*). Of what was he afraid? Perhaps he had not served the Creator appropriately. "**His father**"—he embraced his father's quality (*middah*), that is, "the Fear of Isaac." Isaac served the Creator with the quality of fear, as suggested in the verse "the Fear of Isaac" (Gen. 31:42).

FOR FURTHER THOUGHT

Abraham, Isaac, and Jacob function, for Levi Yitzhak, as both the historical figures of Jewish history and the embodied representations of the divine qualities of love, fear, and beauty (or truth). The proof-text for the association of Isaac with fear is cited in our lesson (Gen. 31:42). Jacob would not otherwise spontaneously respond to the world, to his life, with fear. Rather, he attains that quality by associating himself with his father. In this sense, we might say (with Levi Yitzhak) that he chose to develop that *middah*, that he came to "dwell in the land of his father."

Of course, Levi Yitzhak has further support for this association in the double meaning of the word "sojourn" (*megurei*). The root *g-u-r* has the meaning both "to sojourn" and "to fear or dread." So Jacob dwelt in the "land of his father's fear." What is the nature of that fear? It is not so much fear regarding the vicissitudes of life. Isaac certainly knew them and maintained a fairly even temper. Nor is this fear of God's punishment. Again, the vicissitudes of life would not have been experienced by Jacob as punishment; rather, perhaps, as chastisement and therefore as what God determines to be correct in the moment. Thus, his fear emerges from the awareness of both the privilege and the responsibility of living before God. Standing before God demands constant attention, impeccable behavior and awareness, and pure devotion. Failure to do so is not so much a sin as an insult, reflecting obtuseness, inattentiveness, and self-concern.

The phrase "perhaps some sin would impede" the fulfillment of God's promise comes from Berakhot 4a:

> R. Ya'akov bar Iddi pointed to a contradiction. One verse reads: "Remember, I am with you, I will protect you wherever you go" (Gen. 28:15); and the other verse reads: "Jacob was greatly frightened" (Gen. 32:8)! [How could Jacob be afraid if God has made such a grand promise? The answer is that] he thought that some sin might cause [God's promise not to be fulfilled].

Levi Yitzhak expands this from the particular context of Jacob's fear of facing Esau to reflect a constant attitude, one that we might take on as well.

Of note is how Levi Yitzhak contextualizes the ground of this fear: perhaps my behavior is the source of communal suffering; my deficient devotion to God the cause of woe. It is the self-examination that each of us should undertake when witnessing the suffering of others. When people suffer, even if we can see some external force (of which we are not in control) at work, we are called on to recognize that we may also play (or have played) some role in the collective problem. This fear is not—at least need not be—a morbid fear of making a mistake. Rather, it is an invitation to see our subtle and intimate connection with all others, to sense our participation in our own suffering and the suffering of others. Yet, we can also play a role in the potential redemption of the whole of creation. What Levi Yitzhak offers is the possibility of a productive, positive, redeeming awareness of the potential of sin (inattentiveness, self-concern) as a means of building moral social awareness.

Questions for Reflection

1. Levi Yitzhak seems to create a parallel between serving God "in each and every moment" and rejoicing when we see that "Israel is blessed with goodness in this world." How do you understand this connection? What is the connection between serving God and joy? What is the connection between rejoicing in the good of others and serving God? How might the fear of God also be a source of joy?

2. When others are suffering, do you always feel connected to their pain? What might be the source of distance that a person feels from other people's suffering? Why do you suppose Levi Yitzhak insists particularly that we share in others' suffering, even before he invites us to examine our own deeds?

3. Does the leap that Levi Yitzhak makes from the suffering of others to the possibility of our culpability make sense to you? Are we guilty for everyone else's suffering? Could Levi Yitzhak be voicing the antecedent for Heschel's claim, "In regard to cruelties committed in the name of a free society, some are guilty, while all are responsible"?

 ## Taking It into Your Life

Compassion is the active interest in the well-being of others. It reflects an awareness of connectedness to others, even when that awareness is painful (when they are suffering; when we suffer with them). It is a willingness to remain engaged with the good of others, even when we cannot do anything to help.

The antithesis of compassion is not disinterest; it is pity. Pity is the recognition of others' suffering while reserving to oneself the right to turn away, to dissociate from the pain that suffering arouses, to deny any involvement in the suffering of others. It holds others at arm's length and coats the heart in protective armor. It feigns concern while escaping responsibility for care.

We will take Levi Yitzhak's instructions literally. For the next week, make a practice of listening to the news or reading the newspaper carefully. Whenever you hear/read a story that involves the suffering of others, particularly when it is someone distant from you, pause to consider the full implications of the trouble reported. Imagine what the home of the afflicted looked like. Imagine their families and friends. Make up the story of their lives to this moment. Connect this suffering to your own experience. Consider that this person is in your immediate community, that this is happening to someone you know. Feel the pain of their suffering.

Now, investigate what it might mean to say, "I have played some role in this." That is, can you imagine lines of connection, implications of action or inaction, of attention or inattention that tie you to this event? Can you hold this awareness without slipping into meaningless exaggeration of guilt or without denying all connection? How does finding connection to the suffering of others affect your feeling of connection to their lives in a broader sense? What is the feeling in your heart? Do you sense connection or disconnection—to others, to your own feelings? How does it feel to know your own pain at others' suffering, even as you do continue living your own life moment-to-moment without suffering? What do you discover about the difference between compassion and pity?

Another interpretation regarding the verse above: "Jacob settled in the land of his father's sojourn, the land of Canaan" (Gen. 37:1).

Here is the principle: we are to consider our deeds carefully to make sure that they are all done for the sake of heaven (cf. *Tur, Orach Chayyim* 231), since whatever the blessed Holy One created in this world was created only for God's glory (cf. Avot 6:10), even material things. So when we sit to eat or drink, our intention and focus should be for the sake of our physical health so that we might serve our Creator. Similarly, when engaged in sexual intercourse our intention should be to fulfill the mitzvot connected to that act.

So, then, regarding whatever physical activity this world presents us, our intention should be for the glory of heaven, and in this manner we will raise the holy sparks to their root. In every thing we find some physical love or fear or beauty. But when we sense a desire to eat or drink, or to engage in any other desirable worldly activity, and we intend it instead as love of God, we raise up the physical desire to a spiritual desire. In this manner we separate out the holy spark in the food or any other thing.

This is the mystical meaning of ritual hand-washing (*netilat yadayim*). *Netilah* is synonymous with raising up, as in "He raised them [*vayenatleim*], lifted them up" (Isa. 63:9). So this means that when we wash our hands, we raise and lift the "three hands": "the great hand" (Exod. 14:31; *yad hagedolah*), "the raised hand" (Exod. 14:8; *yad haramah*), and "the strong hand" (Exod. 13:9; *yad hachazakah*), which signify the three higher qualities (*middot*) mentioned above (love, fear, beauty; see Zohar III 246b). We lift and raise them up to their root by means of our intention.

Similarly, this is the mystical meaning of the blessing "Who brings forth bread from the earth" (*hamotzi lechem min ha'aretz*). Bread (*lechem*) signifies holiness (the mystery of *lechem* = 3 x *HVY"H* = 78). Earth (*eretz*) signifies earthiness and materiality. So, we bring forth bread—that is, holy sparks—from the earth—from materiality and the realm of external forces. When we follow this path, we indicate the strong, powerful love that we have for God. There is no better path than this, for wherever we go on this path, in everything that we do— even extraneous things—we serve our Creator.

This is the mystical meaning of "If only you could be my brother, nursing at my mother's breast; then I could kiss you when I met you in the market [and no one would despise me]" (Song 8:1). Consider: there is a love that is hidden and a love that is revealed. The hidden love is that between loving partners, which is kept private. The revealed love is that between a brother and sister, who sometimes will kiss each other in public without any shame, because of their great love for each other. This is the meaning of "If only you could be my brother, nursing"— that is, "If my love for You could be as a brother loves a sister, even if I met You in the market I could kiss You." That is, even when I find sparks of Your holiness in material, physical things, even there I could kiss You, raising them to their source in the mystery of "a kiss." I would not think of any physical desire. This love is fierce love, as in "love is as fierce as death" (Song 8:6).

In addition, this is how we should conduct ourselves: whatever it is that God brings on us we should receive with ease of spirit and joy, as the Sages said regarding the phrase in the *Shema* (Deut. 6:5) "with all your might" (*me'odekha*): "whatever measure [*bekhol middah umiddah*]

God metes [*moded*] out to you, acknowledge [or, thank; *modeh*] Him greatly [*me'od me'od*]" (Berakhot 54a). Further, they taught, "Whatever the Merciful One does, He does for the good" (Berakhot 60b). Whatever comes our way, we should trust and believe that there is some great good in it, for "nothing bad comes from Him" (Lam. 3:38). The model for this is Nahum of Gamzu, whose great trust and belief in God led him to say regarding everything that came his way, "even this is for the good" (*gam zu letovah*) (Ta'anit 21a). In this manner he would sweeten the difficulties that befell him, transforming them to compassion, making of the bad, good.

This is the way we should approach our work in raising divine sparks. Consider the verse "Who brought forth water for you from the flinty rock" (Deut. 8:15). Water symbolizes love and compassion, while "rock" symbolizes force and power. So "who brought forth water for you"—that is, who brought forth love—"from the flinty rock"— from the force of the judgment that befalls you—in the end they are transformed into good. This comes about by means of our pure and faithful thoughts; that we have faith that whatever God does is for the good. In this manner, we display fierce, powerful love for God. This was the sort of trust and faith that Jacob had. The Torah says, "**Jacob settled in the land of his father's sojourn**" (*megurei aviv*), and Rashi says, "He desired to live in tranquility." That is, his constant approach was to seek to live with tranquility and ease of spirit, to be able to receive everything for the good, even in the land of his father's fear." Even when fear and terror (*magur vaphachad*, the quality of his father, Isaac) came upon him, he accepted it all with tranquility and ease of spirit, due to his great piety and trust in the blessed One.

FOR FURTHER THOUGHT

Levi Yitzhak ties together two seemingly unconnected qualities of spiritual awareness, suggesting that each one leads to the other in a circular, mutually reinforcing manner. He begins with the practice of raising holy sparks to their root. This is accomplished by training the mind to notice that the whole of human experience—love, fear, glory, appreciation of beauty—is a means to remembering God. When we pay attention to how our hearts respond to the world, where our attention is attracted (or repelled), to the content of our thoughts and feelings, we have the capacity to transform that awareness from a private, self-satisfying experience to a prompt to serve God. When we are able to notice our experience (and not take it for granted, not claim it as something that is merely happening to us), we can appreciate it more deeply and allow it to direct us toward God.

The second practice that Levi Yitzhak offers is that of Nahum of Gamzu. It is one of appreciation, gratitude, and suspension of judgment, allowing us in any moment to discern that "even this is for the good." This practice also calls us to step out of our private, self-centered orientation to consider that whatever is happening is the only possible consequence of all the conditions antecedent to this moment and that therefore there is some fundamental "goodness" or rightness to it (even if painful, even if amelioration, restitution, or resistance is called for).

The first practice has to do with how we train ourselves to see the world, such that it leads us to God. The second trains us to see God, transforming how we see the world. In the end, Levi Yitzhak suggests that this is how Jacob lived his life, balancing the two practices, using them both to remain balanced and at peace. It is an invitation to us to do the same.

Levi Yitzhak expands and deepens his didactic teaching regarding the first practice with examples drawn from common rituals. He points—in shorthand—to the ritual of washing hands and eating bread. These, he argues, might remain for us simple, mundane, and self-serving acts. But when we pay attention, bringing proper attention and awareness to the act, we can find God in them. Regarding the washing hands, Levi Yitzhak refers to a teaching of the Zohar that identifies *yad hagedolah* with great compassion/love (*rachamim*), *yad hachazakah* with limitation (*gevurah*), and *yad haramah* with the middle way (*tiferet*). With regard to eating bread, he refers to a teaching of R. Isaac Luria. In both cases, his intention is to demonstrate how, in the most commonplace and routine rituals and acts, it is possible to notice God's presence and so to raise up the holy sparks in the mundane.

The mundane, the worldly, is the only place where we can find God. That is the realm that we inhabit. We might think that we have to transcend this world, to look for God only in the ethereal, the otherworldly, beyond our physical and material needs and activities. Not so, says Levi Yitzhak. It is in just this world—"in the market"—that we might meet God. If we can let go of our diffidence, our fear, our embarrassment, we might be able to meet God, embracing and kissing like loving siblings. Perhaps Levi Yitzhak senses that people who say they are looking for God wind up hiding, even running away, when the opportunity arises to meet God. We miss the opportunities to give and get love, even when they are right before us in our daily affairs, in the most mundane circumstances. If we were to open our hearts in love—a third practice that links the first two—we would find that ease of spirit, the inner peace that we crave, cradled in God's loving goodness.

 ## Questions for Reflection

1. How do you respond to the suggestion that nothing that we do should be for our own personal pleasure? Isn't part of the joy of being alive the delight in our capacity to experience everything? How would you explain Levi Yitzhak's teaching in your own terms? What does it mean to you to "lift up holy sparks"? Is this practice in competition with your own enjoyment of the experiences of your life?

2. What do you imagine it would be like to "kiss" God in the marketplace? How would you recognize God? What would the kiss be like? Consider the quality of loving siblings that Levi Yitzhak plays on: Where does that love rest? Does it ever sleep? Why would it burst forth so passionately upon meeting in the market? Where do you sense this sort of love in your life?

3. In your experience, what is the relationship between responding with love to what is happening and perceiving God's goodness in the world? What is the relationship between developing and maintaining an attitude of gratitude and finding God in the world?

 ## Taking It into Your Life

"If only you could be my brother, nursing at my mother's breast; then I could kiss you when I met you in the market and no one would despise me." This is what the lover says to the beloved in Song of Songs (8:1). It might be what we say to every person in the world. Consider going through your daily routine, looking at each person as your brother or sister, as someone familiar, trusted and trusting, whom you would welcome with a kiss and embrace and who would naturally and enthusiastically respond in kind. Open your heart to each person as if he or she were loving and beloved. Allow the armor that you wear on your heart to slip away. Let go of posturing, of pretense, of persona—know that you are acceptable just as you are, without fear of shame or embarrassment. Welcome each person, seeking to meet them fully, as they are, without judgment, without expectation, without projections. Notice what you learn about yourself. Notice what happens to your sense of the quality of your life. Notice when and where you find holy sparks, where you sense God's presence.

> "When the time came for her to give birth, [...] he [i.e., one of the twins] put out his hand.... But just then he drew back his hand, [and] out came his brother; [and she said, 'What a breach you have made for yourself!'] So he was named Peretz. [Afterward his brother came out, on whose hand was the crimson thread;] he was named Zerach" (Gen. 38:27–30).

Consider this teaching of the Sages: When a fetus resides in its mother's womb, a lamp is lighted over its head, by which it sees from one end of the world to another. That is to say, this child still possesses the holiness it had before it left its original location. Then, an angel comes and strikes the fetus on its mouth, at which point the child forgets what it knew up to this point (Niddah 30b).

When the fetus is about to emerge into this world, it is aroused by arousal from above, just at the entrance to the world. At this point it has the capacity to hold its thoughts solely on serving God, without any obstacles. But God wants us to have the opportunity to devote our souls and bodies in divine service, and to that end God removes that arousal from above, and there remains only a separating partition. In this God gives us free will, the capacity to choose the good and spurn the bad.

Now, if we take stock with ourselves in truth, we would say: "This world, in the end, is really bad, and all its pleasures are only passing, ephemeral, and corruptible ("the more flesh, the more worms," Avot 2:7). The true good is only in serving God, and this work will endure for me forever. So, how should I abandon the good to choose the bad? I take it upon myself from now on to cleave in devotion to God." Coming to that conclusion, we regain the capacity to return to our original state. Because this process purifies our physical being, what remains in us are the qualities we had when we first emerged into this world from the womb. As a consequence, the partition ceases to exist; we break a breach in the partition. Through it then shines a great light, radiating from the face of the Living Sovereign. The light that shines on us is like the radiance (*zerichah*) of the sun.

This is the meaning of these verses: "**When the time came for her to give birth,**" that is, when our soul is born, "**he put out** [*vayiten*; lit., he gave] **his hand,**" that is, the blessed Holy One gives us the sense of arousal from above. But, when we grow older, the blessed Holy One removes this arousal (as we explained), and a sort of partition remains called "**hand.**" Still, some small residue remains as well, so that when we purify ourselves, becoming fully transparent before God, we then break through (*poretz*) the partition, as it says, "**He was named Peretz.**" And, it is known that the blessed Holy One calls Israel "brother" (Zohar II 55b), as it says, "For the sake of my brothers and friends" (Ps. 122:8). This helps us to understand the subsequent verse in our lesson: "**Afterward his brother came out ...; he was named Zerach.**" After our efforts, the blessed Holy One shines (*zerichah*) the great radiance of God's face on us.

FOR FURTHER THOUGHT

The story of Judah and Tamar is remarkable both in its subject matter and in its implications. The birth of Peretz from this questionable union—Tamar was both a "local girl" (Moabite) and Judah's daughter-in-law—leads eventually to the birth of David, king of Israel, model, and progenitor of the Messiah. While Levi Yitzhak does not refer to this fact, it lies behind this teaching, deepening the implications of our spiritual work.

In his familiar manner, Levi Yitzhak lifts the narrative of the birth of Peretz and Zerach out of its context, reading it as a description of human spiritual development. We are born spiritually aware and open, supported and energized by God. There is something sweet in this image—in the suggestion that childhood's open-eyed wonder and spontaneous spiritual awareness are gifts from God. We know all too well how that wonder and innocence are squelched, negated, and overwhelmed by our experiences with the adults in our lives, by our education, by our losses, frustrations, and hurt. We tend, as well, to experience that loss as a negative aspect of growing up, but Levi Yitzhak suggests that it is a consequence of God's initiative and intention. God withdraws the "arousal" with which we were born, placing a barrier to block our perception of the Divine. God's desire is that we then generate our own enthusiasm and energy to break through, to once again experience the warm glow of the divine presence, to bask in the light of God's face. The work of growing up, then, is indeed a return to a form of innocence. We overcome the separation of space, time, and heart to turn again to the glowing, welcoming, loving face of the one who birthed us, to our original knowledge of God's great love.

Perhaps Levi Yitzhak connects this image with the line of the Messiah to suggest that the enlightenment that we experience as a product of our spiritual work is an aspect of the coming of the Messiah. The effort that we apply in our inner work has an effect on the outer work of redeeming the world.

 ## Questions for Reflection

1. We tend to identify our freedom of choice with accountability, moral responsibility. Is that why Levi Yitzhak says we were given the power to choose? What is the difference between moral accountability and spiritual initiative, if any? Are they connected at all? Should they be? How do you connect your spiritual striving with your moral muster?

2. The verses demand that Levi Yitzhak do something with the image of the hand. What does it mean to you that here "hand" means "partition"? Is God's hand pushing us away, preventing us from reaching God? Is it extended for us to grab hold of, to reach out for? Whose hand is actually separating us from God if God is the "brother" who shines forth even after his hand has been withdrawn? How might your understanding change if you understood "he gave his hand" to signify God giving us power, authority? How would that meaning change your sense of the partition?

3. Can we use this passage to shape a vision of what the Messiah—or the messianic enlightenment—might be? What do we need to do to experience ultimate redemption? Who makes it happen? What will the experience be like?

Taking It into Your Life

The metaphoric image of Peretz in this lesson is of the one who experiences a "breakthrough." There is a tension in contemplative practice between appropriate (even necessary) effort toward a goal or end and the risk that attachment to the ends may impede awareness of what is true (and good) in the moment. Further, when we exert effort, striving to make something happen, we risk becoming self-centered, thinking that "results" depend on our effort, that we have to "make something happen" when, in the end, it is God who brings all things to pass, and our self-directed, self-centered activity may at best only get in the way and at worst do violence to ourselves or to others. Perhaps what we might aim for is effort and rest, application of intention and attention to what simply "is."

How can we work with these two aspects of effort? One way might be in the physical realm. A simple exercise might be to hold our hands overhead and grasp the right arm at the wrist with the left hand. Pull the right arm toward the right, while holding and resisting with the left. Exert as much force as you can (comfortably, safely) with your right arm while restraining and remaining steadfast with the left. Hold for about thirty seconds. Let go. Observe the sensation in both arms. Reverse the exercise. Observe.

Did you have any sense of "breakthrough" from this exercise? When were you able to recognize it? Did you have any sense of what might constitute "success" for you in this exercise? What did you notice about your inner thoughts: Were you focused on one hand or the other? Did you have any judging or complaining thoughts? How did these thoughts affect your sense of "success" in the exercise? What was your experience of the period of relaxation between the two halves of the exercise and at the end? What is the role of rest in effort? Are "breakthroughs" final and complete or temporary and partial? Where do we find enlightenment in this process?

Mikkeitz

"Now Joseph was the vizier [of the land;] he was the broker distributing rations to all the people of the land [*am ha'aretz*]. [And Joseph's brothers came and bowed low to him, with their faces to the ground]" (Gen. 42:6).

We can identify two categories: "the people of *YHVH*" (*am YHVH*) and "the people of the land" (*am ha'aretz*). The "people of *YHVH*" are the tzaddikim, and the "people of the land" are those who are tied to worldly materiality, and it is necessary to break (*lishbor*) them of that attachment.

This is the sense of our verse: "**Joseph was the vizier ... the broker**" (*hamashbir*)—that is, he was the ruler who broke (*meshaber*) those people who have to be brought higher. They have to be raised up so that they might be called "the people of *YHVH*." That is the meaning of "**broker**" (*hamashbir*), having to do with breaking (*shever*) the "people of the land" so that they might be called the "people of *YHVH*."

FOR FURTHER THOUGHT

This lesson is one way of reading the verse. It certainly makes sense on its surface and has the tone of a chastising preacher, doing what it takes to break people of their bad habits, their coarseness and taste for the material. The image of breaking is quite violent, however, suggesting not merely shattering old habits but also smashing heads and hearts. This does not quite seem in the spirit of Levi Yitzhak. He is generally much more compassionate toward the common folk, more likely to acknowledge the impediment of their having to make a living, to emphasize their native capacity to transcend their earthliness.

An alternative reading—tenuous perhaps, but creative—would be based on the second meaning of the root *sh-b-r*: to buy grain.

As a noun, *shever* means "grain." Could it be that Levi Yitzhak is suggesting that the work of the leader, the tzaddik, is to nurture and raise up the seeds of holiness in the "people of the land"? Or, is the role of the tzaddik to provide the people with the food that they need to grow out of their rootedness in their earthly concerns? Perhaps we are to hear the double meaning in an agricultural sense. That is, to prepare the land to receive seed—to then produce what grows upward, which rises from the ground toward the heavens— one needs to break up the earth. Earth is only productive when it is tilled, broken up, and turned over. This is the work of the leader with his people, and it is this that will produce grain—sustenance, spiritual food—the *shever* by which the "people of the land" come to be called the "people of *YHVH*."

Questions for Reflection

1. The colloquial sense of *am ha'aretz* is "ignoramus." Is that Levi Yitzhak's sense of that term here? Of what might we say these people are ignorant? What do the *am YHVH* know?

2. What does it take to break a habit? Can it be done by violent means? Does it work with tough love (compassionate resistance and clear directives)? How have you experienced the process of changing deeply rooted habits?

3. Most of our habits are adaptive; they serve to protect or comfort some vulnerable aspect of our hearts and minds. To change, we need to learn that the original events that created the adaptive behavior have changed, that we can survive and thrive without the habit, and that continuing with the habitual behavior is actually harmful to us. How does this schema fit with the nurturing aspect of *shever*? How might you apply this to your own personal, spiritual growth?

Taking It into Your Life

Levi Yitzhak identifies *am ha'aretz* as the person who is rooted in earthliness, in materiality. That would be most of us, on some level. That is, we seem to be hardwired to respond to intimations of lack and fear of insufficiency. This is true with regard not only to food but also to all aspects of life that bring us a sense of safety, security, and well-being. We respond with fear, aggression, depression, resistance, and selfishness when we sense that anything we feel we need is insufficient in the moment or may be taken away or fall short in the future. And when we have enough in the moment, we try to guarantee that we will continue to have enough, again responding with fear, aggression, depression, resistance, and selfishness. While the autonomic nervous system may be the source of these responses, we can use our higher brains, our consciousness and conscience, to over-come them and to redirect our energies. This is the goal of spiritual practice and of Levi Yitzhak's teaching.

As you make your way through your life, pay attention to the moments that register the sensation of "hungry." Notice the quality of the feeling, where it manifests in your body. Observe the context of the feeling—is it lunchtime or dinnertime? Are you at work, stuck in traffic, on the phone with a family member? Are you tired, sad, frustrated, afraid? What will satisfy this hunger? Which foods do you gravitate toward when you feel this particular pang? Do you notice any associations from your past connected with this feeling? Will any foods actually address this emptiness?

Can you learn from this process what sort of nurturance might be the most effective response to your "hunger"? Is it always to eat? Might it be to take a nap or a walk? To call a friend? To sit with the feeling and look deeply into its source, to notice how the sensation changes when it is observed rather than responded to? When you notice your own "fam-ine," can you turn to a helpful "broker" (*mashbir*) to provide you with food (*shever*), to help break (*lishbor*) your habitual responses and act more wisely, growing in spiritual awareness?

"[Now Joseph was the vizier of the land;
it was he who dispensed rations to all
the people of the land.] And Joseph's
brothers came and bowed low to him,
with their faces to the ground. When
Joseph saw his brothers, he recognized
them; but he acted like a stranger toward
them [and spoke harshly to them. He
asked them, 'Where do you come from?'
And they said, 'From the land of Canaan, to
procure food.']" (Gen. 42:6–7).

What does Scripture mean to teach us when it tells us that Joseph **"acted like a stranger toward them"**? Apparently it is to tell us about the righteousness of Joseph the tzaddik. Joseph had dreamed that his brothers would bow down to him, as it says: "There we were binding sheaves [in the field, when suddenly my sheaf stood up and remained upright; then your sheaves gathered around and bowed low to my sheaf]" (Gen. 37:7); and "[He dreamed another dream and told it to his brothers, saying, 'Look, I have had another dream:] And this time, the sun, [the moon, and eleven stars were bowing down to me.' And when he told it to his father and brothers, his father berated him. 'What,' he said to him, 'is this dream you have dreamed? Are we to come, I and your mother and your brothers, and bow low to you to the ground?']" (Gen. 37:9–10). But, Joseph's brothers rejected his claim to dominion over them.

Now, it is only natural that when one person overpowers his fellow, and the latter knows that this is the case (that the former has actually gained power over him), it causes psychic pain and emotional distress. But, if someone gains power over another and it is unknown, if the latter does not know who it is who has gained control, the psychic pain is not as acute.

So in our case, Joseph had power over his brothers, as his dreams had come to fulfillment—indeed, his brothers were now bowing down to him. But, still, they did not wish that he have any dominion over them or that they should bow down to him. So this was the righteousness of Joseph the tzaddik: when they bowed down to him, and it was evident to him that he had overpowered them, he realized that it would cause them psychic pain to know that they were bowing down to him. Therefore, Joseph the tzaddik, when his brothers were bowing down to him, **"acted like a stranger to them,"** so that they would not suffer, knowing that he had gained power over them with the fulfillment of his dreams. He let them think that they were bowing down to someone else. He let them think that he was the king, and so it did not bother them that they were bowing down to some king. That is why our verse emphasizes that they bowed down to him, but **"he recognized them"**—he acknowledged them, knowing that they would experience intense emotional distress, so **"he acted like a stranger toward them"**—so that they would not experience distress knowing that it was he, Joseph, their brother, who had power over them.

If this is the case, then we can understand why it was that Joseph the tzaddik did not inform his father that he had risen to high position and that he was still alive. Joseph understood that his dreams would come to pass and that his brothers would come to bow down before him. If he had told his father [that he was still alive and that he was the vizier in Egypt] and his brothers came down to Egypt and then bowed before him, they would suffer knowing that he had bested them. If his father knew, they would surely know as well. That is why he did not inform his father, so that he would not cause pain to his brothers. That way they could ultimately come down to Egypt and bow down before him, and not know to whom they were bowing, and just think that they were bowing before some king or other.

FOR FURTHER THOUGHT

The Joseph story is one of the more elaborate and literary sections of the Torah. Each moment, each movement, each element invites investigation and interpretation. This literary analysis is not only a modern phenomenon, as we learn from Levi Yitzhak. This scene— the arrival of the brothers before Joseph, their prostration before him, and his caustic response to them—is as dramatic as it is opaque. What was Joseph thinking? Why did he respond as he did? What are we to make of his charade and his seizure of one brother?

As the story unfolds, we get the impression that Joseph is playing with his brothers, testing them to know their true intentions, their feelings toward him, their relationship to his full brother Benjamin. In this sense, his response is fully intentional and part of a larger plan that he is hatching in the moment. The classical commentary *Or Hachayyim* (R. Hayyim ben Attar, 1696–1742, Morocco, Italy, and Jerusalem) senses this and responds to these verses as follows:

> He saw them as brothers would see one another, and he recognized his own brotherly feeling toward them. Still, he behaved as a stranger (as it says, "He recognized them; but he acted like a stranger toward them"). That is, since they did not recognize him, they would not suspect anything if he spoke harshly with them, believing him to be a stranger. Joseph behaved in this manner so that the brothers would be forced to bring Benjamin down to him, as we see from

the conclusion of the story. He also wished to test them through the unfolding of the story, to know their thoughts and feelings toward him when they were in a similar situation (with Benjamin). In the end, he learned that they regretted what they had done to him, considering it a sin.

Other commentators read Joseph's reaction as one of fear. He recognized his brothers and feared that they would recognize him and reveal his true identity (Ramban). As we see later, Joseph felt constrained in his position in the court and needed to prepare the way for introducing his family to Pharaoh and resettling them in the land of Egypt.

What Levi Yitzhak suggests, however, is quite different. He senses a dimension of tension here unlike the other commentators. Joseph is the embodiment of righteousness and connection. He is *yoseph hatzaddik*, Joseph the righteous, Joseph the tzaddik. He represents the emerging Hasidic tzaddik, who is then in turn *tzaddik yesod olam*, the foundation of creation, the conduit through which the divine flow is directed toward all creation (the *sephirah Yesod*). How could he be cruel to his brothers? How could he behave in any manner that is not of the highest quality? Could this be Levi Yitzhak, who suffered terribly at the hands of the opponents of Hasidism, explaining why he sought no compensation, took no revenge?

Levi Yitzhak reveals the apologetic aspect of his teaching at the start: this narrative is "to tell us about the righteousness of Joseph the tzaddik." He relates the Torah narrative, referring to Joseph without any title until he applies his teaching. At that point, he again calls him "Joseph the tzaddik." And, when Levi Yitzhak adds his explanation of why Joseph did not inform his father that he was alive in Egypt, he is again "Joseph the tzaddik." In all, Levi Yitzhak teaches us that this passage is to instruct us how to behave toward other people. He directs us to the inner awareness of the righteous person, concerned always for the well-being of the other. Even when the righteous person has been harmed by others yet gains the upper hand, he does not exercise his power over them, even when righteous anger or indignation might seem in order. Saving the heart of another is more important than saving one's own face.

Questions for Reflection

1. How do you respond to Levi Yitzhak's instructions? Does it make sense to you to let miscreants off the hook? Would you protect the feelings of a person who has slighted you, let alone having caused you harm or pain?

2. What do you think is the connection between Levi Yitzhak's emphasis on Joseph having protected the feelings of his brothers and his identification of Joseph as a "tzaddik"? Is he inviting his listeners to take Joseph as a model and to strive to be tzaddikim like him? Is he suggesting that the true tzaddik (like Levi Yitzhak) is able to subjugate or efface his ego such that he can always look out for the well-being of others? Are these two connected? How do you see yourself in this?

3. In light of the previous question, if Levi Yitzhak is offering Joseph as a model (or exemplar) of the true tzaddik, the kind of leader that the Hasidic movement put forth, do you feel that it is a model that makes sense today? What other qualities do you imagine such a leader might need? What might be the outcome today of having such leaders? Could you be such a leader?

Taking It into Your Life

Ramban offers a second explanation of the meaning of our verse:

> "He acted like a stranger toward them": he acted like a stranger in that he spoke harshly with them, responding with anger, as if no one was to appear before him to procure food. Joseph then challenged them: "How did you get here? Where did you come from?" The brothers then replied, "From the land of Canaan, to procure food." When they told him this, they jogged his memory, and he then realized that they were indeed his brothers. That is the sense of verse 8, where we read a second time: "Joseph recognized his brothers." He gained better recognition and truer awareness.

We might see in this a depiction of our own responses to being startled. Our hearts contract. We build ourselves up, revving up our power to protect ourselves against what has surprised us. We lash out in anger, seeking to subdue what we fear is attacking us. If we can attain some presence of mind, if we can take a breath and pay attention to what is truly occurring, then we may be able to recover without doing damage to others, or to ourselves. We gain time to reconsider, to assess our situation, and discern a wise response. In particular, in light of this narrative, we are able to recognize in the other, in what has startled us, our brothers, our selves. We recall our interconnectedness; we recover our openhearted love for all others.

As you make your way through your day, watch for those moments when your breath gets caught in your throat. Attend to when your heart races or your chest contracts. Observe when your shoulders tighten, your hands form fists, your stomach tenses. Note every sign of surprise and startle. In response, take a deep breath. Take another breath. Ask a question—of yourself or of others—to buy time. Look carefully at the one opposite you. Listen to his or her voice. Consider that she or he is not there to attack you, to harm you—or that he or she has no power to do so. See if you are able to relax in the moment. Look carefully again. Where is the brother or sister in the one before you? What can you recognize in this person that might help you recover, change course, and pursue another, more peaceful and compassionate course of action for yourself and for the other?

"On the third day Joseph said to them, 'Do this and you shall live, for I fear God. If you are honest men, let one of you brothers [be held in your place of detention, while the rest of you go and take home rations for your starving households; but you must bring me] your youngest brother, [that your words may be verified and that you may not die.'] And they did accordingly" (Gen. 42:18–20).

According to a plain reading of the text it would seem that the statement "**I fear God**" should have preceded "**Do this and you shall live.**" Further, the final statement "**And they did accordingly**" suggests that they fulfilled the instructions immediately. But did they not bring Benjamin until much later, after they had returned to their father and come back to Egypt afterward, with their father's agreement? Yet "**they did accordingly**" suggests that they did so immediately!

Look at it this way: this is proper instruction for the way we should behave. When people stand against us (i.e., "attack us"), we should judge them for merit, thinking that they are doing this out of fear of God. Since we then do not suspect that they are acting out of wickedness, but out of reverence for God, our hearts are drawn to them. We are thereby reassured that they will finally approach us with peace, since in our hearts we have drawn nearer to them.

When Joseph said, **"Do this and you shall live, for I fear God,"** he hoped to revive their spirits, thinking, "This way my heart will be drawn to you, once you understand and believe that I fear God. Further, you will understand that I am not approaching you (heaven forbid!) with wickedness. And, when I tell you to 'bring me your **youngest brother,'** I do not do so out of hatred or wickedness."

When the text then says, **"And they did accordingly,"** this is what they did immediately: they believed him that he feared God and that he was not acting from hatred. That is why it says immediately afterward the brothers said, "Alas, we are being punished on account of our brother, etc." (Gen. 42:21), that is, they took responsibility on themselves and did not say that Joseph acted out of hatred toward them. He, after all, feared God, and it was they who brought about the circumstances they now faced.

FOR FURTHER THOUGHT

This passage challenges the assumptions that seem to be at play in the Torah narrative. That is, in the Torah, Joseph intentionally alienates himself from his brothers, charging them as spies and seemingly threatening their freedom and their lives. Levi Yitzhak suggests that we read this in a completely different manner. He depicts Joseph as not threatening but reassuring them! Joseph understands a subtle but important psychological dynamic that he hopes the brothers will employ. That is, when we can shift our assumptions about someone who opposes us, who threatens us, we might find a way to break down the conflict and find a peaceful solution.

Levi Yitzhak suggests that one who stands against us may be acting out of fear of God. That is, their intention may not be self-centered or self-serving, nor may it be mistaken or misplaced. Rather, it may flow from their perception of how to serve God. Moreover, it may be intended to arouse fear of God in us, so that we will respond differently, so that we will behave with greater impeccability. When we reconfigure and reconceptualize our situation, we see our opponent differently. When we impute to him or her positive motivation or at least find room to understand her or his intention, our hearts can open in response. We hear more clearly, we think more creatively, we respond with greater flexibility, compassion, and wisdom.

Still, Levi Yitzhak's suggestion is problematic: it may be interesting spiritually, but is it safe? Could he have meant to use this as a response to Cossacks and hooligans, and would he have meant us to use it today in a world seemingly so much more violent, so much more dangerous—so much less susceptible to spiritual manipulation?

Yet, this is his teaching. He wants us to understand that the brothers' ability to hear him report, "I fear God," caused them to open their hearts to him, to relax in his presence, and to respond differently. Joseph's self-revelation as God-fearing created the conditions in which the brothers could more easily face their guilt and shame, acknowledging their responsibility for Joseph's disappearance and their present difficulty. Alternatively, the brothers could respond with more force rather than guilty passivity, with greater candor and a desire for engagement. And so, perhaps, Levi Yitzhak's prescription is not wholly one of passivity, still requiring the opponent to act with compassion and justice or face resistance. Indeed, his suggestion opens up more possibilities of negotiation, creating the likelihood of a more peaceful, more just resolution.

Finally, it must be noted that this text is unclear and somewhat ambiguous. That is, Levi Yitzhak writes using the third-person masculine pronoun for all of the parties involved. So we could also read his prescription in this manner: when we shift our perception of our opponent, realizing that he is acting out of "fear of God," we draw *his* heart toward *us*. In this version, when Joseph reveals, "I fear God," he means to say, "By this means your spirits will be revived, because automatically my heart will be drawn to you, because you will believe that I fear God." This approach is somewhat problematic—or difficult to grasp—because it suggests that our attitude toward another changes his or her feelings toward us. Difficult as this may be, it is worth our consideration. Perhaps we can generate more positive energies in the world by means of our attitude toward others, changing their hearts by our awareness.

Questions for Reflection

1. Is it possible—more, is it wise—to follow Levi Yitzhak's instructions in all cases? When someone attacks us, will our inner assessment of them, our sentiment toward them, really protect us? What can this possibly mean in moments of physical danger? What is the place of this "mindfulness instruction" in moments of physical danger?

2. If the circumstance is not that we are being attacked but that someone "stands against us," that is, opposes us, challenges us, argues with us, differs from us—can Levi Yitzhak's proposal work? How?

3. Is it really possible to do this? What prevents you from responding to other people with an open heart, with the assumption of good intentions, so that they will turn to you in peace and love? What are the obstacles in other people's hearts that prevent their hearts from being drawn to us, to opening to change and reconciliation?

 # Taking It into Your Life

Levi Yitzhak clearly and directly offers us a practice, a way to behave in our lives. He suggests that the first step in transforming a conflict is the transformation of our own hearts. We are asked to judge others for merit, to impute to them God-fearing intentions. In doing this, our hearts are opened, and we are drawn to them with care and concern.

In our text, however, Joseph's brothers were not the ones who understood this practice, but rather Joseph, the "aggressor." He revealed his fear of God to them in the hope of softening their hearts, piercing their fear, to help them resolve the conflict. Indeed, as Levi Yitzhak points out, it was Joseph's fear of God that moved them to confess their guilt for Joseph's disappearance and for their current predicament. So, apparently, this is a practice that can be employed from both sides of a conflict.

Is there an element of Gandhian nonviolence here? What makes this practice so powerful is that it assumes the humanity of the oppressor. The protester stands firmly in the face of aggression and oppression, declaring, "I fear God." It is meant to melt the heart of the other. It generates the crack in the immoral defenses of the oppressor. Eventually, this moral stand demands, impels, revives the sense of shared humanity in the oppressor, leading to justice and reconciliation.

As you make your way in your life, watch for moments of conflict. Notice when you feel constrained, limited, shut off, or denied by another.

Witness the story that you tell yourself about the other person, about his or her motivations, mental or emotional stability or rightness, moral quality. Observe your inner response to his or her position. Do you become rigid? Do you become aggressive? Do you continue to speak and to listen, or do you close off and withdraw? How do you imagine you are perceived by the other? What story can you conceive she or he has told about you? Consider how you might employ Levi Yitzhak's instruction. What can you do to melt your heart, to transform your image of the other, thus possibly drawing him or her toward you in love?

Vayiggash

"[But when they recounted all that Joseph had said to them,] and when he saw the wagons that Joseph had sent [to transport him, the spirit of their father Jacob revived]" (Gen. 45:27).

In this manner Joseph sent a message to Jacob not to fear exile, for it is what will turn events toward redemption, just as the bad is the cause (*sibbah*) of the good. What was the form of the message? The word **"wagons"** (*AGaLot*) is derived from the word for "circular" (*IGGuL*). The turning of events (cause, *sibbah*) is likened to a wheel, something circular. Absolute compassion is like focused light (a line), but the processes (causes, *sibbot*) of transformation are circular.

FOR FURTHER THOUGHT

Rashi comments on this phrase (cf. Gen. R. 94:3):

> "Joseph gave him a sign": What portion of the Torah had he been studying at the time that he departed from Jacob? That of the substitute heifer (*eglah aruphah*; Deut. 21:1–6). This is what the verse signifies when Scripture reports that Jacob saw "the wagons [*agalot*] that Joseph had sent" instead of saying "'that Pharaoh had sent" (since earlier in Gen. 45:17–20 it had indeed been Pharaoh who had sent the wagons).

Levi Yitzhak clearly based his teaching on this precedent. Why didn't he refer to it directly? What prompted his alternative teaching?

Apparently Levi Yitzhak is referring, if only obliquely, to a concept developed in Lurianic Kabbalah (cf. *Etz Chayyim, Sha'ar Shevirat Hakelim*, ch. 9:8). Divine emanation can occur in one of two manners: it can be directed in a focused way, as a line (*yashar*), or it can expand from a point in a circular, spherical way (*iggul*). The line is considered to be a willed form (not quite natural), emanating directly from *Ein Sof*, and is of a higher degree than the circle. The circle's shape is reminiscent of that shape formed by the original contraction/*tzimtzum* and is considered more natural than the line. These two aspects of divine emanation interact and affect the inner divine and natural process in the world.

In this light, Levi Yitzhak invites us to see below or beyond the surface of the Rabbinic narrative reported by Rashi. It is not just that Joseph has maintained his holy status in idolatrous Egypt, as the midrash would have it. Joseph is sending Jacob a message about a much larger matter: the nature of life in exile, the life into which Jacob and his descendants were about to sink. This exile will not be—is not even now—a final destination; it will turn to something new. It is a necessary stage in the divine process. Exile is the precondition for redemption (cf. Gen. 15:13–16). More, Jacob's descent to Egypt will set in motion the forces that will turn the wheel of fortune, that will move processes forward to cause the emergence of redemption. The divine will—the line—is all compassion and love; God desires our service, given freely in response. That will is present in the world, moving back and forth between God and the world. But, it needs a mechanism by which it can come into being. The wheel of life—that one thing leads another, that one thing follows another, that one thing forces the emergence of the next and draws its successor in train—is that mechanism.

His message to us: do not turn away from whatever you face— including suffering (exile). Remaining present to it, accepting that it is true in this moment, makes possible the perception of change, the emergence of some new situation. This is how exile is the precedent for redemption, how bad leads to the good; it participates in and helps generate the energy that leads to its own transformation and end.

Questions for Reflection

1. The midrash, Rashi, and Levi Yitzhak all hold that Joseph sought to communicate with Jacob by means of a symbol (the wagons). This may seem obscure. Consider, though, what symbolic forms you may employ in your communication. Flowers? Chocolate? A book? Could there be other, even more "obscure" messages that you have sent? Why might

this sort of communication be of value? When does it work best (and can it work all the time)?

2. The midrash assumes that Jacob would doubt that Joseph was still alive. Levi Yitzhak seems to feel that Jacob knew Joseph was alive but feared going down to Egypt (keep in mind the scene in Gen. 46:1–4). Which makes more sense to you? Even if the latter makes sense, do you feel that Jacob feared exile? What is the role of the anticipation of exile in the biblical narrative? What is its meaning to Levi Yitzhak, and what is he communicating to his audience?

3. What is your response to Levi Yitzhak's teaching that the "bad is the cause of the good"? Does all bad necessarily lead to good? If the wheel turns and bad leads to good, why doesn't good lead to bad? What do you take away as the spiritual teaching that Levi Yitzhak offers?

 ## Taking It into Your Life

This lesson invites us to investigate with great care the turning of the wheel, the truth of impermanence and transformation. Whatever we see in the moment—about which we then form opinions, upon which we make plans—is always subject to change. While we need to move forward based on our perceptions and plans, we are also called to constantly investigate again what is true—to discern if our current plan, our present course of action, is appropriate. There is no aspect of our lives about which we are more concerned, and least able to see change, than our own beings, our identities and bodies. Observing change can be taxing, but it is a source of liberation, and therefore energizing.

Consider a "morning mirror" meditation. One morning, spend some time meeting yourself in the mirror. Get to know your face, your body, your mannerisms as you start your day. This is the "me" who you will take with you out into the world. As you go through your day, allow yourself to notice your face in the washroom mirror, in the window as you pass a shop, in the glass door as you are entering or leaving. Who are you meeting in this moment? Is it the same "me" you met in the morning? What is different? What is the same? Reflect in the evening on the image you meet once again in the mirror. Who is the "me" you meet then? What has changed? What has remained the same?

If you notice change, what do you sense is its nature? Has gravity affected you? Has the wind blown your hair? Are your eyes more tired? Do you, perhaps, see yourself differently according to your mood, to what you have eaten, to what happened to you during the day, to your feel-ings toward yourself in the moment? Who is the "me" in the mirror—the reflection, or your perception of the reflection, or your feelings about the reflection, or the being who is reflected there?

What do you find remains the same? Your nose? Your ears? Your thoughts? Investigate carefully. What do you learn about change and perma-nence? Can this be liberating, an opening to meet each moment with hope? Can this be a promise of redemption, even when facing exile?

"I Myself will go down with you to Egypt, and
I will bring you up, yes, up again; [and Joseph's
hand shall close your eyes]" (Gen. 46:4).

We can understand this in light of our experience: When students have limited awareness, their teachers have to constrict themselves significant-ly [to connect with them]. But, when students attain a level of greater, more expanded awareness, their teachers do not need to constrict them-selves as much.

This lies behind our verse. In the Land of Israel, Jacob served God through expansive awareness. He feared that in leaving the Land he would not be able to serve God as well. In response, God promised to constrict [and so direct] the flow of blessing and inspiration to him, even if Jacob's awareness was limited outside the Land.

So read our verse this way: "**I Myself will go down with you to Egypt**"—God (as if it were possible) will constrict Himself to those who serve God, even when outside the Land. "**I will bring you up, yes, up again**"—when you come to the Land of Israel, you will attain a more expansive state.

There is a further implication in the last phrase, "**yes, up again**" (*gam aloh*): (as if it were possible) the *Shekhinah* will also be raised up. That is, when Jacob is in the Land of Israel, serving God on a high plane, then (as it were) the *Shekhinah* is raised up. Thus the last phrase *gam aloh* refers to the *Shekhinah* (as it were).

FOR FURTHER THOUGHT

In the biblical narrative we are meant to hear in God's promise to Jacob an echo of the night dream at Beth-el. There God promised to be with Jacob throughout his travels and travails and to bring him safely home to the house of his father. Many years have passed since that promise and its fulfillment upon Jacob's return. Yet, God repeats the promise to be with Jacob and to bring him back to his homeland. This time, however, Jacob will not live to enjoy the return. He will have to be satisfied to know that Joseph will be at his side to the end and that God will accompany him as well.

Levi Yitzhak hears in this a deeper message, based on the Zohar (II 16a):

> R. Yehuda said: When the blessed Holy One said, "I Myself will go down with you to Egypt," do you imagine that the *Shekhinah* would go down with Jacob at that very moment? Rather, it means that when Jacob's descendants experience decline (*yeridah*), the *Shekhinah* also goes down. That is the sense of the verse, "I Myself will go down with you to Egypt, and I will bring you up, yes, up again." So long as there is ascent, then I (as it were) also experience ascent. But, when you experience decline, then (as it were) "I Myself go down with you." Once Joseph and his brothers died and the people experienced decline (as the bondage began), the *Shekhinah* rose and went down with them. In the same manner as these (the Israelites) declined, so did these (the *Shekhinah* and her retinue).

God promises Jacob that the experience of exile will not signal abandonment by or separation from God. The *Shekhinah* will be with them (and of course, we learn this from the Sages as well; Num. R. 7:10: "R. Natan taught: Beloved is Israel, for wherever she went into exile, the *Shekhinah* went with her").

Levi Yitzhak reads this and extends the lesson from the Egyptian exile to his own experience. The Torah is not speaking only of living in the Land of Israel versus exile in Egypt. He senses that the experience of exile is not merely distance from the Land of Israel, nor only of physical subjugation or oppression, even though that was what he and his people suffered. Rather, he understands that closeness to God is the experience of "living in the Land" and distance from God is "exile." Expansive consciousness and awareness is "living in the Land"; constricted consciousness and contracted awareness is "exile."

On the basis of this model, Levi Yitzhak extends God's promise to all of us. He tells us that when we are in more limited states, God will be with us, providing support, waiting for us to grow toward God. When we devote ourselves to study and prayer, to serving God with our whole awareness, we grow in spiritual capacity. As we grow, God "grows" as well, expanding, becoming perceptible in more subtle ways, revealed behind more layers of hiddenness. As our awareness grows, we are more and more able to acknowledge God as sovereign, raising up the quality of God's rule (*Malkhut*). God ascends from constriction to expansiveness, from lower to higher levels, as we grow spiritually. We raise the *Shekhinah*, the *sephirah* of *Malkhut*, toward full reunion with God, toward wholeness, toward the end of exile in all of its forms.

 ## Questions for Reflection

1. The process of constriction and limitation is for the sake of bringing God's overwhelming light and essence into the world. Therefore, to be accessible to one of limited awareness, God willingly enters into a constricted state. What is your experience of feeling God's accessibility when your own consciousness is constrained? Where do you find God when your awareness is limited? Can awareness of your own limited state serve to spur spiritual growth and perception of God?

2. Levi Yitzhak seems to suggest that it is not possible to remain at a high spiritual level all the time. How have you experienced the movement from greater to lesser awareness and back again? How do you respond to that movement? What do you feel when you move from one state to another? How do you sense your connection to God in each moment?

3. What do you make of the association of "Land of Israel" with "expanded consciousness"? Does that change your sense of the nature and goal of spiritual practice? How? How does it affect what you understand it means to be a Zionist?

 ## Taking It into Your Life

Prov. 3:6 is a key text in Hasidic spirituality: "Know God in all your ways, and He will make your way straight." The challenge of spiritual life is to open to God's presence in each and every moment, in each and every situation. Jacob's fear, as Levi Yitzhak portrays it, was that should his consciousness become limited he would not be able to perceive, and so also serve, God fully.

Many of us struggle with the idea that God can be present in a circumstance that otherwise is painful, tragic, or unjust. It may be that we confuse God's being present in a moment with God's causing the circumstances of the moment. We respond to our suffering, saying, "Why is God doing this to me?" We also look for a "silver lining" or some other redeeming aspect in the situation, identifying that as the presence of God, leaving the rest to be just "bad," a realm in which God is not present. If we cannot find this good in the moment, we feel abandoned by God, as if God were absent.

Levi Yitzhak is pointing us to a different way of experiencing our lives. God goes with us into every situation. God is present in each circumstance. This does not make events morally or personally "good." Rather, it is God's presence itself that is good, and that is redeeming. It is a reminder that it is possible to be in this world, to survive as a feeling, compassionate, and just human being despite our suffering and the suffering of others. God's presence is an invitation to remain present, not to run away, not to deny, not to hide. It offers us the opportunity to connect with our own hearts and with the hearts of others in the moment. That God is present keeps us focused and clear and may also energize us to greater awareness and action in the face of suffering and injustice.

Watch carefully as you make your way through your life for those moments when you feel your heart constrict. What prompts this reaction? From what do you withdraw? What do you push away? When do feel yourself cry out, "God, where are You?" When do you sense yourself alone, distant from God? In these moments, pause and take a breath. Bring your awareness to the sensations of your body, the tightness in your chest, the pain in your heart, the tears in your eyes. Identify the feeling and respond, "It is just *this*. This is what is happening *now*." Continue with this response, and observe. If you sense any greater balance, even if you still feel pain or your own suffering, try to add this phrase: "And God is present." Do not think about or analyze the statement, rather simply "report": "It is just *this*. This is what is happening *now*. And God is present." Observe, over time, what your experience is of each such moment. How do you sense God's presence from moment to moment, from limited consciousness to greater awareness?

An alternative interpretation of "Joseph hitched his chariot to go up to Goshen to

> meet his father [Israel; he presented himself
> to him and, embracing him around the
> neck, he wept on his neck a good while]"
> (Gen. 46:29).

What is the intention of the Torah in telling us that Joseph hitched his own chariot? Would it not have been enough simply to tell us that he went up to see his father?

Rather, we can learn from this. We should each investigate all of our deeds with careful scrutiny, so that we not behave like animals (heaven forbid!). We should weigh everything, so that we might discern some indication of how we might better serve the Holy One, and then do it! But if we cannot find such a hint, it would be "preferable to sit and not do."

Accordingly, we should each of us weigh our actions carefully beforehand, so that what we do will be fulfilled. By our good deeds we will become a chariot for the *Shekhinah*. This is the significance of the Torah telling us that "**Joseph hitched his chariot**"; he embraced this practice.

Now, Joseph was surely looking forward to the pleasure of seeing his father. But, then, he thought, "If I am anticipating such pleasure from this, how much more joy would I experience if I were to actually see the face of the blessed Holy One (as if it were possible)." This realization shifted his awareness so that he was truly able "**to go up to ... meet his [F]ather**"! It is only after deep devotion in mitzvot and prayer, exhausting ourselves in the effort, that we slowly slip out of our physicality and experience the emanating spirit of the Holy One dwelling in us. This light would be like seeing the face of "our Father," the blessed Holy One, directly. Joseph, the tzaddik, due to his righteousness, must have enjoyed a very fine, sparkling light, a portion of the Divine from above. Through this act he truly accomplished something—the joy at seeing "his father"—and so thereby became a chariot for the *Shekhinah*.

FOR FURTHER THOUGHT

We know of other instances in which someone important took on a menial task: Abraham saddling his donkey to set off to the *Akedah*; Balaam saddling his donkey to pursue fame and fortune in cursing Israel. We understand it is a sign of personal commitment and investment in the action. But something is different here. Levi Yitzhak directs us not only to the action, but also to the intention.

Again, note how Levi Yitzhak cites this verse. He leaves out the name Israel, indicating that he intends to read the verse, "Joseph hitched his chariot to go up to see his [F]ather." Yes, the narrative is clear, and Joseph goes to meet Jacob, his father, but Levi Yitzhak sees through this event to a deeper meaning. Nothing that we do takes place merely on the physical plane. Our actions are all superficial—unless we learn to "investigate all of our deeds with careful scrutiny," weighing the possible meanings, the potential outcomes of our acts. What are we looking for? How can this act that I am about to undertake lead me to see God more clearly in the world? How can my deeds reveal God's presence, peeling back the garments that obscure the Holy One?

Levi Yitzhak offers us instruction to help in this process. We are to engage in prayer and doing mitzvot with such fervor, with such intense concentration, that we exhaust our physical bodies. This, in turn, helps us detach our consciousness from the particularity of our individual experience, to open to the glorious light that suffuses all of creation, the divine soul that fills our being. This is one way to describe what it means to become a chariot for the *Shekhinah*. When we lose our particular, individualistic self-awareness and open to the interconnectedness of all being, we testify to the whole world being filled with God's glory, declaring God sovereign. We become God's very throne in the world.

 ## Questions for Reflection

1. Joseph merited becoming a chariot for the *Shekhinah* because he engaged fully in the process of greeting his father. Are there shortcuts to spiritual experience? Could Joseph have had this experience merely from thinking about it? Can we?

2. Joseph merited this revelation because he took on the task personally. Can spiritual experiences be experienced vicariously? Can we rely on others to do for us? How can we get others to do for themselves and not look outside for someone else to "get them high"?

3. Are you disturbed by Levi Yitzhak seemingly demeaning Joseph's joy at seeing his father after all these years, equating it (in a sense) to other physical pleasures or "distractions" (like sex or prowess or possessions)?

Is this a meaningful teaching—that even our "normal" emotional connections with family and friends are not to be valued as highly as our connection to God? Might we take it as a caution that we not confuse feeling good with *devekut* (deeply cleaving to God)? Is there a conflict between our human connections and our attachment to God? Can they serve each other?

Taking It into Your Life

Levi Yitzhak points to two types of action: that which is animal-like, and that which emerges from thoughtful reflection. The latter, however, apparently also has a quality of "unknowing." That is, when we attain—through prayer and mitzvot—a degree of concentration on God, we lose all sense of our physical selves and feel only the Divine flowing through us. What would it take to move from one state to the other?

First, we have to develop the capacity to sense the impetus to act, regardless of what we are setting out to do. After all, in going to meet his father, Joseph was not undertaking anything dishonorable or even self-serving! Rather, Levi Yitzhak tells us that every act has a quality of animal behavior when it is not considered, when it does not emerge from reflection.

So, first, during some period of time, pay attention to each change in direction, every shift in activity you undertake. When you notice that you have done something new, even if it is momentary, even if it does not distract you from your original activity, pause to reflect: What prompted this action? Boredom? Fear? Outer distraction? Physical or emotional discomfort? Something else?

After such reflection, see if you can sense the arising of these sorts of impulses before you act. Pause first and notice what you feel pulled or called to do. Breathe in this moment to help establish some balance between the competing pulls of continuity and change. From this point of balance, consider what the change might bring: is it wise; is it helpful; does it contribute to fulfilling your obligations to yourself or to others? Consider: Where is God in this new act? How might this new act express deeper, truer devotion to God? If you cannot sense satisfying answers to these questions, it would be "preferable to sit and not do."

When you have undertaken this exercise over a period of time, observe the level of your concentration during the original activity. Do you find that you are distracted or have the impulse to change more, less, or the same?

When you engage in this sort of reflection, do you notice any difference in how you experience the sensations of the body? What is your sense of fatigue, or boredom, or tension? Do you feel in any way that you are more prepared, open, ready to receive God's presence, to serve as a chariot for the *Shekhinah*?

Vayechi

"Assemble and hearken, O sons of Jacob;
/ Hearken to Israel your father" (Gen. 49:2).

Why does this verse repeat the word "hearken" (*veshimu*)? Consider this section from the Zohar (III 196a):

> R. Eleazar opened the verse: "Who is among you that fears *YHVH*, who hearkens to the voice of His servant [he walks in darkness and has no light]" (Isa. 50:10). What is the meaning of "who hearkens to the voice of His servant"? This verse has been established by the Companions to refer to prayer, thus: Regarding one who is regular in attending the synagogue to pray and one day does not go, the blessed Holy One asks after him. He says: "Where among you is the one who fears *YHVH*, who hearkens to the voice of His servant who now walks in darkness and has no light?" ... What is the sense of the phrase "who hearkens to the voice of His servant"? It refers to that person who prays every day. He hears that voice by which the blessed Holy One praises him, calling him His own servant. "Hearkens to the voice"—which voice? The voice of the one who is called "His servant." It is great praise that issues forth regarding him, that he is His servant. Moreover, this voice echoes throughout all the heavens that he is the servant of the Holy King. This is the meaning of "who hears the voice of 'His servant.'"

The tzaddik hears at all times that voice that announces in heaven that he is the servant of the King. When we are meritorious before God, when we gather together, we hear the heavenly voice that declares, "Give honor to the children of Jacob."

This, then, is what Jacob said to his sons: "**Assemble and hearken, O sons of Jacob**"—hear the heavenly voice that refers to you as "the children of my servant Jacob." The gathering of Israel moves their hearts to do *teshuvah* and to purify their hearts. This is the sense of the next phrase, "**Hearken to Israel your father.**" You will hear and also understand my words, by which I point you to the mystery of the final redemption (Pesachim 56a).

FOR FURTHER THOUGHT

Bringing the passage from the Zohar helps Levi Yitzhak develop a wonderful and subtle interpretation of the verse in Genesis. As he points out, the verb "hearken" (*veshimu*) is repeated, and it is not clear (aside from the demands of biblical poetry) why this should be. The passage in the Zohar relates to two different acts of hearing: the one who prays each day hears God calling her "God's servant" and God hears the prayers of the one who prays each day. Levi Yitzhak extends this from the (mere) act of prayer to all holy devotions—the work of a tzaddik. In response to these devotions, God proclaims each day the praise of the tzaddik, which the latter hears.

Levi Yitzhak sets up this image and then transforms it further by reading it into Jacob's deathbed scene and beyond. His reference to the "gathering of Israel" is likely to refer to the new phenomenon of followers of Hasidic tzaddikim, who gathered regularly on Shabbat and festivals to learn from their teacher and to be inspired to deeper spiritual practice. Gathering around Father Jacob for instruction and inspiration is here a model for the later Hasidim. Seeing each other's dedication and desire inspires greater dedication, or *teshuvah*, to bring the final redemption.

When we gather together—to celebrate, to worship, to do good works—with loving hearts, we are inspired to be better people. We recognize the potential that is in each of us to do good, to live lives of compassion, of integrity, of honesty; the presence of other people striving to manifest those qualities encourages us to do the same. In that state, and as a product of that activity, we prepare ourselves to hear the holy message: there will be redemption, the end of exile will come, and our behavior will play a role. Our hearts and eyes are filled with light, and we can see beyond our current distress to ease and well-being.

The Zohar clearly is concerned with encouraging people to attend daily prayers. Levi Yitzhak seems to be concerned with establishing a sacred community of practice. In both cases, engaging in the prescribed practice is offered as a way to experience a deep connection with God, an awareness of God's pride in us and in our works, and with bringing redemption.

Questions for Reflection

1. Which supports your experience of spiritual awakening—or moves you to *teshuvah*: being alone or being with other people? Does it vary over time or in different situations? Are there different experiences that each context supports or impedes?

2. The passage to which Levi Yitzhak refers at the end of his lesson follows:

   > R. Simeon ben Lakish said: "And Jacob called to his sons, and said, 'Gather yourselves together, that I may tell you' [that which will befall you in the end of days]"(Gen. 49:1). Jacob wished to reveal to his sons the [mystery of the] end of the days, whereupon the *Shekhinah* departed from him. He said, "Perhaps (heaven forbid) there is one unfit among my children, like Abraham, from whom came Ishmael, or like my father Isaac, from whom came Esau!" His sons answered him, "Hear O Israel, *YHVH* our God *YHVH* is One." They said: Just as there is only One in your heart, so in our heart there is only One." In that moment our father Jacob opened and exclaimed, "Blessed be the name of God's glorious kingdom for ever and ever." (Pesachim 56a)

   Why do you suppose Jacob was prevented from revealing the mystery of the end of days to his sons? What was revealed in this moment instead? Which is more important for bringing about the end of days, a true redemption? What prompts you to recall and to declare that there is one God or to acknowledge God's sovereignty?

3. How do you understand the image in the Zohar of hearing a divine voice declaring, "You are My servant"? Would you like to hear that about yourself? Can you imagine how that might come about? Do you merit this today? What do you think qualifies one to be called God's servant?

Taking It into Your Life

Mindfulness practice, and perhaps all spiritual practice, might be described as helping us to be more able to "show up." When we are more fully aware of all that is happening in the moment, attentive to our inner lives, to our bodies and emotions, we are more present to what is transpiring. How we respond will be a more accurate expression of our true self. We will be less likely to shade things, to prevaricate, to tilt things in our favor. Our "yes" will be a full "yes," and our "no" a more honest "no."

The passage from the Zohar suggests that "showing up" regularly is what constitutes spiritual life and allows us to experience its benefits more fully. That is why we call this work spiritual "practice." We do it over and over, but not for the sake of perfecting the practice. Rather, we return over and over to learn—and express—fidelity, trustworthiness, interest, resilience, courage, hope, trust, and joy. We engage again and again both to train the mind and heart and to provide them with the ground in which to nurture what they learn. And when we do so in a community, we offer—and receive—support in our endeavors.

Select one practice that you can do each day for an extended period of time, perhaps starting with something small, both to support "success" and to better notice outcomes. It might be reciting one particular blessing each day, offering thanks (to God, a partner, the store clerk) each day, writing in a journal, doing a body practice, and so on. The goal is to keep "showing up" even when interest flags, even when it may appear that "nothing is happening." Persist. Persevere. Engage over and over. Investigate, inquire, attend, observe, engage, feel. After several months, reflect. What new voices have you heard in response to your "showing up"? What does it mean to you now to be a faithful servant? How do you feel your heart—and your hope—now?

> Further, a different way of interpreting "Issachar is a strong-boned ass, crouching among the sheepfolds. When he saw how good rest is, [and how pleasant was the country, he bent his shoulder to the burden, and became a toiling serf]" (Gen. 49:14–15).

Pay attention to the nature of your mind. Notice that so long as your thoughts of devotion to the Creator have not emerged into speech, your thoughts have no rest. But, when thought comes to speech, then thought has rest.

Read this in our verse. "**Issachar**" represents thought. "**Crouching**" represents rest, and "**among the sheepfolds**" (*mishpetayim*) signifies when thought comes to speech, represented by the lips (*sephatayim*).

The Book of Genesis

It is there (in the lips, in speech) that thought finds rest. That is the significance of the phrase **"he saw how good rest is."**

Or, we can interpret: "Issachar is a strong-boned ass, [crouching among the sheepfolds]" (Gen. 49:14).

The essence of the reward (*sakhar*) that we receive derives from our experience of bodily desires in our youth. True awareness and conscience arise only after age thirteen. It is then that we are immersed in the passions of youth, but that is also when we can break these physical desires, instead to serve God. It is for this endeavor that we receive a reward. But if we have never experienced worldly desires, we will not receive this reward.

So, our verse: **"Issachar is a strong-boned ass."** "Issachar" can be read, "There is a reward" (*yesh sakhar*); **"strong-boned ass"** (*chamor garem*): we receive recompense because the materiality (*chomriyut*) in which we are immersed brings us a reward (*gorem sakhar*).

For Further Thought

Here are two different approaches to becoming balanced in our lives, to attaining a degree of freedom out of which we might serve God. In the first, Levi Yitzhak pays attention to the inner experience of thought. He knows well how distracting thoughts can be. He has received the teachings of the Baal Shem Tov: when we notice the presence of strange, distracting thoughts, rather than banish them, we are to use their energy to turn them to service of God. But what can we do to stabilize and root thoughts of service of God in our busy, distractible minds? Here, Levi Yitzhak applies a different teaching of the Besht: immediately upon sensing the arising of an inclination to serve God or a holy thought, turn that impulse into action. One form of action, and a primary concern of the Hasidic teachers, is speech. It is in speech that we engage in prayer and Torah study and in so doing energize and activate the divine power in speech. So by bringing our thoughts of devotion to God into speech, we ground them, and us, giving us stability in our service of God.

The association of Issachar with thought is based on *Sefer Yetzirah* 5:1, which links twelve elemental letters with twelve elemental experiences. These twelve are then associated with the twelve tribes. R. Avraham ben David of Posquieres (twelfth century) associates the experience of thought with Issachar, and this serves as the source for Levi Yitzhak.

The second aspect of attaining balance has to do with our physical awareness. We first learn about the world through our senses and through engagement with the physical realm. Our curiosity leads us to touch, taste, feel, and play with whatever comes our way. Even as we grow in sophistication, adding speech to our powers of expression and reason to our mode of investigation, we are still attracted to the physical world. This is the realm of eros, which includes not only the sexual but also the sensual, and draws us always to those activities that seem to be life affirming (eating, sexual relations, building, reaping). Only when we fully engage in learning about the world, interacting with it, enjoying it, learning about how it works, can we truly learn how to control and direct our erotic selves. Knowing and recognizing the arising of erotic urges and pulls, we are able to direct them properly (as Levi Yitzhak would have it, toward service of God). The balanced heart/mind/body/spirit is the reward for this effort.

 ## Questions for Reflection

1. How do you understand Levi Yitzhak's teaching that bringing thoughts to speech gives them a place to rest? What is the significance of speaking what you are thinking? How does that affect your understanding of your own thoughts? How does bringing thoughts to speech help you assess the validity of those thoughts, their import or the need to continue thinking them?

2. As much as the Hasidic tradition validates physical experience (since there is no place or time where God is not present), it also inherited the negative attitudes toward the body of medieval piety. What does it mean to you to "break physical desires"? Must all physical pleasures be negated? What have you found to be a meaningful way of balancing the spontaneous urges and desires of the body (and person) with your "higher" intentions—moral, interpersonal, and spiritual?

3. Life has certainly changed since Levi Yitzhak's day. Life expectancies are likely more than twice those of his era, and the curve of the life cycle is much longer. Still, even today, thirteen-year-olds are dealing with all of the urges and confusions of puberty and emergence into adolescence. What have you found to be helpful in supporting young teens in directing their physical urges and yearnings? What sort of language have you found to be meaningful and accessible for teens that might help them view their physical experiences as a source of spiritual knowledge? How can the process of coming into physical maturity be presented as a spiritual process as well?

 ## Taking It into Your Life

One way of describing divine service is to make God the focus of our attention and to make us worthy of God's attention. This suggests that having thoughts of devotion to God may manifest in speech or deed, without necessarily being expressed directly to God. How we behave, what we say, and what we intend with our acts and words will reflect the depth of our devotion and service.

For this practice, we first must spend some time bringing the rush of thoughts that run through our minds into some sort of clarity. For that, meditation can be helpful. It is a practice of bringing sustained, calm, nonjudgmental attention to the thoughts that arise and pass away, without clinging to them, without having to "think" them. While this practice is best accomplished when not engaged in any other activity, ultimately one would want to be able to do this even when engaged in active life. So as you make your way through your life, pay attention to the stream of thoughts that accompany your everyday activities. What runs through your head as you shower? As you eat? As you drive to work or to visit a friend? As you cook or clean or rest?

Becoming aware of the thoughts is a first step. Once we are aware that there are thoughts, and even of what they are, we can begin to assess what we would like to think, what would be skillful and beneficial. We would like to direct our attention to serving God. We may come to a point where we say (to ourselves), "May the mind through which these thoughts pass be directed always to love and fear of God." This mind may be less ruffled by the rush of thoughts; more of the thoughts that do pass through may be thoughts worthy of being directed toward God.

But our lives are not lived in contemplation. We interact with people, we do things in the world. How can the mind that we are directing toward God come to rest in the midst of the busyness of life? By bringing the same intention to our words and deeds. "May the mind through which these thoughts pass *and* which directs me to do this word or deed be directed toward the love and fear of God." Our speech and acts may become vessels in which our intention comes to rest. Our words and deeds will become the resting place of our devotion to God, and our service will be well grounded.

Practice. Observe. Reflect.

Further, a different way of interpreting "Gad shall be raided by raiders, [but he shall raid at their heels]" (Gen. 49:19).

The Talmud (Baba Batra 10a) teaches that we are supposed to give *tzedakah* before we pray. The spiritual benefit of *tzedakah* is that it cuts off the power of the "husks" or external covering (*kelippot*), so that afterward we are able to pray with a pure heart. The spiritual benefit of prayer (and prayer signifies cleaving and connection) is that through our prayers we connect our selves to the blessed Holy One. We are mortal and finite, we have an end, but the blessed Holy One has no end. So, when we pray we ascend from the level of "end" (*sof*) to "no end" (*ein sof*).

This is how we should read our verse: "**Gad**" (*G"D*) signifies "benefiting the poor" (*G"omel D"alim*); "**shall be raided by raiders**" (*gedud yegudenu*) suggests "cutting off the power of the *kelippot*." "**He shall raid at their heels**" (*vehu yagud akev*)—when we attach our selves to the blessed Holy One, "He" will cut off that which has the quality of the heels (*ekev*), which is the "end." In this manner, we enter the realm of "no end."

Further, another way of interpreting the verse "Gad shall be raided by raiders, [but he shall raid at their heels]" (Gen. 49:19).

We know that more than the householder does for the poor person, the poor person does for the householder. When we pray, we should consider ourselves a poor

person, who is nothing, as it says: "Prayer of
a poor person [*tephillah le'ani*] who is faint"
(Ps. 102:1).

It works this way: When we consider our selves as something, we are
faced with accusers, and we are not able to cut off *kelippot*, except for
those that are on our own spiritual level. But we have no power to
affect those above or below us, since we have no connection to them.
But when we give no consideration to our selves and make our selves
as a poor person, then we can cut off the *kelippot* in all the levels
below us.

This is how we then can read our verse: "**Gad**" (*G"D*) signifies
"doing good for the poor" (*Gomel Dalim*). When we make our selves
poor (*dal*) and lowly and then pray, then we do good for God (as
in "more than the householder, etc."). Then, "**he shall be raided** (by
raiders)" [God will act to empower us] and "(we) **shall raid at their
heels**"—cutting off down the lowest levels that are called "heel."

FOR FURTHER THOUGHT

One concern of the Hasidic movement was to revive and energize traditional Jewish practice. Hasidic teachers regularly refer to
the verse in Isaiah (29:13) "My Lord said: Because that people has
approached [Me] with its mouth and honored Me with its lips, but
has kept its heart far from Me, and its worship of Me has been a
commandment of men, learned by rote" as a reproach to their followers and as an invitation to see that it is possible to serve God
not by rote but with lively, active, and personal involvement. Of all
traditional Jewish practices, daily prayer is the one that is offered
with the lips and most likely to be performed without connection to
the heart. In these two lessons, Levi Yitzhak employs the same verse
from our parashah to wake up the act of prayer.

In both instances, Levi Yitzhak opens up the Rabbinic play on
the name Gad, treating it as an acronym for the act of "doing good
for the poor" (*Gomel Dalim*) (Shabbat 104a). This verse invites an
investigation of how doing loving-kindness affects the cosmic drama of cutting off the *kelippot*, of releasing the divine sparks and
bringing about divine unification. Levi Yitzhak offers two different
ways in which we can enact loving-kindness. First, he addresses

the human plane: we can give *tzedakah*. This he derives from a passage in Baba Batra 10a: "R. Eleazar used to give a coin to a poor man and straightway say a prayer, because, he said, it is written: 'I in righteousness shall behold Your face [*ani betzedek eche-zeh phanekha*; Ps. 17:15].'" Giving *tzedakah* and prayer can both be done in a perfunctory manner, to fulfill the commandment. But the passage from the Talmud suggests that in giving *tzedakah* we have the potential of a personal revelation of the Divine. God may appear directly to us.

With this in mind, Levi Yitzhak opens up the prayer experience. Giving *tzedakah*—overcoming selfishness, relinquishing whatever causes us to be hard-hearted or fearful—purifies the heart. When we are in this state, God may more fully appear to us, and through prayer we may connect more directly to God (see Rashi on Gen. 30:8, where he connects the word *naphtulei* with "connection" and also prayer, *tephillah*). With proper intention, giving *tzedakah* leads to the sort of prayer through which we can cut off the *kelippot*, attach ourselves to God, and attain to the experience of *ein sof*.

Levi Yitzhak also extends the act to doing good for God. The model for this is from the Talmud (Baba Batra 10a): "R. Yohanan said: What is the meaning of the verse 'He who is generous to the poor makes a loan to *YHVH*' (Prov. 19:17)? Were it not written in the Scripture, one would not dare to say it: 'The borrower is a servant to the lender' (Prov. 22:7)." He may also have in mind the lesson in Lev. R. 34:10, where giving to the poor—even prompted by the pestering of imposters—saves us from punishment. That is to say, the one who is in a position to give is not superior to the one who receives, but vice versa. By generating the response of the donor, the poor person creates the means by which the donor gains merit; the donor is indebted to the recipient. So when we make ourselves poor before God and then pray, we invite God's response. We make ourselves poor but in effect also shift God to a position of one who receives. God, now indebted to us, empowers us to cut off the *kelippot*, even down to the lowest levels. God is in need of us to fulfill the perfection of creation. God's neediness both invites our prayer and is the result of our prayer. And our prayers ultimately energize the redemptive dynamic in the world.

Questions for Reflection

1. What is your experience in giving *tzedakah*? Does it help purify your heart? What are the *kelippot* that you imagine or experience to be cut off by giving *tzedakah*? Does giving *tzedakah* move you to pray in any way—or facilitate your prayer?

2. Prayer is often depicted as something we offer to God, a transaction between two beings. Levi Yitzhak suggests that prayer is connection; the means to attachment to God, the experience of *ein sof*. Have you ever experienced this sort of prayer? Is it something you would like to attain? What practices do you imagine might support this sort of prayer experience?

3. Why do you imagine that "when we consider our selves as something, we are faced with accusers"? What is it about emptying our selves of all self-concern that allows us to stand unencumbered and unopposed before God? Have you had any experience that helps you understand this claim?

Taking It into Your Life

Consider taking on R. Eleazar's practice, particularly in light of the lesson in Lev. R. 34:10. According to your means and your personal plans for giving charity, get a few rolls of nickels, dimes, or quarters from the bank. Empty the coins into a small bag or sack that you can easily carry in your pocket or purse. As you make your way through the day, be prepared to give to each and every person who asks for charity.

Make this a practice that engages your whole awareness. When you see the person on the street or when he or she approaches you, stop for a moment and feel the sensations of your body. Notice contraction, fear, disgust, compassion, interest, apathy—whatever arises. Feel where you tense, where you might feel nervousness. Breathe into the sensation. Next, look carefully at the person before you. Look for the eyes, see the contours of the face, let the fullness of the person's being come into focus. Now, reach into your bag, take out one coin, and place it in the person's hand or cup. As you move on or turn away, bring the image of this person to mind.

Pray. Pray for the well-being of this person. Pray for yourself. Pray for people you know who are sick. Pray for the world. Connect your prayer to the image of the person to whom you gave *tzedakah*. Reflect on the verse "In giving *tzedakah*, I see Your face."

"Naphtali is a hind let loose, which yields
lovely fawns" (Gen. 49:21).

It works this way: when deep faith in the blessed Creator flows into us,
we begin to sing and praise God.

It is known that "faith" is also called "legs." So when Torah tells us
that "**Naphtali is a hind let loose**," it means to tell us that he has strong
legs on which it is easy to get around. The spiritual meaning is that
Naphtali has deep faith in God, that is, strong "legs." By means of this
faith, he gives *imrei shepher*, that is, "beautiful words"; his deep faith
leads him to sing and praise God with beautiful words.

This is also the spiritual meaning of the translation of Yonatan
ben Uziel, where he suggests that great singers came from the tribe of
Naphtali. We can understand this on the basis of what we said above:
because of their great faith in God, they constantly sing beautifully
before God.

FOR FURTHER THOUGHT

Jacob's testament is one of the older passages in the Bible, archaic in
form and in language. The clear meaning of this particular verse is
not easy to come by. In *JPS Torah Commentary: Genesis* (Philadelphia:
Jewish Publication Society, 2001), Nahum Sarna offers three possible interpretations.

The most common interpretation of the first phrase—*Naphtali
ayalah sheluchah*—holds as we have translated here, a poetic image
of a wild, free deer, in the hill country of the north. The second
phrase is not so clear. What does this "hind" give over? What is the
sense of the phrase *imrei shapher*? The first word may be connected
to an Aramaic word, *imra*, which means "lamb." And *shapher* does
mean "beautiful" (the Rabbis take the meaning of the shofar to be
shipru ma'aseikhem, "improve, make beautiful your deeds"). So, the
meaning of this phrase can, indeed, be "which gives lovely fawns."

But Levi Yitzhak seems to prefer to connect with the Hebrew
sense of *imrei*, having to do with speech (from the root *aleph-mem-
resh, emor*). There is no fixed meaning of "beautiful words," but song
is a particular form of speech, one that is energized both by the power

of the words and by the force of the melody. What is the connection between the "hind let loose" and the "beautiful songs"? Could it be that it is in the experience of freedom one is forced to find a firm foundation? Is a life without external boundaries or constraints one in which faith becomes a means to stability, to orientation? Could song be a means of expression, as well as a means to generate such faith?

A further point of reference is Levi Yitzhak's association of "legs" with "faith." In the world of associations of Kabbalah, the legs are associated with two of the lower *sephirot*: *Netzach* and *Hod*. These two qualities are identified in the Zohar as "two companions who are never separated." They are the foundation for the upper *sephirot*. They hold up the whole structure and need one another to keep it stable. And, of course, it is our legs that hold us up. Without both of them, we could not stand, we could not walk, we would not be balanced. That is the foundation of faith.

 ## Questions for Reflection

1. Why are faith and legs related? What is it about having two legs that gives us "faith" that we can stand firmly? Is faith something you can stand on? Does faith support us, or do we have to support our faith? Are we talking about faith "in" something or faith "about" something? What is your experience of these two types of meanings?

2. How do you understand the claim that the natural product of faith is song and praise of God? What is the difference between this sort of song—emerging from faith—and Anna in Siam "whistling a happy tune"?

3. Can we use this teaching working backward as well? That is, when we find ourselves praising God or perhaps even just singing, can we ask ourselves what produced that emotional response? That is, what is the faith that generated the song? And then, from that, can we find the "legs" that supported us in that moment and train to stand on them in the future?

 ## Taking It into Your Life

This text invites us to investigate both standing meditation and walking meditation. Fundamentally, there is no difference between these forms and what may be more familiar, sitting meditation. The goal is to pay attention and to wake up.

In standing meditation, one simply stands, hands at the sides or clasped together in front. The point of focus is in the sensations of the feet. Feel the weight of your body resting on the soles of your feet. Notice how the limbs of your body and your torso stack up over your feet. Observe the position of your head, how it rests aligned with your neck, spine, and legs. Pay attention to the more subtle sensations of moment-by-moment adjustments that your body automatically makes to keep you upright. As still as you may stand, you are also always moving. Feel that.

Standing meditation is a way to experience what it feels to be "grounded." Our feet and legs help us feel rooted to our spot. Once you have inhabited this position for some time, you might experiment with moving out of stillness—and out of balance. Intentionally allow yourself to sway subtly, and notice how your body both works to hold you up, even as you lean out of center, and what it takes to remain rooted in your position, without falling over. Sense where you are moving toward a point of imbalance, where you might fall out of your place, and then come back to stillness. This is one aspect of the "faithfulness" of our legs, of standing on two feet. This is part of the association of "faith" with legs.

Returning to a standing position, in stillness, prepare for the walking meditation. Begin by shifting your weight to one leg, slightly lifting the other foot off the floor, and then returning it to the floor. Shift to the opposite leg and repeat. Do this a few times. Then shift your weight to the first leg, and move the other foot forward one step. Pause and then rock back to a standing position. Repeat with the other leg and foot. Repeat with the first leg and foot, and place your weight on the extended foot. Pause. Bring the back foot forward to meet the other. Pause. Repeat with the other leg and foot. Keep your attention in the sensations of the leg and foot. Once you begin to feel yourself in the rhythm of walking, you can continue, shifting your weight, moving your foot, bringing your leg forward. Again, notice the way in which each step requires the participation of both legs, how feet alone, legs alone, body alone cannot walk. This, too, is part of the "faith" of the legs.

The Book of
Exodus

Shemot

An alternative interpretation of "God looked upon the Israelites, and God knew" (Exod. 2:25).

This will help us to understand the verse "[O *YHVH*! I have learned of Your renown; I am awed;] O *YHVH*, by Your deeds in these years [vivify them; in these years] make them known! Though angry, may You remember compassion" (Hab. 3:2). Consider it by way of a parable: A poor person asks a wealthy one to fulfill his request and petition because it is in the power of the wealthy person to do so. The latter has to then connect his awareness to the suffering of the poor person in order to feel compassion for him. Surely, when the wealthy person connects to the suffering of the poor person, he will fulfill his request, because the wealthy person has the capacity to be compassionate toward the suffering poor person and to fulfill his request.

So it is when Israel is suffering: they cry out in prayer to God to have compassion on them, because the blessed Holy One always fulfills the requests of the people Israel. Therefore, we have to try to connect our thoughts and our prayers with the blessed Holy One. (After all, prayer, *tephillah*, means "connection" [cf. Rashi on Gen. 30:5].) In this way the blessed Holy One will connect to us (as it were), in order to have compassion on us. This is the sense of our verse: "**God looked upon the Israelites, and God knew.**" The term "**knew**" (*vayeida*) is also a term for "connection" (as in "Adam knew [*vayeida*] his wife"; Gen. 4:25). This is also how "**God knew.**"

In this light, the verse from Habakkuk has deeper meaning. "In these years make them known [*todi'a*]": suffering arises in and is a product of the dimension of time. In the realm beyond time there is no suffering, nor sorrow or grief at all. So, "in these years"—that is, in the midst of time, regarding the suffering that arises due to time—"make known" (*todi'a*)—connect to this. When You, God, connect to this suffering, then "though angry, may You remember compassion."

FOR FURTHER THOUGHT

What was it that God came to know by looking at, seeing the Israelites? From Levi Yitzhak's parable, it appears that looking includes the mental process of "taking notice," in which one connects one's own awareness with that of the person before one. God, the "wealthy person," responds to the petition of the "poor person" (Israel) by sensing directly, internally, the suffering of Israel. This generates the compassion that sets redemption in motion.

If only it were so straightforward! In the parable, Levi Yitzhak suggests that it is the wealthy person who needs to pay attention, to connect with the suffering of the poor person, in response to the petition. To allow the parable to stand as he set it up would suggest that God does not know our situation, that God would need to act intentionally to connect with us. Instead, when he interprets the parable, he emphasizes that we—the petitioners—need to connect ourselves to God through prayer. It is this reaching out on our part that completes God's connection to us and energizes God's compassion. God—apparently—would have fulfilled our requests in any event, but there is a higher level of response when God responds from connection, with compassion.

Levi Yitzhak complicates and deepens this lesson by bringing in the verse from Habakkuk. He reads the verse as our prayer to God. We beseech God to connect with us, we who are trapped in the vagaries of time, whose suffering emerges from our mortal finitude. By connecting with us, we pray that God will be filled with compassion for us, even when we are caught up in rage, savaged by our own suffering.

 Questions for Reflection

1. In your experience, do you respond more favorably to the requests of another person when you connect with them in some manner? How do you feel when you do connect in that way? Do you look to make such connections, particularly when you are faced with someone in need, or does their suffering cause you to turn away? When, how, why?

2. What arouses compassion in you? Do you feel it more strongly toward individuals or groups? Toward people near to you or far away? People familiar to you or strangers? What is your sense of the role of compas-

sion in your life, particularly in response to feeling connection to other people?

3. When you get angry, what helps you reconnect with the object of your anger? What do you do to dissipate your anger and return to a peaceful relationship?

 ## Taking It into Your Life

In most of the traditional commentaries the phrase in Habbakuk "in these years" is seen as referring to exile. Truly, that is a source of suffering. But Levi Yitzhak goes beyond this to a different understanding of "in these years": it is the dimension of time. He teaches that suffering arises in and is a product of the dimension of time. Indeed, our deepest anxiety, our greatest fear is our own death, which is what gives the passage of time some dimension. It is because we know we are finite that we sense the passage of time, all change in our lives. That awareness provokes responses of various sorts: greed, apathy, disgust with the world. Even when we hide from our mortality, we suffer as we experience the passage of time. When we are enjoying something, we know that it might end, and we suffer. When we are in pain, we fear that it will never end, and we see the unfolding of time as ongoing suffering.

Levi Yitzhak says, "In the realm beyond time there is no suffering, nor sorrow or grief at all." This realm is, perhaps, in the upper *sephirot* (particularly *Binah*, where negativity is sweetened and undone). One reason that in this upper realm there is no suffering is because in that sphere there are no distinctions: no good or bad, no water or land, no before or after. It is the realm in which all of history is present as one moment, in which all events and eventualities exist equally without sequential relationships. In that realm, from that perspective, there would be no reason for, no source of, suffering. All things would be known as ultimately good. There would be no "what if?"; nor would there be any "but why?" In the absence of the unfolding of time, there is no suffering.

Our experience of suffering in time is due to our tendency to get caught in it—and so, in a sense, to "fall behind." Something happens and we notice it and decide that we like it or don't like it. When we like it, we grab onto it, seeking to avoid change, denying that time moves on and something else is coming into being. Because we like one thing, we lose touch with, become dislocated from, the next thing. When something happens we don't like, we reject it. In that moment, we set ourselves apart from what is, denying its reality and truth. Again, we lose touch with and step out of connection with what is and so miss what comes next. Dislocation, disconnection, and dissociation are the products of our denial of the moment. This is the source of our suffering.

To accept what is in the moment—and not get caught in denial—is one way to be liberated from suffering. This is not to give up on easing pain, on confronting injustice. Rather, it is an invitation to do so out of a degree of acceptance of what is, without contention. A tool for remaining present to what is, even when painful, even when unjust, even when it makes us sad, is to respond with compassion. When we offer ourselves compassion for what causes us pain, we are able to see it more clearly, accepting it for what it is. Compassion eases our return to the moment, our reconnection with what is.

As you make you way through the day, notice the moments in which you feel constriction, in which you are in contention with what is happening. Stuck in traffic? On the slow line at the grocery? Confronted with more work than can be done in a day? Notice your reaction. Feel the withdrawal from what is transpiring taking place in your heart. Offer yourself compassion for the suffering that arises from that disconnection. Sit with the awareness. Take a breath. Reconnect with what is true, and consider how you would like to interact with it. What is called for in this moment? What can you do to ease your suffering? How can you connect with what is true, and how can you remain present to it, even as you seek to change it?

"Though angry, may you remember compassion."

"And YHVH said, 'I have marked well the plight of My people in Egypt and have heeded their outcry because of their taskmasters; [yes, I am mindful of their sufferings. I have come down to rescue them from the Egyptians and to bring them out of that land to a good and spacious land, a land flowing with milk and honey, the region of the Canaanites, the Hittites, the Amorites, the Perizzites, the Hivites, and the Jebusites]. Now the cry of the Israelites has reached Me; [moreover, I have seen how the

Egyptians oppress them. Come, therefore, I
will send you to Pharaoh, and you shall free
My people, the Israelites, from Egypt']"
(Exod. 3:7–9).

When we want some good or other from the blessed Creator, our
fundamental intention should not be to satisfy our personal ends.
Rather, our intention should be that with this boon we would be better
able to serve the blessed Creator with a full heart. When Israel was in
Egypt, their awareness was limited, and their outcry emerged from
their personal needs. They did not cry out for God to save them from
their suffering so that they would be better able to serve the blessed
Creator, to then be called the "people of *Adonai*," because in Egypt their
awareness was constrained.

But, the blessed Holy One benefited them in two ways. One was
that God saved them from their suffering at the hands of the Egyptians.
The second, greater benefit was that God received their outcry as if
they had been crying out on God's behalf, that is, as if they had cried
out that God save them from their suffering so that they may be called
the "people of *Adonai*."

This is hinted at in our verses. **"I have marked well the plight of
My people"**—that they want to be My people. So, too, in the verse
"Now the cry of the Israelites has reached Me"—as if the fundamental
intention of their outcry was for **"Me,"** for My sake. They cried out
their desire that I save them so that they might serve Me.

This is how we can then interpret the earlier verse **"I have ... heeded
their outcry because of their taskmasters"**—they cried out only for
themselves only due to their taskmasters, because they were in Egypt
in bondage, where their awareness was constrained.

FOR FURTHER THOUGHT

Levi Yitzhak, with his characteristic precision, reads these verses
carefully and finds hints of divine intent in them. The prayerful
outcry of the Israelites (*tza'akah* is one word for prayer) draws God's
attention. In the first instance, their cry seems to be the result of
the oppression of the overseers. We can imagine that its content
was primarily "save us from this suffering." God hears this and
understands that their hearts and consciousness are constricted
because of their suffering: "I am mindful of their suffering." The

word "mindful" here, of course, is from the root *yod-dalet-ayin*: to know intimately, to connect with, to feel in concert with.

This awareness sets up Levi Yitzhak's reading of the second phrase regarding Israel's cry. Having taken note of their suffering, and having realized both the nature of their limited awareness and also having connected with their hearts, God experiences something new: "Now the cry of the Israelites has reached me." Out of God's deepening awareness of the state of the Israelites, it is possible for God to sense their cry differently. God senses the suffering of the Israelites but also knows deeply and directly that their true intention, could it be expressed, would be to serve God with love. Their concern would be for the sake of the wholeness of creation, for God's delight in connection. That prayer, in its deepest root, in its truest core, is for God.

We often think that our spiritual endeavors can only be effective when we are fully aware of our intentions and undertakings. Levi Yitzhak suggests that even when our awareness is limited, when we are constrained in our own *Mitzrayim* (Egypt; lit., Narrow Place), in some fundamental way we are still oriented toward God. And God knows this, then acting on our behalf. God listens carefully, hearing our true deep desires even when we can't express them directly—to serve God with a full heart. Knowing this, how can we use this lesson to help us hear ourselves more deeply, for God's careful listening to "hear us into prayer"?

 ## Questions for Reflection

1. What might come of modeling our behavior on God's: hearing in other people's words a higher message, a kinder, less selfish intention? What might be the benefits? If this were a parent-child relationship, would this be a healthy approach to child rearing? What are the dangers of intervening too soon, of impeding self-realization, self-awareness, clarity of expression and intent? How can we find a balance, making our best effort while trusting God's deeper listening?

2. Levi Yitzhak instructs us to forgo our personal desires, transforming them into a desire to serve God. How might this serve to deepen our spiritual awareness? What might we learn about our desires when we devote them to serving God?

3. Yet, is there a danger that we may use "serving God" as a cover for seeking to fill our selfish or more base needs? Think of the song from *Man of La Mancha*—"We're Only Thinking of Him"—when, of course, the singers are only thinking of themselves. When are you able to express your needs and desires clearly, and when do you hide them (from others or yourself)?

 ## Taking It into Your Life

Sylvia Boorstein, noted mindfulness teacher, is wont to say, "The natural response of the awakened heart is compassion." We might translate this into Levi Yitzhak's terms: "The natural response of the awakened heart is devotion, the desire to serve God with a full heart." In our lesson, Levi Yitzhak reminds us that God knows this truth and with compassion responds to us and our needs on that basis, making it possible, in the end, for us to finally fulfill that expectation.

If we now know this truth as well, how shall we come to embody it, to live it out? We might turn our attention to the ways in which we experience limited consciousness, constricted awareness, closed-heartedness. Do not look only for those big events in which the heart and spirit shut down—in the face of death or illness, major life transitions, times of danger. Look as well at the moment-to-moment experience of suffering. What is your habitual response to making a mistake? What are the words you use (even if heard only in your heart) in response to being delayed, interrupted, impeded, contradicted, criticized, or challenged? How do you feel when you accidentally break a glass, bang your finger with a hammer, ding the car door? All of these are moments in which the heart may close and awareness shrink.

Each of these instances, and dozens of others throughout the day, are moments in which we close ourselves off from God to focus only on our individual needs, our personal sense of suffering. As you bring your attention to these moments, you have the opportunity to hear your response as the impetus for prayer. It may be initially "I don't want to feel this way." Over time, this may evolve into "I don't want to feel this way, because it makes me feel bad and I don't like how I react in response." Further: "I don't want to feel this way, because I don't like how I act in response, and I truly wish to be kind, compassionate, and just." Finally: "I don't want to feel this way, because I want to devote my life energy to serving God, manifesting God's love and compassion in the world."

"[And He said, 'I will be with you;] that shall be your sign that it was I who sent you. [When you have freed the people from Egypt, you shall worship God at this mountain']" (Exod. 3:12).

Keep the following text in mind, as it is how we shall understand our verse: "Your ointments yield a sweet fragrance, your name is like emptied oil—therefore do maidens love you" (Song 1:3).

But, first we will interpret this other verse: "[Moses said to God, 'When I come to the Israelites and say to them, "The God of your fathers has sent me to you,"] and they ask me, "What is His name?" what shall I say to them?' And God said to Moses, *'Ehyeh-Asher-Ehyeh.'* He continued, 'Thus shall you say to the Israelites, "*Ehyeh* sent me to you"'" (Exod. 3:13–14).

The righteous person who serves God must know every day that whenever he or she attains any degree of spiritual awareness, there is another level of awareness beyond this one that she or he does not yet understand. The degree of awareness now attained is still nowhere near complete understanding. Thus, he or she must know that there is still something they lack in their understanding, yet even when they finally attain that degree of awareness, there will still be another one deeper within yet to be attained. This process is endless. Whatever you might understand, know that it is still not complete. You still must strive to attain the level beyond this one, since you do not yet comprehend it. You must then know, at all times, that you are not yet complete, and what you lack, as well. This is what Elijah revealed: "There is no one who comprehends you at all" (*Tikkunei Zohar* 17a). The best among those who serve God are they who know that they have not yet attained any level of completeness, and yet desire and yearn to rise even higher than their present level....

This, then, is how we should understand the phrase: "Your ointments yield a sweet fragrance." "Oil" signifies good deeds, as in "Let your head never lack for oil" (Eccles. 9:8; see Eccles. R. 9:7). When is it, then, that "your ointments yield a sweet fragrance"? When "your name is like emptied [*turak*] oil"; when it appears to you that you are always empty (*reik*), always lacking and so not yet complete, and you desire to attain the next level of awareness. When you sense this "emptiness," then your "oil" smells fragrant.

Further, this helps us to understand the phrase "therefore do maidens [*alamot*] love you." When we sense that we have still not attained any degree of completeness and that God is hiding from us, it is so that we endeavor to draw nearer to God, attaining an even greater level of awareness. This is like the parent teaching the child to walk, moving away all the time so that the child will make the effort to move closer. This is how we can understand the phrase "therefore do maidens [*alamot*] love you": "like this child [*alumaya*]." It appears to us that God is hiding, withdrawing, just as a parent who teaches a child (*elem*) to walk. Thus, with every degree of awareness we attain, we sense that there is another one even beyond it that we still do not comprehend and that this is to draw us closer to God. This is why righteous people always sense their lack and yearn to perfect themselves further.

So this is how we can understand our verse from Exodus. Moses had asked, "Who am I that I should go to Pharaoh, that I should bring the Children of Israel out of Egypt?" (Exod. 3:11). Out of his great righteousness Moses felt he lacked something, that next level of awareness. In his own eyes he was still on a low level and always felt his lack. To this God responded: "**That shall be your sign that it was I who sent you**," and that you do indeed perceive this prophecy clearly. When you sense your lack always and ask, "Who am I?" (*Mi anokhi?*), this [experience of lack] itself is "**your sign that it is I who sent you**." This is the path of truly righteous people who know what they lack, that they do not yet perceive the full meaning of serving God. "**That shall be your sign**" that your prophecy is clear is your sign that I sent you.

FOR FURTHER THOUGHT

What, in fact, are we to understand to be the sign that Moses was indeed God's emissary? We might say that it is God's promise to be with Moses in Egypt (which will be fulfilled in its own clear manner then). Or, it may only be confirmed when Moses brings the people out of Egypt to the mountain *and* when they then spontaneously respond in devotion and worship of God.

Perhaps it is the latter that Levi Yitzhak had in mind. The event at the mountain, of course, was *Matan Torah* (the giving of Torah), the revelation of God's very being and the invitation to cleave to God wholeheartedly. That invitation continues even today. Our spiritual challenge is to make up for the failure of the generation of the desert, to enter into Torah and to attach our hearts, minds, and souls to God. If we are always en route to Mount Sinai, if we are always climbing that mountain to meet God face-to-face, then the door is open for Levi Yitzhak to introduce his spiritual teaching into the Torah narrative.

This lesson is grounded in a core teaching of the Baal Shem Tov: God draws us closer, but also withdraws from us, so that we will constantly strive to come closer to God. The manifest world cloaks the true nature of existence: "The whole of creation is filled with God's glory" (Isa. 6:3). We see things and imagine them to be self-existent and separate one from the other. This misperception leads us to feel that God is far away. And, even if we strive to perceive God, we approach that endeavor with the same eyes and assumptions with which we see the world. We will be looking for God as a distinct entity, something outside of ourselves, something that we can grasp, hold on to, analyze.

The Baal Shem Tov challenges that assumption and calls us to deeper awareness: "There is no place devoid of God." When we investigate this lesson, we come to realize that deepening our awareness of God in the world requires more refined means of perception. We come to understand that whatever awareness we attain, in our consciousness of having attained awareness we fall back into our analytic, separate self, the self that is aware of self and other and so is not fully connected with God. In that sense, we are always working to supersede our current level of understanding.

But, we should not think that this is dependent on our effort alone. God is calling us. God is drawing us nearer. As illustration, Levi Yitzhak employs what is clearly the Baal Shem Tov's teaching: the parent drawing the toddler forward by withdrawing. This image, based on the pun *almut* (Ps. 48:15) / *alamot* (Song 1:3) / *alumaya* (child), appears in many books of Levi Yitzhak's generation (students of the student of the Besht). Further, although absent here, this word also suggests *olamot* (worlds), suggesting that we are drawn deeper and deeper into the perception of worlds within worlds, levels of existence where we attain a more refined and purified awareness of God—of the uniqueness, oneness, and "onlyness" of God. The constant awareness of the need to push on, to see beyond this moment's perception, is the sign that we are indeed connected to God, drawn onward by God's loving withdrawal, inviting us to deeper consciousness and connection.

Questions for Reflection

1. In the next chapter in Exodus, in response to Moses's continued doubt and fear, God does indeed give Moses a sign: the staff. What is your experience with regard to "signs" that reassure you in your life? Do you have "talismans," good-luck pieces, mementos that you hold on to as indications of your well-being, of a promise of hope or security? How do they work? What has been your experience of their power in your life?

2. Have you ever asked God for a sign, to support you in your life? Have you ever received one? What was it like? How did it function? If you have not, what do you imagine one would be like? How would you know it as a sign?

3. Levi Yitzhak proposes a radical but wonderful definition of the sign of spiritual engagement: the very fact that you are aware of your spiritual process is the sign that you are connected with God and on the right path. Is that satisfying to you as a sign? Is it self-defining and self-justifying? Does it inspire you? How, why?

Taking It into Your Life

It is possible to read Levi Yitzhak's description of spiritual practice as grim—negative in its presentation of human capacity and critical of spiritual seekers as all potentially egotistical strivers. We can read it the opposite way, however. Spiritual practice, and mindfulness, can be described as the intentional practice of curiosity. It emerges from the constant question "What is true?" While folk wisdom may dismiss curiosity (after all, it "killed the cat"), consider the delight of children discovering the world, and themselves in it, each day. Remember the thrill of understanding—whether it was a moment in a science lab, a clear perception of historical processes, or the truth of another person's being. Reflect on the relief of discovering a painful perception to be a misperception and the freedom that discovery offered. This is what Levi Yitzhak is inviting us to find in our spiritual lives.

While Levi Yitzhak portrays this dynamic in the negative—remembering that we lack understanding or that we have not yet attained awareness—it is possible to frame it in the positive. In each moment we are invited to recognize what we know, what we have learned, what we are now aware of, and to delight in it. That delight is legitimate ("therefore do maidens love you"), and it provides the energy that drives spiritual practice. But it needs to be applied, and not experienced as an end in itself. So even as we sense the delight in awareness, we are invited to then turn to our understanding, to our experience, and ask, "Is this true?" This is not to deny our experience. This is not to challenge our perception. Rather, it is an invitation to reengage in inquiry, in practice. We ask, "Is this true?" and then dig in again to our lived experience. We investigate our lives, our experiences, our perceptions. It may be that over and over we answer "yes"—but if we keep asking the question honestly, eventually we will have to answer "no" because, of itself and by nature, things (we) will change, and something else will now be true. And what a discovery that will be!

Realize each moment as a discovery. Treat every moment as an invitation to inquiry. Do not take for granted what you know, what you perceive, what you think, but ask, "Is this true?" Welcome the question, and open your heart to the new in each moment.

Va'eira

"It is the same Aaron and Moses to whom
YHVH said, ['Bring forth the Israelites from
the land of Egypt, troop by troop.'] It was
they who spoke to Pharaoh king [of Egypt to
free the Israelites from the Egyptians;] these
are the same Moses and Aaron"
(Exod. 6:26–27).

Rashi comments, "There are places (in the Torah) where Aaron
precedes Moses, and where Moses precedes Aaron. This is to tell us
that they were equal, one to the other."

Now, it is clear that God spoke only with Moses, as for instance the
verse, "God spoke to Moses [saying to him, 'I am *YHVH*']" (Exod. 6:2).
From this we might be inclined to think that Moses is greater than
Aaron. That is why our verse says, "**It is the same Aaron and Moses
to whom YHVH said**, etc." Even though the word came to Moses,
nevertheless Aaron was still Moses's equal, even in this instance.

In turn, it was Aaron alone who spoke to Pharaoh. Moses had said,
"I am of impeded speech" (Exod. 6:30). In response we read, "Aaron
will be your prophet" (7:1). From this we might be inclined to think
that Aaron is greater than Moses. That is why our verse says, "**It was
they who spoke to Pharaoh ... these are the same Moses and Aaron**."
Regarding speaking to Pharaoh they were equal. This is the simple
meaning of the text.

An alternative interpretation: We are enjoined to serve the Creator
in each and every moment with reverence and fear, and to find the
good in other Jews, and not to cause them any pain.

The starting point of divine service is fear, and from this fear
ultimately we come to delight. Moses symbolizes fear: he merited
complete wisdom, and "the foundation of wisdom is fear of *YHVH*"
(Ps. 111:10). Delight is represented by Aaron. The letters of his name
spell *NaHa"R A'* (*aleph*): from the *aleph* in the word "fear" (*yirah*:

yod-resh-aleph-hei), one comes to delight, which itself is called a river (*nahar*): "a river emerges from Eden" (Gen. 2:10; *eiden* means "delight"). Thus, from fear one comes to delight.

But the quality of fear does not apply to the Creator. God experiences delight from the start, wishing to pour out goodness and blessing for Israel. "And more than the calf desires to suck, the cow wishes to suckle" (Pesachim 112a). So when our verse says, "**It was they who spoke to Pharaoh king of Egypt to free, etc., these are the same Moses and Aaron**," Moses comes first. In the human plane, fear must come first, and this is represented by Moses. But in the phrase "**It is the same Aaron and Moses to whom YHVH said**," Aaron comes first. In God's realm, the delight comes first, arising immediately.

FOR FURTHER THOUGHT

Here are two very different ways to interpret these verses: on the level of *parshanut*—that is, classical Torah commentary—and on the level of kabbalistic symbolism and spiritual dynamics. In the first instance, Levi Yitzhak unpacks Rashi's claim that Moses and Aaron were equal. That might seem to be a radical assertion. God makes clear (Num. 12:6–9) that Moses excelled Aaron and Miriam and clearly stood head and shoulders above all other people. How could Rashi say they were equal? Levi Yitzhak suggests that they were equal without being the same. Moses could speak directly with God—"face-to-face" (Deut. 34:10)—while Aaron could speak to Pharaoh as Moses's mouthpiece. Each had an important role to fill; each was indispensable to the mission. Neither could do what the other did. They were equally important without being the same.

In the second lesson, Moses and Aaron cease to be human figures, serving instead as representatives of spiritual qualities and dynamics. The verse from Psalm 111 is used regularly to suggest the primacy of the divine *sephirah*, or quality of *Chokhmah*, Wisdom. Here, Levi Yitzhak employs it to make the argument that in our spiritual work, we must first connect with the qualities associated with Moses: wisdom (*chokhmah*) and fear (*yirah*). The connection between these two is very powerful. When we pay close attention to the nature of life—its fragility, its unpredictability, its fleetingness, its seeming emptiness—that is, when we deepen our wisdom, we experience fear. Not fear of "what will happen," but the fear that arises from awareness "that things happen." This fear turns us to God, out of gratitude for the capacity to know the truth of reality; out of devotion to the source of all existence; out of joy in the experience of life at all, delight in awareness of God's grace. God, who is the source of all existence and embodies all that is, has no experience of fear. Rather, God delights in being able to do good, to offer blessings. That delight exists without anything else having to take place, without any other instigation.

The association of Moses with fear is based on *Tikkunei Zohar* 5b: "Fear is connected to humility: 'the consequence of humility is fear of *YHVH*' (Prov. 22:4). One who has fear of God is brought to the quality of humility.... This is the level of Moses: 'Moses was very humble' (Num. 12:3)."

Questions for Reflection

1. We have been having a broad political debate in our country about the meaning of equality: is it equality of access or is it equality of outcomes? What is equitable, and what is out of balance? How do you understand Levi Yitzhak's teaching in this light? Do you have a sense of which position—if either—he might hold in our contemporary debate? Does it make sense to you that people can be equal without being the same? How have you experienced that in your life? When?

2. Moses speaks to God, and Aaron speaks to Pharaoh. Which of these personalities would you like to embody? Which one attracts or repels you? In the Torah, we know which one wielded more power. Which one does today? Why? Is that a good thing, to your mind? Why or why not?

3. Levi Yitzhak posits that fear of God is the starting point for spiritual growth. In this selection, he identifies delight as the state that emerges from fear. The more common pairing is fear-love. How do you understand the connection between fear of God and love of God? Have you experienced that movement in yourself or observed it in someone else? Why do you imagine that fear of God must precede love of God? And, how does love then lead to delight?

Taking It into Your Life

All human beings are not equal in their abilities; they are all equal in value. Yet, we frequently find ourselves comparing ourselves to others, finding ourselves lacking or seeing ourselves superior to them. What would it take to see the world on this model of Moses and Aaron? How can we develop the inner balance, the inner awareness of the truth, so that we might be fully present both to ourselves as we are and to others as we meet them, without hiding anything, without denying anything about ourselves or them?

Let us make this a practice. Make a list of what you consider to be your best traits and also a list of the things that you feel you lack or that you do not do well. For a period of time, simply review these lists each day, and as you read each trait, pause and feel into your body, heart, and mind to examine if this is true. Notice when you resist acknowledging this truth. Notice, as well, when you discover information or awareness that may call that observation into question. When you are clear about your awareness of this trait as it truly exists, respond, "That is true." Feel the truth in your body.

When you feel stable in your awareness of your truth—or at least that you can come to that truth without too much struggle—begin to apply this to others. As you meet them, seek to see them for their full beings. Notice what they can do that you cannot, and praise them for it. Notice what you can do that they cannot, and hold them with appreciation nonetheless. In each interaction, as you recognize your traits and capacities and those of the person before you, respond with "This is true." And be at peace.

"But I will harden Pharaoh's heart [that I may multiply My signs and marvels in the land of Egypt.] When Pharaoh does not heed you [I will lay My hand upon Egypt and deliver My ranks, My people the Israelites, from the land of Egypt with extraordinary chastisements]" (Exod. 7:3–4).

Take a look at the commentary of the *Or Hachayyim* on verse 7:4 where he asks: If God has already hardened Pharaoh's heart, what sense does it make to then say he will not listen to Moses and Aaron?

First we need to understand the following: in the plague of frogs Moses said to Pharaoh, "So that you will know that there is none like *YHVH* our God" (Exod. 8:6), and at the plague of wild beasts he says, "So that you will know that I *YHVH* am in the midst of the land" (8:18). How shall we understand the change in his language? In these two instances surely God performed two great miracles in two different ways. One miracle was in the form of the Ten Plagues. The second was in hardening Pharaoh's heart so that God might smite him with great plagues.

These two types of miracles are hinted at in our verse. **"But I will harden Pharaoh's heart that I may multiply My signs and marvels"** expresses God's intention: "This is how I will multiply My signs and marvels: Pharaoh will not listen to you." That is, because Pharaoh will refuse to listen, I will be able to multiply the miracles. This is one type of miracle. **"I will lay My hand upon Egypt and deliver My ranks, My people the Israelites, from the land of Egypt with extraordinary chastisements,"** this is the second kind of miracle.

(The end is missing....)

FOR FURTHER THOUGHT

This is classic Levi Yitzhak. He finds a problem that someone else raises and shows that it is not really a problem. He senses in our verses that there must be two different acts that God is pointing to: hardening Pharaoh's heart, and Pharaoh failing to listen. To help tease out these two themes, he identifies another seeming repetition, one where there is also a subtle difference. In the plague of frogs, Moses informs Pharaoh that he is to learn that there is no other God but *YHVH*; with the plague of swarming beasts, Pharaoh is to learn that it is this very God who is at work in the land of Egypt. Levi Yitzhak applies these two positions to our verses: there are two different types of response in Pharaoh, reflecting two kinds of miracles that God performs. One miracle is demonstrated in Pharaoh's resistance to Moses's entreaties, bringing about the wondrous Ten Plagues; the other miracle is that God then performs wonders, bringing Israel out from Egypt. God's name is made great in both ways, Levi Yitzhak claims, even through Pharaoh's intransigence.

As always, the issue of God hardening Pharaoh's heart is problematic. Here is one way to understand it, in light of Levi Yitzhak's lesson. The first aspect of miracle that Levi Yitzhak identifies is that of the Ten Plagues. In each of them, in increasing intensity, God caused great suffering to the people of Egypt. The natural response of a caring, sensitive human being would have been compassion. Pharaoh, even as the "bad guy" in the biblical and Rabbinic narratives, was still a human being. In response to the plagues, he *could* have responded differently. In fact, we might even say, he would have been *compelled* to respond differently, to respond *only* with compassion for his people (and, of course, the same outcome could have resulted had he been compelled by his fear of God's power, instead of by compassion). He would not have been free to consider any other option, to truly assess what would have been the best course for him and for his country. God hardened Pharaoh's heart to create *greater* room for action, greater freedom of will. Had Pharaoh only followed the natural dictates of his heart, he would not have been choosing freely, and quite possibly God then would not have been able to perform the other miracles needed to bring the Israelites out of Egypt. In this manner, it was indeed a miracle that God could cause Pharaoh not to hear Moses's threats and not to pay attention to what was set before him so clearly. The miracle overcame the natural response of the human heart (compassion or fear).

This explanation may be a bit of a stretch, but it does offer a way of understanding Levi Yitzhak without having to resort to the perverse perspective he uses elsewhere: the suffering of the wicked (or the nations) in the service of promoting Israel is a form of *kiddush Hashem*, sanctification of the divine name, and so really a benefit to those who suffer. And it challenges us to look even more closely at our spontaneous reactions to events in our lives, to ask—even against our natural instincts and strongly held values—"What is true here? What is the wisest response in this instance?"

 ## Questions for Reflection

1. What is the nature of the human heart? Is its natural inclination toward compassion and loving-kindness (such that it requires divine intervention to prevent Pharaoh from acting compassionately and letting the Israelites go)? Or is there no tendency of the heart one way or the other, and the real marvel is that we have free choice before God's ultimate knowledge and power?

2. Levi Yitzhak holds that it is not only in the manifest power that God exhibits through the plagues but also in Pharaoh's foolish audacity before the God of the Universe that God's greatness is demonstrated. How do you respond to this idea? Do we mean something like this when we marvel not only that our people have persevered ("*vehi*

she'amdah la'avoteinu velanu / God has saved us through the generations," as we declare in the Passover Haggadah), but also that evil has been overcome? In our post-Holocaust world, in our post–Bosnia/Kosovo/Rwanda/Syria world, can you retain any part of Levi Yitzhak's worldview? How is God present even in conflict?

3. In our lives, our attention runs among our memories of the past, our imaginings of the future, and our experience of this moment. What we experience in the moment becomes the past, and inevitably we look back to see what it looks like now. Sometimes it appears different from what it was like in the moment. How we understand the past shapes our experience of the present. If we survive trauma (or simply make our way through the suffering of life), which interpretation do you find more helpful: "It is just what happened" or "There was a reason behind it"? Which seems healthier to you? Which is Levi Yitzhak doing? How shall we respond?

 ## Taking It into Your Life

Most of us have a sense of knowing, intuitively, what to do in most situations. True, there are often instances in which we are asked to make a decision or respond to a problem and we have to reflect, to mull, to evaluate, before coming to a conclusion. Still, for the most part, we make our way through the day just doing the next thing. We pick up the phone when it rings. We get something to eat when we are hungry. We brush our teeth before going to bed. And we also respond to our partners or our children from moment to moment, to their wants and needs, in the exigencies of the moment. We usually feel that however we respond is the natural and correct response, and we simply act.

On reflection, you may be able to recall an instance in which your spontaneous reaction was ultimately a bad response, a thoughtless response. Recognizing that to be true in interpersonal interactions, we might extend that to the more mundane, almost automatic actions we take. Should we pick up the phone right now, in mid-thought, mid-sentence? Is eating now, in response to this pang, truly the correct response? How well am I brushing my teeth?

The challenge is not to "think" about what we are doing or about to do. Rather, what we are invited to do is to be more fully present to whatever it is we are doing—to be aware. In mindfulness practice, we develop awareness—plain awareness, direct awareness, unmediated awareness—of the present moment, free of bias, impulse, preference, and even a "system" of values. To be mindful is to recognize in the moment what is true and discern what is wise in response, not to react automatically, even "naturally."

As you move through your day, bring your attention over and over to what you are doing. Feel it in your body. Notice how you hold yourself, how you sense your body in motion, how you find yourself in relation to others. Notice each moment that you feel movement arise. What is its source? Can you sense the impetus to pick up *this* book in *this* moment; to make *this* call at *this* moment; to respond in *this* manner to *this* person? What does it feel like first thing in the morning when you place your feet on the floor? Can you bring awareness to that moment, to then sense the next moment, rising to go to the bathroom? To brush your teeth? To shower? Each of these acts is a choice, and we can become more aware, from moment to moment, of these choices, toward the end of being even more present, even more aware of how we respond in moments of even less import. We may, in this manner, uncover our natural heart of compassion.

"And Moses said to Pharaoh, 'You may have this triumph over me: for what time shall I plead on your behalf [and your courtiers and your people, that the frogs be cut off from you and your houses, to remain only in the Nile?]' 'For tomorrow,' he replied. And [Moses] said, 'As you say—that you may know that there is none like *YHVH* our God'" (Exod. 8:5–6).

Moses said to Pharaoh at the plague of frogs, "**You may have this triumph over me**, etc."; "**And [Moses] said, 'As you say—that you may know that there is none like *YHVH* our God.**" The reference "**our God**" means to say "this is *our* God," specifically the God of Israel, the people who arose in God's mind at the beginning of all beginnings and for whom all was created; they are the origin of all thought, the people in whom God takes pride (*mitpa'eir*). That is why Moses said to Pharaoh, "**You may have this triumph over me** [*hitpa'eir alai*]: **for what time shall I plead on your behalf …?**" That is, he informed Pharaoh that there is power in the prayer of a tzaddik, who is able to effect whatever he wills, turning judgment into compassion; and that God does miracles for His people Israel outside of the natural order. Israel is the first thought of all, above and beyond nature. So Moses was precise in saying, "**There is none like *YHVH* our God.**" This is the quality of "I am the first and I am the last" (Isa. 44:6)—and it is like the vowel *cholom*.

At the plague of wild beasts Moses informed Pharaoh, "On that day I will set apart [the region of Goshen, where My people dwell], so that no swarms of insects shall be there, that you may know that I *YHVH* am in the midst of the land" (Exod. 8:18). That is, know that even in the natural order I am present: right in "the midst of the land." The nature of that miracle—that God set apart Goshen so that no wild beasts would be there—did not require a change in the order of nature. The miracle was garbed in the natural order. This is the quality of "there is no God beside Me" (Isa. 44:6)—and this is like the vowel *shuruk*.

Further, Moses informed Pharaoh of the third quality: "I am the last" (Isa. 44:6)—which is like the vowel *chirik*. We see this in his words: "In order that you may know that there is none like Me in all the world. I could have stretched forth My hand and stricken you and your people with pestilence, and you would have been effaced from the earth. Nevertheless [I have spared you for this purpose: in order to show you My power,] and in order that My fame may resound throughout the world" (Exod. 9:14–16). God cuts off and uproots the wicked so that they might recognize God's sovereignty. Even the lowest level, those sparks that have fallen into the realm of the externalities (*kelippah*) (may the Merciful One save us), even they must ultimately recognize God's sovereignty. So, when Moses informed Pharaoh, "There is none like Me in all the world," he meant even in the lowest level God is present, and there is no place devoid of God. So, he meant specifically "all the world": even in its most material, physical aspects, God is still present.

Finally, at the plague of hail, Moses informed Pharaoh, "So that you may know that the earth is *YHVH*'s" (Exod. 9:29). With this, Moses told him of even one more level, beyond the thinking of the philosophers. They think (heaven forbid) that God is not involved in this lower world, for God is too exalted to do so. Moses told Pharaoh that this is not the case. Rather, God oversees all the creatures of the world, bringing them to life—from nothingness to being—from moment to moment. God's providence (*hashgachato*) extends to all extant things. Even when gentiles pray to God, God hears their prayer and helps them, as King Solomon prayed, "Or if a foreigner who is not of Your people [Israel comes from a distant land for the sake of Your name—for they shall hear about Your great name and Your mighty hand and Your outstretched arm—when he comes to pray toward this House, oh, hear in Your heavenly abode and grant all that the foreigner asks You for. Thus all the peoples of the earth will know Your name and revere You, as does Your people Israel; and they will recognize that Your name is attached to this House that I have built]" (1 Kings 8:41–43). This was Moses's intent when he said, "The earth is YHVH's" (Exod. 9:29): God's interest and concern extend to these lower realms, and from His exalted heights he considers all inhabitants of the land. With the plague of hail Moses did not pray to compel Pharaoh to warn the people to go inside, since he knew that he would not do so, as it says, "I know that you and your courtiers still do not fear YHVH" (9:30). His prayer was to bring Pharaoh to acknowledge, "YHVH is in the right" (9:27). Moses prayed so that Pharaoh would come to know that God hears the prayer even of a stranger, for God's providence extends over all creation. So Moses's meaning was precisely "the earth is YHVH's" (9:29).

FOR FURTHER THOUGHT

This is one of the more literarily well-shaped and clearly expressed expositions in *Kedushat Levi*. Levi Yitzhak uses it—on its first level —as a means to distinguish among the various ways that Moses expresses the point of the plagues: to make known that Israel is God's own people, that God has power over Pharaoh, and that God has sovereignty in the world. In this, he points to an important liter-ary strand in the Torah and helps us to sense the deep drama of this confrontation between Moses and Pharaoh.

On another level, this is a presentation of classical Hasidic thought: God is above, below, and permeates all existence, and God's provi-dence is over all things, in all moments. Levi Yitzhak connects the "above, below, and permeates" trope to another Hasidic trope: that God's very, sustaining, life-giving power is present in the world through the letters of Creation. So, God's presence in the world is represented by the shape of three Hebrew vowel-letters: the *cholom* (a *vav*, or line with a dot over it), the *shuruk* (a *vav*, or line with a dot next to it in the middle), and the *chirik* (a dot below the line).

Each of these corresponds to one of God's modes of manifestation in the world: above or beyond nature; in or through the natural order; and below the "natural" world, in the realm of the fallen sparks, even to the *kelippot*, or husks, that imprison those holy sparks. The inspiration for the association with vowels and its implications for God's presence in all creation is rooted in the Zohar (II 158a) and connected to the verse "I am the first, I am the last, and there is no god but Me" (Isa. 44:6).

The comprehensive matrix that Levi Yitzhak creates in this manner is impressive enough. But, he goes beyond that with his lovely conclusion, where he extends his model beyond the classical concern only for Jewish practice, for the role of Jews in redeeming the world. He invites all people, all strangers (gentiles; *nokhri*), even Pharaoh, to recognize that God hears their prayers. Everyone who prays, prays ultimately to God. Levi Yitzhak does not quote the verse from Malachi, but suggests it: "For from where the sun rises to where it sets, My name is honored among the nations, and everywhere incense and pure oblation are offered to My name; for My name is honored among the nations—said *YHVH* of Hosts" (1:11). We are all struggling against our inner and outer blindness to see that truth, to experience God in all places, at all times, in every circumstance.

 ## Questions for Reflection

1. What helps you recognize God's power in the world? When do you sense that power as coming from the outside, working "on" the earth, and when do you sense it emerging from life itself, "in the earth"?

2. Is it your experience to look for proof that God is active in the world, in your life? What kind of test is sufficient for you? Have you ever rejected the proof emerging from a test you set? Have you ever accepted it? When, how, why?

3. What do you make of Levi Yitzhak's final turn, to invite the prayers of all people, including Pharaoh? Does this suggest that he does not find Pharaoh to be the complete villain, the absolute negation of Israelite holiness? Who have you identified as "Pharaoh," outside the bounds of decent, moral community—and might you find a way to include their prayers with yours?

Taking It into Your Life

"The Holy One is the Place of the world [*Makom*]. God's existence is above all worlds, below all worlds, surrounds all worlds, within all worlds, fills all worlds" (*Peri Ha'aretz, Kedoshim*: R. Menahem Mendel of Vitebsk, based on Zohar III 225a). This conception stands behind Levi Yitzhak's teaching, represented in the three vowels and the three speeches of Moses. How can we develop this consciousness in our lives?

We might use R. Menahem Mendel's formulation as a meditation. Sitting comfortably, bring your attention to the breath. Rest in the breath for a period of time, until you sense a degree of balance in your awareness. Then, slowly recite the teaching. Pause with each phrase, and bring your awareness to sensing God's presence and existence in that orientation. So, "above all worlds"—extend your awareness above your head, and extend upward beyond your imagination to encompass all creation above you; "below all worlds"—extend your awareness below you, through your seat and soles of your feet, down into the earth to its core; "surrounds all worlds"—feel yourself surrounded by the air in the room, by the room itself, by the world outside, by all creation; "within all worlds"—sense your innards, investigating down into the smallest capillary, alveolus in your lungs, oxygen molecules flowing in your blood, vitamins at work in your cells, atoms constructing your body; "fills all worlds"—sense the vital force that enlivens you, that you experience as being "alive," how that fills you entirely. Repeat slowly, reciting the phrases, bringing awareness to mind and heart and body. Observe how this affects your awareness of God's presence in you and in the world. Pray from that awareness.

Bo

"[Then *YHVH* said to Moses,] 'Hold out your
arm toward the sky that there may be
darkness upon the land of Egypt, a darkness
that can be touched.' Moses held out [his arm
toward the sky and thick darkness descended
upon all the land of Egypt for three days.
People could not see one another, and for
three days no one could get up from where
he was;] but all the Israelites enjoyed light in
their dwellings" (Exod. 10:21–23).

Check out Rashi's comments where he focuses on the phrase **"a darkness
that can be touched"** (*veyameish choshekh*). Further, consider that our
text says, **"All the Israelites enjoyed light in their dwellings,"** when,
to follow what preceded, it should have said, "For all the Israelites
there was no darkness." We can explain this starting with the midrash
(Exod. R. 14:2): "Where did this darkness come from? From the
darkness above, as it says, 'He made darkness His hiding-place round
Him' (Ps. 18:12)." From this we learn that the darkness in Egypt came
from the same darkness about which it is written, "He made darkness
His hiding-place round Him"—which refers to the hidden light.

Consider further the teaching in the Talmud (Shabbat 34a): "[R.
Shimon bar Yohai, upon leaving his cave] placed his gaze on him and
turned him into a pile of bones." What is the significance of "placed
his gaze on him"? More, don't we know that "punishment is not good
for a tzaddik" (cf. Prov. 17:26)! Here is how to understand this: God's
brightness is endless (*ein sof*). When it arose in God's thought to create
the world it was "because God wished to be known as merciful, etc."
(Zohar III 257b). Therefore, God constricted His brightness so that it
might be received according to the spiritual capacity of the recipient:
to the realm of the seraphim according to their qualities; to the realm
of the *chayyot* and other angels according to their qualities; and so then

throughout all of the supernal realms. These realms remain fixed at one spiritual level, just as they were at the time of their creation, so that they will not be annulled in the light of *ein sof*, nor fall to a lower state. This is hinted at in the verse, "With two [wings] it covered its face and with two it covered its legs" (Isa. 6:2)—"its face" so that they would not look above their station and so be annulled; "its legs" so that they would not look below their level. But Israel, God's holy people, create garments for the light from their devotion to Torah and mitzvot and so constantly rise up level after level.

But the wicked of the nations who have neither Torah nor mitzvot remain only on one level. When it becomes necessary to break them, they are shown the supernal light. They have neither Torah nor mitzvot from which to create garments and rise up level by level, and this is their downfall. This is the meaning of the passage above—"he placed his gaze on him"—this is the appearance of the supernal light. Those who do not attach themselves to Torah and mitzvot are not able to make garments by which they might tolerate this supernal light pouring out on them. As a consequence, they are turned into "a pile of bones."

Now we can understand the phrase "**a darkness that can be touched**." The verb translated "**touched**" (*veyameish*) can signify "to remove"; "**darkness**" refers to the constriction of the supernal light. So, *veyameish choshekh* means that God removed the constriction of the divine light so that its pure, unlimited power might pour out on them (the wicked). For those who had no Torah or mitzvot, this was their downfall. But, "**all the Israelites**"—who have Torah and mitzvot by which to make garments, to rise up level by level—"**enjoyed light in their dwellings**"—they experienced more of the divine light.

Now we can also understand the teaching of the Sages (Nedarim 8b): "In the time-to-come the blessed Holy One will remove the sun from its sheath: the righteous will be healed in its light, and the wicked will be judged." The "sun" is the supernal brilliance; "its sheath" refers to the process of constriction. This teaching tells us that God will reveal the full brilliance by removing (reversing) the constriction, and thereby "the righteous will, etc."

FOR FURTHER THOUGHT

This lesson builds from the classical mystical conception of Creation: the outflowing of God's light into lower, coarser levels of existence by means of constriction. The light was limited, contained, and garbed in the material forms of this world, hidden, screened. That the light was so contained permitted lower, more physical forms of life to exist in God's presence; should the light shine full force, its purity and brightness would overwhelm and nullify those forms. So while the containers and garments obscure God, they also make possible the existence and persistence of the lower realms, realms in which conscious beings turn to recognize God as sovereign.

This conception feeds into Hasidic spiritual practice. That is, even though God's divine light is hidden from us for our benefit, our role as God's people is to reveal that light, to strive to live more fully in its presence. As Levi Yitzhak tells us here, we accomplish that through our study of Torah and a life of doing mitzvot. Citing a passage in the Zohar (I 66a), we learn that our positive deeds create supernal garments for our souls. These garments will protect us from that supernal light in the world-to-come. Thus, as we purify our selves through Torah and mitzvot, we become more able to perceive and tolerate ever greater degrees of the supernal light. Thus prepared, when God in the time-to-come removes the sun (that is, the source of the divine light) from its sheath—its container, the garments that limit its power—the righteous (those who study Torah and do mitzvot) will be able to tolerate its light, having grown ever more transparent before it. But the wicked will be doomed by it. They will not be able to stand before it; they will be nullified, turned into "a pile of bones."

The imagery of light and darkness here is somewhat paradoxical. God's light is so powerful—so pure, originating in *ein sof*, in endless power and clarity—that it makes all else appear to exist in the dark. And anything that stands before it is overwhelmed by its purity such that it no longer can be perceived; it is nullified, disappearing as if in darkness. (I am reminded of a movie, I believe *THX 1138*, by George Lucas, in which there is such a scene: the space pure white, filled with blazing light in which there is no depth, no direction, no presence or absence.) Yet, the process of nullification can be positive. That is, if one is aware of movement toward the light, of divestment of corporeality or concern for the physical, if one attains an unbounded awareness of the emptiness of all things, of the lack of independent existence in the light of God's true presence in all existence, then the experience of nullification is to be striven for. Paradoxically, then, our study of Torah and doing mitzvot are to prepare us to be absorbed into the totality of divine light (redemption), while the wicked who have no access to these practices will be nullified, to become the empty shells they truly are.

Questions for Reflection

1. How do you understand that the study of Torah makes it possible both to know that the divine light is hidden and also to reveal it? How do you understand that doing mitzvot makes it possible both to know that the divine light is hidden and also to reveal it?

2. How do you understand that engagement in spiritual practice helps us prepare to stand before the full divine light and be healed by it?

3. Have you ever had the experience of disappearing before the Divine? When, how? Was it your experience that this was positive or negative? When, how, why?

Taking It into Your Life

We have all been told not to look directly at the sun, and it must be something like that to which our teachers are referring when talking about a light that nullifies all else in its presence. An aspect of this image is that of holding a candle or even a torch before the sun, where its small light becomes nothing in the brilliance of the greater. Here are two practices you might employ to enter into this awareness.

You might choose to meditate on a candle. Sitting in a relaxed but attentive position, allow your eyes to settle on the flame. You may notice your retina adjusting subtly, allowing the light in, but protecting your eye from the brightness of the flame. Do not focus too tightly on the flame; allow your gaze to soften, opening up around the flame, letting more light into your eyes. Hold your vision steady, allowing more and more of the light of the flame to fill your field of vision. Continue to sit in this manner, bringing your full attention over and over to the image of the flame and its light as you sit.

You may want to repeat this over several days or weeks, to develop your capacity to remain connected to the flame and to open to the light. After some time, you may want to reflect: What is your experience? What do you sense happens to the other objects in your field of vision? If you are not aware of those objects in the moment, have they disappeared? Has the light overwhelmed them? What was your sense of the quality of your mind in those moments? How self-aware were you when the light most fully filled your field of vision?

An alternative meditation is one of inner vision. Sitting comfortably, yet alert, allow your attention to rest in your breath. When you sense a degree of balance, begin an inner, visual inventory of people. Begin with the people you live with, and then include the rest of your "people"— parents, siblings, and extended family; in-laws, their children, and their children; your co-workers and their families; your immediate neighbors; and so on. As you bring the people to mind, imagine them joining you in your room. As each person comes to mind, place them in the group, and "see" the whole group together. Allow the group to grow, but never lose sight of all the members—so, periodically you may wish to remain with the image of the group, to make sure "everyone is there"—including yourself. Keep adding and adding, allowing new people, new faces to rise in your mind's eye. After some time, you may sense that there are no more faces appearing. Hold the whole group in your inner awareness. Sometime later you may want to reflect: What was it like to be among so many people? What was your feeling toward the group as it grew, as each new person came to mind and joined in? What was your sense of where you were, of how central or peripheral or otherwise situated you were? How self-aware were you in the whole of the group?

"Moses said, 'Thus says *YHVH*: [Toward midnight I will go forth among the Egyptians]'" (Exod. 11:4).

There are two points from which we might come to our devotion to the Creator. One derives from our witnessing miracles and wonders, where God changes the course of nature, doing as God wills. From this display of power we recognize that God rules over all, and all creatures are obligated to serve God in fear.

The second way is the recognition of the truth: God created everything by the word of His mouth. Therefore, God has the capacity to change them as well. This awareness is surely better. The force of this perspective diminishes the significance of knowing God through miracles…. The one who comes to this true awareness is not dependent on knowing God's miracles; they have no significance. This person has attained a higher degree, and so miracles are not wondrous at all; since God created everything, it is in God's power to do with them as God wills.

This is the significance of the question of the Wise Child at the seder: "What about statutes and laws and ordinances that *YHVH* your God commanded you?" This child understands that there are no wonders from God's perspective; it is clear that God can change nature as God wills, since God created everything. But the Passover offering and matzah represent serving God because of the miracles and wonders that God performed. So, the Wise Child asks, "Why do we still do them? Do we not have a more perfect, truer awareness of God, and nothing that God does is a wonder to us?" It is this question to which the Haggadah responds, "We do not eat after the Passover offering *afikoman*." Matzah and the Passover offering indicate miracles and wonders, and this mode of devotion is permanent. But, the second form of devotion is not permanent—one can only arrive at it after sanctification and purification through constant devotion. Therefore, the form of devotion that results from awareness of miracles and wonders remains forever.

This is why the Sages taught, "The last taste of the seder must be that of matzah" (Pesachim 119b)—and when the Temple stood, this was the Passover offering. This was so that the taste would remain, indicating serving God out of awareness of miracles and wonders. This tells us that this form of devotion is sustained forever. That is why we continue with this form of religious practice, so that service of God will not budge from our mouths and the mouths of our descendants. This is not the case of that true awareness, which can only be attained by the greatest devotees, who are in continuous connection with God and never fall from that state.

Now we can understand the response to the Wise Child: "We do not eat after the Passover offering *afikoman*." This is so that the taste should remain in our mouths, such that the service of God motivated by awareness of miracles and wonders will not pass away. Therefore we need to continue with this form of devotion that is based on miracles and wonders. This explains the clear question of the Wise Child, "What are the statutes?" and not "Why do we do these?"

FOR FURTHER THOUGHT

Once again we meet the "two types" formula. This time, however, the "true" position is one that is not advocated for the masses; it is not a model for the students of this lesson. Levi Yitzhak tells us that true perception is that God is Creator of all, not only in the past, but also from moment to moment. That being so, what we perceive to be the "natural course of events" and perhaps even the "laws of nature" are only the present, immediate manifestation of God's will. Whatever God intends in a given moment is what unfolds in the course of creation right now. From this perspective, there is nothing that can be predicted, that as a matter of course must come to pass. Therefore, there is nothing to be learned about God through the upending of the "course of nature," a miracle. The world is full of wonder from moment to moment; every instant is the awesome manifestation of God's love in this particular configuration, as God desires.

The less laudatory position is one that perceives God changing the course of events out of love of Israel, making miracles for their sake. This perspective may not be the truth, but it is what most of us can hold in our minds most of the time. One thing that makes miracles seem special is that they are dramatic. They catch our attention because they are out of the ordinary. They overwhelm us with their power. In response, we tell stories, recounting the miracle, recalling God's love. We ritualize this process, adding performative acts to dramatize the telling, to concretize the experience of God's love in the past and the present. That is what the seder is about (as well as much of the rest of our religious practice). We return over and over to our rituals, to the retellings and the reenactments, so that we will remain connected in a lively manner to our experience of the miracles that God has performed—and performs—for us.

While this may not be the highest, truest form of devotion, it is the safest. It is possible to imagine that someone who perceived the truth—like the Wise Child in Levi Yitzhak's telling—would no longer feel compelled to participate in the rituals of a community who see miracles as remarkable events, as something beyond nature. Indeed, such a person would need no ritual to remain connected to God. Each breath, every beat of the heart, the falling of a leaf, the rising of the sun, the movement of the air, everything would be constant evidence of God's love—manifest in the continued existence of the universe in this moment.

This may be an accurate response to the truth, but it is unacceptable within Hasidism and the normative Jewish living. Despite the pull of this "truth," it might have seemed dangerous to Hasidic teachers, fearful as they were of accusations of being crypto-Sabbateans and heretics. We may not have to worry about that today. Nevertheless, we are well warned not to give up on the power of ritual and religious practice. They are the ground of communal coherence and cohesiveness, of collective consciousness and historical continuity, of education and enlightenment. Levi Yitzhak promoted the importance of the perception of the "truth," and we need to strive for that view and share it with others. But we, like Levi Yitzhak, also need to remember that that view is rooted—given stability and nourishment—in the rites, rituals, and practices of tradition.

 ## Questions for Reflection

1. What is your sense: are miracles events that take place outside of the order of nature? Have you witnessed or experienced such miracles in your life? Do you have a sense of these miracles still reverberating in your life experience from the past?

2. Why do you imagine that it would take such effort to attain the "awareness of truth" as Levi Yitzhak describes it? Why would this be a perception reserved for the elite?

3. How does this teaching help you understand the conservative element of the Hasidic revolution? How do you sense this—if at all—in your own life?

 ## Taking It into Your Life

Modern Jews have a mixed relationship with the idea of miracles, particularly those that seem "outside of nature." There were those, for instance, who saw the Israeli victory in the Six-Day War as a miracle, perhaps one that unfolded with God's help through nature, but a miracle nonetheless. In the past, communities and families who were saved from destruction created rituals similar to those of Purim to commemorate their salvation—making a connection between their experience and God's miraculous work through nature.

Of a more personal nature, in recent years Jews have come to appreciate more intimately the miraculous nature of human existence. We have been ever more mindful of the awareness prompted by the *Modim* prayer, recognizing "Your miracles that are with us daily" (*nisekha shebekhol yom imanu*). What are these miracles? Is our spontaneous healing from a cold or a cut a miracle? Are the normal workings of the body a miracle (e.g., that the breath returns at all)? Is it a miracle that we are not killed on the freeways? Is the persistence of love, the dedication to relationships even when strained, a miracle? Is generosity, compassion, or altruism a miracle? What are the miracles—in nature, in the daily unfolding of our lives—that we notice and for which we respond with gratitude?

But, what if these are not miracles? If they are only the unfolding of the divine will in the moment, the lawful emergence of life from the conditions of the past, do you sense that they prompt the same sense of gratitude in you? If "all that is" is "just what is," can you sense excitement, hope, devotion, or engagement?

As you sit to feel through these questions, add to your reflections the question, how might ritual help keep the sense of gratitude for the unfolding of all life—of pain and delight, of loss and opening—alive and vital? How do you experience your engagement in traditional practice—or contemporary rituals—as prompts to perceive God's presence in your life?

An alternative interpretation: "Moses said,
'Thus says YHVH: "Toward midnight I will go
forth among the Egyptians""'" (Exod. 11:4).

Israel, a holy people, receive delight and vitality from the Torah and mitzvot of the Holy One. But the delight of wicked people and their vitality is from revolting things (*ma'us*; as we know, swine delight in revolting things, Baba Kamma 17b; and this is true also of the wicked). But should a wicked person eventually do *teshuvah*, he then perceives that previously his delight came from something revolting.

In this light we can understand the Sages' teaching (cf. Beitzah 16a): "When Shabbat comes, the Holy One gives Jews an extra soul, and takes it away at the end of Shabbat, as it says, 'He ceased from work and was refreshed [*shavat vayinaphash*]' (Exod. 31:17). Once it (Shabbat) has ceased (*kevan sheshavat*), woe, that soul is lost (*vay avda nephesh*)!" What is the relationship of the verse of Scripture and the conclusion "once it has ceased"—when Shabbat ends is this soul not lost? We can explain this in light of the two teachings: "If Israel had only observed two Shabbatot properly, they would immediately have been redeemed"; "If Israel had only observed that first Shabbat [no nation or people would have ever ruled over them]" (Shabbat 118b).

Shabbat signifies *teshuvah*, since the letters of *ShaBBa"T* are *TSh"B*. From this we learn that on the holy Shabbat Jews do *teshuvah* and so realize that that in which they found delight during the week was actually from something revolting. They then are at pains when the next week arrives not to experience delights from the same things as they did in the week that has passed (heaven forbid). This comes about because on Shabbat the Holy One gives them an extra soul, that is, the delight in the Torah and mitzvot of the Holy One. When they do *teshuvah* and fear (that they will return to their previous delights), "since they ceased" (*kevan sheshavat*; made Shabbat; did *teshuvah*) and thus gained an extra soul, "woe to that soul which is lost" on the weekdays, which come and yet are like they were before.

Therefore, they really do need two Shabbatot, one on which to do *teshuvah*, on which to understand that their true purpose is to gain delight from serving God through Torah and mitzvot. On the second Shabbat, then, they would experience that true delight. Yet, when they came out of Egypt they experienced great spiritual clarity ("even a maidservant saw at the Sea more than even the prophet Ezekiel saw"; *Mekhilta, Beshallach* 2). Therefore, if they had kept that first Shabbat, if they had derived that true delight from Torah and mitzvot, they would have been fully redeemed. But, now that we are burdened with corporeal coarseness, we need at least one Shabbat to purify ourselves and do *teshuvah*, to then gain the second Shabbat in which we might experience the delight in God's Torah and mitzvot.

FOR FURTHER THOUGHT

This lesson comes as the core of a larger teaching, explaining why Moses addressed the people in Egypt from a lower level of prophecy. The answer has to do with the fact that the people were mired in the lowest levels of impurity there, and God first had to act to bring them up a notch or two before they could receive the full message of Moses's pure prophetic voice. To illustrate this point and to describe the dynamic at work in Egypt, Levi Yitzhak turns to an experience that his listeners would understand: the power of Shabbat to elevate and transform the heart.

He uses a teaching from the Talmud to depict this process, yet his interpretation of the passage is novel. It seems, in context, that this lesson is to teach how special Shabbat is, how it is unlike any other of the commandments, any of the other gifts and blessings bestowed by God on Israel. This brief lesson is the proof-text, the source of the teaching that on Shabbat Jews who keep the day are given an extra soul. When Shabbat departs, the person experiences a loss, deflation (perhaps to be brought back by sniffing the spices at *Havdalah*).

But Levi Yitzhak transforms this. He suggests that when we experience Shabbat, our eyes are opened and we look at the difference between our weekday lives and our true life in Torah and mitzvot. We know a deeper delight and then, in comparison, grieve over the emptiness and grossness of our previous pleasures. We might yearn to be able to go back to our weekday sleep, to the simple (but "revolting") pleasures of the mundane world, but cannot once we have tasted the richness of Shabbat delight. Seeing what is possible, we are renewed even in our weekday lives, bringing a bit of Shabbat with us, such that on the succeeding Shabbat we are able to see ourselves even more clearly, growing from week to week.

Questions for Reflection

1. Levi Yitzhak suggests that the extra soul on Shabbat makes us grieve going back to the weekday, particularly if we remain the person we previously were. Have you ever experienced Shabbat in that manner? Does having Shabbat prepare you for the week ahead or make it harder to go back? How are these two related?

2. Shabbat is a day of *teshuvah*—on it we return to our essential soul. Levi Yitzhak suggests that the *teshuvah* comes about because Shabbat points up the emptiness and vanity of our regular activities. Do you experience Shabbat as *teshuvah*? Which way does it work for you?

3. Since Shabbat happens so regularly, could this teaching offer us another way to see our spiritual lives in terms of a path, with regular moments of pause to consider where we are, of regular, ongoing growth that is also never finished?

Taking It into Your Life

In 1990 Rabbi Harlan J. Wechsler published a book titled *What's So Bad about Guilt? Learning to Live with It Since We Can't Live without It* (New York: Simon and Schuster). It is an investigation into the psychological role that guilt plays in our emotional lives and its significance for religious and moral growth. It comes to mind in relation to this text and the practice it suggests. That is, Levi Yitzhak believes that Shabbat offers us a perspective from which we can observe our mundane, weekday lives—and from that perspective we will see ourselves lacking. We will find our lives repulsive and so seek to change.

There is something harsh in his term—*ma'us*, abhorrent, revolting, repulsive. Yet, surely it applies to some or another act we have performed, some way in which we behaved in the past about which we feel great shame and guilt. The challenge when we see this aspect of our lives, or even those things that we find embarrassing or painful, is not to be overwhelmed by our negative reaction. We are neither to run away from the fact that we behaved in this manner nor to castigate and punish ourselves. To do so would be to become fixed in that moment in the past, unable to do any sort of *teshuvah*.

Rather, we are invited to recognize what was *ma'us* in the past and experience regret for that act or behavior. Regret incorporates a sense of sadness, the sting of recognition of having caused pain and damage to our own personal value, lessening ourselves in the world. But the emotion of regret is not so strong as to prevent recognition of who we are today. It allows us to say, "That was then. I certainly did that thing. But I do not today, and I am committed from now on not to do so again." Liberated in the moment from the bonds of the past, we are free to act differently now and into the future. And this process is one that happens in steps, over time, as we grow in awareness and in inner strength.

"You shall say, 'It is the Passover sacrifice to YHVH, [because God passed over the houses of the Israelites in Egypt when He smote the Egyptians, but saved our houses']" (Exod. 12:27).

Consider: we call the festival known in the Torah as "the festival of matzot" by the name *Pesach*. Where is there any suggestion in Scripture that we should call this festival by the name *Pesach*? Throughout the whole of the Torah this festival is called "the festival of matzot"! We can derive the answer from this verse: "I am my beloved's and my beloved is mine" (Song 6:3). We tell the praises of the blessed Holy One, and the blessed Holy One tells the praises of Israel. We experience this when we put on tefillin: in them is written the praise of the blessed Holy One; and the blessed Holy One puts on tefillin in which is written the praise of Israel.

This helps to explain what is taught in *Tanna deBei Eliyahu* (ch. 17), that it is incumbent on us to praise other Jews. God derives great pleasure when we praise them. This is connected to the tefillin, from which we are not to remove our attention (Menachot 36a). Indeed, it is a mitzvah to continuously engage in the mitzvah of tefillin. One way is to constantly tell the praises of Israel, to connect with the tefillin worn by the Master of the Universe, in which is written the praise of Israel (as the Sages teach, Berakhot 6a: "What is written in the tefillin of the Master of the Universe? 'And who is like Your people Israel ...' [1 Chron. 17:21]"). The other way is to tell the praises of the blessed Holy One, which is written in our tefillin, in which God is praised (in its four sections: Deut. 6:4–9; Deut. 11:13–21; Exod. 13:11–10; Exod. 13:11–16). In this manner we will constantly be telling the praises of God, and God will be telling our praises.

The name "festival of matzot" is praise of Israel, as we learn from Rashi on the verse, "And they baked unleavened cakes of the dough [that they had taken out of Egypt, for it was not leavened, since they had been driven out of Egypt and could not delay;] nor had they prepared any provisions [for themselves]" (Exod. 12:39):

> This tells the praise of Israel who did not say, "Should we go out into the wilderness without provisions?" but had faith and set out. This is echoed in Scripture: "I remember in your favor the devotion of your youth, your love as a bride—how you followed Me in the wilderness, in a land not sown" (Jer. 2:2)—what follows immediately after this? "Israel is holy to *YHVH*."

So, the name "festival of matzot" tells Israel's praise, since they promptly baked their cakes of matzah [and set out]. That is why Scripture calls this festival "matzot," as if God were praising Israel. But, we call the festival *Pesach*, in praise of God: "You shall say, 'It is a *pesach* offering to *YHVH*, who passed [*pasach*] over, etc.'" This is praise of God, as in "I am my beloved's and my beloved is mine."

An alternative interpretation of "You shall
say, 'It is the Passover sacrifice to *YHVH*
(*zevach pesach hu lYHVH*)" (Exod. 12:27).

When we speak words of Torah or prayer, this is *pesach*: *Pe"h Sa"Ch*
("the mouth speaks"). When we speak we must take care to make
the aspect of *hu* (that is, "He"—the hidden One) *lH'*, it should be
revealed.

FOR FURTHER THOUGHT

The first lesson could easily have been a pre-Passover sermon. It
includes a reference to Song of Songs, intimately connected to that
holiday, and also emphasizes the faithful love shown by Israel following God into the wilderness, as recalled by Jeremiah. Further
it emphasizes the key elements of the festival, implicit in its two
names—the festival of matzot and Pesach. While we might employ
historical analysis to answer Levi Yitzhak's initial question regarding
the distinction between these two terms, what he offers as an explanation is surely more moving.

Let us consider the framework he offers. Lying behind the Exodus narrative are traditions from the agrarian and herding roots of
Israelite culture. The offering of a springtime animal sacrifice from
the flocks (called *pesach*) was an expression of gratitude to God
for renewing life and sustenance after the winter. So, too, was the
ritual proscription of leavened cakes at the turning of the season to
spring and the ripening of the grain crops so essential to life. But
the narrative of the Torah links the *pesach* offering and the eating
of matzah to events in the Exodus. The *pesach* was in response to
God's dramatic acts in the last of the plagues, an acknowledgment
of our dependence on God for our liberation. The matzot were
prepared in haste, testimony to our faith in God as our liberator.
It is this to which Levi Yitzhak points, and the basis for his argument that each of the names of the festival refers either to God or
to Israel.

I included the short second lesson to reflect back on the first
(which I trust is what Levi Yitzhak would have wanted). In contrast
to the first, it does not focus solely on Passover. Rather, it speaks
in general of "Torah study and prayer," or possibly all devotional

speech. Whatever we speak with awareness should have the effect of bringing to the surface, making visible or apparent, that God is in everything, even when most hidden. Hasidic teachers regularly identify the third-person masculine singular pronoun *hu* as referring to the hidden aspect of God (and in Hebrew the third-person is called "the hidden one/*nistar*"). I think that Levi Yitzhak also wishes us to stay with the common shorthand reference to God—*H'* (which generally signifies *Hashem*, the Name of God). But, perhaps he wishes us to recognize it as the final *He* of the Divine Name *YHVH*, which signifies the *Shekhinah*. She is the aspect of God most present in this world, most evident in the material realm. Through our speech we are to bring the hidden aspect of God into relation with, present in, the dimension of revelation. This seems to resonate with the theme of the first lesson, in that it deepens the quality of "telling God's praise" with the matzah. It is a reminder, particularly when we ourselves finally sit at the Passover seder table, that what we are talking about is how God is found in all moments, in all things. That discussion is ultimately liberating, as it is echoed by God's praise for us, God's constant endeavor to help us out of servitude to full spiritual freedom.

 ## Questions for Reflection

1. When are you aware of being a person in whom God might glorify (in your deeds, in your attitudes, in the quality of your relationships)? When would God speak of you as "Israel, in whom I glory"? How do you (in your deeds, in your word, in the quality of your relationships) glorify God?

2. There is a Rabbinic association between the verse "And all the peoples of the land will see that the name of *YHVH* is inscribed on you, and they will fear you" (Deut. 28:10) and the tefillin placed on the head (Berakhot 6a). What do you imagine or hope will be recognized by other people as "the name of *YHVH* inscribed" on you? How might your behavior, your way of being, be a constant song of praise of God?

3. What do you sense is the difference between your speech in Torah and prayer and the rest of your talking? Do you think that there should be any connection between these two realms of expression? How might you make your "secular" expression into Torah and prayer—without becoming mute or unable to engage in normal conversation?

Taking It into Your Life

A key teaching of the Baal Shem Tov is that if we know that God is hidden, then God is not really hidden. The most profound form of exile is when we do not even know that God is hidden. Once we realize that "the whole earth is filled with God's glory" (Isa. 6:3) and "there is no place devoid of God," (Tikknei Zohar 91b), it becomes possible to perceive God in everything. God will be hidden in plain view.

This is a conundrum. In order for God to be present to us, God needs to be garbed, hidden in the physical manifestations of creation. Yet, creation has no independent meaning—its only value or meaning is as the screen pointing to God behind it. To work to perceive God is to empty the manifest world of its independent meaning. Yet, learning to see that all is God is to understand how even the garb in which God is clothed, even the screen behind which God hides, is yet God.

How to engage in this practice? We might take a note from the first lesson and focus on the mutuality of "I am my beloved's and my beloved is mine." In the first half of the verse, we are invited to devote our whole being to our beloved, to God. We hold nothing back for our own use, for our private enjoyment, for our personal glory. Everything is devoted to God, all is recognized as tribute to God, all is God. We—in our beings, in our thoughts, in our emotions—belong to God and are meant to be wholly integrated, connected, unified with God.

So, as you move through your day, begin with the awareness of dedication: everything you come upon—a thought, a feeling, a sensation, food, work, a vision, people—is devoted to God. In this thought and inner action, you are still in a position of duality—of you and God. But in pursuing this practice, you may more and more automatically find that whatever comes your way you experience as already belonging to God, already in God's dominion. Keep at this, seeking to sense how everything reveals God, how God is not hidden at all.

Then turn to "my beloved is mine." Sense how everything that reveals God, the fullness of God that is the whole of creation, flows back to you. Notice how you delight in God's glory, how you are sustained by the manifest and manifold forms in which God is garbed. The particulars of creation thrill the senses and engage us. God is hidden everywhere, and we are constantly (and pleasantly) surprised to find God over and over again.

What a wonderful game this is: not "hide-and-seek" but "hide-and-seek-and-find."

Beshallach

"Then sang Moses and the Israelites this
song to *YHVH*, they said to say: ['I will sing
to *YHVH*, for God has triumphed gloriously;
horse and driver God has hurled into the
sea']" (Exod. 15:1).

The primary experience of joy is in the heart. So, why do we feel
compelled to put words into song when we feel joy? The reason is that
the joy in the heart ends after a short time, an hour or so; but when we
put the joy we feel into words, those words affect us in turn, and the
joy expands.

This is how it was for Israel when the Sea split before them. They
wanted to increase their joy and remain delighting with their Creator,
and they didn't want this joy to cease. Therefore they opened to the
realm of speech, and divine beings joined in singing to Him, to increase
their joy. This is the intent of our verse: **"Then sang ... they said to say**
(*az yashir ... vayomeru leimor*)"—they **"said"** words in order that they
will be able **"to say"** even more. (If we do not interpret in this manner,
then the concluding word "to say" [*leimor*] makes no sense; all of the
people sang together, so to whom would this have been addressed?)

Another meaning, similar to how we have interpreted elsewhere:
The essence of delight and joy derives from meriting to serve our
Creator. God created upper and lower worlds without number; worlds
that also serve Him, the realms of the seraphim, *chayyot*, and *ophanim*.
For all that, "*Yah* chose Jacob" (Ps. 135:4), that we in particular also
should serve God. Therefore, the devotions that we offer our Creator
are themselves a great delight for us.

This is the meaning of our verse **"Then sang Moses and the
Israelites"**: What was their song, and what was their joy? That they
could recite **"this song to *YHVH*"**! They delighted in the fact that
they merited to sing before God. That is the sense of **"they said to say"**:
whatever they **"said"** emerged from the fact that they merited **"to say."**

Or we can interpret this verse as follows: Why does the word for "**sang**" appear in the Hebrew as if it were in the future tense (*yashir*), rather than in the past tense (*shar*)? With God's help, we will explain this in light of the teaching of the Baal Shem Tov regarding the verse "*YHVH* is your shadow" (Ps. 121:5). God relates to us similar to a shadow. However we move, so moves our shadow. This is how the blessed Creator acts in response to us, following our behavior in turn. So, when Israel were redeemed from Egypt and they sang this song, so at the same time did the blessed Holy One sing this song.

Further: the word "**sang**" (*yashir*) grammatically suggests making something happen, generating the action. So read the verse this way: "**Then sang**"—Israel brought about through their song—"**this song** *of YHVH*"—that the blessed Holy One should also sing "this song"—"**and they said to say**"—they said that God should say this song as well.

An alternative interpretation of the verse "**Then sang Moses...**": Rashi (on the basis of Sanhedrin 91b, which notes the odd formulation *yashir* in the future, versus *shar* in the past) comments, "This means to suggest that the idea to sing arose in thought."

How shall we understand Rashi? In general, when we see the greatness of the Creator, we respond trembling with fear and awe, and it is impossible to experience any pleasure in the midst of this terrible fear. But the truth is that God pours out blessings afterward, and that is surely pleasure. So, when we perceive God's greatness and are seized with fear, we can yet settle our hearts knowing that afterward we will receive great pleasure from this experience.

This pleasure has the quality of song. In this instance (at the Sea), Scripture reports, "The people feared *YHVH*" (Exod. 14:31), and in that moment of fear they were not able to derive pleasure. They were only able to bring to mind the delight that would follow. This explains Rashi's comment: in the moment of fear, it arose in their hearts to sing a song, and that is the delight that follows fear.

FOR FURTHER THOUGHT

These four teachings offer us a rich complex of ideas and experiences on which we might reflect. This verse offers Levi Yitzhak the opportunity to deepen our understanding of the role of song in the Hasidic community, how singing represents a spiritual practice.

Singing is not just fun, and it is not only to create an atmosphere in which something else might take place. It is a natural response to the experience of God and a necessary response to a relationship with God. Singing is a method for connecting directly to sensation, to focus awareness on the experience of the moment. It helps extend that awareness beyond its momentary arising, so that we might more fully enter into it. What is more, the experience of singing connects us to the source of that experience or awareness, to God. It both brings the power of God's vital force into us and the world and raises our awareness beyond our personal and immediate situation to connect with the divine realm.

Levi Yitzhak, in these four teachings, concretizes the power of singing by associating it with four experiences.

1. We sing to sustain and extend an otherwise ephemeral experience of awareness of God.
2. We sing in response to our awareness of the great blessing of being in relationship with God, of connecting with God.
3. We sing to energize the reciprocal flow of energy, represented in God's song in response, concretizing "arousal from below," bringing God's reply.
4. We sing as an expression of our awareness of the possibility of resting in impermanence, trusting in God's love and care even in the midst of fear and confusion.

It will pay to consider the question, is Levi Yitzhak talking about four different experiences or one experience that has four different aspects, four ways of entry? My sense is that it is the latter. The experience of joy arising in the heart may come from many sources— of them, though, we can surely list the following: doing mitzvot; having awareness of God's presence in our lives; having awareness of God being responsive to us in our lives; and trusting that God takes care of us, even when that is not apparent in the moment. When we feel the joy that arises from sensing God's presence in our lives, the pleasure that is generated in devotion to God, we surely want to extend and sustain that feeling and wish to encourage an even greater response from God. Reaching out to God to stimulate God's response, we thrill when it comes, speaking and singing of it. Trusting in God to remain present in our lives, we respond, attentive to the joy implicit even in suffering. In each instance, it is song—coming to voice, expressing our pleasure and delight concretely—that captures the spiritual dynamic and generates spiritual energy.

Questions for Reflection

1. Levi Yitzhak claims that by bringing experience (joy) into speech/song, we extend the experience. Has this been true in your life? When, how? What might it mean practically for you to connect inner experience/feelings with speech and song?

2. The image of God acting as our shadow is often meant to tell us that "what goes around comes around"—that is, how we behave toward others is how God will respond to us. How is this present in this lesson, and how is the message here different? How do you sense that your actions affect God? Can you "compel" God to act?

3. There is a difference between experiencing fear and experiencing the fear of God. Yet Levi Yitzhak seems to suggest that a lesson might be learned from the latter to help us deal with the former. How do you understand that fear of God prepares us for and is preliminary to joy? How might holding that awareness help you face the concrete fears that arise in your life today?

Taking It into Your Life

Singing seems to cover just about all aspects of a spiritual life: as the means to extend and make more manifest our spiritual awareness; as the expression of our joy; as a way to connect with God and thus affect the world; and as a method for responding to times of stress, anxiety, fear, or imbalance. There are surely physiological as well as psychological components to this. Hasidic spirituality intuits both of these elements and adds others. In particular, singing is one activity that connects us directly to the vital force, the *chayyut*, that enlivens us. The *chayyut* is divine energy; we might even say it is the essence of God in us—without it, we could not exist. As we move breath through our bodies in song—that is, in a focused, controlled manner—we come into more direct contact with that force. We sense it moving in and out of our bodies. We respond to the movement of the music—up and down the scale, higher and lower in pitch, louder and softer, faster and slower—and perceive our own spiritual experience. We come to know directly what the mystical tradition teaches: "The *chayyut* comes and goes, moves back and forth" (a play on Ezek. 1:14). When we are concentrated in our singing, we feel our whole bodies engaged, sensation spreading out through the limbs. It is as if the origin of the sound rises from our deepest core; the note starts from the soles of our feet and moves not only out through our mouths but also out the top of our heads. Singing can engage us fully and express completely the fullness of our spiritual awareness.

Take one or another of the teachings here as a model. Pay attention to your own experience. (When do you sense joy? When do you sense fear or another difficult emotion? When do you desire God's complementary response to your actions?) As soon as you notice the awareness, respond with "Hallelujah." Simply saying a word—as Levi Yitzhak tells us—helps extend the awareness. Repeat. Repeat and bring the word into song. Perhaps you know a melody for Psalm 150 or simply its concluding verse, "Let all that has breath praise God," *Kol haneshamah tehallel yah*. Perhaps you favor a wordless *niggun* to which you might add this word. Maybe another word and another melody come to mind. Whatever works for you, bring the experience into song. Sing not only one time through. Sing over and over. Sing out loud. Breathe deeply. Sense your body. Feel the vibrations of the voice and body in song. Listen as loudly as you sing—God sings along with you in response.

"*Yah* is my strength and might; this is my own salvation. [This is my God and I will glorify Him; the God of my father, and I will exalt Him]" (Exod. 15:2).

We Jews, through our prayers and good deeds, arouse compassion, great goodness, effulgent blessing to flow from God onto all the worlds. This is, indeed, God's desire: that through our good deeds God's goodness will extend to all the worlds.

But we must understand that when fulfilling God's will, even that is from God, as the Sages taught (Kiddushin 30b): "Were it not that the blessed Holy One provided help, no one would be able to stand against the evil inclination [*yetzer hara*]." Thus, everything is from God; even our capacity to fulfill God's will and to draw down goodness ultimately comes from God. So what does it mean to say that God desires that we, through our good deeds, should draw down blessing and that God's goodness then come about through our deeds? Doesn't everything come from God, and God helps us to do His will, to draw down God's goodness on all the worlds? And, so, in the end, isn't it God who does the good, and isn't everything from God?

The following was a favorite teaching of my teacher and rabbi, the sainted R. Dov Baer, and it can help us to understand. Think in terms of this analogy: We might give a difficult problem to one of our children to solve, asking the child to explain this or that passage in a sacred text. Now, even though the child does not have the understanding to answer the question him- or herself, we help the child to understand it, and we derive great pleasure from doing so. Even though our child doesn't understand the matter until we explain it him or her, we get pleasure attributing the solution and understanding to our child. And so God deals with us. God is our parent. Even though all of our efforts ultimately rest on God's help; and were it not that the blessed Holy One helped us we would not be able to succeed (against the *yetzer hara*); and we would not be able to accomplish God's will without God's help—God still desires that our efforts be attributed to us. When we do that which draws down God's blessing and great goodness, God calls this our doing.

Accordingly, this is how we can understand this verse: "**Yah is my strength and might**"—the strength and power and might that we have to do God's will, and to thank and praise and to sing before God, to draw down God's great goodness for us and all the worlds, all is from God. Nevertheless: "**this is my own salvation**"—God attributes the salvation we experience to us. This is the sense of "**this is my own**" (*vayehi li*)—even though everything is from God, still "**this is my own**"—God attributes it to our doing.

FOR FURTHER THOUGHT

Here Levi Yitzhak confronts the conundrum of the non-dualistic theology of the Baal Shem Tov and the Maggid of Mezritch. All is God. Physical reality is real only to the extent that we recognize it as a manifestation of God, and not as having separate existence. As such, physical reality doesn't really exist as we perceive it; rather, all is God. This applies to us as well. We, like the rest of physical reality, do not exist except as manifestations of the Divine. Yet, our sense of being separate from God—and from other people, and from nature—is both necessary and false. It is necessary to enable us to perceive anything—and thus have the capacity to recognize God as God and to desire to serve God, to act with will. But the goal of this endeavor is to discover that there is nothing but God and that our sense of separate self is false. The more we become aware of how all is God, the more clearly we see through physical reality to perceive that all is God, the more we lose a sense of separate self, the more we recognize that all is just "God God-ding God's Self" in this moment. God desires that we come to know God, not as separate beings, but as the expression of God's will. Yet, to do so, we have to act as if we are separate and as if we act according to our own will, choosing to serve God.

Levi Yitzhak's suggested way out, based on our verse, may seem slick (after all, on some level the whole argument is circular and self-justifying). But it is also consistent with the whole of Hasidic spirituality. That is, God created the world so that God might become known as loving and compassionate. Further, God could not fully manifest as Sovereign without beings who might recognize God as such. So God had to create a world that could sustain itself in some sort of separate awareness. Yet, ultimately, God wants that world to finally be reabsorbed into God's Being, for the consciousness of all creation to be One. As loving parent, God steps back—temporarily—so that we might develop our awareness, our capacity to think, feel, perceive, and understand, crediting us with those capacities so that we might gain confidence. And this is the case in our own lives: we find as we mature that our parents were much wiser than we thought when we were younger, helping us in ways we were unaware of or that we chose earlier to ignore. So we might also discover that what we thought we did "all on our own" we did in concert, with God's help. Indeed, all we ever do is with God's help. Ultimately, should we learn to see clearly, should we succeed in purifying our hearts, we would become "transparent," and it will be clear that all we do is God.

 ## Questions for Reflection

1. Think about R. Dov Baer's analogy. Were you ever in such a situation, as a child or a parent? How easy did you find it as a child to sense that you were actually solving the problem? When did you feel that your parent was doing all the work or that your success was empty? How easy did you

find it as a parent to draw your child out, to help him or her understand when the problem was truly beyond his or her comprehension? How did you avoid creating frustration or inducing a sense of failure? What does it take to instill a sense of competence rather than dependence, a sense of engagement and interest rather than laziness and avoidance? How does your understanding of the analogy help you investigate your own relationship with God?

2. In the long term, do you think that it is conducive to reaching God's ends—that we should realize that all is God—for God to let us think "this is my own salvation"? Is this balanced at all for you by remembering "*Yah* is my strength and might"? Why or why not?

3. How do you sense that your good deeds bring about the flow of goodness from God into the world?

Taking It into Your Life

The issues of consciousness and self-consciousness are problematic. The danger of growing awareness of God is that it may induce a degree of self-consciousness: "Look at how deeply I have come to perceive the nature of creation!" With each step along the path of spiritual growth, we risk just such thoughts—slipping down several levels in one mindless musing. False modesty, however, is equally damaging. To deny that we have power or to deny that we have come to a newer, deeper perception would prevent us from acting honestly in the moment. We could play "After you, Alphonse" with God all day, and in the end nothing would get done.

Levi Yitzhak offers us a method to try to remain balanced while still opening and growing in our spiritual lives. First we declare, "*Yah* is my strength and might." We turn to our lives, we look deeply at the unfolding from moment to moment, and come to recognize that without God as our help, without God's vital force pulsing through us, we would not exist. But why do we exist? We exist to effect God's end: that life and goodness may most effectively shower down on all creation. We have the power to do that—because we exist, because we are aware of God and of God's help—and should we not act, the world will be the poorer.

As you make your way through the day, pay attention to the shifting inner awareness that arises in each changing situation. When do you feel fully confident and competent? In that moment, turn your attention to God and respond, "*Yah* is my strength and might." Attribute your success and power to God. In moments of uncertainty, of unease or insecurity, turn your attention to God and respond, "But this is my own salvation." Attribute your capacity to remain present, to move forward, to the power that God gives you. Watch and notice when you are clear about which response to apply in the moment and when you feel in between. What does that tell you? Over time, which phrase do you feel is more prevalent? Does it remain the same? What is your experience?

"For liberators will go up on Mount Zion to judge Mount Esau; [and dominion shall be YHVH's]" (Obad. 1:21).

We read in the Talmud (Sukkah 52a):

> R. Yehudah expounded: In the time-to-come the blessed Holy One will bring forth the evil inclination [*yetzer hara*] and slay it in the presence of the righteous and the wicked. To the righteous it will have the appearance of a towering mountain, and to the wicked it will have the appearance of a hair. These will weep and those will weep; the righteous will weep saying, "How were we able to overcome such a towering mountain?" The wicked will weep saying, "How is it that we were unable to conquer this hair?"

So, in the time-to-come, when the blessed Holy One does miracles and wonders for us, and the nations make battle against us, oppressing us, at that time the *yetzer hara* will surely seem to them like a towering mountain. If it only seemed like a hair, they would surely allow us to go to our land, and they would not oppress or pressure us. So, certainly the *yetzer hara* appears to them like a mountain, even though in truth it is only a hair. It is for this reason that God comes to judge them.

This is the meaning of our verse: "**Liberators will go up**" in the future "**on Mount Zion**": "liberators" are righteous Israel, to whom the *yetzer hara* appears like a mountain. They will go up this mountain "**to judge** [the] **Mount** [of] **Esau**"—they will judge (Esau) because they (Esau) perceived the *yetzer hara* to be a mountain, when they will ultimately come to see that it is only a thread.

185

FOR FURTHER THOUGHT

Here we have an example of how, in the Hasidic literature, the *yetzer hara* is not so much an entity, an opposing being, a force of its own, as it is misperception. This misperception may be the result of willful ill will, of unexamined passion or desire, of fear or anger or jealousy or greed—but it is still only misperception. The nations—Esau—oppress the people of Israel because they sense that somehow Israel's well-being stands before them like a mountain, over against them, blocking them, resisting them. If they only knew that they could live in peace with Israel and that the effort of toleration, acceptance, and compassion takes as little effort as lifting a hair, they would be amazed. But apparently they do not see this, and so they will be judged.

Do pay attention to the two different "mountains" in this teaching. "Righteous Israel" ascend the mountain that they perceive in the future—their deeper perception of what it took to overcome the *yetzer hara*. It is from that vantage point that they will judge Esau for their misperception of the true nature of the *yetzer hara*. That is, even now, for both Israel and Esau, the *yetzer hara* is neither mountain nor hair; it is merely what stands before us in each moment, demanding clarity of vision, openness of heart, willingness to let go of our story and ask again, "What is really true?" This may be a difficult practice, but it is not so great as to be a "mountain." The righteous simply undertake the practice and from it overcome the seduction and misperception of the *yetzer hara*. It is merely what is demanded to live a righteous life; it is just what is called for in the moment. Those who are not righteous, in this sense, feel always that they are faced by mountains, that what is asked of them in the moment is more than they can do. Yet what is asked may simply be to lift a hair.

It is interesting to think about what Levi Yitzhak had in mind, writing at the end of the eighteenth century, when he imagines a future messianic Jewish immigration to the Land of Israel. Surely he was aware of the significant Hasidic migration to Safed, Tiberias, and other holy cities in Palestine. He could not have imagined (and who knows, perhaps he too would have protested) the Zionist movement that would arise not even fifty years or so after his death. But his words are so evocative and prescient.

The Zionist interpretation of this text is complex in our contemporary situation. Holding on to a story of innocence—à la Levi Yitzhak—is just as likely to cause continued suffering to the Jews as it is to Esau (and Yishmael). What may be more important is to hear in Levi Yitzhak's narrative a caution to us in all of our dealings: we cannot by default count ourselves to be "righteous Israel." We may very well be closer to the nations, to Esau, who are unable to see clearly and are overwhelmed by what we perceive to be the mountain standing before us. If only we could let go of our story, if only we were prepared to face our fears before confronting others, we might find that we can easily move forward, as easily as picking a hair off our shirt.

Note: Levi Yitzhak refers to this verse from Obadiah in the middle of his commentary on Exodus because this verse appears in the traditional prayer book following the morning recitation of the Song of the Sea. There may be no connection in the text of the Torah, but the compilers of the siddur created a liturgical association. The Song itself ends, "You will bring them and plant them in Your own mountain, the place You made to dwell in, O *YHVH*, the sanctuary, Adonai, which Your hands established. *YHVH* shall reign forever and ever" (Exod. 15:17–18). To this the siddur appends: "For sovereignty belongs to *YHVH*, who rules the nations. For liberators shall go up on Mount Zion to judge Mount Esau; and dominion shall be *YHVH*'s. *YHVH* shall be sovereign over all the earth. On that day *YHVH* shall be One and God's name One" (Ps. 22:29; Obad. 1:21; Zech. 14:9). In this manner, the siddur extends the sentiment of the Song from our people's beginning to the eschatological end of time.

 ## Questions for Reflection

1. Levi Yitzhak connects the term *moshi'im* to "righteous Israel." In our translation we have this word as "liberators," but it could mean "deliverers" or "saviors" or "victors." Which of these terms would you apply to the righteous who resist the *yetzer hara*? What do you imagine qualifies these righteous to then serve in that capacity? When, how, why? Which

do you think might apply to you? Is this a role that you might like to play? Why or why not?

2. How do you understand the nature of the *yetzer hara*? Is it an entity that stands outside of the human heart, psyche, and soul? What do you imagine it might mean to "slay" the *yetzer hara*? In your own experience of grappling with the *yetzer hara*, would it be better to work with the *yetzer hara*, to see if it can be subdued or redirected, or for it to be slain altogether? When, how, why?

3. In this passage, Levi Yitzhak suggests that the *yetzer hara* is closer to warped or incorrect perception than it is to an external entity or force. What does this mean to you? What do you "see" as standing in your way of doing the right thing all the time? When do you sense that you are facing a mountain, and when do you feel that your opposition is merely as flimsy as a hair?

Taking It into Your Life

One summer at camp, my stepson went on a long bicycle trip. He reflected on his experience, particularly regarding how to approach the difficult hills. His sense was that it was better to work with the bike, to continue pedaling and finding a way to make it up the hill, than to look ahead and get off the bike at the bottom and walk up. He felt that it took more energy to walk up, and that most often, the people who made the effort found that they could ride up (or most of the way) and enjoyed both the sense of accomplishment as well as the pleasure at the top of the hill.

I found his reflections to be a valuable spiritual teaching. Developing composure, insight, balance, perseverance, compassion, and open-heartedness is not easy. But it is possible. What holds us back, most often, is our own fear, our doubts, our misperceptions of what is called for and what we are capable of doing.

As a way to begin to notice how our minds and hearts work when confronted by a challenge, we need to practice in a controlled manner. Here is one way to approach this process of observation and discovery. It is a simple physical exercise, but it may also be taxing, and so revelatory.

Stand at ease in the middle of the room. Warm up your arms by swinging them easily as you twist your body, allowing one to flap in front of your body as the other flaps in back, switching from side to side as you twist. After a minute or so of this exercise, continue to warm up by raising your arms out to the sides from your shoulders, extending out beyond the fingertips. Slowly rotate your arms in circles, first forward, then back.

When you feel that your arms have warmed up, that they are loose and easy, and you have full sensation in the arms, continue in this manner: bring your arms up in front of you, palms down, shoulder height. Hold this position. Continue holding this position. Remain with your arms out in front of you. Observe. Watch carefully the sensations that arise in your arms and shoulders. What feels like effort? What feels like strain? What feels like pain? What prompts the inner thought "I can't do this"? What prompts the thought "I don't like this"? When do you begin to make deals with yourself, thinking, "I'll count to ten and then I'll stop," or the like? Can you continue beyond that count?

Notice what happens to your breathing as you hold this pose longer. What do you notice about the flow and flux of breath as an indicator of challenges? When you sense shifts in your breathing, how do you respond to these fluctuations? What inner voices do you detect? Do you try to control your breath or use it as a way to remain present? How can staying attentive to breath, as physical sensations shift, help you sustain your presence in this practice?

Continue as long as you possibly can, and then investigate if it is possible to continue beyond that limit. What do you learn about your perceptions? What do you learn about how your perceptions affect your decision-making process? When did this effort feel like "a hair," and when did it feel like "a mountain"? Which was true, and when?

Yitro

"In the third month after the Israelites had gone forth from the land of Egypt, on this very day they entered the wilderness of Sinai" (Exod. 19:1).

Consider: "Rav Yoseph was known as 'Sinai'" (Berakhot 64a), since he had an encyclopedic knowledge of the laws, holding within himself all of the traditions, the whole of the Talmud. It was for this reason that they called him "Sinai."

From this we learn that the term "Sinai" suggests total inclusiveness, for that is the place where all of Torah, the totality of divine speech, is located. Similarly, we know that "voice" (*kol*) is made up of several different components: fire, wind, water. We cannot conceive of all that God's speech might contain. For God there is no difference between "voice" and "speech," since God's speech can contain everything. This was our experience at Sinai, where we heard, "I am [*YHVH*]" (*anokhi*)" (Exod. 20:2) and "You shall have no other [gods before Me]" (*lo yehiyeh lekha*) (20:3), [the first two commandments] at one time from God's mouth. These two utterances contained the whole of the Torah. But no other mouth could accomplish this; human speech can express only one thing at a time.

But when we believe that our very breath and the words that emerge from our mouths arise from the power of the vital energy of the Creator, and that the spirit of God is speaking through us, if we then connect speech to voice, and voice to thought—to the spiritual source and divine vitality—then even though normal speech cannot contain more than one meaning, in this instance it has the capacity to carry several matters on several levels of awareness. This speech then bursts into several parts, since it is divine speech. We witness this in the Torah: of every word of Moses written in the Torah, each word is made up of several matters that then separate out from it, which can be interpreted in many different lights. So, too, every word of the

Tannaim and *Amoraim* contains many matters, since their speech was connected to the source, to divine power.

"Jerusalem, mountains surround it, and *YHVH* surrounds His people" (Ps. 125:2). "Jerusalem" is the Community of Israel (*Knesset Yisrael*; the *Shekhinah*), who is the container of all speech. It is surrounded by mountains, which is to say, the Patriarchs. The sources of holiness in the spiritual, supernal realms surround the Community of Israel. Similarly, we must cleave to the source, so that the source can then illuminate that branch, without any intervening barrier, without any intermixing of the negative. We must connect ourselves with God's holy qualities (*middot*), and we each must do loving-kindness in the world. But the key is that this be full loving-kindness (*chasadim tovim*), the loving-kindness that flows from the source: supernal love (*chesed elyon*), without any negative in it. Even though loving-kindness is good in itself, it can still be mixed with the negative, as the Sages taught (*Midrash Zuta, Kohelet* 7:16):

> Resh Lakish taught: Anyone who becomes compassionate toward the cruel eventually becomes cruel to the compassionate. [From whom do we learn this? From Saul. With regard to Amalek, Scripture reports, "But Saul and the people had compassion (*vayachamol*) [on Agag]" (1 Sam. 15:9), and then later, regarding the priests at Nob, Scripture reports, "He put Nob, the town of the priests, to the sword: men and women, children and infants, oxen, asses, and sheep—[all] to the sword" (22:19). Toward the compassionate he showed no compassion.]

Our loving-kindness must be completely good. So similarly are we to employ our capacity for rigor: we have to overcome our inclination (*yetzer*), subjecting all the negative forces in us to the good. When we then turn to true devotion, we must connect our selves to the source of Truth that is many-sided. We must connect to all of our qualities (*middot*)—our love and rigor, and our compassion, when we come to that point of truth. Then we will comprise all three lines, since Truth contains everything. This is the quality of the letter *shin*, which is made up of three lines.

This, then, is how we can understand our verse: "**in the third month**"—this is the quality of Truth, which is the letter *shin*, woven of the three strands of loving-kindness, rigor, and glory (*chesed, gevurah, tiferet*). When we attain the quality of Truth, we exit all aspects of the negative and are released from all limitations (*meitzarim*). This is what

Scripture meant in reporting "**the Israelites had gone forth from the land of Egypt**" (*mitzrayim*)—they went out from under all forms of servitude to the negative. In that manner all aspects of the negative were subjugated to the good and the Truth. That is the sense of "**on this very day**"—it was with that degree of purity, which is the essence of holiness that "**they entered the wilderness of Sinai.**" They attained the capacity of speech that is "Sinai," speech that contains all things. When we connect with the all-inclusive quality, then our speech is transformed to the quality of "Sinai" containing everything; then by our speech we are able to bring about all sorts of good blessings for the Community of Israel, all sorts of loving-kindness and salvation for the Children of Israel.

FOR FURTHER THOUGHT

This verse invites us to investigate how we can experience Sinai in our lives. That is, in its characteristic manner Torah here says that the people arrived "on this very day" (*bayom hazeh*) at the wilderness of Sinai. We are challenged to understand how what happened in the past can be happening now, this very day, in our lives as well.

Levi Yitzhak offers us a very sophisticated, yet classically Hasidic approach. He turns to the event of Sinai, which was speech, direct communication from God to Israel. God spoke—a very human act, perhaps uniquely so. Still, God's speech is different from human speech, in that it can communicate more than one thing at a time; one speech-act can communicate more than one content. Yet, since it is speech, it must in some way be related to our human form of communication. So Levi Yitzhak tells us how we might share in the divine form of speech. He invites us to practice lifting our awareness to so purify our consciousness and intention that even our human speech might carry more than one meaning—something that Moses, the *Tannaim*, the *Amoraim*, and (we assume) the contemporary tzaddik can do.

In this, we are to work at unifying our inner intention. All that we do must be devoted to the good: our loving-kindness, our rigor and limitation, our compassion must be purified so that it is truly good. In this regard, Levi Yitzhak's reference to the *Midrash Zuta* is challenging. He reminds us that compassion is not apathy, nor does seeing the good in all things allow us to stand by, accepting all things. Loving-kindness and compassion must be balanced with rigor yet devoted solely to the good, without any hidden negatives. Levi Yitzhak again represents this form of unification in terms of language, in the form of the letter *shin*, made up of three lines joined together. This symbolizes the balancing of loving-kindness and rigor in the central quality of truth, of compassion.

Finally, Levi Yitzhak presents the image of Jerusalem surrounded by hills. Jerusalem, in kabbalistic symbolism, is the tenth *sephirah Malkhut*, the *Shekhinah*, and *Knesset Yisrael*, the Community of Israel. The lowest of the *sephirot* is connected to the quality of speech, the particular articulation of phonemes, words, and sentences. It is an expression of rigor and limitation, since it cuts up the undifferentiated, totally inclusive flow of sound, that is, voice (*kol*), represented by *Tiferet*. In this image, we are to surround our speech, purifying it with the power of the Patriarchs, who themselves represent loving-kindness, rigor, and compassion. In this manner, we connect *Shekhinah* to *Tiferet* and raise it all to the highest level of Thought. This is all to the end of purifying our speech, so that it might participate more fully in the totally inclusive flow of the divine vitality, coming closer to expressing the undifferentiated wholeness of divine Truth.

 ## Questions for Reflection

1. When are you able to express in words all that you know in your heart or soul? In your experience, what facilitates that form of communication, and what impedes it?

2. Instrumental music is not a product of human voice, yet it is equally evocative, emotionally, and spiritually moving. How is your experience of instrumental music different from your experience of words that are sung? When, how, why? How might the capacity for instrumental music to contain many different "meanings" help you understand "voice/sound" (*kol*) as being all-inclusive of meaning, while "speech" (*dibbur*) is limited, limiting? What sort of speech have you found that can contain multiple meanings—and still be meaningful?

3. Levi Yitzhak teaches that in bringing the qualities of *chesed*, *gevurah*, and *tiferet* together and directing them only to the good, we are able to touch the all-inclusive totality of Truth. Have you ever had such an experience? When, how? What was it like? Why do you think that Levi Yitzhak

(and the Hasidic tradition) considers this speech a source of power, one that can even redirect divine plans?

Taking It into Your Life

The well-known yoga chant *om* can be spelled, and also pronounced, *A-U-M*. The movement of sound originates in the diaphragm, at the foundation of the breath. In moving up the windpipe, it produces vibrations in the larynx; the sound is then shaped by the throat and oral cavity at the rear of the mouth. This is the "Ah" sound. The sound then moves forward, shaped by the cheeks, the roof of the mouth, the tongue, and finally the somewhat pursed lips to produce the "U" sound. The lips then close, cutting off the airy vowel sound produced by the unimpeded breath, and shifting vibration to the lips, teeth, nasal cavities, and possibly chest, producing the "M" sound. Doing this, we will have expressed one continuous sound without pronouncing an actual word.

Experiencing this sound in our bodies may help us understand the concept of "voice" (*kol*) as undifferentiated, all-inclusive sound. Clearly, at any point in producing the chant, if we were to bring our teeth together, shape our lips differently, or move our tongue or cheeks, we would make a different sound. Depending on the degree of change in the shape of the oral cavity, we will likely come closer to articulating a phoneme, the beginning of speech. Further, Levi Yitzhak teaches, "'Voice' (*kol*) is made up of several different components: fire, wind, water." If you hold your hand before your mouth as you make this sound, you will easily sense that these three elements are present in your breath—but it will not be quite so easy to sense them when you hold your hand in front of your mouth as you speak.

Stand at ease, allowing your shoulder blades to slide down your back, tucking your tailbone slightly, and letting your head float easily at the top of your spine. Tilt your head back slightly, so that the flow of air from your diaphragm up through the windpipe and out the mouth is nearly straight, unimpeded at the top of the throat. Feel your diaphragm moving up and down. Draw breath down to the bottom of your lungs and then let it flow out, making the sound of the sea as it passes out through your mouth. Feel where the constriction in your throat produces that sound. Slowly, as you take the next several breaths, attempt to lower the source of that sound into your chest and diaphragm. Allow yourself to simply articulate a low, "belly-produced" *aaahhhh* sound. After that sound is rooted in your diaphragm, slowly sense its movement through the chest and oral cavity so that you can, with slight adjustment, begin to shape the *ah* to *uuu*. When that movement is established, close your mouth and hum *mmmm*. Finally, connect this process to your inner awareness: your intention to manifest the most balanced expression of love, strength, and compassion, to be an expression of the Truth. Repeat.

Practice this as a form of prayer.

"*YHVH* said to Moses, 'Go down, warn the people [not to break through to *YHVH* to gaze, lest many of them perish. The priests also, who come near *YHVH*, must stay pure, lest *YHVH* break out against them.'] But Moses said to *YHVH*, ['The people cannot come up to Mount Sinai, for You warned us, saying, "Set bounds about the mountain and sanctify it."'] So *YHVH* said to him, 'Go down, [and come back together with Aaron; but let not the priests or the people break through to come up to *YHVH*, lest He break out against them']" (Exod. 19:21–24).

Rashi interprets [God's second instruction to go down (Exod. 19:24)], "'Go down': Warn the people a second time. We rouse someone before the deed, then we rouse them again at the time of the deed."

Moses had such deep and abiding faith in the words of the blessed Creator that, with great energy, he would fulfill God's words as soon as he heard the command from the mouth of the Creator. Now Moses was certain that just as he trusted the words of the blessed Creator and would not trespass His words, so was the faith and heartfelt behavior of every other Jew. But we are not at the same level as Moses, who knew God face-to-face; who saw the greatness of the blessed Creator always; whose faith sustained him in keeping the commands that issued forth from God, never to trespass His will. He was always attached to God and at a high level of enlightenment.

This is revealed in the verses above. "**YHVH said to Moses, 'Go down, warn the people.' But Moses said to YHVH, 'The people cannot come up to Mount Sinai, for You warned us.'**" That is, Moses said to

God, "Why should I return to say this to them again? You already commanded them once, and certainly they will not trespass Your words!" It was inconceivable to Moses that there might be anyone in the world who would violate the command of the blessed Creator, since he was at such a high level of spiritual attainment. He was certain that it would be impossible for anyone to contravene the command of the blessed Creator. That is why "**YHVH said to him, 'Go down'**" a second time. God said to Moses, "You are so advanced that you are always attached to Me. Therefore it is hard for you to imagine that anyone might transgress My commandment. '**Go down**'—that is, go down from your high attainment—and see that at the lowest level it is possible to trespass My command. Therefore, you need to go a second time to warn the people."

FOR FURTHER THOUGHT

The starting point for this teaching in the Torah is easy to understand. In Exod. 19:12, in preparation for the momentous day, God tells Moses, "You shall set bounds for the people round about, saying, 'Beware of going up the mountain or touching the border of it. Whoever touches the mountain shall be put to death.'" So, in our passage, Moses is puzzled by God's second instruction. Levi Yitzhak recognizes this problem too and adds a dimension to the narrative that we might not have sensed before: Moses may not be asking the simple question of why God repeated the instructions. He is asking because he cannot understand the need for any instruction from God to be repeated.

This is certainly a challenge to anyone who holds a position of leadership, and it is also a challenge to us in our own behavior and practice. Aren't there times when we believe we have given instructions or told someone something, only to find that they have not understood or have not made plans to fulfill our directions? Haven't there been times that we have not paid attention, that we have experienced our own inner reservations or hesitations, and needed to be prodded, reminded, or roused to do what is called for in the moment? In this instance, God tells Moses that if he truly wishes to lead and serve the people, he needs to "go down" to their level, to truly understand "where they are at" and so be able to communicate with them in the manner they need.

Note that Rashi's interpretation regarding rousing (*mezarzim*) the people appears connected to Exod. 19:24, the second time Moses is instructed to "go down." The first time, in verse 21, Rashi ignores the instruction to "go down" and comments only that Moses is to "warn them that they are not to come up the mountain." Regarding Moses's response in verse 23, Rashi expands: "'The people are not able': I do not need to warn them; they have been warned and waiting for the past three days; and they are not able to go up, since they do not have permission." Levi Yitzhak explains the circumstances according to Rashi's commentary on verses 21 and 23. Yet, he chose to quote Rashi's comment on verse 24. What was he pointing to? There is a tradition (Yoma 28b) that "those who are zealous [*zerizim*] in doing mitzvot strive to do them as soon as possible." We learn this from Abraham, who arose at first light to saddle his donkey to fulfill the divine command at the *Akedah* (Gen. 22:3). And, in turn, we learn that although it is permissible to perform the mitzvah of circumcision any time on the eighth day, those who are zealous strive to do so as soon as possible. But not all people have the quality of energetic arousal (*zerizut*). It takes most people time to internalize what is called for; they need to be warned that something is coming and then reminded when the time has arrived. Moses, whose consciousness was perfected and whose devotion was pure, did not need such help. God's instructions were to help the people develop their capacity to be more like Abraham, more like Moses.

Questions for Reflection

1. Rashi offers useful pedagogy; Levi Yitzhak, instruction for leaders. How do you resonate with his image of Moses's inability to conceive of what passes for "normal" among the Israelites (and most people)? What practices, mitzvot, and behaviors do you assume "everyone" does? How do you respond when you meet people who don't? What reminders do you need, and what have you found others need?

2. Levi Yitzhak describes the situation in which the "word" of instruction comes directly "from God's mouth." Yet, we "only" hear God's word from Torah. Do you sense that this gives us more or less incentive to fulfill the "word" immediately? Are there other modalities in which we "hear God's command" and must immediately respond? What happens when we follow that voice yet others do not accompany us?

3. Levi Yitzhak puts the instructions to "go down" to the lowest level in God's mouth. How does this affect how you hear Levi Yitzhak's tone at the end of this selection—that is, is he condescending toward the Israelites or loving? In this version of the story, how does God feel about our "normal" behavior versus Moses's? How should we feel? Should we strive to be like Moses? Why or why not?

Taking It into Your Life

Just as mindfulness helps us maintain a balanced awareness without being distracted or seduced by the myriad thoughts that cross our minds, it also helps us make good choices. That is, we may experience physical urges, feelings in the body that prompt a response. For example, when we feel an itch, we often spontaneously, and largely without thought or decision, move to scratch it. Or we hear a fly buzzing and wave our hand to brush it away. Another example: we sense something as hunger and respond by getting something to eat. Or we feel fatigue and reach for something caffeinated. Sometimes each of these responses may be appropriate, but for the most part, we simply act without thinking, without awareness.

Acting without thinking is like thinking without thinking: both are thoughtless, mindless. Just as we hope to become more mindful of our inner lives, attending to the arising of feelings and thoughts, investigating what is true in the moment, so we can become mindful of our actions. So, with our thoughts we seek to steady our attention opening the possibility of choice in how to respond to the flood of feelings, images, plans and memories, so that we might direct our attention toward compassion for ourselves or others. Similarly, we can bring our attention to our physical actions, to move with integrity, with intention. With practice, we can become more able to bring awareness to our actions, so that what we do is what we fully intend, so that our behavior—from the most minor movement to our grandest gesture—will arise from intention, bringing the greatest harmony and balance to our lives and the lives of those around us.

Let us apply this to eating. Even as we plan for and anticipate special meals, much more of the time we simply dive in and eat. For this practice, begin (if possible) with the food preparation. Engage with the food, noticing its color, shape, texture, smell. Appreciate its current, unprepared state. Acknowledge your appreciation for its existence now. As you go through the steps of preparation, pay attention to the movements of your body. Notice what is required to cut, chop, mix, grate, stir, measure, and so on. Each of these acts can engage your whole body and focus your awareness.

When the food is ready, set it before you and observe its cooked/prepared state. Notice change. Notice the response of your body—salivation, growling stomach, anticipation, frustration, happiness, disappointment. Take a first bite, chew slowly, noticing all aspects of taste and flavor. Notice the physical actions required to bring a bite to your mouth. Notice the change in your mouth, where you sense flavors, the urge to swallow. Have you taken more food on your fork before you have finished this bite? Developing awareness in this manner can extend to all of our other actions. Each moment of specific consciousness supports us in making clear, intentional choices in how we move in our lives, in how our bodies express the truth we seek to live. Indeed, we may be able to attain the level of Moses, whose actions were fully consistent with his intention, to do God's will.

"I [*Anokhy*], YHVH, am your God [who brought you out of the land of Egypt, the house of bondage]" (Exod. 20:2).

The Sages taught: "[*ANoKh"Y* represents the initial letters of the words] Pleasant Speech Given in Writing (*A"mirah N"e'imah K"etivah Y"ehivah*)" (Shabbat 105a). Consider this in light of the teaching that we are to strive to fulfill the verse "I place *YHVH* before me always" (Ps. 16:8).

Now, it is impossible to hold our attention always on God. But, when we serve God in order to bring ease and delight to the blessed Creator, this delight itself arouses us to connect our thought with the blessed Creator. *Amirah* is speech (*dibbur*), which cannot be constant, whereas that which is written is permanent.

So understand now the lesson above: "Pleasant Speech" (*amirah ne'imah*)—this is when we serve the Creator in order to bring God delight (*ne'imah* is a way of speaking of delight)—"Given in Writing" (*ketivah yehivah*)—this is a way of arousing us always, in each moment, to connect our thoughts to the blessed Creator.

FOR FURTHER THOUGHT

This lesson echoes one from *Beshallah*, in that it focuses on the difficulty of sustaining inner awareness. In the earlier lesson, the instruction was to bring delight into speech and song to sustain it; here the response is to bring the otherwise transitory delight of serving God into a more permanent form, something like writing. Yet rather than our writing something, it is our contact with written sacred speech that is eternal (i.e., Scripture) and always a delight that will help us develop a sustained awareness of God (*devekut*).

This is a curious lesson. It represents one pole of the Hasidic spiritual awareness: the goal is to attain a degree of attachment (*devekut*) to the Divine, and to be in that state always. Yet, it is also well known and acknowledged that "continuous delight is no longer delightful" and "the vital force [*chayyut*] comes and goes." This lesson suggests that while it may not be possible to be continuously connected to God, always bringing God delight, it may yet be possible to be engaged in the effort, always aware of that as our goal—and for that to be delightful.

The quotation from Shabbat 105a with which Levi Yitzhak begins his commentary is part of a more extended section that opens with the question "From where in the Torah do we learn that *notarikon* is a legitimate method of interpretation?" R. Yohanan and the Sages offer different interpretations. We might expect that the Rabbinic willingness to engage in word- and letter-play, imputing meaning through letter associations (i.e., *notarikon*), would attract a Hasidic teacher. Letters are the building blocks of Creation, the fundamental elements of speech. Prayer and Torah study are key practices in Hasidic life because they are verbal; they are primary means to sanctify speech, to raise the letters of Creation back to their source. In the Talmud, R. Yohanan learns the legitimacy of *notarikon* from the word *Anokhi*, reading it as "*A"na N"aphshi K"etavit Y"ahavit*," "I Myself have written my spirit into this which I have given you." Levi Yitzhak found the teaching of the Sages to be more meaningful here. Thus, he chooses to point us to the significance of our speech (*amirah*), that it has the capacity to bring God delight (*ne'imah*). That pleasure will be sustained longer, will have greater effect, when we connect it to the writing that God gave us (*ketivah yehivah*)—or, alternatively, when we bring that Scripture as a gift to God.

 ## Questions for Reflection

1. The lesson of R. Yohanan in the Talmud seems to be a more spiritual teaching: God's very being is in the Scripture God gave us. Yet the thrust of kabbalistic-Hasidic spirituality urges us to move beyond our role as

recipients of God's grace, to do our part in perfecting God's creation. There is great merit in "doing for" God. Which mode suits you more: to be the recipient of God's grace or to be active in raising creation back to God? Does one mode suit you at different times? When? How do you understand that variation?

2. In *Beshallach*, Levi Yitzhak urged us to connect our awareness of joy to speech and song. How is this lesson similar, and how is it different? Which do you sense is more sustaining or creates greater permanence: speech/song or writing? Why, how?

3. When do you feel most that your speech delights God? Why? Recognizing this, do you think that you might bring that awareness into other modes, other periods of speech? How might this help you understand what it means to experience some aspect of *devekut*?

 ## Taking It into Your Life

Levi Yitzhak offers profound insight: it is of the nature of human existence that it is impossible for us to hold our thoughts steady, on one object, permanently. Indeed, we might say that it is impossible for us to do any one thing intentionally, permanently. Still, he offers a practice by which we might move in that direction: to set an intention, to experience it in an embodied fashion, and to return to it over and over. In that manner, it will not be that we attain the fulfillment of the intention permanently, once and for all, but that we are permanently (more or less) engaged in returning to, following that intention. This is essentially the instruction for mindfulness meditation. It is the basis of developing mindful awareness.

You might experiment with this practice outside of meditation. That is, it may be salutary to seek to bring God pleasure from our acts, returning over and over to that behavior. You need not choose anything particularly exalted or holy. You might choose any number of simple acts to return to over and over: holding a smile on your face; noting your posture (and the degree of tension or relaxation in your body); saying "thank you" for your life with each breath; kissing your partner every time you see him or her— even if you did just a minute before; and being gracious in simple interactions—holding doors, ceding right-of-way on the road, and saying "thank you" for small acts.

The goal is not "success" in the deed. It is to bring our awareness over and over to our intention to perform it and to note our experience in the moment we do so. It is as much the sense of returning to awareness over and over as the act itself that wakes us up from moment to moment. When we notice that we are not doing this one small act, rather than responding with criticism and judgment ("There you go again, unable to do even this one little thing") we are invited to recognize the opportunity to fulfill our intention ("Oh, I'm not smiling—what a treat it is to feel my face change as I start to smile again"). The constant attention to the need to bring attention is how we build awareness, stability, and persistence, creating a trend toward consistency and *devekut*.

An alternative explanation of "I, *YHVH*, am your God [who brought you out of the land of Egypt, the house of bondage]" (Exod. 20:2).

The Sages taught:

> **"I, *YHVH*, am your God."** Why does Scripture say this? It is because at the Sea God appeared to the people as a young man, but at Sinai God appeared as an elder, full of compassion. And, should you then claim that there are two divinities, God declares, "I am [your God]: I am the one who was at the Sea and I am the one here at the giving of the Torah."

How shall we understand that at the Sea God appeared as a young man and at the giving of the Torah God appeared as an old man, and that anyone might think, seeing these two images, that there are two powers that control the world?

We will refer to the teaching of the AR"I *z"l*, who taught: Pesach is the experience of limited awareness (*mochin dekatnut*), but Shavuot is the experience of expanded awareness (*mochin degadlut*). Let me explain to you what he means by limited and expanded awareness. There are two degrees of tzaddikim. One serves the blessed Creator for the sake of the world-to-come. This form of devotion is called by Rambam (*Hilkhot Teshuvah* 10:5) "not for its own sake" (*shelo lishmah*). There is another tzaddik who serves the Creator "for its own sake"— that is, not for his own good, but only to bring joy to the Creator, to bring God ease.

But, do not think that the first degree is worthless. That is not so. Rather, one who is wise is able to serve the blessed Creator for the sake of the world-to-come and still his devotion can be "for its own sake." Consider: When parents provide a young child, who has no understanding, with new clothes, the child may prance around delighting in the clothes with no thought at all for the parents' feelings. But an older child who has understanding will wear those clothes in his parents' presence in order to bring pleasure to them, deriving great pleasure from this. So it is in our matter. Anyone who is a "wise child" can serve the Creator "not for its own sake"—that is, for the sake of the world-to-come—and it will yet be "for its own sake" since the intention will be to wear beautiful garments [in the world-to-come] *and* so that the Heavenly Parent will derive pleasure and joy from this. Indeed, God cannot bear His children's suffering. This, then, is what the Sages intended when they taught, "That which was done originally not for its own sake will come to be done for its own sake" (Pesachim 50b). It is possible to desire good things so as to bring ease of spirit to the Creator.

So the state of serving God for one's own good and "not for its own sake" is called "limited awareness," which we understand as limited understanding (*katnut hasekhel*). This is like the little child above who behaves only for its own delight. But, when God graces one with wisdom and so is able to raise up the quality of "not for its own sake" to that of "for its own sake," this is "expanded awareness," like the older child above who is able to act with wondrous wisdom. So we can say that "limited awareness" is a garment for "expanded awareness"—for without the limited state we would not be able to attain the expanded awareness.

This is what the AR"I *z"l* meant when he taught that on Pesach the people had limited awareness. In Egypt they were in a constricted state (*katnut*) and served God not for its own sake, as Scripture says, "I have heard the cry of the Israelites [that has come about] due to their taskmasters" (Exod. 3:7). This is also what the Haggadah means when it says that "originally our ancestors were idolaters" in Egypt. Surely this is not to say that they really worshipped idols, only that they served God not for its own sake, and this is called "idolatry" since, in the end, one is serving oneself and not serving the blessed Creator "because He is Master and Ruler"—and this is "limited awareness." But, on Shavuot they experienced "expanded awareness." After they received the Torah and said, "We will do and we will obey" (Exod. 24:7), they surely served God for its own sake, and this is called "expanded awareness."

This is what the Sages meant when they said that "at the Sea God appeared to them as a young man": their perception was a child's perception, limited awareness (*mochin dekatnut*). But "at the giving of the Torah God appeared like an old man": that is, they served with expanded awareness (*mochin degadlut*), with great wisdom like an elder, which is "for its own sake." "And, should you then claim that there two divinities"—that is, you might think that these are really two different forms of divine service—Scripture says: "I am" (*anokhi*)—I am who I was. That is: one who is wise serves God in only one manner—raising "not for its own sake" up to the level of "for its own sake." Even devotions or prayers that may be for one's own good can still be offered with the intention of bringing pleasure to the Creator. There are not two "divinities" (ways of doing things), only one, for from the "not for its own sake" we can make "for its own sake" as well.

FOR FURTHER THOUGHT

One aspect of the spiritual transformation initiated by the Baal Shem Tov was a revival of a more "democratic" spirituality. That is, he believed that all people had the capacity to perceive the Divine in all things, to see through the garments of gross corporeality, and to raise up the world to its divine reality. While his ideal was soon abandoned—perhaps because it was not possible for most people to take on the spiritual practices necessary—his ethos remains in early Hasidic writing, such as our passage.

Levi Yitzhak regularly employs the trope of "two types of tzaddikim"—yet, if we pay close attention here, he breaks this trope open altogether. He presents the first "tzaddik" as someone who serves God to gain the world-to-come, "not for its own sake." We might think that this approach is deficient, yet Levi Yitzhak immediately disabuses us of that perception: "Rather, one who is wise is able to serve the Creator for the sake of the world-to-come and still his devotion can be 'for its own sake.'" The first "tzaddik" is not a tzaddik as we come to know him in later Hasidic literature (or even as we find him in *Kedushat Levi*), and this "tzaddik"—even in his deficient state—can actually be engaged in practices that lead to becoming a full-fledged tzaddik.

Further, the Baal Shem Tov taught that God—rather than being aloof, residing in the seventh heaven, as much exiled from Israel as Israel from God—was fully present in this world. It may be that Israel is in exile and that God experiences that distancing and separation as well. But God waits yearning, constantly calling to us to find Him.

What the Baal Shem Tov taught was that it is both impossibly difficult and infinitely possible for us to do so. God wants nothing more than to be found. That is what spiritual practice is for, and even though it is difficult, "God cannot bear His children's suffering," and so it is not impossible. That is why Levi Yitzhak teaches that even the act that seems so base—to serve selfishly, for one's own good, "not for its own sake"—is the ground out of which true devotion emerges: "That which was done originally not for its own sake will come to be done for its own sake."

Levi Yitzhak deepens this lesson by associating it with the argument from the midrash: the One God who was at the Sea is the same God who was at Sinai, and therefore you must not think that there are two powers at work in the world. We are neither to think that there is more than one God nor that there is more than one way to God. *Every* way to God is the way to God, even when it is self-centered, even when it emerges from limited awareness—so long as we wake up on that path and transform our awareness (eventually). Similarly, no way is a way to God unless it ultimately leads to expanded awareness, selfless devotion, and transcendence. In that sense, we are always on the path, yet all depends on attention, awareness, and intention to move meaningfully and in the right direction.

Here is the full text of the mishnah from Rambam (indeed, it pays to look at the whole of ch. 10):

> All who engage with Torah in order to receive a reward, or to prevent suffering, do so "not for its own sake." All who engage with it not out of fear or to receive a reward, but due to love of the Master of All, whose commands are in it, do so "for its own sake." The Sages taught that one should constantly engage in Torah, even if not for its own sake, since from engaging not for its own sake one will come to engage for its own sake. Therefore, when we teach children, women, and the general population, we start by teaching them to serve God from fear and in order to receive a reward. But as their intellect grows and they increase in wisdom, we increasingly reveal to them the true secret of Torah, little by little; we accustom them to this matter with ease [*benachat*], until they attain full awareness, and come to know God, and serve God out of love.

Questions for Reflection

1. The original formulation of the passage from Pesachim 50b relates to the study of Torah: "That which was done originally not for its own sake...." It might be more accurate, however, to translate "for *her* own sake," that is, the sake of Torah, the purpose for which She exists. We might be even more radical and identify "Her" with *Shekhinah*: our devotions are for the sake of raising the *Shekhinah*, easing her pain. Reread Levi Yitzhak's teaching, substituting either of these ideas, and consider what it then means to serve God "for its/her own sake."

2. Have you had the experience of receiving a gift of clothing (or the like) and then wearing it when you knew you would see your benefactor? Do you recognize the dynamic of both being pleased to have something new and attractive and wearing something new and attractive as a way of pleasing your benefactor? How did your joy for yourself affect your pleasure for your benefactor? How did your desire to please your benefactor affect your own pleasure? Was it ever the case that the benefactor did not notice or did not acknowledge your efforts? How did you feel then?

3. When do you feel most engaged in your spiritual life? What does it feel like when you do not feel so engaged? Do you imagine that it might be possible for even your "down" times to become spiritually informed? Why or why not? How might you go about making this so?

Taking It into Your Life

It is interesting that Levi Yitzhak uses the image of the gift of clothing for this lesson. Surely it had significance in the social-economic conditions of his community—and it resonates today as well. Beyond that, however, is the possible connection to be made between the clothing of his parable and the "garments" that cloak and obscure (but also reveal) God in the world. Indeed, Levi Yitzhak uses this very language in speaking about the relationship of limited awareness (*mochin dekatnut*) and expanded awareness (*mochin degadlut*): "We can say that 'limited awareness' is a garment for 'expanded awareness'—for without the limited state we would not be able to attain the expanded awareness." It is possible, therefore, that directly engaging with the "garment"—secondary, deficient as it may be—with awareness brings us directly to the core, to God. Connecting to this world, seeing it for what it is in its fullness, is a way of opening to awareness.

Clothing not only serves to protect and decorate, but it also honors and identifies us. "The true honor of the princess's garments is inward" (Ps. 45:14). Even when we get dressed and pay attention to our clothes, in the end we are expressing our care for our selves. We want people to see us truly, for who we are, and not what we look like.

As you move through your day, from the time you put on the first piece of clothing, bring awareness to the sensation of clothing on your skin. Notice how it covers you. Notice which piece of clothing comes to your attention when. When do you see your reflection, and what is your response? How do you see yourself in other people's eyes? How does your clothing help you remember your inner life, point you toward your soul?

Mishpatim

"[Then He said to Moses, 'Come up to *YHVH*
with Aaron, Nadab and Abihu, and seventy
elders of Israel, and] bow low from afar'"
(Exod. 24:1).

The blessed Creator has, as it were, two qualities: "far" and "near."
The quality of "far" is when we believe that the light of the blessed *Ein
Sof* (i.e., God) is antecedent to all beginnings, and there is no creature
that is able to perceive it. It actually is impossible to perceive God in
thought, since human thought is constantly changing and renewed,
but the blessed Holy One is antecedent to all things. There is not even
an *ophan* or a seraph that can perceive Him, since He is beyond all
perception. This is the quality of "afar": He is distant and separate
from all perception.

The quality of "near" is when we believe that the blessed Creator
fills all worlds, is in all worlds, surrounds all worlds and there is no
place devoid of Him, for "the whole world is full of His glory" (Isa.
6:3). This is the quality of "near." We have to believe in both of these
qualities, both "far" and "near." This is the sense of the verse "Peace,
peace to the far and the near—said *YHVH*" (Isa. 57:19). The Holy
One extends all sorts of blessings into the world for the sake of that
tzaddik who believes that the Holy One is both far and near.

There are also the qualities of "love" and "fear." Now, we only
fear that which is over and beyond us. This is the quality "far," which
engenders "fear" in us. But from that which is "near" we receive
"love." So, when it says, "**bow low**" it implies experiencing the quality
of "fear" (since we make ourselves low in this manner), and therefore
it says, "**from afar.**" From the quality of "far" they perceived the aspect
of "fear."

Alternatively, we can interpret this according to the AR"I *z"l*, who
wrote in his instructions for reciting the *Aleinu* prayer, regarding
the phrase "and we bend the knee" (*va'anachnu kor'im*): through our

prostration we draw down great flow of blessing from the blessed *Ein Sof* into all the worlds. This is the significance of God instructing the men to **"bow low"**: draw down great fullness from that distant source.

FOR FURTHER THOUGHT

Levi Yitzhak notes the paradoxical invitation that God extends to Moses and the others: "come up" to God, but then also "bow low" before God. It is as if God both wants to be close, intimate with us, but also to preserve a degree of distance. How does this work? Does God change from one moment to the next? Is the divine intent confused?

Of course, there is only one God and only one intention: to be connected to us. The difference in how we experience God, apparently, is in us. There are times that we feel near and times that we feel far; there are times that we sense a deep love and intimacy with God, and times when we are aware of God's greatness and power, God's awesome grandeur, and we feel distant from God. Both experiences are true and accurate. Both point and lead us to connection with God. The challenge in spiritual practice is to recognize when we sense each quality of heart and to know how to respond in each instance.

Levi Yitzhak adds to, and so complicates, his teaching. He makes the connection between the prostration invoked in this verse and the common experience among his listeners of bowing before God when reciting the closing prayer of each daily service. He refers to the teachings of R. Isaac Luria, the mystical master of sixteenth-century Safed. Luria expanded the kabbalistic practice of joining mystical concepts to common acts, intending that the act bring about changes in the divine realm. In this particular instance he refers to the book *Peri Etz Chayyim* (*Kri'at Hatorah* 5, end). He teaches that the physical act of bowing suggests drawing down fullness from God:

Aleinu: We have already taught that from the phrase "and we bend the knee" (*va'anachnu kor'im*) to the end of the prayer, our intention is in the realm of *atzilut* with all of its enclosures. But at first we have to direct our attention to all of the other worlds that precede it in this way: "It is incumbent upon us to praise the Lord of all" (*la'adon hakol*)—this is the realm of *beriyah*, since that realm is called "the

Lord of all the earth"; "the Creator" (*yotzer bereishit*)—this is the world of *yetzirah*; "who did not make us" (*shelo asanu*)—this is the realm of *assiyah*, where the husks reside, and it is for that reason that in this phrase we mention the other nations in the mystery of *assiyah*, since they "bow to vanities and nothings." "But we bend the knee—before the King, King of kings the blessed Holy One"—this is now the realm of *atzilut*. In this manner we connect all of the worlds.

This would suggest that the experience of fear of God and the consequent sense of distance are neither to be avoided nor to become an impediment to truly serving God. Indeed, it appears that from the position of prostration we not only succeed in drawing down great blessing but also raise our awareness to the highest divine realms.

 ## Questions for Reflection

1. Have you resolved for yourself how to hold these two aspects, "far" and "near," at one and the same time? When you sense God filling all, in, around, and pervading the whole of the cosmos, are you also aware of God's inscrutability? Can you feel in your body both God's distance and closeness?

2. Do you associate "far" with "fear"? When, how? Do you associate "love" with proximity? When, how? Could drawing near actually make it more likely that we will sense how far we are from God? But, if "near" and "love" are connected, why does Levi Yitzhak want to introduce "fear" into this moment?

3. What are the implications of realizing that God precedes all thought and is beyond our perception? What other modalities might we employ to improve/deepen our perception of the Holy One?

 ## Taking It into Your Life

Let us investigate the relationship of these four qualities: fear, far, love, near. It is not so clear that the only relationships are love/near and fear/far. Consider: When we love someone, that love can extend over distances of space and time. It is not only when in their presence that we love them. On the other hand, there are forms of love that can be too close, even invasive. When someone loves us in this way, we can experience a degree of fear. Then, indeed, proximity might be frightening. (One might ask if this type of love is, in fact, love. Surely, we would not include what masquerades as "love" in an abusive relationship. But, clearly there are parents who love their children very much, yet whose love can be smothering, even if well intentioned.) On the other hand, distance may also induce fear in one who loves. Both physical and emotional distance can do so. And proximity may induce fear—in the sense of awe, in the sense of lack of control, in the awareness of one's capacity to hurt one's beloved.

As you make your way through your day, pay attention when you sense the emotions of love and fear. As you note them, note as well the source. Does news of events halfway around the world raise fear? Does a phone call from a distant friend rekindle love? Does a near miss on the freeway induce fear? Does a hug remind you of love? What are the qualities of love and fear? Are they always opposite? Do they sometimes reinforce one another? Might one lead to another? Is fear always bad and love always good? When and how? How do you respond to fear? How do you respond to love? Do you run toward one and from the other? What would happen if you held your ground in both instances? What might you learn from fear? What might come from staying present to, but not running toward, love?

"Moses went and reported to the people all the commands of *YHVH* and all the rules; [and all the people answered with one voice, saying, 'All the things that *YHVH* has commanded we will do!']" (Exod. 24:3).

Rashi holds that this event took place before the giving of the Torah, where the people received and were bound by the seven laws of the descendants of Noah, as well as the Red Heifer, honoring parents, Shabbat, and the other laws given at Marah. But, Ramban (on Exod. 24:1) challenges that view, saying that it is not correct to say that this verse refers to the Noahide laws or what was said to them at Marah (cf. Exod. 15:25 and *Mekhilta*, *Vayasa* 1) and that they had already heard what Moses now says. Further, he argues that the word "reported" (*vayesappeir*) should only apply to new matters that Moses now tells them.

It seems to me that Rashi has it right, and according to the sense of the Talmud (Shabbat 88a), this took place before the giving of the Torah (as explained by the *Or Hachayyim*). However, we still have to explain the clear meaning of the phrase "**Moses went and reported to the people**." Rashi holds that this means that Moses communicated to them the seven Noahide laws, the Red Heifer, civil laws, and Shabbat. But regarding these matters the phrase "**reported** [*vayesappeir*] **to the people**" is not really appropriate. We would have expected "he commanded the Children of Israel" or "he spoke to the Children of Israel." So in all, we still do not have a clear understanding of the significance of the verb "**reported**."

Here is how we can understand it. Indeed, they did receive these commandments at Marah, and the seven Noahide laws were given long before this. Here, Moses "**reported**" to the people the great import of their having fulfilled those seven laws and the others that were commanded at Marah; how much the blessed Holy One delights in their fulfillment of these mitzvot; and how all the worlds and souls are dependent on their acts. Moses reported the great significance of the mitzvot that Israel observed (those seven and the laws given at Marah).

From this we can see that the phrase "**reported to the people**" does not refer to giving new mitzvot, since they had already been given. Rather, Moses reported to the people the great worthiness and delight that Israel generated by keeping those mitzvot. And once Israel heard the great delight that the blessed Holy One takes in their keeping those commandments, the great blessing and joy and rejoicing that Israel thereby bring to all the worlds from keeping the commands of the blessed Creator, they responded directly, saying, "**All the things that YHVH has commanded we will do**." That is to say, "We desire the mitzvot even more so that we might delight the blessed Holy One, that the blessed Holy One might pour out even more blessing and life in response to our doing mitzvot." That is the significance of the phrase here "**All the things that YHVH has commanded we will do**": "We desire even more the mitzvot of the blessed Creator."

FOR FURTHER THOUGHT

With this lesson, we enter into one of the moments in the Torah that prompted the Sages to declare, "There is no absolute chronological order in the Torah" (cf. Rashi on Exod. 19:11). The Torah is (uncharacteristically) silent with regard to the date on which the Torah was given. After having identified the date on which the people arrived in the wilderness of Sinai, the Torah continues with an account devoid of precision, leaving it to the Rabbis to interpret the narrative so they can make the giving of the Torah fall on the fiftieth day after the Exodus. Moreover, as the story unfolds from chapters 19 through 24, it becomes even more unclear when and how the events took place. When, precisely, were the laws of chapters 21 through 23 given to Moses (not to mention those mentioned in Leviticus 25, specifically noted as having been given at Mount Sinai)? What is meant by Exod. 15:25, "There God gave them statutes and judgments, and there He tested them"? How shall we understand the sequence of events mentioned here in chapter 24 in relation to the details in chapter 19?

As Levi Yitzhak notes, there is a difference of opinion among the Rabbinic commentators on the Torah. The *Or Hachayyim* on Exod. 24:1 gives us a sense of that debate, as well as insight into Levi Yitzhak's thinking:

> The plain meaning of these verses makes clear that this passage stands in its proper chronological place, after the giving of the Torah, and there is no need to offer more proofs. Further, R. Abraham ibn Ezra, Rashbam, and Ramban all agree with this position.
>
> Still, I have seen in the *Mekhilta* a rationale that contradicts this position, arguing that on the fifth day (of the month of Iyar) Moses paused in his ascent and descent of the mountain to build the altar mentioned here in *Mishpatim*. At this altar he made a covenant with them on the basis of some of the mitzvot that they had already received: one teacher said the seven Noahide laws, another said the laws given at Marah, and there are even those who would include the laws mentioned in Leviticus 25–27. From this we learn that these all took place before the giving of the Torah, and it was with regard to them that Moses made the aforementioned covenant. The people had not yet made any covenant regarding any of the commandments they had received. Moses was testing them, to know if of themselves they would keep the covenant regarding those earlier commandments, even though God had not yet obligated them fully. Perhaps this is what God meant above when He instructed Moses, "And relate [*vetageid*] to the Children of Israel" (Exod. 19:3), which the Sages taught means God instructed Moses to attract them with words of *aggadah* (Shabbat 87a). So what we

have here was also to attract the people, to determine if they of their own accord would swear to obey the earlier commandments.

In this passage we can see the possible roots of Levi Yitzhak's commentary: Moses does address the people regarding their observance of the earlier laws, in some manner inspiring them to take on all those to come at Sinai. Of course, Levi Yitzhak applies his own particular approach: that our deeds must be directed to bringing delight to the Creator. Moses neither commanded nor instructed the people here; rather, he reported to them the significance of their acts. In observing the earlier set of commandments, they brought delight to God. Learning this, they responded spontaneously, with whole hearts: "All that God has said with regard to our observance of the first set of laws we will do with regard to whatever God asks of us. We so thrill to know the capacity we have to bring joy and delight to God, we will do whatever is asked of us."

The seven Noahide laws were derived by the Rabbis from verses early in the book of Genesis. They include not committing murder, not worshipping idols, not engaging in licentious sexual relations, not eating flesh from a living animal (without slaughter), not cursing God, not stealing, and establishing laws (cf. Sanhedrin 56a). This is a form of Rabbinic "natural law."

 ## Questions for Reflection

1. The teaching that "there is no absolute chronological order in the Torah" can be either liberating—freeing us to read the Torah as mythical narrative, a dream rather than a record—or frustrating, a "dodge" employed by the Rabbis to deal with internal inconsistencies in the Torah. How do you respond to this teaching?

2. How do you understand the nature of the laws in the Torah? Are they divine instructions? Are they mediated by Moses, and so somewhat human in nature? How would you have responded had you been standing at the foot of Mount Sinai when Moses brought these words to you?

3. Does it change your sense of the significance of the Torah given at Sinai to think that there was already a body of law that had been given beforehand? How? Why or why not?

Taking It into Your Life

A classical Jewish explanation for mitzvot is that they are meant to "smelt" and purify people (cf. Lev. R. 13:3; *Tanchuma, Shemini* 7). That is, the mitzvot are for our good. The Hasidic approach is to acknowledge this to be true, but to look beyond. That is, as Levi Yitzhak says, performing the mitzvot is a key method of bringing delight to the Creator, which in turn brings great blessing to the world. The motivation for bringing delight to God is just that, and whatever blessings derive from that will be secondary. Indeed, on some level, the world is sustained by Israel's deeds, so the benefit extends far beyond any personal or parochial concern.

The idea of doing everything to bring another delight or pleasure is attractive, but we also recognize how it can be problematic. We know how "people pleasers" suffer, acting against their own interests, and we have seen the negative consequences of their behavior. Still, what might it mean to bring God delight through our actions? Would it be solely by performing the commandments? What would be the necessary inner intention? What is the role of will and willingness in this regard?

Of course, we don't know with certainty what is truly pleasing to God. Can we gain some insight from taking this experiment to the human plane? How would you undertake to bring pleasure to the people you meet in your life? Start with the people closest to you. How well do you know what brings them pleasure? Is there only one thing? Does it vary with time and circumstances? Does it vary with whom they are dealing? What impediments might there be to you, in particular, bringing delight to this or that person? What might you have to know about yourself and your inner experience, limitations, reservations, prejudices, fears, and limits?

Try this practice for a week. Observe your inner experience. When did you feel you succeeded? How did you feel doing so? What did it take on your part? What prevented you from succeeding? How did you feel then? What would have been required to succeed in those moments?

This inquiry is purely for the sake of discovery. There is no risk of failure. Even in the moments that we might act mistakenly, our intention will be upright, and our capacity to recover and make good strong. But the possibility of learning about our own hearts, as well as how to bring delight to our loved ones, to our friends and neighbors, and to God will increase in response to the depth of our investigation and our desire to learn from it.

> "Now the appearance of the glory of *YHVH*
> was like a consuming fire [in the sight of the
> Israelites on the top of the mountain]"
> (Exod. 24:17).

Through our devotions—in studying Torah and in prayer—we bring great delight to God above. Now, if you wish to know if God does indeed delight from your service, you can discern this if you sense that your heart burns like fire, blazing always to serve God, and if you have desire and inclination to serve the Creator. These feelings are proof that God does delight in your devotions. Therefore you receive help from above, being sent holy thoughts into your heart.

This is the sense of **"the appearance of the glory of YHVH, etc."**: if you want to know if you see **"the glory of YHVH"** and that the blessed Holy One delights in you [and your actions], then the sign will be **"like a consuming fire"**—if your heart burns like fire.

FOR FURTHER THOUGHT

Here Levi Yitzhak lifts the verse from the Torah out of its context in order to teach about spiritual experience. His assumption, in doing so, is that the Torah is not a mere document. It is the living interface between the Divine and Israel. It is neither history nor a simple law code. Rather, its words have eternal meaning and power because they are applicable to—more, they speak directly to—the lives of everyone who reads it, in every age, in every place.

The scene from which our starting verse is taken is quite dramatic and suggestive. Moses is ascending the mountain, invited by God to approach. There are great preparations, and he is accompanied part of the way by colleagues, assistants, and supporters. Yet, in the end, he must go on alone. Levi Yitzhak reads this as a description of spiritual work, of divine service. We work together in community to build capacity in ourselves, supporting each other in our endeavors. We grow and gain in confidence from the support of others. Yet, in the end, we each do our own work. We ascend the mountain on our own. Yet, what happens in our heart and the "product" of our devotions are often shrouded in cloud, obscured from others and perhaps even ourselves.

Levi Yitzhak finds instructions to help us gain a sense of direction in the midst of uncertainty, to discern if our devotions are rightly directed. To this end, Levi Yitzhak plays with the word "appearance" (*mareih*). He reads it as if it meant something like a mirror, which reflects the appearance of that before it. If we direct our attention toward God, devoting our study and prayer to bring God delight, we may see the purity of our devotions reflected in God's glory. But that reflection will not be visual. Rather, we will sense in our hearts the increased passion to devote ourselves to God. Indeed, that inner fire will have been fed by the holy thoughts sent there from the heavens, measure for measure, in response to our service.

Exod. 24:16 reads: "The Presence of *YHVH* abode on Mount Sinai, and the cloud hid it for six days. On the seventh day He called to Moses from the midst of the cloud." This chronology is somewhat confusing, since it is not clear when this took place, nor is it clear if this means that Moses entered the cloud before God called to him or after. Rashi comments:

> "The cloud hid it"—The Sages differ on this matter. Some say that these were the six days from the new moon [until Shavuot, the day the Torah was given].
>
> "On the seventh day He called to Moses"—So to speak the Ten Commandments. Moses and all the Israelites stood there, but Scripture honored Moses. Another interpretation: the cloud covered Moses for six days following the Ten Commandments, and they began the forty days of Moses's ascent to receive the Tablets. This also teaches that all who enter into the camp of the *Shekhinah* need to separate themselves for six days.

This is quite suggestive in terms of our spiritual practice. During the six days of the week, we engage in our devotions, Torah study, prayer, deeds of loving-kindness, and so on. We build up our spiritual energies, always moving toward Shabbat. On the seventh day, God calls to us. We are given the time to pay attention, to notice what is happening in our hearts. We can sense how our devotions are "reflected back" to us in the quality of our experience, the climate of our hearts. Levi Yitzhak may not have had this schedule in mind, intending that we "take our internal temperature" on a regular basis. In either case, this teaching is quite powerful: we can look toward the "glory of God" and see it reflected back in our own hearts. Our efforts may be reciprocated, our devotions inviting holy thoughts from heaven in response.

Questions for Reflection

1. Accepting, for the moment, the premise that God might delight in your actions, would you want to know if God did or did not? Why or why not?

2. Which is more important to you: the effect of your actions on God or the outcome of your spiritual practice in your life? Does it matter if God delights in our deeds if, in the end, the consequence is that we are enthused and fired up in our devotions? Why or why not?

3. In a previous lesson we met the metaphor of God as our shadow, doing as we do in response. Here, Levi Yitzhak offers a different image: God is our mirror. The purity of our devotions is reflected back to us in the increased energy we feel in our devotions. Does one appeal to you more? Which one? Why? What are the implications that each has for you in your spiritual work?

Taking It into Your Life

"As face meets face in the water, so is the heart of one person toward another" (Prov. 27:19). This verse says that we can see the quality of our heart reflected in the heart of the person before us. The Gaon, R. Eliahu of Vilna, comments:

> Just as water reflects back according to the face that is presented—if one distorts his face, that is what the water will reflect—so is one person's heart to another. If your heart is positively directed toward another person, he will respond in the same manner, even if the latter doesn't really know what is in the heart of the former.

Malbim (Bible commentator R. Meir Leibush ben Yechiel Michel, 1809–1879) comments:

> The heart pumps blood to the limbs to bring them life, and the limbs send back the best blood in return to the heart. In that way, the heart returns to us that which it receives from us. This is the way it is, as well, with water: when we look into it we see our faces. The face that the water reflects back to us is the face that it received from the one who is looking in the water.

What the heart receives it turns around and returns. In that way, the heart tells us what is going on in us, since the quality of each part of our body will be seen in the heart. Thus, the heart is the seer regarding our inner forces, and the prophet of good or ill. This is true, as well, in the reflection that comes to us from looking in water.

Mayor Koch of New York City was famous for asking people, "How am I doing?" It is easy to hear that as the cynical pandering of the politician. But often we don't have a clear sense of how we're doing. We have a feeling, perhaps, but we are unsure. One way to check out how we're doing, to get a read on our own inner state, might be to look carefully at how people respond to us. Do they look us in the eye? Do they share their hearts easily with us? Do they hold us to be trustworthy? Do they look away when we approach? Do we find that we are met by receptivity or resistance? Do we find welcome or woe? When we are met with a frown, a scowl, a worried look, we might inquire, "Is that my reflection?" When we see a healthy, glowing countenance before us, we might want to know, "Could that be me?" as well.

How do you hear the messages of your heart? What do you want to hear? What are you prepared to hear? What does it tell you about how your body is doing? How friendly are you to your back, your belly, your head? Where do you turn to look carefully at the state of your heart? How might you learn to hear God's voice, through the prophet of the heart, the seer of the face reflected back to you?

Terumah

"[Tell the Israelite people to bring Me gifts;]
you shall accept gifts for Me from every
person whose heart so moves him. And
these are the gifts that you shall accept from
them: gold, silver, and copper" (Exod. 25:2–3).

We are all obliged to serve the Creator in action and in thought. By means of our intention and holy thought we raise up the *Shekhinah* from the dust. Our deeds are so that we will raise ourselves up, to become better people.

This is how we can interpret our verse. "**Every person whose heart so moves him**" (*asher yidvenu libbo*)—this refers to thought, by which "you shall take up My elevation" (*tikchu et terumati*), that is, the *Shekhinah* will be raised up and exalted (*yitromem*). "**These are the gifts that you shall accept from them**" (*haterumah asher tikchu mei'itam*)—this is the inner elevation (*hitromemut*) that we take for ourselves, which comes about through action. That is the sense of "**gold, silver, and copper**," which signify sacred devotion.

FOR FURTHER THOUGHT

Levi Yitzhak teases out two different movements, represented in the self-referential "gifts for Me" (*terumati*) and the plain "gifts" (*haterumah*). The former suggests an offering to God, which is problematic: of what material object can it truly be said "we give it to God"? Doesn't the world and all that is in it belong to God? King David said this very thing: "All is from You, and it is Your gift that we have given to You!" (1 Chron. 29:14; cf. Avot 3:7). So, it cannot be a physical gift that we offer God. Instead, Levi Yitzhak senses that this is about how we connect with God: through our inwardness, our thoughts and intentions. Our heartfelt urgings ("whose heart so moves him") are not material and can have a profound effect on the world, even on the state of the *Shekhinah*. Actually, it is not that we give anything material to God, but our offering is in the act of raising up, a play on the root of *terumah*. God is raised up in the aspect of the *Shekhinah* through our inner intentions and thoughts.

But in a classical move of Hasidic *mussar* (ethical teaching), Levi Yitzhak reminds us that spiritual devotion alone is not enough. We must also give attention to our behavior in this world. So we are to raise up our own beings as well. The reference to "gold, silver, and copper" is an oblique nod to the three *sephirot*: *Gevurah* (Rigor, Judgment), *Chesed* (Love), and *Tiferet* (Beauty, Balance) (cf. Zohar II 90b). These qualities represent the highest manifestation of human endeavor. To devote one's loving emotion to God, to turn fear of worldly things to reverence for God, and to devote whatever delight and glory one might experience to God is a practice that cleanses and uplifts one's interpersonal interactions.

In this manner, Levi Yitzhak invites us to read this verse as instruction for spiritual practice. We are to devote our inner awareness and intention to raising the *Shekhinah*, to bringing all existence under God's dominion. And we are to devote our energies to making our behavior match the divine qualities. Spirituality and ethics meet as we make our hearts a tabernacle, a place where God can dwell in holiness and joy.

 ## Questions for Reflection

1. Another name for the *Shekhinah* is *Malkhut*, the representation of God's dominion and reign. Does it make sense to you, in your life, to see your actions as testimony to God's sovereignty? When, how? What of your actions do you see in that light?

2. What do you sense is the connection between raising or exalting yourself and improving yourself? Have you any experience of ecstasy or delight as a motivation to behave better? Have you any experience of seeing yourself in a new light, as standing taller than you had thought, as a prompt to acting better? Can you think of any other analogous examples in your life?

3. Does it make sense to you to subsume all behavior under the dynamic interaction of love, fear, and beauty/glory? Why or why not? What else do you think may need to be included?

Taking It into Your Life

Once again we are invited to pay attention to the connection between thought and action. Spiritual practice is not solely an inner process; it demands support through the body and expression in the world.

There are four possible arrangements of these two elements:

1. Intention and action are aligned and enacted spontaneously together.
2. Intention—inner awareness—prompts action.
3. The call to action prompts inner awareness.
4. Lack of inner awareness and lethargy fail to bring about action.

Let's pay attention to numbers 2 and 3. As you make your way through the day, notice when you have an inner sense of God's presence: stirring of the heart, awareness of gratitude, joy, love, diligence. Allow the feeling to fill your body and awareness. Get to know it well. Then observe: How does this feeling become manifest in the world? How does it become action? What might you do to express actively your sense of thanksgiving, joy, love, or diligence? How might your inner experience translate into action on behalf of others?

Alternatively, watch carefully which actions you naturally gravitate toward or what is called for from you. How do you speak to or reach out to friends or loved ones? Are you moved to offer charity or do some kindness to a stranger? Note the action, and claim it as your offering. Reflect on it, and allow it to stimulate an inner awareness of kindness, devotion, and love. Notice when you exercise self-restraint—avoiding harming others or yourself. Reflect on this moment, and allow it to resonate with your true intention to raise the *Shekhinah* from the dust, to be one in whom God might delight.

> "Exactly as I show you—the pattern of
> the Tabernacle and the pattern of all
> its furnishings—so shall you do"
> (Exod. 25:9).

Rashi comments (regarding the last phrase "**so shall you do**"), "And so shall you do throughout the generations." But the *Tosafot* reject this, arguing that the altar that Moses built was not the same as that built by Solomon (cf. 2 Chron. 4:1), and Ramban also argued against this position.

But we can explain Rashi's comment so that it makes sense. The phrase "**so shall you do**" refers to something else. Surely the pattern of the Tabernacle and its furnishings had to be described in detail regarding height, size, weight, and measurement, since these were to be the garment and the form for their interior, spiritual holiness. According to the prophetic vision of Moses and all Israel at Mount Sinai, and the manner in which they drew down spiritual holiness through their service, to that extent and according to that pattern would the "garment" have to be made, which is to say the form of the furnishings and the Tabernacle according to that pattern.

But the Sages taught that "no two prophets prophesy in the same style" (Sanhedrin 89a). Rather, the prophetic spirit appears to each one according to his quality and according to the manner in which he serves God. In this light Moses and the generation of the wilderness could only create the form of the Tabernacle and the pattern of its furnishings (which are the garment for the spiritual lights of holiness) according to their spiritual quality, the nature of their devotions, and their prophetic spirit that they perceived at Mount Sinai.

Thus, this is how we can understand our verses: "**Exactly as I show you, etc.**"—according to the limits of your prophecy, so shall be "**the pattern of the Tabernacle and ... its furnishings.**" "**So shall you do**" throughout the generations—that is, in every future generation when you desire to build a Sanctuary, its pattern shall be according to the prophecy that shall be attained then; according to that form shall you make the Sanctuary and its furnishings. So Solomon created the form for his according to his devotions and the spirit of prophecy that he attained.

In this light, there is no problem with Ramban's challenge, that Solomon's altar was not like that which Moses made. The opposite is the case: the instruction was *not* to make the same form always. Only according to the spirit of prophecy of the time should we form here below the pattern of the furnishings. We can explain this further: the phrase "**so shall you do**" refers back to the earlier phrase "**exactly as I show you.**" In other words, "just as you are not permitted to change these instructions, but to do only as I have shown you, so shall you do in the future—just as I show you, according to the prophets that will be in that generation."

FOR FURTHER THOUGHT

Here is Ramban's commentary:

> I don't think that Rashi is correct, that Solomon would be obligated to make the Temple according to this pattern—after all, the altar that Solomon made was twenty cubits long and twenty cubits wide (cf. 2 Chron. 4:1; the original was five by five cubits, Exod. 27:1).
>
> The seeming redundancy of "Make Me a Sanctuary" (Exod. 25:8) and our verses is rather to encourage and inspire the people. So it says, "Make Me a Sanctuary"—an enclosure, and furnishings "like a king's sanctuary and a royal palace" (Amos 7:13)—"so that I might dwell among them"—in that palace, on the throne of glory that they will make for Me there. "Exactly as I show you—according to the pattern" of this Tabernacle that I said I would dwell in "and the pattern of the furnishings." Scripture then repeats itself to say "and so shall you do," meaning "all of you, with enthusiasm and diligence." And this redundancy appears again later, when we read, "And the Israelites did according to all that *YHVH* commanded Moses, so they did" (Exod. 39:32). Because this was the command, Scripture says, "And so shall you do" (*Vekhein ta'asu*).

This is suggestive, leaving room for any future construction of the Sanctuary or Temple to be done according to the designs of the later builders—so long as the construction is ultimately fitting, "like a king's sanctuary and a royal palace." This is taken up by Levi Yitzhak, but expanded, deepened, and enriched by his sensibilities.

His point is powerful, and in its time (and perhaps in ours as well) quite revolutionary. Levi Yitzhak is not afraid for Scripture to bind future generations to do as Moses and the Israelites did. He invites this connection, because he senses that Moses and the Israelites were inspired: living in God's presence, sustained by manna, in touch with the deepest aspects of spiritual awareness and prophecy. He wants his people—and even us, as well—to sense that this same sensitivity is possible, is even called for (commanded!) by the Torah in every generation. "So shall you do—throughout the generations into the future" means "you shall respond to God's invitation to draw near and to make a place in which God might dwell—just as was done in the wilderness."

Levi Yitzhak makes a radical claim: the leaders of each generation must participate in prophetic inspiration, and he and his fellow tzaddikim are such leaders. They are empowered to innovate because they are following in the pattern and practice of Moses and the Israelites. That authority comes from God, in that it emerges from prophetic awareness of God's will and intention. The implications of this revolutionary claim (even in the midst of a conservative, perhaps reactionary culture) in practice are seen in the following story:

> When Rabbi Noah, son of Rabbi Mordecai (of Lekhovitz, d. 1834), assumed the succession after his father's death, his disciples noticed that there were a number of ways in which he conducted himself differently from his father and asked him about this.
>
> "I do just as my father did," he replied. "He did not imitate, and I do not imitate." (Martin Buber, *Tales of the Hasidim: The Later Masters*, 157 [New York: Schocken Publishing, 1948])

Questions for Reflection

1. Which Jewish practices do you feel are fixed and unchangeable throughout the generations? Which Jewish practices do you feel are meant as models, from which we are to take inspiration in shaping our response today?

2. What do you sense distinguishes the two categories above? How do you feel when you change a practice—adding or subtracting, expanding or contracting it? From where do you draw your energy and inspiration to do so?

3. What do you imagine (or what have you experienced) to be the practices that would bring about the "prophetic" awareness of which Levi Yitzhak speaks? What would that consciousness be like? Is that something to which you aspire? Why or why not?

Taking It into Your Life

Rabbi Noah rejects his disciples' complaint that he is doing things differently from his father by saying, "I do not imitate." The simple meaning of the story is that he was not imitating his father, but the implication may extend farther: he may not even wish to imitate himself. That is, when returning to a practice or a season or a prayer, he may seek to engage with it as if it were the first time, such that his response will be true to that moment, and not an "imitation" of what he had done before.

His aspiration is to know God in the moment, to respond as the occasion demands, to answer God's call as he perceives it this time. We seek spiritual direction to develop this very sensibility. We can also bring our attention to our daily endeavors, and particularly our religious practices, to begin to notice where we have fallen into habit and to seek ways to wake up to what is called for in the moment.

Pay attention to the most mundane activities: brushing your teeth, how you soap up in the shower, how you put on your socks and shoes, how you butter your toast or make your coffee. In each activity, are you aware of how you move your body? Do you perform the actions in the same manner every day? While it is true that there is a certain degree of grace in finally learning to tie our shoes in first or second grade, and it does save us time not to have to think about it now, still how do we use that "freedom"? Where are your mind and heart in those moments? On the radio? In conversation? Distracted, empty, reaching out into the future, planning...? What might happen in that moment if you were to bring the whole of your awareness to that one activity? Even if you were to tie your shoes (or whatever) just as you have for years, would paying attention make the experience different? How might paying attention in this way bring about change? What might you do—internally or externally—so that you would not be "imitating" the "you" who tied his or her shoes yesterday? What might you do—internally or externally—so that you would not be "imitating" the "you" who prayed these prayers yesterday or last week? How can you come to know how to build a dwelling place for God in your heart appropriate to this moment, this day, this "you"?

"Look, and follow the patterns for them [that are being shown you on the mountain]" (Exod. 25:40).

Rashi comments, "['Look here on the mountain to see the pattern that I show you':] This tells us that Moses had difficulty understanding how to form the menorah until the blessed Holy One showed him [the form of a menorah of fire]."

How shall we understand this? Doesn't it say with regard to the other furnishings of the Tabernacle, "Exactly as I show you—the pattern of the Tabernacle, etc." (Exod. 25:9)? And why particularly did Moses have difficulty with how to fashion the menorah?

Look: when all the worlds direct their attention to the blessed Creator, seeing only that pure supernal brightness that is above all the worlds, that great brightness induces fear and terror to the point that they cease to have independent existence. They have no delight because of the fear and terror that they experience to the point that they are nullified out of existence. Their essential joy is only when they return to their separate existences and the brightness of the blessed Creator contracts itself, garbing itself in the raiment of the worlds. That is when they experience joy.

This is implied in the teaching (Ta'anit 29a) "When Adar comes in, we increase in joy." "Comes in" (*mi-shenikhnas*)—when the worlds return to their separate existence, they garb themselves in the flow of light from the blessed Creator, just as the word *Adar* suggests "garment" (as in "Elijah's cloak," *aderet eliyahu*; 2 Kings 2:13). It is then that they "increase in joy." But before that, when they are gazing (at God's brightness) they are filled with fear to the point of ceasing to exist....

This helps us to explain our passage. How is it possible to perceive the supernal light that has not yet been contracted in the lower worlds? It is through inner fiery enthusiasm to connect with the blessed Creator. By means of that passion we are able to perceive that supernal brightness that has not yet been garbed in the lower worlds, from which the vital force descends to all the lower worlds, as Scripture says, "From the light of the face of the King there is life" (Prov. 16:15).

The menorah signifies that flow of light that has not yet been garbed in the lower worlds. This is what puzzled Moses. He wondered how to cleave to and perceive that supernal brightness. The Sages hint that the blessed Holy One showed him a menorah of fire, signifying that by fiery enthusiasm he would be able to attain it. That is the meaning of "[a menorah] of fire." But all of the other furnishings of the Tabernacle signify that flow that has been garbed in the lower worlds, and that surely was not difficult for Moses to perceive.

FOR FURTHER THOUGHT

Levi Yitzhak has brought together two teachings: one is about the process of the flow of divine light/power and blessing (*shefa*) and our response to that awareness; the other is about how we can prepare ourselves to energize that process.

Levi Yitzhak places these experiences in relation to the menorah and its creation. Gazing at the menorah no longer is tied to the very physical process of forging a metal lampstand. Rather, the menorah represents the source of divine blessing, the infinite, undifferentiated divine light. The light of the menorah represents the fiery enthusiasm that is required if we are to engage in energizing the flow of divine blessing and creation into the world. That is, the flow is facilitated and focused by the movement of the physical toward the spiritual, of the manifest multiplicity of created beings toward the undifferentiated oneness of *ein sof*. But as Levi Yitzhak reminds us, that ascent is not undertaken lightly. It is terrifying—because it brings about (or is brought about by) the dissolution of individual separate consciousness—the nullification of being. There is no joy in that moment, since there is no personal awareness (there is no fear either, it having been transcended/sloughed off in nullification). There is joy only later, when we return to our individual consciousness, bringing along the divine flow. It is for that reason that we need to develop our enthusiasm, our passion to serve God and to raise our consciousness toward perceiving the undifferentiated source of all being.

Levi Yitzhak may be referring to the fiery furnace into which Moses tossed the talent of gold to create the menorah. Over and over Moses forgot how to make the menorah. He could not bring the source of divine light into the physical world. Instead, he had to go to the source. The furnace—the light of which (to melt metal, smelt it, and prepare it for use) is white hot and blinding—symbolizes the light of *ein sof*. Moses, at God's instruction, finally was willing to ascend, to look toward that brightness from which all creation emerges. He tossed the gold into that fiery furnace. Gold—which is reddish in color—is associated with the *sephirah Gevurah*, or the quality of fear. Moses brought his fear forward, giving it over to stand fully in the presence of *ein sof*. His willingness to do so was necessary to energize the process by which God ultimately brought the physical menorah into existence. Rather than being embarrassed by his inability to understand God or ashamed that God had to act to create the menorah, Moses happily received both instruction and the finished product.

This is the message of our lesson. We have the capacity to move between this world of multiplicity and physicality and that of undifferentiated, pure spirituality, but it is demanding. We must be willing to experience the fear and terror that accompany the loss of our individual selves, our separate consciousness, so that we might perceive the light of *ein sof*. But, we should be assured of the joy that we will experience when we recognize the good that comes of our doing so—the blessing that flows into the world by our actions. To find the will and energy to do so, we are invited to gaze upon the miraculous menorah to inspire passionate, fiery enthusiasm, so that we might climb the spiritual mountain toward God.

Questions for Reflection

1. How, if at all, does this lesson help you expand the meaning of "fear" as a potentially positive spiritual experience? When might fear be a positive motivating force? When might fear actually be attractive?

2. How do you understand the place of joy in this process? Is it delight at having survived? Is it renewed joy in being alive and in the world? Is it pleasure at having participated in bringing down blessing into the world? Is it delight in the knowledge of God's love? All of these? More?

3. How do you generate spiritual enthusiasm?

Taking It into Your Life

The "eternal light" (*ner tamid*) in synagogues is a symbolic representation of the light that would shine from the menorah, illuminating the Tabernacle through the night. With this lesson in mind, we might employ the *ner tamid* in our spiritual practices, using it to develop spiritual passion and enthusiasm (*hitlahavut*) in our prayers.

Consider using the *ner tamid* as a point of focus for meditation. You may wish to do this when there is no service going on or try to arrive some time before services begin. When you arrive in the synagogue, find a place to sit where you might be less likely to be disturbed and where you will also have a clear view of the *ner tamid*. This may be farther toward the back or off to the side, so that you will not have to crane your neck to see it. Settle into your seat, and take a few deep breaths. Train your eyes on the *ner tamid*. Hold it steadily in your sight, softening your vision of whatever is around it. Allow the light of the *ner tamid* to fill the center of your field of vision. As you lose your focus or are distracted, simply take a breath to settle in again, and return your vision to the *ner tamid*. (You can do this at home, of course, with a candle, but the association between the *ner tamid*, the menorah, and the synagogue can be quite powerful. Give it a try.)

How do you experience the light? Is there any moment in which you sense it entering you, moving beyond the receptors in your eyes? What happens to your sense of your connection to the room around you, to the people nearby? How do you sense the beating of your heart as you maintain your connection to the light? How do you sense your breath? Allow a smile to form on your lips. Does that change your experience? How?

Bring your experience into the prayer service in which you next participate. Reflect.

"Make loops of blue wool [on the edge of
the outermost cloth of the one set; and do
likewise on the edge of the outermost cloth
of the other set]" (Exod. 26:4).

Understand this in light of the teaching (Sotah 17a) "'Blue' [*tekhelet*] is similar in color to the sea, which is reflective of the color of the heavens, and the heavens are like the Throne of Glory." Consider this in terms of a parable. When we set out to build a building, it exists first in our thoughts. Then comes the extension of that thought into designs, followed by the actual construction and its ultimate purpose, that is, why we built it, who will dwell in it. From this we see there are four steps: thought, expansion of the thought, action, and fulfillment of the plan. When the original thought is manifest in the construction, and when someone inhabits that building, fulfilling its purpose, then it is filled with goodness.

It is the same with the blessed Creator. At first there is thought: it first arose in God's mind to create the world for Israel's sake; Israel was the purpose of the action. And when that original thought is made manifest, then Israel are filled with all good things. This is the dynamic behind all the miracles that God performs for Israel. We see this in the word "megillah," *megaleh yo"d*. When God's original thought and intention (to create the world for Israel) is made manifest, all four aspects of the parable are combined in a complete unity.

This can be seen, as well, in our opening teaching: "**blue**"—"blue is similar in color to the sea," which is the realm of *assiyah* (the lowest world). "The sea [that is, *assiyah*] is reflective of the color of the heavens [*raki'a*]"—which is expansion, spreading out (as in "to the One who spread [*leroka*] the land over the waters"; Ps. 136:6). "The heavens are like the Throne of Glory"—this is thought. This suggests the four letters of the divine name *HVY"H*, as well as the name *ADN"Y*. The first two letters of the Tetragrammaton, *yod hei*, signify thought; the *vav* signifies extension, expansion; the final *hei* signifies the world of *assiyah*, from which all other worlds are created. The name *ADN"Y* signifies the fulfillment of the action (*assiyah*).

FOR FURTHER THOUGHT

Levi Yitzhak offers a sophisticated reflection on the significance of the Tabernacle. There are many ways in which the construction of the Tabernacle echoes the Creation. In this sense, the microcosm reflects the macrocosm, and the latter is fulfilled and completed in the former. Levi Yitzhak senses this and brings that awareness into the mystical system within which he works. That is, with the appearance of the Tabernacle we see a representation of the fulfillment of God's intention in creating the world: that there might be a people "Israel in whom I glory."

God glories not only in the existence of Israel. More than that, God delights in Israel's devotion to serving and bringing glory to God. In this we see the mutual, almost cyclical relationship between God desiring to bless and Israel delighting God so that God might bless—the relationship between arousal from below and arousal from above.

Levi Yitzhak finds the word "blue" used in the Tabernacle and makes the association to the blue thread in the tzitzit and then to Sotah 17a. The movement in this passage is from below—the Sea—to above—the heavens—and finally the Throne of Glory. In this way Levi Yitzhak suggests that the Tabernacle (and all that went on in it, all that was associated with it) played a role in the movement from below to above, or arousal from below.

Yet he immediately offers a parable that appears to contradict the lesson he just offered. The parable of the builder is told from the perspective of the builder, God. God thought of Israel, and so God created the world and delights in the fulfillment of God's initial intention in Israel's devotion in this world (and, presumably, in the Tabernacle). What this suggests is that the construction of the Tabernacle (in the wilderness, and in our hearts today) is the fulfillment of God's initial thought. Through our actions we complete that movement outward from God.

Yet, at the same time, we climb the ladder from action to thought, following the steps from the *tekhelet*, through the sea and the heavens, all the way to God's thought. Seemingly we start in action—but that is not what Levi Yitzhak is teaching us. Rather we, too, must start with thought, with awareness of our intention to bring God delight; discerning how to do so (through prayer, study, good deeds); enacting those deeds; and sensing fulfillment of our intention in the blessings that flow back to us from God's thought.

In setting out his schema, Levi Yitzhak refers to Zoharic and kabbalistic conceptions, locating the *yod* and *hei* of God's name in the realm of thought (cf. Zohar I 21a), the *vav* extending and expanding the energy of that initial thought, and the final *hei* as the realm of *assiyah*. This realm is not the physical world; rather, it is the lowest of the realms of spiritual emanation from which the physical world emerges. That then invites his connection with God's other name: *ADN"Y*. The realm of *adnut* is the world in which we come to recognize and accept God's sovereignty. We can only legitimately do that in the world in which we live and work. Everything that we do that acknowledges God's sovereignty feeds back into the system that raises the energy back up the ladder to its source, in God's thought. The construction of the Tabernacle—in the wilderness, in our hearts—is both the fulfillment of God's intention and the expression of our thought and intention to accept God's sovereignty, returning the energy of delight to its source in God.

Questions for Reflection

1. Can you think of instances in which you are able to trace the process from initial thought to fulfillment of a plan in your life? How did you experience it at that time, and how do you experience your memory of it now?

2. Have you ever had an experience where you sensed that you—and what you were doing—were fully aligned with God's intention? What was that like? What were the conditions that supported it? Were you able to extend it further into your life?

3. We contemporary Jews are in the midst of a long conversation regarding the names we call God. The masculine terms we use—like "Lord"—are

problematic for many. Here, Levi Yitzhak employs the specific and literal name *ADN"Y* to mean "Lord" or "Sovereign," as a way of recognizing God as "Creator of all that is." What other names or terms might you offer that could be equally suitable (ignoring his delight in the fact that it, like *HVY"H*, is made up of four letters)?

Taking It into Your Life

We spend a lot of our time waiting for things to happen, planning, executing, adjusting, evaluating. Our attention is directed toward the end point, the goal, the fulfillment, creating the possibility that we will pay less attention to what is happening in the moment. To quote John Lennon, "Life is what happens to you while you're busy making other plans." Levi Yitzhak is inviting us to become present to the whole of the process, to notice each stage and to connect them into one complete whole, so that in the moment of the initial thought, the clarification of the intention, we sense the emerging elaboration of the process, the enactment of the plan and its fulfillment—and delight in the initial thought with joy of the fulfillment.

Doing so may seem paradoxical—after all, why do anything if it is just the idea that counts? Further, it may seem that this would focus us on the outcome and perhaps close us off to what is actually happening. Yet this process is actually more likely to energize us to act, while also keeping us open and flexible, present to what is arising and able to adjust to changing conditions.

This suggests our practice: investigate the delight that comes from identifying and articulating an intention. Notice what you truly, wholeheartedly, deeply wish to do or become. Sense it fully in your heart. Allow it to be present without grasping, without forcing things toward your goal. Hold it lightly, and notice how you feel having such an intention. It may be that fulfilling your intention requires many steps, or the participation of other people, or deep transformative change. It may seem impossible to fulfill. Yet, you know that you have this intention. As you make your way through your day, revisit your intention. How clear is it to you now? How does it feel to return to it at this moment? What have you learned about your intention in the course of the day, through your interactions with others, through your own inner experience? How do you understand your intention now? How powerfully do you feel it now? Can you delight in what you know now, in the nature of your intention and your determination to bring about its unfolding?

How does having a clear intention change your awareness of your experience from moment to moment, from day to day? How does having a clear intention help generate delight and joy in the midst of the details of life, the process of enacting that intention? How might this practice help you remain connected to the whole, by connecting the beginning to the end (and experiencing *sof ma'aseh bemachshavah techilah*—what comes about last arose in thought first)?

Tetzavveh

"[You shall further instruct the Israelites] that
they bring to you clear oil of beaten olives
for lighting, [to raising up a light always]"
(Exod. 27:20).

When we pay attention, we can see that the evil inclination (*yetzer hara*) seduces us to follow some improper desire or some perverse love. In this way, it tries to interrupt our devotion to the Creator. The proper response is to smash it (the *yetzer hara*), then to raise up those thoughts and all of our desires to holiness, to service of the blessed Creator. We should meditate in our heart, thinking, "I have this desire for something physical, some foolishness! Shouldn't I have this sort of desire for the Creator, to devote myself to serving God? And if I feel this fear of something material, shouldn't I turn it instead to ultimate fear of standing before God?" When we do that, the bad becomes a throne for the good.

It is for this reason that God made it such that we humans are distant from God. If everyone served God all the time, God would not have as much delight, since continuous pleasure is really not so pleasant. But when we feel far from God yet still smash all barriers to hold fast to serving God, that brings great delight and pleasure to God.

A tzaddik must raise up all of the strange thoughts that people have. That is why a tzaddik sometimes experiences such thoughts, so that he can raise them up through his prayer or speech. God made this, too, for God's own glory. If the tzaddik did not have to also raise up the people connected to him, God would not get so much pleasure from the tzaddik, who serves God always. But since the tzaddik also raises up other people, the increased joy brings God great delight from the tzaddik, even though otherwise he is engaged in constant devotion.

Now, all thoughts are really made up of letters, created through some love or fear. And, all strange thoughts come from broken vessels, which are also called broken letters. And the tzaddik has to raise up all of these.

This is how we should understand our verse. "**You shall further instruct** [the Israelites] **that they bring to you clear** [*zakh*] **oil of beaten olives**": see to raising up everything, all the thoughts made up of letters, that is, the twenty-seven (*Kaph-Zayin*) letters represented by the word "clear" (*ZaKh*); "**beaten**" (*katit*)—those letters that are beaten and broken. "**For lighting**" (*lama'or*): the tzaddik must raise up and draw these broken letters and thoughts to holy illumination. All of this is to the end of "**raising up a light always**" (*leha'alot ner tamid*): when the tzaddik engages in raising up the strange thoughts that come to him from others, then there is ascent and delight from the enlightened devotions of the tzaddik, who is called an "eternal light" (*ner tamid*). He serves God always, yet through raising up the thoughts of others, he brings delight above.

FOR FURTHER THOUGHT

There are three aspects to this lesson. One is to connect the verse to Hasidic spirituality. Levi Yitzhak sees in the word "clear" (*ZaKh*) a reference to the twenty-seven letters of the Hebrew alphabet (including the final forms). Aaron represents the tzaddik who not only has the capacity to raise his (or her) own awareness to God but also is so connected to the people that he senses even their impure or negative thoughts. This is positive in two ways: it serves to raise up all thoughts, even those that individuals are unable to recognize and raise on their own, and it serves to interrupt (briefly) the meditation that connects the tzaddik to the Holy One. These fluctuations in the tzaddik's concentration bring about a fall-and-ascent in the tzaddik's spiritual awareness. The recurring ascent—accompanied by the negative and impure thoughts that are thereby raised up—brings God great delight.

Another aspect of this lesson is to define the character of the tzaddik. In this passage, we see these qualities: the tzaddik is able to serve God at all times; the tzaddik's attention to God is unbroken, unless interrupted from the outside; these interruptions originate in the negative, impure, or strange thoughts of other people; the tzaddik's sensitivity to the thoughts of other people reflects his capacity to connect heaven and earth, the divine *ayin* (infinite formlessness) with mundane *yesh* (limited form); the intimate connection that the tzaddik forms with those who devote themselves to him serves to connect these people to the Infinite; and all three parties—God, the tzaddik, and the people—derive pleasure from this process. God needs the devotions of the tzaddik (both its perfection and its interruption); the tzaddik needs the interruption of the people's thoughts; and the people need the tzaddik to help raise them up. A tzaddik who is not connected to other people may approach perfection, but does not help others—or the world—to attain that state. Again, Aaron represents the tzaddik. So God instructs Aaron to bring to himself the thoughts of the people and to raise them up, even in the midst of his continuous devotions.

The third aspect of this lesson has to do with the Hasidic theory of the role of letters in sustaining Creation. The letters of God's speech bring all into being from moment to moment. Our awareness of the presence and activity of these letters raises them up, returning them to their source. In this manner, the process of emanation and return—similar to the process of returning the *yesh* to its source in *ayin*—makes the world one.

Levi Yitzhak states, "All strange thoughts come from broken vessels." In this, he employs a term that appears only a few times in the Zohar. There the broken vessels are the poor—and the poor righteous who study Torah—for whom God has particular concern. The Psalmist says, "You will not despise a contrite and crushed heart" (Ps. 51:19). We might have been inclined to see the broken letters of the impure thoughts of the people in a negative light. We might have seen the impact of the broken letters—particularly as they emerge in response to the suggestions of the *yetzer hara*—as negative, opposed in some way to God. But in light of the Zohar, we might reconsider. The poor are not poor by choice; the poor would choose to live fuller lives if given the chance. So, too, our thoughts. Were our hearts more balanced, if our minds were clearer, we would choose to serve God with love and devotion, turning every thought, emotion, and awareness toward God. And so the righteous—the tzaddik—seeks them out, looking for those thoughts that ought to have been devoted to God to help them fulfill their true task. Indeed, it is by turning our attention to these thoughts, to these broken vessels, that we mimic God's concern and prevent God's anger.

Questions for Reflection

1. Have you had the experience of a thought, a feeling, or an image coming to you unbidden? What have you done in response? What have you found helps you best deal with surprising, disorienting, or negative thoughts that come to you?

2. Have you ever had the experience of your own thoughts, feelings, or memories capturing your mind or heart? What helps you loosen their hold on your heart or mind? Can you imagine some way in which the goodwill of another person (or even just thinking of it) might help you in these instances? How do you think that might work?

3. What relationship do you have where you feel mutual concern, such that you are improved just by the other's concern for you?

Taking It into Your Life

Some people think that the goal of spiritual practice is to attain something final, to get to some degree of "perfection." In Hasidic spirituality it is otherwise. That is, while the tzaddik has attained a very high level—maintaining *devekut* at all times—that is not the goal. Rather, it is to slip out of complete connection so as to return over and over again. The tzaddik may even welcome the "distraction" of other people's *machshavot zarot* ("strange thoughts"—negative, unskillful, misplaced thoughts). Paying them heed, he is at first distracted but then experiences ascent to connect with God once again—and he realizes his deep connection with his people. He comes to know, over and over, how they suffer, how they struggle to resist the distractions of the *yetzer hara*, how they seek to live up to being God's "holy vessels."

How do you respond to distractions? How often do you experience them as opportunities to pay attention, to notice something new, to revisit your primary focus? How often do you resent them and their source? When you are distracted by other people, how do you respond to them? Is it possible to acknowledge that your attention has been broken, that you have turned to something/someone else, and to give that new focus your attention and concern, even if it is to prepare to turn once again to your original, chosen focus?

As you make your way through your day, notice when you are distracted from what you have given your attention. Scan your heart and mind to hear your response. Do you respond negatively, criticizing either what has distracted you or yourself for being distracted? Feel into that reaction. Notice anger, frustration, fear, or resentment. Notice how you cling to your inner goals. Notice how you assess your goals as more important than those of others (otherwise, why would it be a problem to be distracted?). Or notice how relieved you are to be distracted, freed from the demands of your work, liberated to say, "It wasn't my fault."

Bring compassion to your own heart and soul. Allow that to loosen your grasp on your feelings, on your goals. Notice fully what has distracted you. Who is it? What do they need (what are they doing, why are they doing it, with whom are they doing it)? By turning your interest to the distraction, can you find something that you can do to respond to this need? Can you bring compassion to what has distracted you? In bringing compassion, do you sense that the distraction is not directed at you, is not personal, and so is not so powerful? Can you discover a way to respond that may both limit the distraction and allow you to return to your work— or that may make clear that the distraction is more important?

How can you become one of the righteous whose devotion is to care for God's "broken vessels"?

"Make sacral vestments for your brother Aaron, for honor and glory. Instruct all who are wise of heart, [whom I have filled with a spirit of wisdom,] to make Aaron's vestments, for consecrating him [to serve Me as priest]" (Exod. 28:2–3).

Moses consecrated Aaron to be a garment for the blessed Holy One and His *Shekhinah*. The souls of tzaddikim are vessels for the quality of the supernal qualities (*lemiddot elyonim*).

This is how we should understand our verse: "**Make sacral vestments for your brother Aaron**"—may Aaron's soul serve as garments for the holy—"**for honor and glory**" (*lekhavod uletifaret*)—which is to say, for the blessed Holy One and His Shekhinah. But those "**who are wise of heart**" shall make the garments for Aaron's body. That is why Scripture first says, "**for Aaron**" (*le-aharon*), and then later, with regard to the work of the wise of heart, it says, "**Aaron's (vestments)**" (*bigdei aharon*) (without the direct object).

239

FOR FURTHER THOUGHT

Levi Yitzhak, reading carefully, notices subtle differences in how the text refers to Aaron and to the garments being prepared for him. In the first instance, he suggests that "sacral garments for Aaron"(*bigdei kodesh l'aharon*) does not refer to the outer garments he would wear, but the "sacred garments *of* Aaron," the capacity of his soul to be a garment. That is, his spiritual quality would be such that as much as his body serves as a garment for his soul, his soul would also enclose, protect, and garb the supernal qualities of "honor and glory" (*lekhavod uletifaret*). These two qualities are identified by Levi Yitzhak as the *Shekhinah* and the Holy One (the *sephirot* of *Malkhut* and *Tiferet*).

In the second instance, we are told of "Aaron's vestments" (*bigdei aharon*), where he possesses them. In that sense, they must refer to his own garments, the clothing that he would actually wear. They are not what sanctify Aaron; they are only outward markers.

Levi Yitzhak seems to be referring to a passage in the Zohar (I 217a). The Zoharic symbolism is rich and complex. But, characteristic of the Hasidic enterprise, Levi Yitzhak simplifies the imagery. The upper realms are brought directly into the human heart, that of high priest Aaron and of the tzaddik. There, the Holy One and the *Shekhinah* (*Tiferet* and *Malkhut*) are united. The supernal garment is internalized, turning the imagery from vertical to horizontal. When we wish to engage with the *sephirot*, when we strive to energize the divine qualities, we do so in our hearts and souls. While people may make garments for the tzaddik, that is not his glory. Rather, it is his capacity to create an inner garment to bring together the Holy One and the *Shekhinah*, to bring wholeness to himself and the world, that the tzaddik gains "glory and splendor."

 Questions for Reflection

1. How do you experience the power of clothing to affect your inner state? How do you feel when you put on your tallit? How do you feel when you wear new clothes or clothing that you sense makes you look particularly good?

2. How do you imagine that Moses was able to help Aaron make his soul a garment for the Holy One and the *Shekhinah*? Can you imagine doing something like that yourself?

3. The Zohar suggests that there is a connection between providing clothing for those in need and providing garments for the Holy One and the
Shekhinah. Is this different from what Levi Yitzhak is teaching? How do
you imagine making the act of clothing others a unifying event—in your
heart, in the life of the person clothed, in the world?

Taking It into Your Life

Once again, let us give attention to the function of clothes. For the Romantics,
"natural man" needs no outer covering. The body itself is good and beautiful,
and any attempt to cover it expresses either prudishness or fear. For the
Puritan (and traditional Jewish pietists), the body is an embarrassment, a
sign of our low state, and should be obscured. Levi Yitzhak suggests that
perhaps there is another position. Clothing—and all similar definitions
and limitations—create the form in which the substance can be perceived.
Clothing makes it possible to step back from the elemental sexual attraction
revealed by the naked body, to make it possible to perceive the whole person
who appears before us.

Let us work from the outside in. Pay attention to the clothing you wear.
Notice how it fits you—and how you respond when it fits well, when your
clothing corresponds to the shape and nature of your body (without exag-
gerating or hiding its true shape). How do you feel in your skin when your
clothing feels "just right"? How does this affect your sense of "self," if at
all?

Now turn your attention to how your body is a container for your soul.
How do you feel in your skin? How do you sense the shape of your physical
being? Investigate how you perceive your inner being. How do you sense
your soul? Does it fill the whole of your body, or does it reside in some inner
core, an inner point (perhaps the *pintele yid*, the defining Jewish aspect
of your inner being)? How contiguous is your soul with your body? What
might it take to fill your body with soul, or what does it feel like for your
soul to fill your body? How does your body help you perceive the "shape"
of your soul, who you are in the spiritual sense?

Once you have attained a sense of how your soul resides in your body,
begin to investigate how your soul might provide a "container," garments
for the Holy One. Do you sense your soul to be continuous with God? Is God
separate from your soul? How do they relate one to the other? If your soul
has a "shape" (in the sense of reflecting who you are as a whole person),
how might that shape help create the "garment" for the Holy One?

How do you sense the relation between the unity of your body and soul and the ultimate unification of the Holy One and the *Shekhinah*? What internal work might you do to create the ground in which the Holy One and the *Shekhinah* might find a place of refuge, a home in which they might cohabit in peace?

"They shall receive the gold, the blue, [purple, and crimson yarns, and the fine linen]" (Exod. 28:5).

Rashi explains that it is those very ones who are wise of heart (cf. Exod. 28:3) who would **"receive the gold"** from those who freely brought it as an offering.

We are going to explain why it is that the garments of the priests were made from public monies. Even though it is only the priest who performed the divine service and offered sacrifices, his service was not complete if he did not garb himself in love of his fellow Jews, for the sacrament of any priest who does not love the people Israel is worthless....

"Aaron shall carry the names [of the sons of Israel on the breastpiece of decision] on his heart, [when he enters the sanctuary, for remembrance before *YHVH* at all times]" (Exod. 28:29).

Why did Aaron **"carry the names"** of the tribes (on his heart)? In general, when we invoke the merit of the ancestors we refer to Abraham, Isaac, and Jacob. Now, even though the Sages taught that their names were also engraved on the **breastpiece** (Yoma 73b), this is not specified in Scripture. Rather, only the names of the tribes were to be engraved on the stones.

Now regarding Aaron, Scripture reports that God chose him from among all of the Israelites. When one person is selected from among others, we can only conclude that the choice of this individual is because he is more beloved than everyone else, even to the point that the rest are disdained. And here we might say that the selection of Aaron from among the Israelites was like this. That is why the names of the tribes were inscribed **on the breastpiece:** to demonstrate that God also desires them and loves them.

FOR FURTHER THOUGHT

In these lessons Levi Yitzhak confronts the fundamental problem of "chosenness." That is, if Israel is God's chosen people, how does God relate to the rest of humanity? If Israel is God's chosen people, what is the significance of God having chosen Aaron and his descendants to be priests, elevated above the rest of Israel? To choose one person over another, and even one people over another, seems to create a hierarchy. This was problematic in the early Hasidic movement, when the possibility of all Jews establishing a direct and powerful relationship with God was still a goal.

Levi Yitzhak fudges. In the portion of the first text that we did not reproduce, Levi Yitzhak argues that having chosen Israel out of love, God then would hate those who hate Israel. Yet, this same calculus does not apply to the selection of Aaron as priest. Choosing Aaron and his descendants does not distance the Jews from God's love, or put them at a disadvantage. In this, Levi Yitzhak reveals his awareness of the problem of chosenness. He resolves it in the latter case by interpreting the texts to show that the priests had to enact God's continuing love for Israel, negating or undermining any implicit repudiation of the rest of the Jews. He allows the problem to remain relative to those who hate the Jews, but leaves open the possibility that God still loves—or can love—those gentiles who do not hate Israel (whoever they might be).

The role of the priest is not independent of a relationship with both the people and God. Whatever the significance of having been "chosen," it does not come without responsibilities. Status, ultimately, is still dependent on intention and awareness.

 ## Questions for Reflection

1. In which ways do you know that you are "more" than other people? How do you relate to people when you use your "more"? In which ways do you recognize that there are others who are "more" than you? How do you respond to them when they manifest their "more" in your presence?

2. When you function in a leadership position, how do you recall your relation to those whom you are leading? How do you "carry them on your heart"? In what ways do they "clothe" you with authority, and how do you experience that in your work?

3. In your experience, is it possible to be "chosen" and not be set apart, different, better than? How, when? If not, why not?

 ## Taking It into Your Life

Isaiah says, "Your people are all tzaddikim" (Isa. 60:21). This seems to have been a principle of early Hasidism, and it seems as well to express a contemporary value. The impact of modernity, and particularly feminism, has been to level hierarchies and expand the boundaries of Jewish life and community. Contemporary liberal values challenge all boundaries, pushing us to ask not only "who is a Jew?" but also "what is a Jew?"

Moreover, aspects of Hasidic spirituality push us beyond all separations. There is no duality of God-and-world; all is, ultimately, truly One. When we grapple with this view, we are invited to investigate: What is inside, what is outside? Is there a separation? The ultimate experience is to know "no inside, no outside."

Yet, we live our lives in relationship, and there are real boundaries. What might we take from our lessons here as instruction for transcending boundaries while retaining proper relations with others? Aaron was taught in two ways that he was not superior to the Israelites, that his selection did not remove him from connection with and dependence on them. He did not own his clothing; he was dependent on the people to provide him with the garments required for him to perform his duties as priest. And at all times, he carried the names of the tribes—and so also all their members—on his heart.

How might we do this as well? We might use a "gratitude" meditation. Pause periodically throughout the day to notice whatever is in your hands: car keys, pen, glasses, coffee cup, book, food. Whatever it is, bring your full attention to it. Notice it anew; examine it closely to see clearly its components, its particular characteristics. See if you can discover something new about it. When you have "befriended" this object once again, begin to reflect: Where did you get it? Who had it before you? Where did it come from? How was it made? Who produced it? Who provided the raw materials from which it was made? Where did these people live? Who took care of them? As you expand and ramify this inquiry, notice what feelings arise in you. Curiosity? Wonder? Awe? Gratitude? As you sense the emotion arising, allow it to come fully into your awareness. Make the sensation the point of your focus, connecting it with the investigation you have conducted, tying it to the people you have imagined in this process. Wear this awareness as you continue in your day, as you use this and other implements in your life.

"[Then bring his sons forward; clothe them with tunics and wind turbans upon them. And gird both Aaron and his sons with sashes. And so they shall have priesthood as their right for all time.] You shall then ordain Aaron and his sons" (Exod. 29:8–9).

In this world nothing is whole. For the person who desires the physical pleasures of this world, something is always lacking. Even if he has satisfaction from material things, he still lacks the pleasure of honor, he still feels the desire for sex, and the like. He is always missing something.

This is not the case when serving the Creator. The one who serves God is whole in every way, "for those who seek *YHVH* shall not lack any good" (Ps. 34:11). The delight that comes from serving God transcends all others. The one who is attached to the vital force and the service of the *Ein Sof*, who is complete in every sense of wholeness, such a person who cleaves to God will by definition not lack for anything.

So the verse says, "Fill the hands of [i.e., "ordain"] **Aaron and his sons.**" That is, God instructed Moses to make sure to bring Aaron and his sons to that level of enlightenment where they will cleave only to Holiness, and therefore their hands will be filled with all good things. They will not lack anything when they feel this supernal pleasantness and delight. Therefore their investiture was called "the eight days of filling," for then the *Shekhinah* was among them, and they were filled with delight because of the Holiness.

FOR FURTHER THOUGHT

Material things are not bad in themselves. The desire for things is problematic. Kohelet says, "A lover of money never has his fill of money, nor a lover of wealth his fill of income" (Eccles. 5:9). How can we control our avarice; how satisfy our hunger? It is not through getting more. Rather, it is to sense the fullness of our lives in every moment. When we feel that our hands are filled, when we sense satisfaction and balance in our hearts, we will be able to relate to others in a more open, balanced, and loving manner.

Levi Yitzhak is quite clear: everything is transitory, impermanent. Therefore, desire for things is the cause of suffering—the desire for more, grief at its loss. No matter what we point to in this world—and he identifies both material possessions and emotional attainments—it will prove disappointing as a source of satisfaction. It will ultimately disappear or fade in intensity, and we will want more. That is not the case with spiritual awareness. God is not impermanent, and connection to God, even if it comes and goes, is ultimately fulfilling. We do not possess God, nor do we possess our awareness of God. Rather, we enter into awareness, we develop a consciousness that is not ours. We let go of our personal perspectives, we relinquish our desire to control and manipulate what is. We enter into the realm of God's dominion, the totality of what is—as it is, without wishing it otherwise, completely full in all its fullness, lacking nothing to be just as it is. In that, we find our hands full of all that is, without any lack.

 ## Questions for Reflection

1. This sort of teaching can be dangerous. Could this be a version of "pie in the sky"? Couldn't this sort of teaching be used to tell the hungry to ignore the growling of the empty belly and be satisfied in seeking God? Forget your physical hunger and feed your spiritual hunger? Do you think this is what Levi Yitzhak is saying? Why or why not?

2. Alternatively, imagine this addressed to bourgeois householders, to wealthy Americans. What are the lessons that we can draw from this teaching as a critique of a consumer society, a culture that generates needs for things that they themselves can never satisfy?

3. The phrase "fill the hands of" is actually an idiom for ordination, induction. Yet it is also quite potent as an image. With what would our hands be filled if we were to cleave to the presence of God in our lives? How would we sense it, feel it, know it? In what ways would our sense of

need for things be diminished? How could we sustain that sense of satisfaction; what practices would help us continue to feel our hands "full"? How would we hold our hands in the presence of others? How would others know that our hands are full?

 ## Taking It into Your Life

I recall being on a retreat during which a fellow retreatant received word that his wife might have cancer. His first wife had died of cancer. He could not change the news. There was nothing that he could accomplish by leaving the retreat. He sat, and in a final presentation he reflected:

> The psalm reads: "*Pote'ach et yadekha, umasbi'a lekhol chai ratzon*—You open your hand and satisfy all living things from Your favor" (Ps. 145:16). The subject is God. Yet, we might read it as an instruction for our own lives. I'm sitting here and my heart is breaking. My body is tight with fear. But I take a breath and open my hand, and find balance in the moment. I cannot control what is happening. I can respond, but I know that I don't know what will happen, and so I have to keep opening my hand to receive whatever is, and whatever will be with grace, with willingness, with love.

When we open our hands, releasing our grip on what we "possess," we find that our desire is indeed filled.

> How can we learn to let go of our expectations in the face of what is? How can we learn to let go of our frustrations in the face of what is? How can we learn to let go of our fears in the face of what is? We might adapt a breathing practice that we can bring into every moment of our lives.

Sit easily, attentive, and at ease, allowing your eyes to close. Bring your attention to your breath. Follow the breath from the moment of its arising, through its fullness, and all the way to its conclusion. When you have established a degree of stability in your awareness, add this thought/awareness to each breath:

When breathing in, say to yourself, "I breathe in blessing."

When breathing out, say to yourself, "I breathe out gratitude."

When you start this element of the practice, you might actually want to formulate the words in your mind. But be sure to add to the phrases an awareness of what it feels like to experience blessing, what it feels like to express gratitude. In that way, the words will begin to reflect your felt experience. After a while, you may be able to let go of the words and simply continue with each breath made up of two experiences: blessing and thanksgiving.

After practicing for some time, when you sense that this practice is familiar, carry it out into "the world." From moment to moment, bring this awareness to each breath. As you encounter frustrations—when expectations have not been fulfilled, when things run counter to your wishes—respond with "I breathe in blessing; I breathe out gratitude." As you encounter moments of great satisfaction—when expectations have been fulfilled, when things run directly according to your wishes—respond with "I breathe in blessing; I breathe out gratitude."

You may want to add another concrete physical act to match your inner experience: each time you breathe out gratitude, open your hand, palms up, to receive whatever is, aware of the fullness of the moment.

Ki Tissa

Or we can interpret in this manner: "[When you take a census of the Israelites] according to their enrollment, [each shall pay *YHVH* a ransom for himself on being enrolled, that no plague may come upon them through their being enrolled]"
(Exod. 30:12).

The word *liphkudeihem* infers lack. We should always see ourselves as we are in truth: we have not yet even set out on our path to serve God. In this manner we will have attained some degree of awareness, of spiritual development. But if we were to think (heaven forbid!) that we actually have succeeded in serving God, we would show that we have not attained any understanding of the meaning of serving the blessed Creator.

This is implied in the verse, "**When you take a census** [lift up the heads] **of the Israelites**" (Exod. 30:12) to raise them up to some spiritual attainment, the essential thing is that it be "**according to their enrollment**" (*liphkudeihem*): let them be aware of their spiritual deficiency, as in "but David's place remained vacant" (*vayippakeid mekom David*) (1 Sam. 20:25). In this manner they will come truly to see their "insufficiency" (*pikkadon*), that is, their lack: they have not yet achieved anything in the service of the blessed Creator.

This is hinted at in the phrase "**each shall pay *YHVH* a ransom for himself**" (*kopher naphsho*): *kopher* means "attachment," as in "cover [*vekhapharta*] it inside and out with pitch [*bakopher*]" (Gen. 6:14). When are they attached to God? "**Through their being enrolled**" (*biphekod otam*); once we know our own deficiencies in divine service, then we can truly become connected with the Holy One.

Or, we can interpret in this manner: "When you take a census of the Israelites according

249

> to their enrollment, each shall pay *YHVH* a
> ransom for himself [on being enrolled, that
> no plague may come upon them through
> their being enrolled]" (Exod. 30:12).

This is how it works: If our intention is to pray for others when they are suffering, then we have to lift them up. That is, we have to recognize that this is not only their suffering, it is actually God's, who is our Parent. That is what the Sages taught (Chagigah 15b): "When a person suffers, what expression does the *Shekhinah* use? 'My head is heavy, my arm is heavy.'" We find, then, that in lifting all up to God, the people are saved from their troubles.

This is the meaning of our verse: "**When you take a census** [lift up the heads] **of the Israelites**"—that is, when you raise them—"**according to their enrollment**" (*liphkudeihem*)—do so according to their lack. When the Jews lack the blessings of the Creator, then raise them up. The verse continues to explain how to raise them: "**Each shall pay YHVH a ransom for** his soul" (*kopher naphsho*)—our souls should be "for God," belonging to God.

FOR FURTHER THOUGHT

Clearly Levi Yitzhak associates the word for "enrollment" or "muster" (*pekudah*) with another term meaning "taking note" (*pakad*), particularly noting lack, absence. This resonates in the Hasidic milieu, where humility is the *sine qua non* for true spiritual growth and devotion, and not knowing is a sign of truly knowing.

The quality of humility is the result of knowing that whatever we may think we know is nothing relative to the fullness of what is to be known. Knowing our "lack" is not a sign of deficiency, but an indication of honest appreciation of our attainment. There is a certain pathos here: when we recognize how little we truly know of God, we realize how lonely God must be. However much God may reach out to us, desiring our love and attention, we are able to respond in only the most limited ways. This is reflected, as well, in the sense that our suffering reflects God's suffering. When we notice our own limitations—inflicted on us by enemies, caused by deprivation, manifested in our mortal imperfection—we are directed to God's emptiness, knowing that we have not even begun to know

God. The only response to this knowledge is to offer ourselves completely, giving our souls to the Holy One.

In this light, we see that being mustered into the army of God is no longer a matter of preparing for physical combat. Rather, it is our effort to engage in divine service, in working toward *devekut*. As ever, this requires a capacity to see the truth, to enter into an honest assessment of our own spiritual attainments. This is possible only if we recognize the "Spirituality Uncertainty Principle": we can know either where we stand in spiritual development or the direction we are moving (closer or farther from knowledge of God), but not both at the same time. Levi Yitzhak warns us of forgetting that principle.

 ## Questions for Reflection

1. The value of "self-esteem" seems to be in conflict with this teaching. Can we lift anyone up by telling them they aren't anywhere yet in their spiritual development? Can we really, fully, serve God if we feel that we are always "lacking"? How? Alternatively, Levi Yitzhak may be warning us about the spiritual dangers of too much "self-esteem." Is any sense of attainment just an invitation to egotism and smugness, to sloppiness in our spiritual work? When have you experienced this in your life?

2. How do you feel the balance of "the truth" and "self-esteem" in yourself? In your community? In our culture/society? Can you share this selection from *Kedushat Levi* with others—telling people that they have not yet even started out on the path of divine service? Should you?

3. What do you make of the association of *kopher* and *devekut*, of sticky stuff and cleaving to God? Rather than hiding something or atoning for something, the *kapparah* (here, literally, "atonement") is actually making ourselves "sticky" and attaching ourselves to God. Does making a connection between recognizing the truth of our lives (our lack, insufficiency) and "atonement" help you see a way for atonement to effect a deep connection to God? When, how?

 ## Taking It into Your Life

There are two aspects to the experience of "not knowing": curious investigation and willing self-doubt. Cultivating both can be energizing and liberating. When we meet each moment with open awareness and curiosity ("What is this really?" or "What is this *now*?"), we engage with that moment with new and renewed energy. We meet it with interest, inquiring into its particular qualities, its unique truth. We are less likely to be bored; we find that nothing is "same old, same old." And, when we hold what we know with a light touch, allowing the possibility that our knowledge is incomplete and that we might be wrong in this instance, we are liberated. We are not bound to protect our previous statements or positions but are free to be who we are in this moment, responding to challenge without fear or rancor. We are uninhibited, able to recapture the curiosity that brought us the knowledge we have and to grow into it again. In this manner, we open again and again to awareness of our own impermanence and find our place in the infinite of the Divine.

As you make your way through the day, carry with you two questions: "What is this?" and "What do I know?"

Apply the first to every situation you meet. When faced with a slower car ahead of you, ask, "What is this?" with curiosity about the driver, the traffic ahead of that car, the situation around you—and your own inner state. Are you anxious because you are late? Are you frustrated because you like to go faster? Could it be that there is danger ahead and the driver's caution is protecting you?

When the phone rings, ask before picking up the receiver, "What is this?" What is happening in this moment? How are you feeling? What are your expectations? How do you want to respond ... to everyone?

When challenged by a loved one, ask, "What is this?" What is being asked of me? What am I afraid of? What do I think is going on in the other person? How is he/she feeling? What does he/she want? Can I give it? Can I help? Is it OK for me to say, "I can't help"?

When you assert your position at work or at home, take a breath and ask internally, "What do I know?" Feel out the ground of your certainty, the basis for your assertion. What would it feel like to change your position? What would be the consequence of following another path, of doing things another way? There is a difference between "2 + 2 = 4" and "the right way" to wash the dishes, fold the laundry, drive in traffic, keep the checkbook, speak to children, express affection. Often what we "know" is our habits of mind; asking, "What do I know?" makes possible discovering the needs, concerns, and cares of others. The compassion we bring to our own hearts when we ask, "What do I know?" generates the compassion for the other, the context for us to truly know what is true.

"This is what everyone who is entered in the records shall pay: a half-shekel by the sanctuary weight—[twenty *gerah*s to the shekel—a half-shekel as an offering to YHVH]" (Exod. 30:13).

There are a number of problems of interpretation in this passage:

1. Why a half-shekel and not a whole one?

2. Why are only those aged twenty and older required to pay this tax, and not those younger? If this is a positive commandment, then it should automatically apply equally to one who is thirteen years old (bar mitzvah)!

3. Why is this tax applied specifically to those who go out to battle, as it says: "All those who are able to bear arms" (cf. Num. 1:3)?

Let us approach this by way of analogy: Think of a person who does everything without being settled in his mind. Occasionally he will do the exact opposite of what is called for. That is, he will do good even to those who do not obey his instructions. But a person who acts from a settled mind and balanced consideration—who weighs carefully what to do—will surely act appropriately. To the person who is aligned with him he will do good, and to those who oppose him he will not do good.

This is how it is with the Jewish people. When (heaven forbid) they do not behave properly, by their misbehavior they only merit to draw down blessings on all the worlds, and the blessed Creator pours out blessing only because of His love for His creatures. As a result, the external forces also receive this blessing. The blessed Creator responds to the Jews' behavior and sends down blessing only because of His great love. Therefore, as it were, God is like the one who acts without a settled mind, unable to discern to whom to send blessing and from whom to withhold it. Because there is no one with merit for whom God can send blessings due to merit; therefore, everyone winds up being equal and receives uniformly. God in this state is called (as if it were possible): "acting without a settled mind."

But when the Jews, by their good deeds, merit to direct and draw down blessing on all the worlds, then the blessed Creator does weigh how to distribute the flow: to those who do God's will (Israel, God's holy people) He sends blessing; to those who do not do God's will He does not send blessing. This is because God responds to the Jews' merit.

Now, since God acts through balanced consideration, it appears as if God's mind is divided: benefiting those who do God's will, but not those who do not do God's will. When Israel need to avenge attack and vanquish their enemies in battle, they have to arouse this quality in God: that the blessed Creator (as it were) would weigh out in His mind to whom to send blessing and from whom to withhold it. In this manner, the blessing will come only to Israel, and by default their enemies will be defeated (since blessing comes only to Israel and not to them).

This is the significance of the half-shekel offered only by the twenty-year-olds who go out to battle. They have to arouse this quality of balanced consideration so that God (as it were) will discern how to bless and whom to bless. For sure, in this way the blessing will come only to Israel, and in this manner they will be victorious in their battles. Now, this quality of balanced consideration that seems to signify a divided mind is represented by two letters *yod*: one *yod* here and one *yod* there with a letter *vav* as the balance between them. In this manner, we can see that the quality of balanced consideration is like the letter *aleph*: two *yod*s and a *vav* have the shape of *aleph*. The numerical value of two *yod*s is twenty, which also explains why there are twenty *gerah*s to a shekel.

FOR FURTHER THOUGHT

What a startling way of talking about God! It seems to bother Levi Yitzhak to do so, as he appears to use the term *kevayakhol* ("as it were"; "as if it were possible") much more than in other sections in the book. For all that, it is still important to him to offer this image: God, at times, loses track of His intention, His true desire. God's mind is unsettled, unbalanced. However, when the Jews behave in ways that are meritorious (presumably doing mitzvot, devoting themselves in prayer and Torah study, but possibly just, as he says, only "their good deeds"), then God's mind clears up; God is more settled, and so discerning, even discriminating in how to behave.

The term that Levi Yitzhak uses for this state of mind is "balanced" (*shikul hada'at*). Clearly he uses this to make the connection to "half-shekel." But he also creates the image of the scale, by which one "weighs" (*shokel*) one's decisions. That scale (or balance) is a simple device: a center pole (like the letter *vav*) to serve as fulcrum, two pans (the letter *yod*) to hold the matter being weighed. Together these take the shape of the letter *aleph*. The sum of the two *yods* is twenty, referring to the twenty-year-olds and to the twenty *gerahs* that make up the weight of a shekel. It appears that Levi Yitzhak means to suggest that twenty-year-olds (as opposed to those younger) are more able to recognize the significance of their deeds and so to act in such a manner as to merit God's attention. Their capacity to weigh their deeds causes God to do the same.

To carry the image further: it is only by truly weighing both sides together—that is, both *yods*—that one attains a full measure of a shekel. Thirteen-year-olds are more likely to see things in black-and-white, in absolute oppositions, and so less likely to be truly discriminating in their assessments of circumstances. They may have to work harder to control their *yetzer*, but that does not mean that their minds are settled, or that they are truly balanced in their thoughts. They cannot truly engage in that battle and so are not included in the muster of the half-shekel. And, when the two *yods* together with the central *vav* make an *aleph* manifest, it perhaps points to *alupho shel olam*, the Cosmic Aleph, the blessed Holy One. This capacity for investigation and assessment brings God more fully into the world.

The images that seem to be Levi Yitzhak's true interest are quite striking in their familiarity. Mindlessness and mindfulness, an unsettled mind and balanced awareness are human experiences and central to spiritual practice. In his attempt to call us to greater awareness, to serious attention to the state of our minds and the import of our "good deeds," Levi Yitzhak is willing to make God more human. How radical! How welcome!

 ## Questions for Reflection

1. The term for "settled awareness" is *yishuv hada'at*. *Yishuv* may be related either to the root *y-sh-b* (to dwell) or to the root *sh-u-b* (to return). What is your experience of what it takes to "settle" your mind? What do you sense is the relationship between the two Hebrew roots and this process?

2. What do you imagine is the connection between this lesson and the Rabbinic teaching of the world hanging in the balance at Rosh Hashanah?

This parashah comes between Purim and Passover. Why do you imagine Levi Yitzhak might have brought this into his teaching at this time of year? How might it affect your experience of this season?

3. Does it please you or offend to you think of God's mind being cloudy at times, forgetful of God's true intent, unable to make good decisions? Is it true for you that "good decisions" are only those that benefit the Jews? If not, how might you reread this text in a manner that fits your sensibilities? If so, what do Jews need to do to benefit from those "good decisions," and how might that then also benefit all decent, spiritually devoted people?

Taking It into Your Life

In meditation (as in a mindful life), we set an intention and then experience the constant process of returning to our intention. It is in that return that we build confidence in the possibility of accomplishing our goal, move toward our goal, and learn to assess the value of our original intention. So, for instance, we sit and set an intention to pay attention to the breath, to developing a concentrated, balanced awareness. As we sit, we may become aware that our attention has wandered. We recall our intention and bring our attention back to the breath. This may happen many times. Each times it occurs, we may experience different responses. At times, we may feel delight in being awake and aware in the moment and able to follow through on our intention. At other times, we may feel doubt, frustration, anger, or despair at how easily we stray from our intention. In each instance, noting the quality of our feelings and the nature of our response is important—but only as the context out of which we reconnect with our intention. Sometimes, doubt may lead us to question our original intention. Recognizing doubt as a quality of heart/mind is important, as it allows us to recognize the presence of uncertainty. But we do not have to act on it immediately. Rather, noting it, we can return to our practice.

However, having noted its presence, we can at another time reconsider our intention. What moved us to set it? What was our goal? Do we still hold that ambition? Is it still valuable? What might we do to remain balanced even in the face of our doubt? In this manner, our investigation of our intention may lead us to recognize where it might need to be changed (e.g., pay attention to the breath only for concentration—balance can come later). Alternatively, we may recognize that doubt is one form of hindrance, distracting us from our true intention. This process of investigation and understanding will help us remain balanced in the face of doubt in the future, allowing us to remain connected to our intention.

Bring this awareness into your meditation practice. At the same time, reflect on how this process applies as well to the other intentions you may have in your life: to express love toward loved ones, to be trustworthy in your relationships, to guard your speech, and so on. Notice what it feels like to hold this intention; notice when you are connected to it, fulfilling it; notice when you are not in touch and what it takes to return to it; allow your intention (and the repeated return to it) to support and sustain you, helping you to be discriminating in your actions, balanced in your responses, a blessing to yourself and others.

"The Israelite people shall keep the Sabbath,
[observing the Sabbath throughout the ages
as a covenant for all time]" (Exod. 31:16).

We can explain this verse in light of the teaching (Shabbat 118b):

> R. Yohanan said in the name of R. Shimon bar Yohai: If Israel were to keep two Sabbaths according to its laws, they would be redeemed immediately. [Scripture says: "Thus said *YHVH*: 'As for eunuchs who keep my Sabbaths'" (Isa. 56:4), which is followed by, "'I will bring even them to my holy mountain, etc.'" (56:7).]

When we keep Shabbat appropriately, as it should be, we gain from this Sabbath the vital energy and divine fullness to serve God throughout the week that follows. When we devote ourselves to serving God through the whole week, then it is even easier for us to keep the next Shabbat appropriately. And this continues to build on itself, ad infinitum!

This helps us to resolve a problem raised in a different passage (Y. Ta'anit 1:1, end; 3b): "[R. Levi said:] If Israel were to keep even one Shabbat properly, [immediately the son of David would come]." But in our passage, it speaks of two Sabbaths. In the end, the key is really one Shabbat. When we keep one Shabbat and then serve God with a pure heart the whole following week, it is then easier for us to keep the second Shabbat appropriately. From this we see that the key is one Shabbat, because by keeping one Shabbat we are able to keep the second even easier, and so on.

This we can see in our verse: **"The Israelite people shall keep the Sabbath"**—they will keep one Shabbat—"to do the Sabbath"—that is, the second Shabbat, since observing the second Shabbat will be easier. Thus: **the Israelite people shall keep the Sabbath** to do the Sabbath.

FOR FURTHER THOUGHT

What a wonderful promise. The experience of Shabbat creates the energy to experience Shabbat. Many of us know that in our own lives: we made Shabbat a practice by being invited into the practice. What was once difficult or unfamiliar grew in pleasure, and we entered into it.

There is something enticing about this lesson beyond its application to Shabbat practice. In each of the two quotations from the Talmud, the consequence of observing Shabbat properly is that redemption/the Messiah will come. It is interesting that Levi Yitzhak does not refer to this aspect of these texts, focusing only on the inner experience of energy born of Shabbat observance. He does not suggest that by observing Shabbat properly once the whole cycle of time will cease, that life as we know it will come to an end, entering a time "that is all Shabbat." Rather, the observance of one Shabbat will energize the preparation for and experience of the next Shabbat forever.

Perhaps Levi Yitzhak is offering us a new understanding of what "redemption" or the "coming of the Messiah" might be like. We would sense purpose in our lives: to serve God with a whole heart. We would live with expectation: our weeks would be directed to preparing for Shabbat. We would sense growth in our spirits: Shabbat would lift us, providing inner and outer strength to live in the weekday. One Shabbat will be complete in itself, needing nothing more than what we brought into it from the week before. Yet, that same Shabbat will affect our lives into the week to come. Its spirit will make each succeeding day a form of Shabbat: preparing for Shabbat. In that way, perhaps, Levi Yitzhak is describing a life that will be a time "that is all Shabbat."

 Questions for Reflection

1. What do you remember of your best Shabbat experience? What helped make it special? What of it can you bring into your life today?

2. Have you had the experience of remembering (tasting, feeling, smelling) something from Shabbat during the week? What was that like? How did you feel—nostalgic, sad, refreshed, otherwise? Why?

3. When do you start preparing for Shabbat? How does that affect your sense of the rhythm and flow of your week? How does that affect your sense of how you come into Shabbat and how you experience it? What does it mean for how you leave Shabbat and enter the next week?

Taking It into Your Life

Levi Yitzhak's teaching follows the Hasidic view that spiritual life is meant to be a continuous process of growth, always changing, always moving ahead/deeper. Yet we know that there are also periods of less acuity, less connection. More, this lesson seems to suggest a constant awareness of comparison: "This week's Shabbat is certainly better than last week's."

Yet we also hear in Levi Yitzhak's teaching a profound awareness of the meaningfulness of the "one" experience. That is, there is no Shabbat but this one Shabbat. Whatever we do to observe it, however deeply we immerse ourselves in its holiness, sweetness, and beauty, it is meaningful only for this Shabbat. We can have no knowledge or expectation of its significance or its potential contribution to the next Shabbat. That will depend on how much we are able to draw out of this Shabbat its power and bring that into the week that follows. And even then, we cannot know on Sunday what the impact will be on the following Shabbat. Indeed, whatever awareness we bring into Sunday will only have significance beyond that day if we are able to carry it forward, renewing and deepening it, on Monday. And so on. However continuous Levi Yitzhak suggests this process may be, what he is teaching is the importance of this experience, this one moment, this now.

How can we bring the rest and ease of that day into the hustle and bustle, the rough and tumble of the weekday? Shabbat is the day on which we refrain from exercising our will to change the world. We step back to appreciate God's blessing, the sustaining love present in creation. When we pay attention to precisely what is happening in this moment without trying to make it other, without resisting or insisting, we experience a Shabbat moment. That is rest; that is ease. The weekday is not Shabbat, however. We have permission—no, the obligation—to prevent injustice, overturn the perversion of the good. When we pause to rest in the midst of this work, we are reminded that even this moment is filled with God's presence.

We remember that we are not doing this work alone. We can accept and even bless this moment, so that we are not in contention with "what is," even as we work toward what "should be."

Bring "Shabbat" experience into your weekday. Make it a practice to stop periodically to rest, to catch your breath, during the day. As you move from one activity to another, incorporate some ritual—saying an internal "thank you," washing hands, taking a breath, saying a prayer, singing a *niggun*—to separate one moment from another. Let each activity be the one activity you are doing, with your whole heart, soul, and mind—so that you can bring that energy into the next activity to which you turn. In observing this "one Shabbat" may you find redemption in the moments to come.

> YHVH passed before him and proclaimed:
> ["YHVH! YHVH! a God compassionate
> and gracious, slow to anger, abounding
> in kindness and faithfulness, extending
> kindness to the thousandth generation,
> forgiving iniquity, transgression, and sin—
> remitting—punishment—]" (Exod. 34:6–7).

Rashi cites the Rabbinic teaching that the blessed Holy One wrapped himself like a prayer leader [and said, "If you act before Me according to this rite I will forgive and cleanse you"] (Rosh Hashanah 17b).

My teacher, R. Dov Baer, taught that the thirteen homiletic methods of Torah interpretation are connected to the thirteen qualities of God's love expressed in our verse. The interpretive method *a fortiori* (*kal vachomer*) is linked to the name "God" (*el*), and the quality "compassion" (*rachum*) is linked to the method of interpretation by analogy (*gezerah shavah*).

Here is how we might understand this: when a wealthy person has compassion for a poor person, the former has to see himself like the latter, connecting himself with the suffering of the poor person and the pressure he is under. This is how he develops compassion for the poor person, by seeing himself as the same as the poor person. In this way, compassion extends from the wealthy person to the poor person, and finally the two are equal.

This is how it is (as if it were possible) with the blessed Creator, as it says, "I am with him in his suffering" (Ps. 91:15)—this is how analogy (*gezerah shavah*) functions like compassion.

> Another interpretation: *YHVH* passed before
> him and proclaimed: ["*YHVH*! *YHVH*! a God
> compassionate and gracious, slow to anger,
> abounding in kindness and faithfulness,
> extending kindness to the thousandth
> generation, forgiving iniquity, transgression,
> and sin—remitting—punishment—]"
> (Exod. 34:6–7).

The Sages taught that this signifies that the blessed Holy One wrapped himself like a prayer leader and said, "If you act before Me according to this rite I will forgive and cleanse you" (Rosh Hashanah 17b).

The blessed Holy One surely does not deal despotically with His creatures (Avodah Zarah 3a). Further, Israel is fundamental to creation, as the Sages taught: "In the beginning (*bereishit*; Gen. 1:1): the world was created for the sake of Israel who are called 'beginning' (*reishit*) (Jer. 2:3)" (Lev. R. 36:4). Yet, if God were to judge them according to their actual standing in the exalted realms, they surely would not last a moment. The source of their souls obligates them to be holy and pure in every way, but "there is not one good man on earth who does what is best and doesn't sin" (Eccles. 7:20). How much more so were God to judge them according to God's own supernal holy qualities and great holiness! They are supposed to mirror in their form the One who formed them, as they are known as "God's children" (Avot 3:14), and the king's child is supposed to behave in a royal manner.

But the Creator has compassion for His creatures. Compassion (*rachum*) is linked to the interpretive method of analogy (*gezerah shavah*). God cascades His thoughts to the lower worlds to investigate them and judges them according to the capacities and expectations of material worlds, since the letters making up the word "compassion" (*RaChU"M*) are the same as "material" (*ChOMe"R*). In this manner compassion is surely aroused, just as the wealthy person who looks into the low estate of the poor person and his suffering and extends his thoughts to really see him. He then is compassionate to him and provides for all his needs. In the same way, the blessed Creator garbs His thoughts in the garments of the lower realms and so has compassion for us.

This is signified by the word He **"passed"** (*vaya'avor*)—God passes from the deepest realms of holiness and cascades His thoughts into the most constricted qualities, the lower worlds, to be garbed in our very beings. Then, He **"proclaimed: '*YHVH! YHVH!*'"** and is filled with compassion, love, and grace. That is what the Sages meant in saying that the blessed Holy One wrapped Himself: he wears our qualities, clothed in us. "***YHVH*** **passed before him**" (*al panav*): God's face (*panav*) is the very essence of God's infinite light, without garments (yet God passed up that expansiveness to dwell in our garments).

This functions measure for measure. If we, a holy people, wish to raise our thoughts out of the garments of this world that obscure God, to cleave only to the root of all, the origin of all, yet behave only according to our qualities, then God will act only according to His. That is what the Sages meant when they told us God said, "If you act before Me according to this rite" (Rosh Hashanah 17b): just as I am doing. "Before Me" (*lephanai*): if you pass up your qualities, then I will turn from solely acting according to My qualities to connect with yours. This is the sense, as well, of the verse "I am my beloved's, and my beloved is mine" (Song 6:3).

FOR FURTHER THOUGHT

The Hasidic impulse is to see God's presence in all things and to recognize God's goodness in all moments. A popular teaching was to misquote Lam. 3:38, changing "Is it not from the mouth of the Most High that both bad and good come forth?" to say "The bad does not come forth from the mouth of the Most High." Yet it takes a great effort to see past the suffering in this world to perceive God's loving goodness. This seeming contradiction stands behind Levi Yitzhak's efforts in these two teachings.

Levi Yitzhak ties together a number of strands of interpretation based on these verses. One identifies the terms in this verse as divine qualities, qualities that we should emulate:

> "[And now, O Israel, what does *YHVH* your God demand of you? Only this: to revere *YHVH* your God,] to walk only in His ways, [to love Him, and to serve *YHVH* your God with all your heart and soul]" (Deut. 10:12). These are the ways of the Holy One: "*YHVH*! *YHVH*! a God compassionate and gracious, slow to anger, abounding in kindness and faithfulness, extending kindness to the thousandth generation, forgiving iniquity, transgression, and sin—remitting—punishment—." Further, Scripture says: "All who call

the name *YHVH* shall escape" (Joel 3:5). How is it possible for a mortal to call the name of the blessed Holy One? Just as He is compassionate and merciful, so you be compassionate and merciful.

(*Sifrei, Eikev* 13)

God's attributes of mercy are the model for our behavior. The foundation of spiritual practice—and of ethics—is to emulate the Holy One.

These verses from Exodus, however, also serve a more focused purpose. They are not only how we should behave to be like God. They are also the means by which we can reflect back to God that these are the attributes of the Holy One, reminding God to act accordingly. The passage quoted above from Rosh Hashanah 17b is the basis on which the whole of the order of penitential (*selichot*) prayers were composed, particularly those recited on Yom Kippur. These verses are used in two ways, each mirroring the other: they teach us how we are to behave to be more like God, and they remind God how God wishes to behave toward us.

A problem remains. God and Israel are still pictured in separate camps, each mirroring the other, but not connected. We cannot truly walk in God's ways, and God merely models how we should behave, not truly entering the human sphere. Where is the point of connection? How can that distance be transcended, eroded, transformed? The mystical tradition posits a fundamental unity among God, Israel, and the Torah (Zohar III 73a). Torah is the interface, the place of meeting between God and Israel. We have a shared lot with God in the Torah.

God and the Jewish people engage together in the study of Torah. There are certain fundamental principles, homiletic rules for interpreting Torah. The classical list of R. Yishmael (*Sifra*, opening of ch. 1) contains thirteen principles (*middot*), equal to the number of God's qualities (*middot*) of compassion. In this manner, when we engage in interpreting the Torah, we uncover aspects of God's compassion, meeting God in the Torah. When God acts lovingly and compassionately in the world, God meets us through Torah as well. In this manner, we not only mirror each other, but we also participate in a shared practice: we engage in revealing Torah, activating God's compassion. When we strive to live according to God's qualities (*middot*), God meets us, extending compassion to us and through us.

Questions for Reflection

1. The first of R. Yishmael's principles is reasoning *a fortiori*, drawing inferences from one expansive premise to another that is less inclusive. That is how the wealthy person comes to recognize his connection, his equality with the poor person. Describe how you understand the way this dynamic works. Have you experienced this process? When, how?

2. It is an expression of God's mercy that He does not judge us according to divine standards, but according to human ones. What does it mean to you to consider that God is willing and able to "stand in our shoes," to "see how it feels to live in our garments"?

3. The Thirteen Attributes of God's Compassion are divine qualities. Sylvia Boorstein teaches, "The natural response of the balanced heart is compassion." What does it take for you to discern and manifest the divine qualities in your own heart? How do you imagine that extending yourself to express these qualities helps energize those same qualities everywhere?

Taking It into Your Life

Levi Yitzhak presents an image that is quite powerful: just as the wealthy person connects directly to the poor person, fully feeling his suffering, entering equally into that experience, so does God engage with us. No matter what our status or standing, we are all truly equal. No matter how low we may fall, no matter how distant we feel from God, it is possible for God to reach out to be present to—and in—us.

The fundamental practice is to extend compassion to all others. Levi Yitzhak suggests a number of approaches:

> One: compassion arises from connecting to the suffering and pressure others experience, sensing the ways in which our own experience is the same. The source of the compassion for the other is our awareness of our own suffering. The compassion that we bring to our own experience we then can extend with graciousness and with openness to others.
>
> Another: step out of the frame of reference by which we measure the world, by which we assess and evaluate circumstances, to enter into the frame of reference of others. Imagine that other people are not merely failed versions of yourself. This requires a degree of self-contraction. We must

get our perspectives out of the way to see more clearly, to sense more directly the truth of others' lives. Compassion is required to shift perspective and get out of the way, so that we can then express compassion for those we might otherwise have judged harshly or ignored as different and unworthy.

Another: seek to perceive how others strive to do the best they can, to live their highest ideals. Recognizing the best intention in others inspires us to respond in kind, bringing our full hearts to our interactions. Compassion arises in response to the struggles of others to be compassionate, loving, and just.

As you move through your day, notice when you experience a twinge of pain; sense when you draw back from the experience of suffering. Breathe into that moment and allow the suffering to be present. Respond, naturally, spontaneously, with compassion. Allow that compassion to extend out to others.

As you move through your day, notice when you scoff at, withdraw in revulsion from, demean, or ignore others. Those moments, too, are moments of suffering. Bring compassion to your own pain, and allow it to soften your boundaries. Consider: why would another person choose to live this way, behave this way? How am I like that? Allow your heart to open in compassion.

As you move through your day, pay attention to other people. Investigate the quality of their intention. Where do they express compassion, love, and justice? How are they like you, and you like them?

Vayakheil

[Moses then convoked the whole Israelite community and said to them:] "These are the things that YHVH has commanded you to do: On six days work may be done, [but on the seventh day you shall have a Sabbath of complete rest, holy to YHVH. Whoever does any work on it shall be put to death]"
(Exod. 35:1–2).

The Sages taught that the words "**These** [*eileh*] **are the things**" are the basis for the thirty-nine foundational acts of labor prohibited on Shabbat (Shabbat 70a). This is to say, "these" (*eileh*) refers to the negative external forces, as the AR"I *z"l* taught regarding the verse, "For these things [*eileh*] do I weep" (Lam. 1:16): we have to repair them by means of our labors. That is the sense of the word "**to do**" (*la'asot*)—meaning "repair." And this is what we do on the weekday. But on Shabbat we do not engage in removing the external forces, and therefore it is prohibited to do this labor.

But what is the implication that in this parashah we find the phrase "**that YHVH has commanded you** *to do*" regarding Shabbat, yet with regard to the construction of the Tabernacle (*Mishkan*) we find the phrase "that YHVH commanded *to say*" (Exod. 35:4)?

This is how I see it: even though the people were engaged in fulfilling practical mitzvot in constructing the *Mishkan*, nevertheless their endeavors contributed to the repair of the world of speech. This is hinted at in the phrase "that YHVH commanded *to say*." But on Shabbat we do no labor, instead focusing our energies on mitzvot fulfilled in speech, such as prayer and Torah study (when these practices reach their fullest expression). Nevertheless, through them we repair the world of action. This is hinted at in the phrase "**that YHVH has commanded you** *to do*"—that is, to repair the world of doing.

FOR FURTHER THOUGHT

Levi Yitzhak offers us a creative way to understand the relationship between contemplative practice and spiritual acts in the work of *tikkun olam*. The practical mitzvot we do during the week—the ways in which we act concretely to repair the world—have an impact on the upper realms. In particular, we affect the "world of speech," that is, the realm of the *Shekhinah*. By performing mitzvot, we acknowledge God's sovereignty; we accept the yoke of God's dominion. On Shabbat, when productive work is prohibited, our speech acts affect the physical world. We fill material space with holiness.

The world of speech, in kabbalistic terms, is related to the *sephirah* of *Malkhut*, or *Shekhinah*. The world of doing or action is our material realm. During the week we engage in acts to repair the world, exemplified in this parashah in the construction of the *Mishkan*, but today in *gemilut chasadim* and *tikkun olam* (or perhaps simply in our daily affairs performed consciously). Our attention is often located solely on our human, planetary plane. Levi Yitzhak suggests that if we are not conscious of repairing the world of speech, helping the *Shekhinah*, we are missing the mark. Our intention should be directed toward the plane of the *Shekhinah*, attending to her suffering in exile, helping to raise her up to the Holy One (represented in the world of voice—thus connecting voice and speech). If we are able to do that during the week, then on Shabbat, when we engage primarily in acts of speech (Torah study and prayer), we connect speech and voice, facilitating the flow of blessing into the world. In this manner, we affect the material plane without engaging in work.

There is an intimate and mutually reinforcing relationship between contemplative practice—spiritual practice—and repairing the world. The former grounds and focuses us so that our actions in the world can be effective and reparative. We will see clearly where our deeds separate and where they mend, where we are creating a true dwelling place for the *Shekhinah* and where we let in negative forces; we will know the difference between "These are your gods, O Israel" (Exod. 32:4) and "This is my God—I will glorify Him" (Exod. 15:2).

Questions for Reflection

1. In your own practice, what do you "do" to fulfill Shabbat? What sort of "doing" can you accomplish by "not doing"?

2. In what ways do you recognize your actions as a form of speech? What do you do to communicate your inner state, your spiritual or moral intention, without speech?

3. In what ways do you understand that observing Shabbat contributes to repairing the world—ethically, physically, spiritually?

Taking It into Your Life

Levi Yitzhak says that we have to repair the destruction brought about by the *chitzonim*, the negative forces that result from seeing the world only in terms of its externalities. When we look only at the surface, disregarding the inner value of an object—which is to say, that it is for God's glory—we deny that God's glory fills all creation. We assert, instead, that the world is only material, that it has no meaning beyond its utility. The way in which we repair the damage of the *chitzonim* is to perform our daily labors with a different consciousness, one that connects the material world to the spiritual. Whatever we do, we should be helping to make this world a *mishkan*, a dwelling place for God.

How shall we do that? First, we have to be able to conceive of that dwelling place, what it might be like. That is one reason that we observe Shabbat. It may also be why we meditate, pray, or engage in other spiritual practices. When we focus our attention—in body and mind—on the Divine (or the truth of the moment), we experience the fullness of each moment and know that the world exists in itself, for itself, and our place is interconnected in it. Our sense in the moment is one of peace, wholeness, and gratitude. We, in stillness, in awareness, sense the possibility of perfection.

We come to see through our practice both how perfect the world is in this moment and what the world could be like if love, justice, and compassion were fully present for all people and beings. That vision is inspiring. It does not yet exist, yet it is present in our hearts and minds. We know what it might look like. We sense its potential. When we leave our spiritual practice, when Shabbat ends and we return to the workaday, we bring that vision with us. That which "is" we receive with the same gratitude and appreciation we sensed in our practice. Yet we also apply ourselves through our actions to repair the world, seeking to make our actions and those of others more like what we saw in our practice.

But we also discover new things about this world through our actions. We come to know other people, we learn about their concerns, their needs, their perspectives. We adjust our actions in light of the new information we garner from them. We test our perceptions against theirs and grow in insight. We bring this experience back to our spiritual practice. When we then sit back on Shabbat or sit in meditation, we see the world differently. From this, new perceptions open up, new consciousness grows.

This is the movement between the world of speech, which we repair during the week, and the world of doing that we engage when we sit in spiritual practice. Neither is of value on its own; each is dependent on the other for its fullness, its truth.

Pekudei

We might interpret further the verse:
"These are the records of the *Mishkan*, the
Tabernacle of the Pact, which were drawn up
at Moses's bidding [the work of the Levites
under the direction of Ithamar son of Aaron
the priest]" (Exod. 38:21).

The Sages taught, "Blessing cannot dwell in that which is numbered or measured" (Ta'anit 8b). Yet, the work of the Tablernacle (*Mishkan*) was accomplished with measured, precise calculations, and still blessing filled it! We will consider this in light of the verse: "Your eyes are like the pools [*bereikhot*] in Heshbon" (Song 7:5).

Balaam's behavior epitomizes the nature of the evil eye (cf. Avot 5:19): wherever he turned his gaze he cursed that thing. How did this work? The wicked one will, in looking at something, separate it from the supernal source of the wellspring of life—since he lusts after that thing and thinks that it has some intrinsic value. But he does not gaze upon the divine power in it.

But, of Israel it is written, "Your eyes are like the pools in Heshbon" (*bereikhot becheshbon*): even to that thing that can be measured (*cheshbon*), that can be counted and accounted, this gaze brings no harm, because they see the power of the Creator in each and every thing they look at. They connect that thing to its source, and through this glance they draw down blessing pouring forth from the supernal wellspring onto that thing. When it says, "Your eyes are like the pools" (*bereikhot*), it means that your eyes have become like blessings (*berakhot*) and wellsprings of divine flow, even for that which has a measure.

Thus, when it says, "**These are the records of the *Mishkan***" and in the *Mishkan* everything was measured and counted several times over, and its number (*cheshbon*) taken—still blessing and the *Shekhinah* dwelt in it. More than that: the accounting, the numbering and measuring, was for a higher purpose. That is the significance of the phrase "**which**

270

were drawn up at Moses's bidding." Since the accounting took place at Moses's instruction and he was connected to God in supernal holiness, blessing was added to that which was measured.

FOR FURTHER THOUGHT

Rashi comments on Num. 15:39:

> "So that you do not follow your heart and eyes in your lustful urge"—The heart and eyes are the scouts for the body, procuring for it the opportunities to sin. The eye sees, the heart desires, and the body sins.

His comment draws from *Midrash Tanchuma*, *Shelach* 15, where the verb "procuring" (*mesarserim*) appears as a noun, "middlemen" (*sarsurin*). The sense is that the eyes and heart pimp for the body, finding opportunities to devour and possess what it desires. Levi Yitzhak is sensitive to this, as well, and unpacks the inner dynamic that leads to sin. When we look at something, we can either see it as an object for our possession and control, that we might claim for our own, or we can see it as the garment of the Holy One, inseparable, incorruptible. The acts of counting, numbering, and measuring can be ways of exercising control. When we know the number of things, we set a limit: this many and no more. When we measure something, we separate it from a larger totality; we determine its extent. Often, the act of numbering or measuring is for the purpose of claiming ownership, an assertion of power and of ego.

Levi Yitzhak reminds us of this danger and invites us to turn our gaze into one of appreciation, not of appropriation. Rather than counting and measuring to gain control, we can number and assess to witness again and testify to God's glory, which fills all creation—as a whole and in its parts. In this manner, we connect the discrete parts to the whole. We let go of our desire to establish our sovereignty over things, acknowledging instead God's dominion.

This is the basis of Levi Yitzhak's wonderful pun on the verse from Song of Songs, "Your eyes are like the pools in Heshbon." The "pools" (*bereikhot*) are the source from which all creation flows, the wellsprings of God's enlivening power. When we testify to that through our appreciative gaze, we follow the stream back up to its source in the pools, recognizing that they are the source of blessing (*berakhot*). Rather than separating off, we reconnect, testifying to ultimate unity in God.

Questions for Reflection

"Rashi comments: 'The eye sees, the heart desires, and the body sins.' We might have thought that the teaching would say, 'The heart desires and the eye observes,' following the order of our verse ('follow your heart and eyes'). Rather, that which the heart does not desire the eyes do not see at all" (*Toledot Ephraim*).

1. Does this teaching make sense to you? Where do you sense the root of your desire: in the heart, the mind, or the soul? What have you experienced to be the source of desire, the root of greed?

2. Contemporary literary criticism has made us aware of the role of "gaze" and the power held by the one who gazes. The masculine gaze, which commodifies the feminine and the female, permeates much of literature, cinema, and the marketplace. What does our lesson have to offer us in response?

3. In your experience, what is the connection between a stingy eye (cf. Prov. 23:6, *ra ayin*; Deut. 15:9, *vera'ah einekha*) and an evil eye (as Levi Yitzhak presents it here)? How does this play out in Levi Yitzhak's teaching? How have you experienced this in your own life? How do you work with the impulse to possess, the need to own, the resistance to sharing?

Taking It into Your Life

Levi Yitzhak teaches us that we have to train our gaze—not only in the sense of where we place it, but also in how we view what comes into our field of vision. You may recognize how it is both possible to look blankly at something, seeing it without really paying any attention to it, and how it is possible to notice something out of the corner of your eye and turn quickly to see it, to take it all in, to answer fully, "What was that?" In neither case have we given that which our eyes perceive its full due. It either has been ignored, and so denied its existence, or it has been possessed, denied its integrity and its dignity as God's creation.

Our job is to train our eyes to see appreciatively. The first step is to become aware of the act of seeing. This may seem cumbersome, but it is helpful. As you go through your day, pay attention to what you see. Notice it. Name it. Describe it to yourself. Pay attention to what is in the foreground and the background. Notice what catches your eye. Look for what you are missing.

Become familiar with your habits of seeing, and begin to reflect on how they represent habits of mind. What we look at with interest is frequently what we find pleasant, desirable, or beautiful; what we want, hunger for, or lust for. What we turn away from is frequently what we find ugly, disgusting, or painful; what we would want to remove, annihilate, or end. Allow the feelings that arise in association with your view to come to consciousness. Simply note, without judgment.

On the basis of what you learn, experiment with noting whatever you see and responding, "There is God, too." Observe how that helps you let go of what you seek to possess, how it helps you remain connected to what you would deny. Reflect.

An alternative explanation: "These are the records of the Tabernacle, [the Tabernacle of the Pact, which were drawn up at Moses's bidding,] the work of the Levites under the direction of Ithamar son of Aaron the priest" (Exod. 38:21).

This is how it is: The Holy One constantly pours out love and compassion on His people Israel. Even when (heaven forbid!) something bad happens to Israel, it is only so that in the end good will come to Israel. But if (heaven forbid!) no good will arise out of this evil, then God does not send it on Israel. The principle is that if God sends malevolence upon Israel, it is only so that afterward good will arise from it.

This is hinted at in our passage. "Levi" signifies the quality of judgment, and "priest" (*Kohein*) suggests the quality of love. The phrase **"the work of the Levites"** refers to the quality of judgment, and **"under the direction of Ithamar son of Aaron the priest"** refers to the quality of love. This means that the aspect of judgment is under the power of love. When it will produce love, then judgment is allowed to do its work; but if no love will emerge from it, then judgment is not permitted to execute judgment.

This is the implication of the phrase **"These are the records of the Tabernacle"**: the Tabernacle (*Mishkan*) suggests the sweetening

> of the judgment, that is, sweetening the suffering of Israel. This
> comes about through "**the work of the Levites under the direction of
> Ithamar son of Aaron the priest.**"

FOR FURTHER THOUGHT

We must be careful when reading this text to remember that
Levi Yitzhak is talking about the suffering of Israel, the people as
a whole, and not individual suffering. He assumes that there is a
special, unique, relationship between God and Israel, one that will
allow no ultimate evil to prevail over Israel; ultimately, Israel will
be redeemed from suffering and from exile. In that sense, we have
faith that whatever tribulations we may suffer as a people, they are
always filled with the promise of future blessing. In the end, love
must prevail.

This is not meant as counsel for one who suffers, suggesting that
it must necessarily be for the good. This may be your faith, but it has
yet to be discovered and proved for the one who suffers—and it may
not be true, in the end. The only lesson that we might take relative
to individual suffering is the imperative that we bring love (*chesed*)
with us into every interaction. Our love may be the only counter-
balance to the suffering of others. It is no small thing to offer that.
It may be enough.

The identification of the priest with love (*chesed*) is rooted in the
verse "And of Levi he said: Let Your Thummim and Urim be with
Your man of love" (Deut. 33:8). The priests derived from the House
of Levi, but they alone employed the oracular Urim and Thummim
to divine God's purpose. So the priests are also identified as "Your
man of love" (*ish chasidekha*). The Levites, in several different ways,
are identified with violence, limitation, and rigor (cf. Genesis 34;
Exod. 32:26–28; Num. 1:53–54). These elements ultimately emerge
in Kabbalah, with the Levites identified with the left side and with
the aspect of judgment, and the priests identified with the right side
and with love.

The final association of "the records of the Tabernacle" with this
system may be as follows. The Hebrew root *p-k-d* can suggest "absence,
lack," and so perhaps stand in for judgment, the side of constriction.
The *Mishkan* would signify love and expansiveness. Once again the
left is bound up in the right, judgment sweetened in love.

Questions for Reflection

1. Is it acceptable to you to say that evil will only be allowed to unfold if in the end love will arise? What sort of love do you imagine is meant here? How have you found that love can emerge from evil? Does this make it any more possible to tolerate the suffering caused by evil? Can this "sweeten the judgment"?

2. How do you understand the image of "judgment" being under the control of "love"? In what ways, if at all, have you experienced enacting "judgment" while still holding on to love, still looking for love to prevail?

3. This teaching may be useful as a way of talking about the persistence of the Jewish people, even after the Holocaust. Perhaps it is only possible to do so now, decades after its conclusion. What do you sense to be the timeline by which we might discern the love that emerges from evil? In your experience, is it necessary to have "faith" to wait to see such love emerge? What kind of faith? What kind of theology might emerge from such a teaching?

Taking It into Your Life

Levi Yitzhak invites us to develop a degree of faith. Whatever befalls us cannot ultimately be bad. It may be painful in the moment; it may cause suffering that will not find relief. But in the end, it will be good: it will lead us to love.

This is a great challenge. It does not relieve us of our obligation to prevent suffering, to alleviate pain, and to work for justice. Indeed, that may be precisely how the bad becomes the good, how the love is generated.

There is an additional element to this teaching. That is, in the midst of our work for justice—fighting the forces of evil, preventing those who would cause harm to others—can we retain faith that ultimately good will emerge? What would be the impact of holding such faith? Perhaps we would be able to do our work more lightly, while no less seriously, with no less concern. In some sense, this might mean recognizing that as much as the good depends on our acts—individually and collectively—ultimately it is not in our hands. God will bring the good. We can loosen our shoulders, take a deeper breath, smile. We might even find room for compassion for our opponent. Neither he nor we are independent actors. He is doing what he is doing out of the conditions of his life. He is in pain, just as we are in pain. The good that will finally emerge will be for his benefit, too.

We do not own the good. It is God's blessing to bestow. Can we live in the light of the faith that knows God's goodness, even now, in the midst of the bad? Can this heart of compassion be the love that flows from evil?

Notes

1. Collected and edited by Aharon Yaakov Greenberg, Yavneh Publishing, Tel Aviv 1993, seven volumes.

2. It is important to note here: there is no one "Hasidic teaching" on God or any other spiritual topic. Nonetheless, there are general themes that can be discerned among the students of the Baal Shem Tov, the "founder of Hasidism," and R. Dov Baer, the Maggid of Mezritch, who made Hasidism a "movement." I admit that I will be selective, offering those that I have found meaningful that have generated a significant response among my students and others today.

3. This review of the spiritual views of the Baal Shem Tov and the Maggid of Mezritch are cursory and focused on their significance for this book. I encourage you to read further on this topic. In particular, I would recommend three books by my teacher, Dr. Arthur Green, which can serve both as background to this book and as an invitation to a much larger conversation regarding contemporary Jewish theology and spirituality:

   - *Seek My Face: A Jewish Mystical Theology* (Woodstock, VT: Jewish Lights, 2003).
   - *Ehyeh: A Kabbalah for Tomorrow* (Woodstock, VT: Jewish Lights, 2003).
   - *Radical Judaism: Rethinking God and Tradition* (New Haven, CT: Yale University Press, 2010).

4. We should not ignore the fact that we have neighbors, fellow Jews, who are Hasidim. Their practices are rooted in the time of R. Levi Yitzhak. They, too, attempt to live out these important teachings from the late eighteenth century, but with a difference. They do not try to adapt the teachings to the twenty-first century, instead adapting their lives and worldviews to the texts. Their bodies may reside here and now, but their souls and minds interpret this world as if they were there and then. Sadly, we find that this sometimes results in friction between Hasidim and modern Jews (and others), conflicts of values and worldviews. For us to access the riches of *Kedushat Levi* and other Hasidic books we need not—and perhaps must not—turn our backs on important contemporary values: pluralism, tolerance, freedom of the individual conscience, and equality of all people, genders, sexual orientation, and religions. For this reason, throughout the translation I have often identified the reader/actor as female or male, specifically Jewish or simply "us," hoping thereby to invite everyone to find his or her place in these teachings, overcoming what might otherwise be unpleasant conceptual obstacles.

5. Martin Buber, *Tales of the Hasidim* (New York: Schocken Press, 1947), 222.

6. Ibid., 229–230.

7. Ibid., 209–210.

8. Ibid., 222.

9. Regarding this translation: As with most other classical Jewish texts, *Kedushat Levi* is addressed to a male reader. It accepts the fact of gendered language to speak of God. As noted above, I have tried to change the form from instructions to an anonymous male reader to an invitation to our pluralistic, integrated community. I hope I have succeeded in making the teachings more inclusive and embracing. Yet I know that I have not succeeded completely in changing the gendered language R. Levi Yitzhak sometimes uses to speak of God. To do so often would have led to cumbersome circumlocutions or clumsy language. I have done the best I saw how, and I beg your willingness to enter into the text as teaching without regard to the gendered language.

In the main, I have relied on the Jewish Publication Society translation of Scripture: *JPS Hebrew-English Tanakh: The Traditional Hebrew Text and the New JPS Translation*, 2nd ed., electronic version (Varda Book Publishing, 2002). Yet, I have made changes to bring the language in line with what R. Levi Yitzhak was reading, to communicate more clearly the point of the text.

When I have incorporated passages from the Babylonian Talmud or Midrash Rabbah, I have based my translation on the Soncino translations (digital version, Judaica Press, 1973 and 1983) but have changed them substantially to speak to a contemporary audience.

Bible Study / Midrash

Passing Life's Tests: Spiritual Reflections on the Trial of Abraham, the Binding of Isaac *By Rabbi Bradley Shavit Artson, DHL*
Invites us to use this powerful tale as a tool for our own soul wrestling, to confront our existential sacrifices and enable us to face—and surmount—life's tests.
6 x 9, 176 pp, Quality PB, 978-1-58023-631-7 **$18.99**

The Messiah and the Jews: Three Thousand Years of Tradition, Belief and Hope *By Rabbi Elaine Rose Glickman; Foreword by Rabbi Neil Gillman, PhD; Preface by Rabbi Judith Z. Abrams, PhD*
Explores and explains an astonishing range of primary and secondary sources, infusing them with new meaning for the modern reader.
6 x 9, 192 pp, Quality PB, 978-1-58023-690-4 **$16.99**

Speaking Torah: Spiritual Teachings from around the Maggid's Table—in Two Volumes *By Arthur Green, with Ebn Leader, Ariel Evan Mayse and Or N. Rose*
The most powerful Hasidic teachings made accessible—from some of the world's preeminent authorities on Jewish thought and spirituality.
Volume 1—6 x 9, 512 pp, Hardcover, 978-1-58023-668-3 **$34.99**
Volume 2—6 x 9, 448 pp, Hardcover, 978-1-58023-694-2 **$34.99**

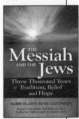

Masking and Unmasking Ourselves: Interpreting Biblical Texts on Clothing & Identity *By Dr. Norman J. Cohen*
Presents ten Bible stories that involve clothing in an essential way, as a means of learning about the text, its characters and their interactions.
6 x 9, 240 pp, HC, 978-1-58023-461-0 **$24.99**

The Genesis of Leadership: What the Bible Teaches Us about Vision, Values and Leading Change *By Rabbi Nathan Laufer; Foreword by Senator Joseph I. Lieberman*
6 x 9, 288 pp, Quality PB, 978-1-58023-352-1 **$18.99**

Hineini in Our Lives: Learning How to Respond to Others through 14 Biblical Texts and Personal Stories *By Rabbi Norman J. Cohen, PhD*
6 x 9, 240 pp, Quality PB, 978-1-58023-274-6 **$16.99**

The Modern Men's Torah Commentary: New Insights from Jewish Men on the 54 Weekly Torah Portions *Edited by Rabbi Jeffrey K. Salkin*
6 x 9, 368 pp, HC, 978-1-58023-395-8 **$24.99**

Moses and the Journey to Leadership: Timeless Lessons of Effective Management from the Bible and Today's Leaders *By Rabbi Norman J. Cohen, PhD*
6 x 9, 240 pp, Quality PB, 978-1-58023-351-4 **$18.99**; HC, 978-1-58023-227-2 **$21.99**

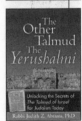

The Other Talmud—The *Yerushalmi*: Unlocking the Secrets of *The Talmud of Israel* for Judaism Today *By Rabbi Judith Z. Abrams, PhD*
6 x 9, 256 pp, HC, 978-1-58023-463-4 **$24.99**

Sage Tales: Wisdom and Wonder from the Rabbis of the Talmud
By Rabbi Burton L. Visotzky 6 x 9, 256 pp, HC, 978-1-58023-456-6 **$24.99**

The Torah Revolution: Fourteen Truths That Changed the World
By Rabbi Reuven Hammer, PhD 6 x 9, 240 pp, HC, 978-1-58023-457-3 **$24.99**

The Wisdom of Judaism: An Introduction to the Values of the Talmud
By Rabbi Dov Peretz Elkins 6 x 9, 192 pp, Quality PB, 978-1-58023-327-9 **$16.99**

Congregation Resources

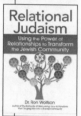

Jewish Megatrends: Charting the Course of the American Jewish Future
By Rabbi Sidney Schwarz; Foreword by Ambassador Stuart E. Eizenstat
Visionary solutions for a community ripe for transformational change—from
fourteen leading innovators of Jewish life.
6 x 9, 288 pp, HC, 978-1-58023-667-6 **$24.99**

Relational Judaism: Using the Power of Relationships to Transform the
Jewish Community By Dr. Ron Wolfson
How to transform the model of twentieth-century Jewish institutions into twenty-first-
century relational communities offering meaning and purpose, belonging and blessing.
6 x 9, 288 pp, HC, 978-1-58023-666-9 **$24.99**

Revolution of Jewish Spirit: How to Revive *Ruakh* in Your Spiritual
Life, Transform Your Synagogue & Inspire Your Jewish Community
By Rabbi Baruch HaLevi, DMin, and Ellen Frankel, LCSW; Foreword by Dr. Ron Wolfson
A practical and engaging guide to reinvigorating Jewish life. Offers strategies for
sustaining and expanding transformation, impassioned leadership, inspired pro-
gramming and inviting sacred spaces.
6 x 9, 224 pp, Quality PB Original, 978-1-58023-625-6 **$19.99**

Building a Successful Volunteer Culture: Finding Meaning in Service in the Jewish
Community By Rabbi Charles Simon; Foreword by Shelley Lindauer; Preface by Dr. Ron Wolfson
6 x 9, 192 pp, Quality PB, 978-1-58023-408-5 **$16.99**

The Case for Jewish Peoplehood: Can We Be One?
By Dr. Erica Brown and Dr. Misha Galperin; Foreword by Rabbi Joseph Telushkin
6 x 9, 224 pp, HC, 978-1-58023-401-6 **$21.99**

Empowered Judaism: What Independent Minyanim Can Teach Us about Building
Vibrant Jewish Communities By Rabbi Elie Kaunfer; Foreword by Prof. Jonathan D. Sarna
6 x 9, 224 pp, Quality PB, 978-1-58023-412-2 **$18.99**

Finding a Spiritual Home: How a New Generation of Jews Can Transform the
American Synagogue By Rabbi Sidney Schwarz
6 x 9, 352 pp, Quality PB, 978-1-58023-185-5 **$19.95**

Inspired Jewish Leadership: Practical Approaches to Building Strong Communities
By Dr. Erica Brown 6 x 9, 256 pp, HC, 978-1-58023-361-3 **$27.99**

Jewish Pastoral Care, 2nd Edition: A Practical Handbook from Traditional &
Contemporary Sources Edited by Rabbi Dayle A. Friedman, MSW, MAJCS, BCC
6 x 9, 528 pp, Quality PB, 978-1-58023-427-6 **$35.00**

Jewish Spiritual Direction: An Innovative Guide from Traditional and
Contemporary Sources
Edited by Rabbi Howard A. Addison, PhD, and Barbara Eve Breitman, MSW
6 x 9, 368 pp, HC, 978-1-58023-230-2 **$30.00**

A Practical Guide to Rabbinic Counseling
Edited by Rabbi Yisrael N. Levitz, PhD, and Rabbi Abraham J. Twerski, MD
6 x 9, 432 pp, HC, 978-1-58023-562-4 **$40.00**

Professional Spiritual & Pastoral Care: A Practical Clergy and Chaplain's Handbook
Edited by Rabbi Stephen B. Roberts, MBA, MHL, BCJC
6 x 9, 480 pp, HC, 978-1-59473-312-3 **$50.00**

Reimagining Leadership in Jewish Organizations: Ten Practical Lessons to
Help You Implement Change and Achieve Your Goals By Dr. Misha Galperin
6 x 9, 192 pp, Quality PB, 978-1-58023-492-4 **$16.99**

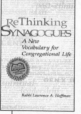

Rethinking Synagogues: A New Vocabulary for Congregational Life
By Rabbi Lawrence A. Hoffman, PhD 6 x 9, 240 pp, Quality PB, 978-1-58023-248-7 **$19.99**

Spiritual Community: The Power to Restore Hope, Commitment and Joy
By Rabbi David A. Teutsch, PhD
5½ x 8½, 144 pp, HC, 978-1-58023-270-8 **$19.99**

Spiritual Boredom: Rediscovering the Wonder of Judaism By Dr. Erica Brown
6 x 9, 208 pp, HC, 978-1-58023-405-4 **$21.99**

The Spirituality of Welcoming: How to Transform Your Congregation into a
Sacred Community By Dr. Ron Wolfson 6 x 9, 224 pp, Quality PB, 978-1-58023-244-9 **$19.99**

Bar / Bat Mitzvah

The Mitzvah Project Book
Making Mitzvah Part of Your Bar/Bat Mitzvah ... and Your Life
By Liz Suneby and Diane Heiman; Foreword by Rabbi Jeffrey K. Salkin; Preface by Rabbi Sharon Brous
The go-to source for Jewish young adults and their families looking to make the world a better place through good deeds—big or small.
6 x 9, 224 pp, Quality PB Original, 978-1-58023-458-0 **$16.99** *For ages 11–13*

The Bar/Bat Mitzvah Memory Book, 2nd Edition: An Album for Treasuring
the Spiritual Celebration
By Rabbi Jeffrey K. Salkin and Nina Salkin
8 x 10, 48 pp, 2-color text, Deluxe HC, ribbon marker, 978-1-58023-263-0 **$19.99**

For Kids—Putting God on Your Guest List, 2nd Edition: How to Claim the
Spiritual Meaning of Your Bar or Bat Mitzvah *By Rabbi Jeffrey K. Salkin*
6 x 9, 144 pp, Quality PB, 978-1-58023-308-8 **$15.99** *For ages 11–13*

The Jewish Prophet: Visionary Words from Moses and Miriam to Henrietta Szold
and A. J. Heschel *By Rabbi Dr. Michael J. Shire*
6½ x 8½, 128 pp, 123 full-color illus., HC, 978-1-58023-168-8 **$14.95**

Putting God on the Guest List, 3rd Edition: How to Reclaim the Spiritual
Meaning of Your Child's Bar or Bat Mitzvah *By Rabbi Jeffrey K. Salkin*
6 x 9, 224 pp, Quality PB, 978-1-58023-222-7 **$16.99**
        Teacher's Guide: 8½ x 11, 48 pp, PB, 978-1-58023-226-5 **$8.99**

Teens / Young Adults

Text Messages: A Torah Commentary for Teens
Edited by Rabbi Jeffrey K. Salkin
Shows today's teens how each Torah portion contains worlds of meaning for them, for what they are going through in their lives, and how they can shape their Jewish identity as they enter adulthood.
6 x 9, 304 pp (est), HC, 978-1-58023-507-5 **$24.99**

Hannah Senesh: Her Life and Diary, the First Complete Edition
By Hannah Senesh; Foreword by Marge Piercy; Preface by Eitan Senesh; Afterword by Roberta Grossman
6 x 9, 368 pp, b/w photos, Quality PB, 978-1-58023-342-2 **$19.99**

I Am Jewish: Personal Reflections Inspired by the Last Words of Daniel Pearl
Edited by Judea and Ruth Pearl 6 x 9, 304 pp, Deluxe PB w/ flaps, 978-1-58023-259-3 **$19.99**
Download a free copy of the *I Am Jewish Teacher's Guide* at www.jewishlights.com.

The JGirl's Guide: The Young Jewish Woman's Handbook for Coming of Age
By Penina Adelman, Ali Feldman and Shulamit Reinharz
6 x 9, 240 pp, Quality PB, 978-1-58023-215-9 **$16.99** *For ages 11 & up*
        Teacher's & Parent's Guide: 8½ x 11, 56 pp, PB, 978-1-58023-225-8 **$8.99**

The JGuy's Guide: The GPS for Jewish Teen Guys
By Rabbi Joseph B. Meszler, Dr. Shulamit Reinharz, Liz Suneby and Diane Heiman
6 x 9, 208 pp, Quality PB Original, 978-1-58023-721-5 **$16.99**
        Teacher's Guide: 8½ x 11, 30pp, PB, 978-1-58023-773-4 **$8.99**

Tough Questions Jews Ask, 2nd Edition: A Young Adult's Guide to Building a
Jewish Life *By Rabbi Edward Feinstein*
6 x 9, 160 pp, Quality PB, 978-1-58023-454-2 **$16.99** *For ages 11 & up*
        Teacher's Guide: 8½ x 11, 72 pp, PB, 978-1-58023-187-9 **$8.95**

Pre-Teens

Be Like God: God's To-Do List for Kids
By Dr. Ron Wolfson
Encourages kids ages eight through twelve to use their God-given superpowers to find the many ways they can make a difference in the lives of others and find meaning and purpose for their own.
7 x 9, 144 pp, Quality PB, 978-1-58023-510-5 **$15.99** *For ages 8–12*

The Book of Miracles: A Young Person's Guide to Jewish Spiritual Awareness
By Lawrence Kushner, with all-new illustrations by the author.
6 x 9, 96 pp, 2-color illus., HC, 978-1-879045-78-1 **$16.95** *For ages 9–13*

Children's Books

Around the World in One Shabbat
Jewish People Celebrate the Sabbath Together
By Durga Yael Bernhard

Takes your child on a colorful adventure to share the many ways Jewish people celebrate Shabbat around the world.
11 x 8½, 32 pp, Full-color illus., HC, 978-1-58023-433-7 **$18.99** *For ages 3–6*

It's a ... It's a ... It's a Mitzvah
By Liz Suneby and Diane Heiman; Full-color Illus. by Laurel Molk

Join Mitzvah Meerkat and friends as they introduce children to the everyday kindnesses that mark the beginning of a Jewish journey and a lifetime commitment to *tikkun olam* (repairing the world). 9 x 12, 32 pp, Full-color illus., HC, 978-1-58023-509-9 **$18.99** *For ages 3–6*

What You Will See Inside a Synagogue
By Rabbi Lawrence A. Hoffman, PhD, and Dr. Ron Wolfson; Full-color photos by Bill Aron

A colorful, fun-to-read introduction that explains the ways and whys of Jewish worship and religious life. 8½ x 10¼, 32 pp, Full-color photos, Quality PB, 978-1-59473-256-0 **$8.99** *For ages 6 & up*
(A book from SkyLight Paths, Jewish Lights' sister imprint)

Because Nothing Looks Like God
By Lawrence Kushner and Karen Kushner

Real-life examples of happiness and sadness—from goodnight stories, to the hope and fear felt the first time at bat, to the closing moments of someone's life—invite parents and children to explore, together, the questions we all have about God, no matter what our age. 11 x 8½, 32 pp, Full-color illus., HC, 978-1-58023-092-6 **$18.99** *For ages 4 & up*

The Book of Miracles: A Young Person's Guide to Jewish Spiritual Awareness
Written and illus. by Lawrence Kushner

Easy-to-read, imaginatively illustrated book encourages kids' awareness of their own spirituality. Revealing the essence of Judaism in a language they can understand and enjoy. 6 x 9, 96 pp, 2-color illus., HC, 978-1-879045-78-1 **$16.95** *For ages 9–13*

In God's Hands   *By Lawrence Kushner and Gary Schmidt*

Brings new life to a traditional Jewish folktale, reminding parents and kids of all faiths and all backgrounds that each of us has the power to make the world a better place—working ordinary miracles with our everyday deeds.
9 x 12, 32 pp, Full-color illus., HC, 978-1-58023-224-1 **$16.99** *For ages 5 & up*

In Our Image: God's First Creatures
By Nancy Sohn Swartz

A playful new twist to the Genesis story, God asks all of nature to offer gifts to humankind—with a promise that the humans would care for creation in return. 9 x 12, 32 pp, Full-color illus., HC, 978-1-879045-99-6 **$16.95** *For ages 4 & up*
Animated app available on Apple App Store and The Google Play Marketplace **$9.99**

The Jewish Family Fun Book, 2nd Ed.
Holiday Projects, Everyday Activities, and Travel Ideas with Jewish Themes
By Danielle Dardashti and Roni Sarig

The complete sourcebook for families wanting to put a new spin on activities for Jewish holidays, holy days and the everyday. It offers dozens of easy-to-do activities that bring Jewish tradition to life for kids of all ages.
6 x 9, 304 pp, w/ 70+ b/w illus., Quality PB, 978-1-58023-333-0 **$18.99**

What Makes Someone a Jew?   *By Lauren Seidman*
Reflects the changing face of American Judaism. Helps preschoolers and young readers (ages 3–6) understand that you don't have to look a certain way to be Jewish.
10 x 8½, 32 pp, Full-color photos, Quality PB, 978-1-58023-321-7 **$8.99** *For ages 3–6*

When a Grandparent Dies: A Kid's Own Remembering Workbook for
Dealing with Shiva and the Year Beyond   *By Nechama Liss-Levinson*
8 x 10, 48 pp, 2-color text, HC, 978-1-879045-44-6 **$15.95** *For ages 7–13*

Spirituality / Crafts

Jewish Threads: A Hands-On Guide to Stitching Spiritual Intention into Jewish Fabric Crafts *By Diana Drew with Robert Grayson*
Learn how to make your own Jewish fabric crafts with spiritual intention—a journey of creativity, imagination and inspiration. Thirty projects.
7 x 9, 288 pp, 8-page color insert, b/w illus., Quality PB Original, 978-1-58023-442-9 **$19.99**

Beading—The Creative Spirit: Finding Your Sacred Center through the Art of Beadwork *By Wendy Ellsworth*
Invites you on a spiritual pilgrimage into the kaleidoscope world of glass and color.
7 x 9, 240 pp, 8-page full-color insert, b/w photos and diagrams, Quality PB, 978-1-59473-267-6 **$18.99***

Contemplative Crochet: A Hands-On Guide for Interlocking Faith and Craft *By Cindy Crandall-Frazier; Foreword by Linda Skolnik*
Will take you on a path deeper into your crocheting and your spiritual awareness.
7 x 9, 208 pp, b/w photos, Quality PB, 978-1-59473-238-6 **$16.99***

The Knitting Way: A Guide to Spiritual Self-Discovery
By Linda Skolnik and Janice MacDaniels
Shows how to use knitting to strengthen your spiritual self.
7 x 9, 240 pp, b/w photos, Quality PB, 978-1-59473-079-5 **$16.99***

The Painting Path: Embodying Spiritual Discovery through Yoga, Brush and Color *By Linda Novick; Foreword by Richard Segalman*
Explores the divine connection you can experience through art.
7 x 9, 208 pp, 8-page full-color insert, b/w photos, Quality PB, 978-1-59473-226-3 **$18.99***

The Quilting Path: A Guide to Spiritual Self-Discovery through Fabric, Thread and Kabbalah *By Louise Silk* Explores how to cultivate personal growth through quilt making. 7 x 9, 192 pp, b/w photos, Quality PB, 978-1-59473-206-5 **$16.99***

Travel / History

Israel—A Spiritual Travel Guide, 2nd Edition: A Companion for the Modern Jewish Pilgrim *By Rabbi Lawrence A. Hoffman, PhD*
Helps today's pilgrim tap into the deep spiritual meaning of the ancient—and modern—sites of the Holy Land.
4¾ x 10, 256 pp, Illus., Quality PB, 978-1-58023-261-6 **$18.99**

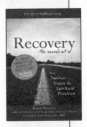

Also Available: **The Israel Mission Leader's Guide** 5½ x 8½, 16 pp, PB, 978-1-58023-085-8 **$4.95**

On the Chocolate Trail: A Delicious Adventure Connecting Jews, Religions, History, Travel, Rituals and Recipes to the Magic of Cacao
By Rabbi Deborah R. Prinz
Take a delectable journey through the religious history of chocolate—a real treat!
6 x 9, 272 pp w/ 20+ b/w photographs, Quality PB, 978-1-58023-487-0 **$18.99**

Twelve Steps

Recovery—The Sacred Art: The Twelve Steps as Spiritual Practice
By Rami Shapiro; Foreword by Joan Borysenko, PhD
Draws on insights and practices of different religious traditions to help you move more deeply into the universal spirituality of the Twelve Step system.
5½ x 8½, 240 pp, Quality PB Original, 978-1-59473-259-1 **$16.99***

100 Blessings Every Day: Daily Twelve Step Recovery Affirmations, Exercises for Personal Growth & Renewal Reflecting Seasons of the Jewish Year *By Rabbi Kerry M. Olitzky; Foreword by Rabbi Neil Gillman, PhD* 4½ x 6½, 432 pp, Quality PB, 978-1-879045-30-9 **$16.99**

Recovery from Codependence: A Jewish Twelve Steps Guide to Healing Your Soul
By Rabbi Kerry M. Olitzky 6 x 9, 160 pp, Quality PB, 978-1-879045-32-3 **$13.95**

Twelve Jewish Steps to Recovery, 2nd Edition: A Personal Guide to Turning from Alcoholism & Other Addictions—Drugs, Food, Gambling, Sex ...
By Rabbi Kerry M. Olitzky and Stuart A. Copans, MD; Preface by Abraham J. Twerski, MD
6 x 9, 160 pp, Quality PB, 978-1-58023-409-2 **$16.99**

*A book from SkyLight Paths, Jewish Lights' sister imprint

Life Cycle

Marriage / Parenting / Family / Aging

The New Jewish Baby Album: Creating and Celebrating the Beginning of a Spiritual Life—A Jewish Lights Companion
By the Editors at Jewish Lights; Foreword by Anita Diamant; Preface by Rabbi Sandy Eisenberg Sasso
A spiritual keepsake that will be treasured for generations. More than just a memory book, *shows you how—and why it's important*—to create a Jewish home and a Jewish life. 8 x 10, 64 pp, Deluxe Padded HC, Full-color illus., 978-1-58023-138-1 **$19.95**

The Jewish Pregnancy Book: A Resource for the Soul, Body & Mind during Pregnancy, Birth & the First Three Months *By Sandy Falk, MD, and Rabbi Daniel Judson, with Steven A. Rapp* Medical information, prayers and rituals for each stage of pregnancy. 7 x 10, 208 pp, b/w photos, Quality PB, 978-1-58023-178-7 **$16.95**

Celebrating Your New Jewish Daughter: Creating Jewish Ways to Welcome Baby Girls into the Covenant—New and Traditional Ceremonies *By Debra Nussbaum Cohen; Foreword by Rabbi Sandy Eisenberg Sasso* 6 x 9, 272 pp, Quality PB, 978-1-58023-090-2 **$18.95**

The New Jewish Baby Book, 2nd Edition: Names, Ceremonies & Customs—A Guide for Today's Families *By Anita Diamant* 6 x 9, 320 pp, Quality PB, 978-1-58023-251-7 **$19.99**

Parenting as a Spiritual Journey: Deepening Ordinary and Extraordinary Events into Sacred Occasions *By Rabbi Nancy Fuchs-Kreimer, PhD* 6 x 9, 224 pp, Quality PB, 978-1-58023-016-2 **$17.99**

Parenting Jewish Teens: A Guide for the Perplexed
By Joanne Doades Explores the questions and issues that shape the world in which today's Jewish teenagers live and offers constructive advice to parents.
6 x 9, 176 pp, Quality PB, 978-1-58023-305-7 **$16.99**

Judaism for Two: A Spiritual Guide for Strengthening and Celebrating Your Loving Relationship *By Rabbi Nancy Fuchs-Kreimer, PhD, and Rabbi Nancy H. Wiener, DMin; Foreword by Rabbi Elliot N. Dorff, PhD*
Addresses the ways Jewish teachings can enhance and strengthen committed relationships. 6 x 9, 224 pp, Quality PB, 978-1-58023-254-8 **$16.99**

The Creative Jewish Wedding Book, 2nd Edition: A Hands-On Guide to New & Old Traditions, Ceremonies & Celebrations *By Gabrielle Kaplan-Mayer* 9 x 9, 288 pp, b/w photos, Quality PB, 978-1-58023-398-9 **$19.99**

Divorce Is a Mitzvah: A Practical Guide to Finding Wholeness and Holiness When Your Marriage Dies *By Rabbi Perry Netter; Afterword by Rabbi Laura Geller* 6 x 9, 224 pp, Quality PB, 978-1-58023-172-5 **$16.95**

Embracing the Covenant: Converts to Judaism Talk About Why & How
By Rabbi Allan Berkowitz and Patti Moskovitz 6 x 9, 192 pp, Quality PB, 978-1-879045-50-7 **$16.95**

The Guide to Jewish Interfaith Family Life: An InterfaithFamily.com Handbook
Edited by Ronnie Friedland and Edmund Case
6 x 9, 384 pp, Quality PB, 978-1-58023-153-4 **$18.95**

A Heart of Wisdom: Making the Jewish Journey from Midlife through the Elder Years
Edited by Susan Berrin; Foreword by Rabbi Harold Kushner
6 x 9, 384 pp, Quality PB, 978-1-58023-051-3 **$18.95**

Introducing My Faith and My Community: The Jewish Outreach Institute Guide for the Christian in a Jewish Interfaith Relationship
By Rabbi Kerry M. Olitzky 6 x 9, 176 pp, Quality PB, 978-1-58023-192-3 **$16.99**

Making a Successful Jewish Interfaith Marriage: The Jewish Outreach Institute Guide to Opportunities, Challenges and Resources *By Rabbi Kerry M. Olitzky with Joan Peterson Littman* 6 x 9, 176 pp, Quality PB, 978-1-58023-170-1 **$16.95**

A Man's Responsibility: A Jewish Guide to Being a Son, a Partner in Marriage, a Father and a Community Leader *By Rabbi Joseph B. Meszler* 6 x 9, 192 pp, Quality PB, 978-1-58023-435-1 **$16.99**

So That Your Values Live On: Ethical Wills and How to Prepare Them
Edited by Rabbi Jack Riemer and Rabbi Nathaniel Stampfer
6 x 9, 272 pp, Quality PB, 978-1-879045-34-7 **$18.99**

Holidays / Holy Days

Prayers of Awe Series

An exciting new series that examines the High Holy Day liturgy to enrich the praying experience of everyone—whether experienced worshipers or guests who encounter Jewish prayer for the very first time.

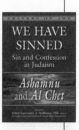

May God Remember: Memory and Memorializing in Judaism—*Yizkor*
Edited by Rabbi Lawrence A. Hoffman, PhD
Examines the history and ideas behind *Yizkor*, the Jewish memorial service, and this fascinating chapter in Jewish piety.
6 x 9, 304 pp, HC, 978-1-58023-689-8 **$24.99**

We Have Sinned—Sin and Confession in Judaism: *Ashamnu* and *Al Chet*
Edited by Rabbi Lawrence A. Hoffman, PhD 6 x 9, 304 pp, HC, 978-1-58023-612-6 **$24.99**

Who by Fire, Who by Water—*Un'taneh Tokef*
Edited by Rabbi Lawrence A. Hoffman, PhD
6 x 9, 272 pp, Quality PB, 978-1-58023-672-0 **$19.99**; HC, 978-1-58023-424-5 **$24.99**

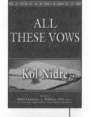

All These Vows—*Kol Nidre*
Edited by Rabbi Lawrence A. Hoffman, PhD 6 x 9, 288 pp, HC, 978-1-58023-430-6 **$24.99**

Rosh Hashanah Readings: Inspiration, Information and Contemplation
Yom Kippur Readings: Inspiration, Information and Contemplation
Edited by Rabbi Dov Peretz Elkins; Section Introductions from Arthur Green's These Are the Words
Rosh Hashanah: 6 x 9, 400 pp, Quality PB, 978-1-58023-437-5 **$19.99**
Yom Kippur: 6 x 9, 368 pp, Quality PB, 978-1-58023-438-2 **$19.99**; HC, 978-1-58023-271-5 **$24.99**

Reclaiming Judaism as a Spiritual Practice: Holy Days and Shabbat
By Rabbi Goldie Milgram 7 x 9, 272 pp, Quality PB, 978-1-58023-205-0 **$19.99**

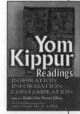

The Sabbath Soul: Mystical Reflections on the Transformative Power of Holy Time
Selection, Translation and Commentary by Eitan Fishbane, PhD
6 x 9, 208 pp, Quality PB, 978-1-58023-459-7 **$18.99**

Shabbat, 2nd Edition: The Family Guide to Preparing for and Celebrating the Sabbath
By Dr. Ron Wolfson 7 x 9, 320 pp, Illus., Quality PB, 978-1-58023-164-0 **$21.99**

Hanukkah, 2nd Edition: The Family Guide to Spiritual Celebration
By Dr. Ron Wolfson 7 x 9, 240 pp, Illus., Quality PB, 978-1-58023-122-0 **$18.95**

Passover

My People's Passover Haggadah
Traditional Texts, Modern Commentaries
Edited by Rabbi Lawrence A. Hoffman, PhD, and David Arnow, PhD
A diverse and exciting collection of commentaries on the traditional Passover Haggadah—in two volumes!
Vol. 1: 7 x 10, 304 pp, HC, 978-1-58023-354-5 **$24.99**
Vol. 2: 7 x 10, 320 pp, HC, 978-1-58023-346-0 **$24.99**

Creating Lively Passover Seders, 2nd Edition: A Sourcebook of Engaging Tales, Texts & Activities *By David Arnow, PhD* 7 x 9, 464 pp, Quality PB, 978-1-58023-444-3 **$24.99**

Freedom Journeys: The Tale of Exodus and Wilderness across Millennia
By Rabbi Arthur O. Waskow and Rabbi Phyllis O. Berman
6 x 9, 288 pp, HC, 978-1-58023-445-0 **$24.99**

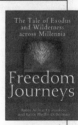

Leading the Passover Journey: The Seder's Meaning Revealed, the Haggadah's Story Retold *By Rabbi Nathan Laufer*
6 x 9, 224 pp, Quality PB, 978-1-58023-399-6 **$18.99**

Passover, 2nd Edition: The Family Guide to Spiritual Celebration
By Dr. Ron Wolfson with Joel Lurie Grishaver 7 x 9, 416 pp, Quality PB, 978-1-58023-174-9 **$19.95**

The Women's Passover Companion: Women's Reflections on the Festival of Freedom
Edited by Rabbi Sharon Cohen Anisfeld, Tara Mohr and Catherine Spector; Foreword by Paula E. Hyman
6 x 9, 352 pp, Quality PB, 978-1-58023-231-9 **$19.99**; HC, 978-1-58023-128-2 **$24.95**

The Women's Seder Sourcebook: Rituals & Readings for Use at the Passover Seder
Edited by Rabbi Sharon Cohen Anisfeld, Tara Mohr and Catherine Spector
6 x 9, 384 pp, Quality PB, 978-1-58023-232-6 **$19.99**

Social Justice

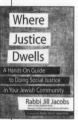

Where Justice Dwells
A Hands-On Guide to Doing Social Justice in Your Jewish Community
By Rabbi Jill Jacobs; Foreword by Rabbi David Saperstein
Provides ways to envision and act on your own ideals of social justice.
7 x 9, 288 pp, Quality PB Original, 978-1-58023-453-5 **$24.99**

There Shall Be No Needy
Pursuing Social Justice through Jewish Law and Tradition
By Rabbi Jill Jacobs; Foreword by Rabbi Elliot N. Dorff, PhD; Preface by Simon Greer
Confronts the most pressing issues of twenty-first-century America from a deeply Jewish perspective. 6 x 9, 288 pp, Quality PB, 978-1-58023-425-2 **$16.99**
There Shall Be No Needy Teacher's Guide 8½ x 11, 56 pp, PB, 978-1-58023-429-0 **$8.99**

Conscience
The Duty to Obey and the Duty to Disobey
By Rabbi Harold M. Schulweis
Examines the idea of conscience and the role conscience plays in our relationships to government, law, ethics, religion, human nature, God—and to each other.
6 x 9, 160 pp, Quality PB, 978-1-58023-419-1 **$16.99**; HC, 978-1-58023-375-0 **$19.99**

Judaism and Justice
The Jewish Passion to Repair the World
By Rabbi Sidney Schwarz; Foreword by Ruth Messinger
Explores the relationship between Judaism, social justice and the Jewish identity of American Jews. 6 x 9, 352 pp, Quality PB, 978-1-58023-353-8 **$19.99**

Spirituality / Women's Interest

New Jewish Feminism
Probing the Past, Forging the Future
Edited by Rabbi Elyse Goldstein; Foreword by Anita Diamant
Looks at the growth and accomplishments of Jewish feminism and what they mean for Jewish women today and tomorrow.
6 x 9, 480 pp, HC, 978-1-58023-359-0 **$24.99**

The Divine Feminine in Biblical Wisdom Literature
Selections Annotated & Explained
Translation & Annotation by Rabbi Rami Shapiro
5½ x 8½, 240 pp, Quality PB, 978-1-59473-109-9 **$16.99**
(A book from SkyLight Paths, Jewish Lights' sister imprint)

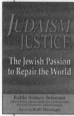

The Quotable Jewish Woman
Wisdom, Inspiration & Humor from the Mind & Heart
Edited by Elaine Bernstein Partnow
6 x 9, 496 pp, Quality PB, 978-1-58023-236-4 **$19.99**

The Women's Haftarah Commentary
New Insights from Women Rabbis on the 54 Weekly Haftarah Portions, the 5 Megillot & Special Shabbatot
Edited by Rabbi Elyse Goldstein
Illuminates the historical significance of female portrayals in the Haftarah and the Five Megillot. 6 x 9, 560 pp, Quality PB, 978-1-58023-371-2 **$19.99**

The Women's Torah Commentary
New Insights from Women Rabbis on the 54 Weekly Torah Portions
Edited by Rabbi Elyse Goldstein
Over fifty women rabbis offer inspiring insights on the Torah, in a week-by-week format.
6 x 9, 496 pp, Quality PB, 978-1-58023-370-5 **$19.99**; HC, 978-1-58023-076-6 **$34.95**

See Passover for *The Women's Passover Companion: Women's Reflections on the Festival of Freedom* and *The Women's Seder Sourcebook: Rituals & Readings for Use at the Passover Seder.*

Ecology / Environment

A Wild Faith: Jewish Ways into Wilderness, Wilderness Ways into Judaism
By Rabbi Mike Comins; Foreword by Nigel Savage 6 x 9, 240 pp, Quality PB, 978-1-58023-316-3 **$16.99**

Ecology & the Jewish Spirit: Where Nature & the Sacred Meet
Edited by Ellen Bernstein 6 x 9, 288 pp, Quality PB, 978-1-58023-082-7 **$18.99**

Torah of the Earth: Exploring 4,000 Years of Ecology in Jewish Thought
Vol. 1: Biblical Israel & Rabbinic Judaism; Vol. 2: Zionism & Eco-Judaism
Edited by Rabbi Arthur Waskow Vol. 1: 6 x 9, 272 pp, Quality PB, 978-1-58023-086-5 **$19.95**
Vol. 2: 6 x 9, 336 pp, Quality PB, 978-1-58023-087-2 **$19.95**

The Way Into Judaism and the Environment *By Jeremy Benstein, PhD*
6 x 9, 288 pp, Quality PB, 978-1-58023-368-2 **$18.99**; HC, 978-1-58023-268-5 **$24.99**

Graphic Novels / Graphic History

The Adventures of Rabbi Harvey: A Graphic Novel of Jewish Wisdom and Wit in the
Wild West *By Steve Sheinkin* 6 x 9, 144 pp, Full-color illus., Quality PB, 978-1-58023-310-1 **$16.99**

Rabbi Harvey Rides Again: A Graphic Novel of Jewish Folktales Let Loose in the
Wild West *By Steve Sheinkin* 6 x 9, 144 pp, Full-color illus., Quality PB, 978-1-58023-347-7 **$16.99**

Rabbi Harvey vs. the Wisdom Kid: A Graphic Novel of Dueling Jewish Folktales in
the Wild West *By Steve Sheinkin*
6 x 9, 144 pp, Full-color illus., Quality PB, 978-1-58023-422-1 **$16.99**

The Story of the Jews: A 4,000-Year Adventure—A Graphic History Book
By Stan Mack 6 x 9, 288 pp, Illus., Quality PB, 978-1-58023-155-8 **$16.99**

Grief / Healing

Judaism and Health: A Handbook of Practical, Professional and Scholarly
Resources *Edited by Jeff Levin, PhD, MPH, and Michele F. Prince, LCSW, MAJCS*
Foreword by Rabbi Elliot N. Dorff, PhD
Explores the expressions of health in the form of overviews of research studies,
first-person narratives and advice. 6 x 9, 448 pp, HC, 978-1-58023-714-7 **$50.00**

Facing Illness, Finding God: How Judaism Can Help You and Caregivers Cope
When Body or Spirit Fails *By Rabbi Joseph B. Meszler*
6 x 9, 208 pp, Quality PB, 978-1-58023-423-8 **$16.99**

Grief in Our Seasons: A Mourner's Kaddish Companion *By Rabbi Kerry M. Olitzky*
4½ x 6½, 448 pp, Quality PB, 978-1-879045-55-2 **$15.95**

Healing and the Jewish Imagination: Spiritual and Practical Perspectives on
Judaism and Health *Edited by Rabbi William Cutter, PhD*
6 x 9, 240 pp, Quality PB, 978-1-58023-373-6 **$19.99**

Healing from Despair: Choosing Wholeness in a Broken World
By Rabbi Elie Kaplan Spitz with Erica Shapiro Taylor; Foreword by Abraham J. Twerski, MD
5½ x 8½, 208 pp, Quality PB, 978-1-58023-436-8 **$16.99**

Healing of Soul, Healing of Body: Spiritual Leaders Unfold the Strength & Solace
in Psalms *Edited by Rabbi Simkha Y. Weintraub, LCSW*
6 x 9, 128 pp, 2-color illus. text, Quality PB, 978-1-879045-31-6 **$16.99**

Midrash & Medicine: Healing Body and Soul in the Jewish Interpretive Tradition
Edited by Rabbi William Cutter, PhD; Foreword by Michele F. Prince, LCSW, MAJCS
6 x 9, 352 pp, Quality PB, 978-1-58023-484-9 **$21.99**

Mourning & Mitzvah, 2nd Edition: A Guided Journal for Walking the Mourner's
Path through Grief to Healing *By Rabbi Anne Brener, LCSW*
7½ x 9, 304 pp, Quality PB, 978-1-58023-113-8 **$19.99**

Tears of Sorrow, Seeds of Hope, 2nd Edition: A Jewish Spiritual Companion
for Infertility and Pregnancy Loss *By Rabbi Nina Beth Cardin*
6 x 9, 208 pp, Quality PB, 978-1-58023-233-3 **$18.99**

A Time to Mourn, a Time to Comfort, 2nd Edition: A Guide to Jewish
Bereavement *By Dr. Ron Wolfson; Foreword by Rabbi David J. Wolpe*
7 x 9, 384 pp, Quality PB, 978-1-58023-253-1 **$21.99**

When a Grandparent Dies: A Kid's Own Remembering Workbook for Dealing
with Shiva and the Year Beyond *By Nechama Liss-Levinson, PhD*
8 x 10, 48 pp, 2-color text, HC, 978-1-879045-44-6 **$15.95** *For ages 7–13*

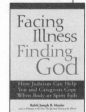

Theology / Philosophy / The Way Into... Series

The Way Into... series offers an accessible and highly usable "guided tour" of the Jewish faith, people, history and beliefs—in total, an introduction to Judaism that will enable you to understand and interact with the sacred texts of the Jewish tradition. Each volume is written by a leading contemporary scholar and teacher, and explores one key aspect of Judaism. The Way Into... series enables all readers to achieve a real sense of Jewish cultural literacy through guided study.

The Way Into Encountering God in Judaism
By Rabbi Neil Gillman, PhD
For everyone who wants to understand how Jews have encountered God throughout history and today.
6 x 9, 240 pp, Quality PB, 978-1-58023-199-2 **$18.99**; HC, 978-1-58023-025-4 **$21.95**
Also Available: **The Jewish Approach to God:** A Brief Introduction for Christians
By Rabbi Neil Gillman, PhD
5½ x 8½, 192 pp, Quality PB, 978-1-58023-190-9 **$16.95**

The Way Into Jewish Mystical Tradition
By Rabbi Lawrence Kushner
Allows readers to interact directly with the sacred mystical texts of the Jewish tradition. An accessible introduction to the concepts of Jewish mysticism, their religious and spiritual significance, and how they relate to life today.
6 x 9, 224 pp, Quality PB, 978-1-58023-200-5 **$18.99**

The Way Into Jewish Prayer
By Rabbi Lawrence A. Hoffman, PhD
Opens the door to 3,000 years of Jewish prayer, making anyone feel at home in the Jewish way of communicating with God.
6 x 9, 208 pp, Quality PB, 978-1-58023-201-2 **$18.99**

The Way Into Jewish Prayer Teacher's Guide
By Rabbi Jennifer Ossakow Goldsmith
8½ x 11, 42 pp, PB, 978-1-58023-345-3 **$8.99**
Download a free copy at www.jewishlights.com.

The Way Into Judaism and the Environment
By Jeremy Benstein, PhD
Explores the ways in which Judaism contributes to contemporary social-environmental issues, the extent to which Judaism is part of the problem and how it can be part of the solution.
6 x 9, 288 pp, Quality PB, 978-1-58023-368-2 **$18.99**; HC, 978-1-58023-268-5 **$24.99**

The Way Into *Tikkun Olam* (Repairing the World)
By Rabbi Elliot N. Dorff, PhD
An accessible introduction to the Jewish concept of the individual's responsibility to care for others and repair the world.
6 x 9, 304 pp, Quality PB, 978-1-58023-328-6 **$18.99**

The Way Into Torah
By Rabbi Norman J. Cohen, PhD
Helps guide you in the exploration of the origins and development of Torah, explains why it should be studied and how to do it.
6 x 9, 176 pp, Quality PB, 978-1-58023-198-5 **$16.99**

The Way Into the Varieties of Jewishness
By Sylvia Barack Fishman, PhD
Explores the religious and historical understanding of what it has meant to be Jewish from ancient times to the present controversy over "Who is a Jew?"
6 x 9, 288 pp, Quality PB, 978-1-58023-367-5 **$18.99**; HC, 978-1-58023-030-8 **$24.99**

Theology / Philosophy

Believing and Its Tensions: A Personal Conversation about God, Torah, Suffering and Death in Jewish Thought
By Rabbi Neil Gillman, PhD
Explores the changing nature of belief and the complexities of reconciling the intellectual, emotional and moral questions of Gillman's own searching mind and soul.
5½ x 8½, 144 pp, HC, 978-1-58023-669-0 **$19.99**

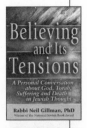

God of Becoming and Relationship: The Dynamic Nature of Process Theology *By Rabbi Bradley Shavit Artson, DHL*
Explains how Process Theology breaks us free from the strictures of ancient Greek and medieval European philosophy, allowing us to see all creation as related patterns of energy through which we connect to everything.
6 x 9, 208 pp, HC, 978-1-58023-713-0 **$24.99**

The Other Talmud—The *Yerushalmi*: Unlocking the Secrets of *The Talmud of Israel* for Judaism Today *By Rabbi Judith Z. Abrams, PhD*
A fascinating—and stimulating—look at "the other Talmud" and the possibilities for Jewish life reflected there. 6 x 9, 256 pp, HC, 978-1-58023-463-4 **$24.99**

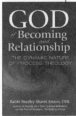

The Way of Man: According to Hasidic Teaching
By Martin Buber; New Translation and Introduction by Rabbi Bernard H. Mehlman and Dr. Gabriel E. Padawer; Foreword by Paul Mendes-Flohr
An accessible and engaging new translation of Buber's classic work—*available as an e-book only.* E-book, 978-1-58023-601-0 Digital List Price **$14.99**

The Death of Death: Resurrection and Immortality in Jewish Thought
By Rabbi Neil Gillman, PhD 6 x 9, 336 pp, Quality PB, 978-1-58023-081-0 **$18.95**

Doing Jewish Theology: God, Torah & Israel in Modern Judaism *By Rabbi Neil Gillman, PhD*
6 x 9, 304 pp, Quality PB, 978-1-58023-439-9 **$18.99**; HC, 978-1-58023-322-4 **$24.99**

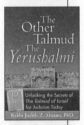

From Defender to Critic: The Search for a New Jewish Self
By Dr. David Hartman 6 x 9, 336 pp, HC, 978-1-58023-515-0 **$35.00**

The God Who Hates Lies: Confronting & Rethinking Jewish Tradition
By Dr. David Hartman with Charlie Buckholtz 6 x 9, 208 pp, Quality PB, 978-1-58023-790-1 **$19.99**

A Heart of Many Rooms: Celebrating the Many Voices within Judaism
By Dr. David Hartman 6 x 9, 352 pp, Quality PB, 978-1-58023-156-5 **$19.95**

Jewish Theology in Our Time: A New Generation Explores the Foundations and Future of Jewish Belief *Edited by Rabbi Elliot J. Cosgrove, PhD; Foreword by Rabbi David J. Wolpe; Preface by Rabbi Carole B. Balin, PhD* 6 x 9, 240 pp, Quality PB, 978-1-58023-630-1, **$19.99**; HC, 978-1-58023-413-9 **$24.99**

Maimonides—Essential Teachings on Jewish Faith & Ethics: The Book of Knowledge & the Thirteen Principles of Faith—Annotated & Explained
Translation and Annotation by Rabbi Marc D. Angel, PhD
5½ x 8½, 224 pp, Quality PB Original, 978-1-59473-311-6 **$18.99***

Maimonides, Spinoza and Us: Toward an Intellectually Vibrant Judaism
By Rabbi Marc D. Angel, PhD 6 x 9, 224 pp, HC, 978-1-58023-411-5 **$24.99**

Our Religious Brains: What Cognitive Science Reveals about Belief, Morality, Community and Our Relationship with God
By Rabbi Ralph D. Mecklenburger; Foreword by Dr. Howard Kelfer; Preface by Dr. Neil Gillman
6 x 9, 224 pp, HC, 978-1-58023-508-2 **$24.99**

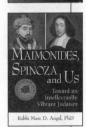

Your Word Is Fire: The Hasidic Masters on Contemplative Prayer
Edited and translated by Rabbi Arthur Green, PhD, and Barry W. Holtz
6 x 9, 160 pp, Quality PB, 978-1-879045-25-5 **$16.99**

I Am Jewish
Personal Reflections Inspired by the Last Words of Daniel Pearl
Almost 150 Jews—both famous and not—from all walks of life, from all around the world, write about many aspects of their Judaism.
Edited by Judea and Ruth Pearl 6 x 9, 304 pp, Deluxe PB w/ flaps, 978-1-58023-259-3 **$19.99**
Download a free copy of the *I Am Jewish Teacher's Guide* at www.jewishlights.com.

*A book from SkyLight Paths, Jewish Lights' sister imprint

Meditation

The Magic of Hebrew Chant: Healing the Spirit, Transforming the Mind, Deepening Love
By Rabbi Shefa Gold; Foreword by Sylvia Boorstein
Introduces this transformative spiritual practice as a way to unlock the power of sacred texts and make prayer and meditation the delight of your life. Includes musical notations. 6 x 9, 352 pp, Quality PB, 978-1-58023-671-3 **$24.99**

The Magic of Hebrew Chant Companion—The Big Book of Musical Notations and Incantations
8½ x 11, 154 pp, PB, 978-1-58023-722-2 **$19.99**

Jewish Meditation Practices for Everyday Life
Awakening Your Heart, Connecting with God
By Rabbi Jeff Roth
Offers a fresh take on meditation that draws on life experience and living life with greater clarity as opposed to the traditional method of rigorous study.
6 x 9, 224 pp, Quality PB, 978-1-58023-397-2 **$18.99**

Discovering Jewish Meditation, 2nd Edition
Instruction & Guidance for Learning an Ancient Spiritual Practice
By Nan Fink Gefen, PhD 6 x 9, 208 pp, Quality PB, 978-1-58023-462-7 **$16.99**

The Handbook of Jewish Meditation Practices
A Guide for Enriching the Sabbath and Other Days of Your Life
By Rabbi David A. Cooper 6 x 9, 208 pp, Quality PB, 978-1-58023-102-2 **$16.95**

Meditation from the Heart of Judaism
Today's Teachers Share Their Practices, Techniques, and Faith
Edited by Avram Davis 6 x 9, 256 pp, Quality PB, 978-1-58023-049-0 **$16.95**

Ritual / Sacred Practices

God in Your Body: Kabbalah, Mindfulness and Embodied Spiritual Practice
By Jay Michaelson
The first comprehensive treatment of the body in Jewish spiritual practice and an essential guide to the sacred. 6 x 9, 272 pp, Quality PB, 978-1-58023-304-0 **$18.99**

The Book of Jewish Sacred Practices: CLAL's Guide to Everyday & Holiday Rituals & Blessings *Edited by Rabbi Irwin Kula and Vanessa L. Ochs, PhD*
6 x 9, 368 pp, Quality PB, 978-1-58023-152-7 **$18.95**

The Jewish Dream Book: The Key to Opening the Inner Meaning of Your Dreams
By Vanessa L. Ochs, PhD, with Elizabeth Ochs; Illus. by Kristina Swarner
8 x 8, 128 pp, Full-color illus., Deluxe PB w/ flaps, 978-1-58023-132-9 **$16.95**

Jewish Ritual: A Brief Introduction for Christians
By Rabbi Kerry M. Olitzky and Rabbi Daniel Judson
5½ x 8½, 144 pp, Quality PB, 978-1-58023-210-4 **$14.99**

The Rituals & Practices of a Jewish Life: A Handbook for Personal Spiritual Renewal *Edited by Rabbi Kerry M. Olitzky and Rabbi Daniel Judson*
6 x 9, 272 pp, Illus., Quality PB, 978-1-58023-169-5 **$18.95**

The Sacred Art of Lovingkindness: Preparing to Practice
By Rabbi Rami Shapiro 5½ x 8½, 176 pp, Quality PB, 978-1-59473-151-8 **$16.99**
(A book from SkyLight Paths, Jewish Lights' sister imprint)

Mystery & Detective Fiction

Criminal Kabbalah: An Intriguing Anthology of Jewish Mystery & Detective Fiction *Edited by Lawrence W. Raphael; Foreword by Laurie R. King*
All-new stories from twelve of today's masters of mystery and detective fiction—sure to delight mystery buffs of all faith traditions.
6 x 9, 256 pp, Quality PB, 978-1-58023-109-1 **$16.95**

Mystery Midrash: An Anthology of Jewish Mystery & Detective Fiction
Edited by Lawrence W. Raphael; Preface by Joel Siegel
6 x 9, 304 pp, Quality PB, 978-1-58023-055-1 **$16.95**

Inspiration

Into the Fullness of the Void: A Spiritual Autobiography *By Dov Elbaum*
The spiritual autobiography of one of Israel's leading cultural figures that provides insights and guidance for all of us. 6 x 9, 304 pp, Quality PB Original, 978-1-58023-715-4 **$18.99**

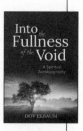

Saying No and Letting Go: Jewish Wisdom on Making Room for What Matters Most
By Rabbi Edwin Goldberg, DHL; Foreword by Rabbi Naomi Levy
Taps into timeless Jewish wisdom that teaches how to "hold on tightly" to the things that matter most while learning to "let go lightly" of the demands and worries that do not ultimately matter. 6 x 9, 192 pp, Quality PB, 978-1-58023-670-6 **$16.99**

The Bridge to Forgiveness: Stories and Prayers for Finding God and Restoring
Wholeness *By Rabbi Karyn D. Kedar* 6 x 9, 176 pp, Quality PB, 978-1-58023-451-1 **$16.99**

The Empty Chair: Finding Hope and Joy—Timeless Wisdom from a Hasidic Master,
Rebbe Nachman of Breslov *Adapted by Moshe Mykoff and the Breslov Research Institute*
4 x 6, 128 pp, Deluxe PB w/ flaps, 978-1-879045-67-5 **$9.99**

A Formula for Proper Living: Practical Lessons from Life and Torah
By Rabbi Abraham J. Twerski, MD 6 x 9, 144 pp, HC, 978-1-58023-402-3 **$19.99**

The Gentle Weapon: Prayers for Everyday and Not-So-Everyday Moments—
Timeless Wisdom from the Teachings of the Hasidic Master, Rebbe Nachman of Breslov
Adapted by Moshe Mykoff and S. C. Mizrahi, together with the Breslov Research Institute
4 x 6, 144 pp, Deluxe PB w/ flaps, 978-1-58023-022-3 **$9.99**

The God Upgrade: Finding Your 21st-Century Spirituality in Judaism's 5,000-Year-
Old Tradition *By Rabbi Jamie Korngold; Foreword by Rabbi Harold M. Schulweis*
6 x 9, 176 pp, Quality PB, 978-1-58023-443-6 **$15.99**

God Whispers: Stories of the Soul, Lessons of the Heart *By Rabbi Karyn D. Kedar*
6 x 9, 176 pp, Quality PB, 978-1-58023-088-9 **$15.95**

God's To-Do List: 103 Ways to Be an Angel and Do God's Work on Earth
By Dr. Ron Wolfson 6 x 9, 144 pp, Quality PB, 978-1-58023-301-9 **$16.99**

Happiness and the Human Spirit: The Spirituality of Becoming the Best You Can Be
By Rabbi Abraham J. Twerski, MD
6 x 9, 176 pp, Quality PB, 978-1-58023-404-7 **$16.99**; HC, 978-1-58023-343-9 **$19.99**

Life's Daily Blessings: Inspiring Reflections on Gratitude and Joy for Every Day, Based
on Jewish Wisdom *By Rabbi Kerry M. Olitzky* 4½ x 6½, 368 pp, Quality PB, 978-1-58023-396-5 **$16.99**

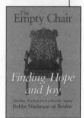

The Magic of Hebrew Chant: Healing the Spirit, Transforming the Mind,
Deepening Love *By Rabbi Shefa Gold; Foreword by Sylvia Boorstein*
6 x 9, 352 pp, Quality PB, 978-1-58023-671-3 **$24.99**

Restful Reflections: Nighttime Inspiration to Calm the Soul, Based on Jewish Wisdom
By Rabbi Kerry M. Olitzky and Rabbi Lori Forman-Jacobi 5 x 8, 352 pp, Quality PB, 978-1-58023-091-9 **$16.99**

Sacred Intentions: Morning Inspiration to Strengthen the Spirit, Based on Jewish Wisdom
By Rabbi Kerry M. Olitzky and Rabbi Lori Forman-Jacobi 4½ x 6½, 448 pp, Quality PB, 978-1-58023-061-2 **$16.99**

The Seven Questions You're Asked in Heaven: Reviewing and Renewing Your
Life on Earth *By Dr. Ron Wolfson* 6 x 9, 176 pp, Quality PB, 978-1-58023-407-8 **$16.99**

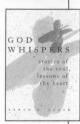

Kabbalah / Mysticism

Ehyeh: A Kabbalah for Tomorrow
By Rabbi Arthur Green, PhD 6 x 9, 224 pp, Quality PB, 978-1-58023-213-5 **$18.99**

The Gift of Kabbalah: Discovering the Secrets of Heaven, Renewing Your Life on Earth
By Tamar Frankiel, PhD 6 x 9, 256 pp, Quality PB, 978-1-58023-141-1 **$16.95**

Jewish Mysticism and the Spiritual Life: Classical Texts, Contemporary
Reflections *Edited by Dr. Lawrence Fine, Dr. Eitan Fishbane and Rabbi Or N. Rose*
6 x 9, 256 pp, HC, 978-1-58023-434-4 **$24.99**; Quality PB, 978-1-58023-719-2 **$18.99**

Seek My Face: A Jewish Mystical Theology *By Rabbi Arthur Green, PhD*
6 x 9, 304 pp, Quality PB, 978-1-58023-130-5 **$19.95**

Zohar: Annotated & Explained *Translation & Annotation by Dr. Daniel C. Matt; Foreword by
Andrew Harvey* 5½ x 8½, 176 pp, Quality PB, 978-1-893361-51-5 **$16.99**
(A book from SkyLight Paths, Jewish Lights' sister imprint)

See also *The Way Into Jewish Mystical Tradition* in The Way Into... Series.

Spirituality / Prayer

Davening: A Guide to Meaningful Jewish Prayer
By Rabbi Zalman Schachter-Shalomi with Joel Segel; Foreword by Rabbi Lawrence Kushner
A fresh approach to prayer for all who wish to appreciate the power of prayer's poetry, song and ritual, and to join the age-old conversation that Jews have had with God. 6 x 9, 240 pp, Quality PB, 978-1-58023-627-0 **$18.99**

Jewish Men Pray: Words of Yearning, Praise, Petition, Gratitude and Wonder from Traditional and Contemporary Sources
Edited by Rabbi Kerry M. Olitzky and Stuart M. Matlins; Foreword by Rabbi Bradley Shavit Artson, DHL
A celebration of Jewish men's voices in prayer—to strengthen, heal, comfort, and inspire—from the ancient world up to our own day.
5 x 7¼, 400 pp, HC, 978-1-58023-628-7 **$19.99**

Making Prayer Real: Leading Jewish Spiritual Voices on Why Prayer Is Difficult and What to Do about It *By Rabbi Mike Comins* 6 x 9, 320 pp, Quality PB, 978-1-58023-417-7 **$18.99**

Witnesses to the One: The Spiritual History of the *Sh'ma*
By Rabbi Joseph B. Meszler; Foreword by Rabbi Elyse Goldstein
6 x 9, 176 pp, Quality PB, 978-1-58023-400-9 **$16.99**; HC, 978-1-58023-309-5 **$19.99**

My People's Prayer Book Series: Traditional Prayers, Modern Commentaries *Edited by Rabbi Lawrence A. Hoffman, PhD*
Provides diverse and exciting commentary to the traditional liturgy. Will help you find new wisdom in Jewish prayer, and bring liturgy into your life. Each book includes Hebrew text, modern translations and commentaries from all perspectives of the Jewish world.

Vol. 1—The *Sh'ma* and Its Blessings
    7 x 10, 168 pp, HC, 978-1-879045-79-8 **$29.99**
Vol. 2—The *Amidah* 7 x 10, 240 pp, HC, 978-1-879045-80-4 **$24.95**
Vol. 3—*P'sukei D'zimrah* (Morning Psalms)
    7 x 10, 240 pp, HC, 978-1-879045-81-1 **$29.99**
Vol. 4—*Seder K'riat Hatorah* (The Torah Service)
    7 x 10, 264 pp, HC, 978-1-879045-82-8 **$29.99**
Vol. 5—*Birkhot Hashachar* (Morning Blessings)
    7 x 10, 240 pp, HC, 978-1-879045-83-5 **$24.95**
Vol. 6—*Tachanun* and Concluding Prayers
    7 x 10, 240 pp, HC, 978-1-879045-84-2 **$24.95**
Vol. 7—Shabbat at Home 7 x 10, 240 pp, HC, 978-1-879045-85-9 **$24.95**
Vol. 8—*Kabbalat Shabbat* (Welcoming Shabbat in the Synagogue)
    7 x 10, 240 pp, HC, 978-1-58023-121-3 **$24.99**
Vol. 9—Welcoming the Night: *Minchah* and *Ma'ariv* (Afternoon and Evening Prayer) 7 x 10, 272 pp, HC, 978-1-58023-262-3 **$24.99**
Vol. 10—Shabbat Morning: *Shacharit* and *Musaf* (Morning and Additional Services) 7 x 10, 240 pp, HC, 978-1-58023-240-1 **$29.99**

Spirituality / Lawrence Kushner

I'm God; You're Not: Observations on Organized Religion & Other Disguises of the Ego
6 x 9, 256 pp, Quality PB, 978-1-58023-513-6 **$18.99**; HC, 978-1-58023-441-2 **$21.99**

The Book of Letters: A Mystical Hebrew Alphabet
Popular HC Edition, 6 x 9, 80 pp, 2-color text, 978-1-879045-00-2 **$24.95**
Collector's Limited Edition, 9 x 12, 80 pp, gold-foil-embossed pages, w/ limited-edition silkscreened print, 978-1-879045-04-0 **$349.00**

The Book of Miracles: A Young Person's Guide to Jewish Spiritual Awareness
6 x 9, 96 pp, 2-color illus., HC, 978-1-879045-78-1 **$16.95** *For ages 9–13*

God Was in This Place & I, i Did Not Know: Finding Self, Spirituality and Ultimate Meaning 6 x 9, 192 pp, Quality PB, 978-1-879045-33-0 **$16.95**

Honey from the Rock: An Introduction to Jewish Mysticism
6 x 9, 176 pp, Quality PB, 978-1-58023-073-5 **$18.99**

Invisible Lines of Connection: Sacred Stories of the Ordinary
5½ x 8½, 160 pp, Quality PB, 978-1-879045-98-9 **$16.99**

The Way Into Jewish Mystical Tradition
6 x 9, 224 pp, Quality PB, 978-1-58023-200-5 **$18.99**; HC, 978-1-58023-029-2 **$21.95**

Spirituality

Amazing Chesed: Living a Grace-Filled Judaism
By Rabbi Rami Shapiro Drawing from ancient and contemporary, traditional and non-traditional Jewish wisdom, reclaims the idea of grace in Judaism.
6 x 9, 176 pp, Quality PB, 978-1-58023-624-9 **$16.99**

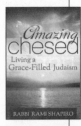

Jewish with Feeling: A Guide to Meaningful Jewish Practice
By Rabbi Zalman Schachter-Shalomi with Joel Segel
Takes off from basic questions like "Why be Jewish?" and whether the word God still speaks to us today and lays out a vision for a whole-person Judaism.
5½ x 8½, 288 pp, Quality PB, 978-1-58023-691-1 **$19.99**

Perennial Wisdom for the Spiritually Independent: Sacred Teachings—
Annotated & Explained *Annotation by Rami Shapiro; Foreword by Richard Rohr*
Weaves sacred texts and teachings from the world's major religions into a coherent exploration of the five core questions at the heart of every religion's search.
5½ x 8½, 336 pp, Quality PB Original, 978-1-59473-515-8 **$16.99**

Aleph-Bet Yoga: Embodying the Hebrew Letters for Physical and Spiritual Well-Being
By Steven A. Rapp; Foreword by Tamar Frankiel, PhD, and Judy Greenfeld; Preface by Hart Lazer
7 x 10, 128 pp, b/w photos, Quality PB, Lay-flat binding, 978-1-58023-162-6 **$16.95**

A Book of Life: Embracing Judaism as a Spiritual Practice
By Rabbi Michael Strassfeld 6 x 9, 544 pp, Quality PB, 978-1-58023-247-0 **$19.99**

Bringing the Psalms to Life: How to Understand and Use the Book of Psalms
By Rabbi Daniel F. Polish, PhD 6 x 9, 208 pp, Quality PB, 978-1-58023-157-2 **$16.95**

Does the Soul Survive? A Jewish Journey to Belief in Afterlife, Past Lives &
Living with Purpose *By Rabbi Elie Kaplan Spitz; Foreword by Brian L. Weiss, MD*
6 x 9, 288 pp, Quality PB, 978-1-58023-165-7 **$18.99**

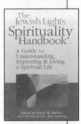

Entering the Temple of Dreams: Jewish Prayers, Movements and Meditations for
the End of the Day *By Tamar Frankiel, PhD, and Judy Greenfeld*
7 x 10, 192 pp, illus., Quality PB, 978-1-58023-079-7 **$16.95**

First Steps to a New Jewish Spirit: Reb Zalman's Guide to Recapturing the
Intimacy & Ecstasy in Your Relationship with God *By Rabbi Zalman M. Schachter-Shalomi
with Donald Gropman* 6 x 9, 144 pp, Quality PB, 978-1-58023-182-4 **$16.95**

Foundations of Sephardic Spirituality: The Inner Life of Jews of the Ottoman Empire
By Rabbi Marc D. Angel, PhD 6 x 9, 224 pp, Quality PB, 978-1-58023-341-5 **$18.99**

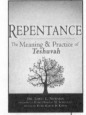

God & the Big Bang: Discovering Harmony between Science & Spirituality
By Dr. Daniel C. Matt 6 x 9, 216 pp, Quality PB, 978-1-879045-89-7 **$18.99**

God in Our Relationships: Spirituality between People from the Teachings of
Martin Buber *By Rabbi Dennis S. Ross* 5½ x 8½, 160 pp, Quality PB, 978-1-58023-147-3 **$16.95**

The Jewish Lights Spirituality Handbook: A Guide to Understanding, Exploring &
Living a Spiritual Life *Edited by Stuart M. Matlins*
6 x 9, 456 pp, Quality PB, 978-1-58023-093-3 **$19.99**

Judaism, Physics and God: Searching for Sacred Metaphors in a Post-Einstein World
By Rabbi David W. Nelson 6 x 9, 352 pp, Quality PB, inc. reader's discussion guide,
978-1-58023-306-4 **$18.99**; HC, 352 pp, 978-1-58023-252-4 **$24.99**

Meaning & Mitzvah: Daily Practices for Reclaiming Judaism through Prayer, God,
Torah, Hebrew, Mitzvot and Peoplehood *By Rabbi Goldie Milgram*
7 x 9, 336 pp, Quality PB, 978-1-58023-256-2 **$19.99**

Repentance: The Meaning and Practice of Teshuvah
By Dr. Louis E. Newman; Foreword by Rabbi Harold M. Schulweis; Preface by Rabbi Karyn D. Kedar
6 x 9, 256 pp, HC, 978-1-58023-426-9 **$24.99** Quality PB, 978-1-58023-718-5 **$18.99**

The Sabbath Soul: Mystical Reflections on the Transformative Power of Holy Time
Selection, Translation and Commentary by Eitan Fishbane, PhD
6 x 9, 208 pp, Quality PB, 978-1-58023-459-7 **$18.99**

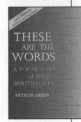

Tanya, the Masterpiece of Hasidic Wisdom: Selections Annotated & Explained
Translation & Annotation by Rabbi Rami Shapiro; Foreword by Rabbi Zalman M. Schachter-Shalomi
5½ x 8½, 240 pp, Quality PB, 978-1-59473-275-1 **$16.99**

These Are the Words, 2nd Edition: A Vocabulary of Jewish Spiritual Life
By Rabbi Arthur Green, PhD 6 x 9, 320 pp, Quality PB, 978-1-58023-494-8 **$19.99**

About Jewish Lights

People of all faiths and backgrounds yearn for books that attract, engage, educate, and spiritually inspire.

Our principal goal is to stimulate thought and help all people learn about who the Jewish People are, where they come from, and what the future can be made to hold. While people of our diverse Jewish heritage are the primary audience, our books speak to people in the Christian world as well and will broaden their understanding of Judaism and the roots of their own faith.

We bring to you authors who are at the forefront of spiritual thought and experience. While each has something different to say, they all say it in a voice that you can hear.

Our books are designed to welcome you and then to engage, stimulate, and inspire. We judge our success not only by whether or not our books are beautiful and commercially successful, but by whether or not they make a difference in your life.

For your information and convenience, at the back of this book we have provided a list of other Jewish Lights books you might find interesting and useful. They cover all the categories of your life:

Bar/Bat Mitzvah	Life Cycle
Bible Study / Midrash	Meditation
Children's Books	Men's Interest
Congregation Resources	Parenting
Current Events / History	Prayer / Ritual / Sacred Practice
Ecology / Environment	Social Justice
Fiction: Mystery, Science Fiction	Spirituality
Grief / Healing	Theology / Philosophy
Holidays / Holy Days	Travel
Inspiration	Twelve Steps
Kabbalah / Mysticism / Enneagram	Women's Interest

Stuart M. Matlins, Publisher

Or phone, fax, mail or e-mail to: **JEWISH LIGHTS** Publishing
Sunset Farm Offices, Route 4 • P.O. Box 237 • Woodstock, Vermont 05091
Tel: (802) 457-4000 • Fax: (802) 457-4004 • www.jewishlights.com
Credit card orders: **(800) 962-4544** (8:30AM–5:30PM EST Monday–Friday)
Generous discounts on quantity orders. SATISFACTION GUARANTEED. Prices subject to change.

For more information about each book, visit our website at www.jewishlights.com